Unlocking the Scriptures for You

LUKE

Lewis Foster

**STANDARD
BIBLE STUDIES**

*From The Library of
Greg Cheatham*

 STANDARD PUBLISHING
Cincinnati, Ohio   40103

Unless otherwise noted, all Scripture quotations are from the *Holy Bible: New International Version,* ©1973, 1978, 1984 by the International Bible Society. Used by permission of Zondervan Bible Publishers and the International Bible Society.

Sharing the thoughts of his own heart, the author may express views not entirely consistent with those of the publisher.

Library of Congress Cataloging in Publication data:

Foster, Lewis.
 Luke.

 (Standard Bible Studies)
 Bibliography: p.
 Includes index.
  1. Bible. N.T. Luke—Commentaries. I. Title. II. Series.
 BS2595.3.F63   1986   226'.407   85-27697
 ISBN 0-87403-163-X

Copyright © 1986. The STANDARD PUBLISHING Company, Cincinnati, Ohio. A division of STANDEX INTERNATIONAL Corporation. Printed in U.S.A.

CONTENTS

PREFACE 7
INTRODUCTION
    Purpose and Overview 9

PART ONE: THE BEGINNINGS
(Luke 1:1—4:13) 21
    Chapter 1: Fulfillment (1:1-80) 23
    Chapter 2: The Reception (2:1-52) 41
    Chapter 3: Preface to Ministry (3:1—4:13) 63

PART TWO: MINISTRY IN GALILEE
(Luke 4:14—9:50) 83
    Chapter 4: The Recruitment (4:14—6:16) 85
    Chapter 5: Sermons to Live By (6:17—7:50) 111
    Chapter 6: Establishing Identity (8:1—9:50) 131

PART THREE: THE WAY TO JERUSALEM
(Luke 9:51—19:27) 159
    Chapter 7: Traveling With the Teacher (9:51—12:59) . 161
    Chapter 8: Answer to Every Lament (13:1—15:32) .. 195
    Chapter 9: The Unexpected (16:1—19:27) 211

PART FOUR: THE FINAL WEEK AND RESURRECTION
(Luke 19:28—24:53) 233
    Chapter 10: The Surprise Beginning (19:28—20:47) .. 235
    Chapter 11: The Last Days (21:1—22:38) 249
    Chapter 12: Trials and Crucifixion (22:39—23:56) ... 267
    Chapter 13: Victory (24:1-53) 291

CONCLUDING NOTES
    Luke: The Author and the Gospel 317

INDEX 341

SUGGESTED READING 351

Maps
1. Where East Meets West 24
2. Where Jesus' Ministry Took Place 71
3. Jesus in Galilee 99
4. Routes to Jerusalem 162
5. Temple Area 252
6. Jerusalem 266

Charts
1. Synoptic Reports 119
2. Jesus' Ministry 169
3. Jesus' Audience 199
4. Gospel Comparisons 334
   Similarities
   Differences

Lists
1. Sayings on the Cross 283
2. Resurrection Appearances 294

Excursus
The Shroud of Turin 287

PREFACE

Approach to Scripture should involve three levels. First, an introductory study provides the background to a passage. It makes clear the setting for the action, the overview of what is covered, and the purpose of its place in the record. This should make the passage come alive. But still the reader has only been viewing the message on the surface.

The second level of study concerns a verse-by-verse treatment of the passage. This is more detailed. It seeks to relate the verses to one another and to other parts of Scripture. Any difficulties in harmony or ambiguities in interpretation or uncertainty as to the true meaning should be confronted. This is good, to probe beneath the surface and come to an appreciation of what each part of the record is saying and how it fits together. But this study is apt to be atomistic. It tends to tear the passage apart in order to examine it bit by bit. Too often, it fails to put the passage together again for the reader to appreciate the seamless-robe quality of Scripture.

This leads to the third level of study. Here a person tries to discern the very heart of the passage. Too often, we stop before we determine the essence of the truths. This requires another summary following the detailed verse by verse study. This time a search is made for the underlying significance of what is recorded, the application to our own lives as well as the thrust originally intended by the inspired author.

The following commentary is laid out with these three divisions in mind for the treatment of each chapter. The reader may use the different parts of the study as he sees fit. It is hoped that he will continue to pursue each of these levels in his own thoughts and in the use of other resources. Further study of

Scripture itself will be most helpful to the better understanding of each portion of Scripture. The Lord affirms:

> So is my word that goes out from my mouth:
> It will not return to me empty,
> but will accomplish what I desire
> and achieve the purpose for which I sent it.
>
> —Isaiah 55:11

Lewis Foster
Cincinnati Christian Seminary
January 1985

Introduction

Purpose and Overview

Plato said that everything has a purpose. The purpose of a knife is to cut; the purpose of a horse is to pull a load. This book has a purpose, too. If, as you read this book, you read the Gospel of Luke along with it—more than you ever read it before—and you understand it better, this book will have achieved its purpose. If you find facts in Luke you see for the first time, if you recognize new lessons for your life, if you discern the real Jesus more clearly and hear what He says to you, Luke will have achieved his purpose, too.

But so many books have been written about Jesus, and so many about Luke's Gospel, how can anyone dare to write another? How can he possibly add anything more? Every writer must answer such a question. As for this book, nothing new can be claimed by way of information, but it has its own way of assembling the data. The material is divided up in a particular way, and each chapter has a special thread to hold it together. Each generation feels Luke's emphases in a little different way. But if there is one area that would justify undertaking this book more than any other, the variety of readers this work is designed to serve would be its plea.

The Readers

To the People

The Jews of Jesus' day had a special term, *'Am Ha-ares,* which denoted "the people of the land" in contrast with the religiously trained teachers of the law. Jesus continually addressed himself to these everyday people, and He received His best responses from their ranks. Today the vast majority of Christians consider themselves untrained in the formal approach to the study of Scripture, but they are hungry for solid food from the Word of God. This book seeks to provide a help to these people as they come to share in the treasures of the Gospel of Luke. This Gospel is particularly appropriate for this audience whether Christian or non-Christian. Luke addresses his work to Theophilus (Luke 1:3), a name denoting someone who yearns to know more about God. The general failure in this group is that they often excuse themselves saying they do not read the Bible more because they do not understand the Bible enough. On the contrary, we do not read the Bible enough to understand it more. To these people, this book urges, "Extend yourself in reading and study."

To the Teachers

Encouraging notes are heard today. Bible-study groups are on the increase. A wider selection of subjects is being offered in Sunday-school curricula. More are attending mid-week Bible studies. The most critical limitation to this welcome development is qualified teachers. The danger here is to have a meeting of individuals eager to study the Word, but for lack of a teacher, they pass the time in sharing experiences and feelings about a passage of Scripture without a study of the meaning intended by the inspired author. Necessary for the teacher is information on the subject, organization of the material, and presentation in a challenging way. The author's hope is that this book will assist teachers in the outlines, backgrounds, and applications of the text. The organization and presentation, however, must be the individual contribution of the individual teacher. To this group, the admonition is "Prepare yourself."

To the Students

One should never cease being a student. All the disciples following Jesus were students. We are blessed today with the number of young people who have become serious students of the Word as they prepare for their lives' work. No matter what area of concentration is chosen, the study of Biblical content will enrich our lives and service. Such chapters as "The Recruitment" and "Traveling with the Teacher" in this book point up the example and teaching of Jesus for those who would follow Him. To the student, the message comes, "Fill your cup."

To the Scholars

Some years ago, my concerned sister told me I should read at least one novel a year just to keep in touch with reality. She was worried lest I become so wrapped up in academia and dusty, scholarly theories that I would lose the realization of problems people live with day by day. It may be presumptuous to hope that this volume has anything to offer to the scholar, but the scholar needs some reminders, too. He is particularly interested in choosing the place to put his attention, to give his emphasis, to dig deeper, and to find something new. Unfortunately, so much effort is given today to depositing words in the proper form-tradition basket or properly labeling to which redactor's theology a thought belongs, or from which level of the church's belief a statement comes, that our attention wanders away from what Jesus actually said, and why Luke wants to tell us about it. This study has not treated each passage trying to address these popular questions, which have bogged down much of today's analyses; but this study suggests a new set of questions to occupy our critical research. It would be profitable to determine in each of these passages the following: (1) What is true to life—then and now—in this passage? (2) What is the unexpected in this passage, both the divine in origin and the human in behavior? (3) What is the key message in this passage? These questions are not directly treated in each instance, but they are urged as worthy of constant attention. Original charts are introduced, both to assist in viewing data and to stimulate explanation concerning Jesus' audiences, His location of ministry, His mode of teaching, and the relationship between the Gospel narratives. (See pages 199, 169, 119, and 334). Luke is a particularly attractive figure for the scholar to concentrate on as a source. Through him, as well as other writers of Scripture, we approach reality, not through the fictional but the factual. To the scholarly, the plea is given, "Direct your attention profitably, with correct starting points and worthy destinations."

To the Preachers

My father was a preacher to the preachers, and he remarked to them on more than one occasion that they were the most difficult audience of all. They were the most critical; they had the hardest, most impenetrable shell; they looked for what they could use on others but refused to apply it to themselves. This may be an exaggeration, but in any case, this volume is intended to be helpful to the preacher. He is constantly searching for new insights from Scripture that he can package and deliver to the people. The best kind of package is one a person can take home and spend time opening and discovering the contents for himself. In a similar way, this book may not have all of the explicit insights you might want to find, but it may trigger thoughts and messages of your own. Illustrations have been included in this study of Luke. Some would consider this incompatible with an objective commentary. On the contrary, illustrations can be an aid to clarity and memory, and need not be a violation of reason and truth. Jesus taught us the high value of good illustration.

To the Individual

Objectivity is good. To see the happening as it actually occurred without our feelings influencing the report about it is what we want, and this is what Luke has investigated and provided for us. But you can feel Luke's love for people, for individuals, that runs deep beneath his objectivity. This does not lead him to be unhistorical or untrustworthy, but it adds a dimension of exhortation to our own lives. This study of Luke is not a devotional work or a sermonizing type of study, but application to an individual's life is expected. It seeks to be objective, but with feeling, even as Luke set the example for us.

In the application of Luke's Gospel, besides seeing Luke's love for individuals, we feel the call to increase our own love for people, being sensitive to their needs and providing sources of help. As we read Luke and see the strong sense of purpose in Jesus' life, His overriding drive to do the will of the Father, may this come through in our own lives. Let us strive to live with the overriding purpose to know and do the will of God. In this type of study, it is not enough simply to note Jesus' style of teaching and preaching, but to incorporate His methods of communication in our homes and at our work, so that His mannerisms and His way of facing life become a life-style for us. Then it is not enough simply to appreciate how Jesus had to struggle uphill against opposition from enemies and misunderstanding among followers, but to endure our own obstacles as we learn from Him and what Luke tells us. Luke wrote for the individual, and he wants us to apply the message.

Synopsis of Luke

Before one lands on a new shore and digs for treasure, it is well to view the countryside from one horizon to the other. From the air, he can see the different sections of the terrain and mark how one part is joined to another. He can see the mountains and the plains, the woods and the fields. Then there are the streams that tie it all together. When finally he arrives at an individual site and begins to dig, he knows where he is and how this place fits into the whole picture. This is the way one should approach the Gospel of Luke—with an overview in mind that helps him understand the deeper studies of the individual parts.

The Beginning (Luke 1:1—4:13)

Luke is interested in people. By introducing a person, Zechariah, Luke informs the reader of preparations for the coming of the Lord. Whereas Matthew tells more about Joseph in describing the birth of Jesus, Luke introduces the person of Mary in a warm, sympathetic way, with all the emphasis given to her role. Two more genuine individuals are introduced in the temple area to receive the baby Jesus, Simeon and Anna. Then the strong messenger of the Lord, John the Baptist, is introduced to complete the action prior to the beginning of Jesus' ministry. These are introduced in the first three chapters of Luke.

Ministry in Galilee (Luke 4:14—9:50)

All of the remaining chapters in Luke can be conveniently divided into three sections: Jesus' Galilean ministry, His trip to Jerusalem, and the final week of His life plus the resurrection appearances and ascension.

Important to the ministry of Jesus in Galilee was His preaching. He preached not only in Nazareth (4:14-30), but in synagogues throughout the land. He proclaimed the good news of the kingdom of God (4:43, 44). It was not long before His crowds outgrew the synagogues, and one finds Jesus preaching and teaching (it is impossible to draw a decisive line between the two) in the out-of-doors. His sermon delivered in the plain (6:17ff.) drew people all the way from Jerusalem to the seacoast of Tyre and Sidon. On another occasion, when people had gathered from town after town, Jesus taught them in parables (8:4ff.). This, too, concerned the kingdom of God.

Another important phase of Jesus' work in Galilee was His

healing ministry. Modern critics have used Luke's emphasis on the miracles of Jesus as a mark against Luke's trustworthiness as an historian. To the contrary, this becomes a mark against the critic who does not allow the possibility of the miraculous. Luke worked as a careful historian, he examined the medical cases with the mind of a trained physician, and he was an honest individual without selfish ambition to gain something by deceit, for he alone stood with Paul in the face of death (2 Timothy 4:11). No man is ready to die for a lie to get ahead. No better witness could give testimony of what he found true in the ministry of Jesus in Galilee. In fact, the healing ministry of Jesus is so woven into the warp and woof of Jesus' activity that the course of events and the climax in Jerusalem at the end would be left inexplicable without it. When Luke tells of the crowds who came to Jesus for healing early in His ministry at Capernaum (Luke 4:40) and how later the crowds were so great they almost crushed Him (8:42), it was a true picture of what was happening in the growing momentum of Jesus' ministry both in word and in deed. Luke gives specific examples of healing: Simon's mother-in-law (4:38, 39), a leper (5:12, 13), a paralytic (5:18-26), a man with a shriveled hand (6:6-10), a centurion's servant (7:1-10), a widow's son (7:11-17), the Gerasene demoniac (8:26-39), the woman who touched Jesus' cloak (8:43-48), Jairus' daughter (8:40-56), and a boy with an evil spirit (9:37-43).

One might conclude that the physician Luke's interest in the sick has led to an overemphasis upon Jesus' power to heal. But this power is seen to work in other ways as well: a miraculous catch of fish (5:4-11), calming the wind and the sea (8:22-25), and feeding the five thousand (9:10-17). One must certainly be aware that all the claims made through the ages in a great variety of sources concerning miraculous healings, both before and after Jesus' time, cannot be true. But this is where the power of Jesus has been manifested in sufficient ways with ample testimony to assure the truth of His claims. It is the combined testimony of His teaching and the nature of His power that demands the credence of man. The power that could feed the five thousand and still the tempest could cleanse a person from leprosy and even raise the dead.

Another important part of Jesus' work was His special ministry to His disciples. He had come to prepare His followers to carry on His work after He was gone. Jesus' regular audiences could have been divided into three groups. Most of the people attended upon occasion to hear Jesus speak and, they hoped, to see Him do His works. Some disciples had left their homes, at least for a time, to follow Jesus from place to place in order to hear His messages and to be identified with a sizable group of regular followers. Finally, there were the Twelve. These were specially chosen, and they received the highest attention of all. Four fishermen had been called (5:1-11). Even a tax collector had been chosen (5:27-32). Only after a considerable period of identification with the larger group of disciples were twelve of them selected by Jesus. He designated them apostles (6:12-16).

Sometimes Jesus addressed His disciples while the people were listening in. At times, further instruction was given after the general audience had wandered away (8:9-18). Some experiences were enjoyed by the disciples alone (8:22; 9:10). Then there were times when the selection was still smaller than the Twelve (Peter, John, and James: 8:51; 9:28).

After Jesus had made at least two general preaching tours around Galilee (4:42-44; 8:1-3), He then felt that the Twelve should be ready to carry out an evangelistic campaign on their own. He sent them out "to preach the kingdom of God and to heal the sick" (9:1-6).

Jesus' impression upon His hearers seemed to rise and fall. Certainly a climax was reached with the mass of people at the feeding of the five thousand (9:10-17). Of all the miracles worked by Jesus, this is the only one recounted in all four Gospel narratives. But soon after this, Jesus' popularity with the crowds waned for a time. His reception with the Twelve, however, reached a new level with the confession of Peter that Jesus was the Christ (Messiah) of God (9:20), and with the experience of the three who witnessed His transfiguration (9:28-36). The spirits of the disciples were burdened, however, when in this same period, Jesus gave the first clear prediction of His coming death (9:22). Soon after this, the disciples failed to drive out an evil spirit from a boy brought to them (9:40) and Luke follows this by telling of an argument that started among the disciples as to which of them would be greatest (9:46). All these events went into the training of the Twelve in the midst of Jesus' public ministry in Galilee.

Another important movement that Luke notes in this period was carried on by those who resisted Jesus. The Pharisees and teachers of the law asked Jesus, "Why do you eat and drink with tax collectors and 'sinners'?" (5:30). On another occasion, when Jesus' disciples had picked some heads of wheat, separated the grain from the chaff, and eaten as they went along on the Sabbath, the Pharisees again asked, "Why are you doing what is unlawful on the Sabbath?" (6:2). On another Sabbath, they were waiting to criticize Jesus while He was healing a man on the Sabbath, but Jesus challenged them beforehand, and they were unable to pursue their plan. "But they were furious and began to discuss with one another what they might do to Jesus" (6:11).

Jesus defended the ministry of John the Baptist, and this became another point of contention with the Pharisees. Luke even inserts an editorial comment at this juncture, "But the Pharisees and experts in the law rejected God's purpose for themselves, because they had not been baptized by John" (7:30). And Jesus proceeded to note their attacks both against John and himself (7:31-35). Jesus did accept an invitation to dine with Simon the Pharisee, but even there, Jesus faced the necessity of reprimanding Simon for his inhospitable reception of Jesus; and then Jesus proceeded to forgive the sinful woman who had shown the reception that Simon should have given (7:36-50).

In this period, Herod was unable to determine what was going on, and whether he dared resist or could afford not to resist Jesus (9:7-9). Herod's beheading of John the Baptist continued to haunt him.

Thus, the Galilean ministry of Jesus was marked by the preaching and miracles of Jesus, the growing number of people who thronged to hear and see Him, the selection and training of the Twelve, and the persistent opposition of the Pharisees and the teachers of the law.

The Way to Jerusalem (Luke 9:51—19:27)

When one reviews these chapters and attempts to plot the route Jesus took in His final trip to the holy city, it is evident that one cannot speak of the "road" to Jerusalem. No one road could traverse the different areas indicated in these chapters. Even the terminology "trip" to Jerusalem, with further explanation that many side trips were taken along the way, places a strain on the wording. All one can do is to follow the steps of Jesus on this fateful journey. It is not the course that He followed in a geographical route that is most important, but the way He proceeded and the things that happened along the way. In fact, one is tempted to ask whether all these things could have happened on this one trip or whether Luke has grouped the succeeding events in a way that the reader can see the teaching and actions of Jesus in a clear, true light. It is not Luke's chronology that is important but the orderly arrangement he uses to fulfill his purpose.

To list a few of the surprising things about the route, Jesus is found just a few miles from Jerusalem in Luke 10:38, but then He is miles away again in 17:11. He starts for Jerusalem through Samaritan territory but ends up arriving from another route entirely—through Perea. These matters will be discussed as they are treated in the chapter division, but in this outline overview, one is eager to see these chapters in their general significance.

One might ask, "Why consider all these chapters as one trip to Jerusalem?" The answer is clearly stated in Luke 9:51: "As the time approached for him to be taken up to heaven, Jesus resolutely set out for Jerusalem." Notes are also given along the way affirming that the trip was continuing (9:53; 13:22, 33; 17:11; 18:31; 19:11, 28). It may be that Luke gathers incidents from several trips to Jerusalem and arranges them in an understandable way leaving the correct impression as to the buildup of response and opposition. Luke does not tell of Jesus' several trips to Jerusalem, as John does; so He inserts incidents that occurred along the way on several trips as though it were in the one trip rather than leave them out entirely. Other reasons may have limited the length of this section. Luke has carefully estimated the length of his entire Gospel because it must fit on a roll of papyrus of about thirty feet. (This was the normal length of one volume.) In all likelihood, he would also estimate the length of major parts of his work so that he would not have to omit portions later for lack of space. Although it is surprising that he would allot so much space to one trip, this may well be significant. He wanted to show the importance of the death, burial, and resurrection of Jesus by giving as much space to going to Jerusalem as he had to all the rest of Jesus' life.

Whereas more deeds of Jesus were recorded in the earlier section (Luke 4:14—9:50), more teaching is given in this section (9:51—19:27). Only four more healings are recorded (a crippled woman [on the Sabbath], 13:10-13; a man with dropsy [on the Sabbath], 14:1-9; ten men with leprosy, 17:12-19; and a blind beggar, 18:35-43). The parables, however, are much more numerous than in the previous section. Some of the most famous are found only in Luke (for example, the good Samaritan [10:25-37], the prodigal son [15:11-32], the rich man and Lazarus [16:14-31], and the Pharisee and the tax collector [18:9-14]).

Although all of this section is lacking in the other Synoptic Gospels just in the form it appears in Luke, nevertheless some of the material is paralleled in different settings. For example, a part of Matthew's record of the Sermon on the Mount is paralleled in Luke's earlier Galilean section as a sermon given in a level place (6:17-49). Other parts of Matthew's Sermon on the Mount are paralleled in this section of Luke (11:2-4, 33; 12:22-31). It is impossible to say whether Matthew has collected sections from Jesus' sermons to give a composite in the Sermon on the Mount; or whether Luke does this in his use of the material, spreading the sayings to different occasions; or whether Matthew's is one sermon of Jesus, and Jesus repeated certain sayings on other occasions as well.

The same main elements are found in this section on the way to Jerusalem that were found in the previous description of the Galilean ministry: Jesus' preaching and healing, the crowds, the disciples, the Pharisees, and growing resistance. Luke's interest in individuals continues: Jesus was in the home of Mary and Martha (10:38-42); He ate in the homes of Pharisees again on two occasions (11:37; 14:1), and the cost of following Jesus, noted in the earlier section (9:57-62), is exemplified in the person of the rich ruler (18:18-30). The crowds, however, continue to grow (11:29; 12:1). The attacks of the Pharisees and experts in the law and the rebuttals of Jesus grow still more severe: the Pharisees said, "By Beelzebub, the prince of demons, he is driving out demons" (11:15); Jesus on another occasion said, "Woe to you [experts in the law], because you build tombs for the prophets, and it was your forefathers who killed them" (11:47).

The whole section ends in a typical Lukan way. That is, the scenes are varied and neatly arranged, building to a climax, but equally faithful to the true historical picture: Jesus predicted His death in a private conversation with His disciples (18:31-34); He healed a blind man at Jericho (18:35-42); He ate in the home of the tax collector, Zacchaeus (19:1-10); and He gave the parable of the ten minas (19:11-26). Jesus was at the threshold of Jerusalem and the fulfillment of the purpose for which He had come.

The Final Week (Luke 19:28—24:53)

With Jesus' triumphal entry into Jerusalem (19:28-44), one senses that the countdown had begun. If the enthusiastic support of the crowds had been calculated each step of the way, it exceeded all bounds here. This is what they had been waiting for. Jesus had declared His Messiahship in His ride into Jerusalem. The enemies of Jesus were beside themselves to devise a plan to counter the momentum of the move toward Jesus.

All four Gospel narratives record this event. In fact, from here to the end of the accounts, all of the Gospel writers follow the same general outline: cleansing the temple (not in John), day of questions, day of Passover, Gethsemane, arrest and trials, the crucifixion, the burial, and the resurrection and appearances.

Definite Lukan touches are felt in the closing scenes of his Gospel, such as the role of the women in the resurrection appearances and the warm, personal glow that lights the appearance to the two on the road to Emmaus. At His ascension, the disciples worshiped Him, returned to Jerusalem with joy, and waited. Luke reserves further word of this scene for the opening of his next volume, Acts. With Jesus' commission to His disciples and the power manifested on Pentecost, the final keystone was dropped into place and the arch was complete, binding man and God together again. Luke's history of redemption was an inspired account of what God wanted man to understand.

Part One:

The Beginnings

Luke 1:1—4:13

CHAPTER ONE

Fulfillment

Luke 1

The opening of Luke's Gospel treats a number of beginnings. When the angel Gabriel announced the birth of a son to Zechariah, it was the beginning of fulfillment. The birth of Jesus in Bethlehem marked the beginning of the visitation when the Word became flesh and lived among His own. The Jewish boy officially became a youth after his twelfth year, and Luke tells of a trip to Jerusalem in the beginning of this period in Jesus' life. Jesus' ministry began with His baptism and temptation trials. Luke gives the genealogy of Jesus, and the beginnings are complete.

Prologue and Preparation

The Setting: Then and Now (1-4)

Professor Cadbury was walking through the stacks in the Divinity School library of Harvard University. He remarked to a student walking by his side that the listings of the library numbered five hundred thousand and that ten percent of the books were about Jesus.

Luke begins his Gospel by noting that, even then, there were numerous reports about Jesus. He does not actually say there were too many. Neither does he say that some had presumed to write about Jesus when they should not have written, but he indicates there is no account like the one he was going to write. It would have a solid basis in the testimony of eyewitnesses. It would be complete, beginning at the beginning. It would have an orderly arrangement, going logically from one event to another. He does not say he will go to the end, but the inference is he will go as far as he can in his own investigation and experience. One is not told whether it includes the second volume, the book of

WHERE EAST MEETS WEST

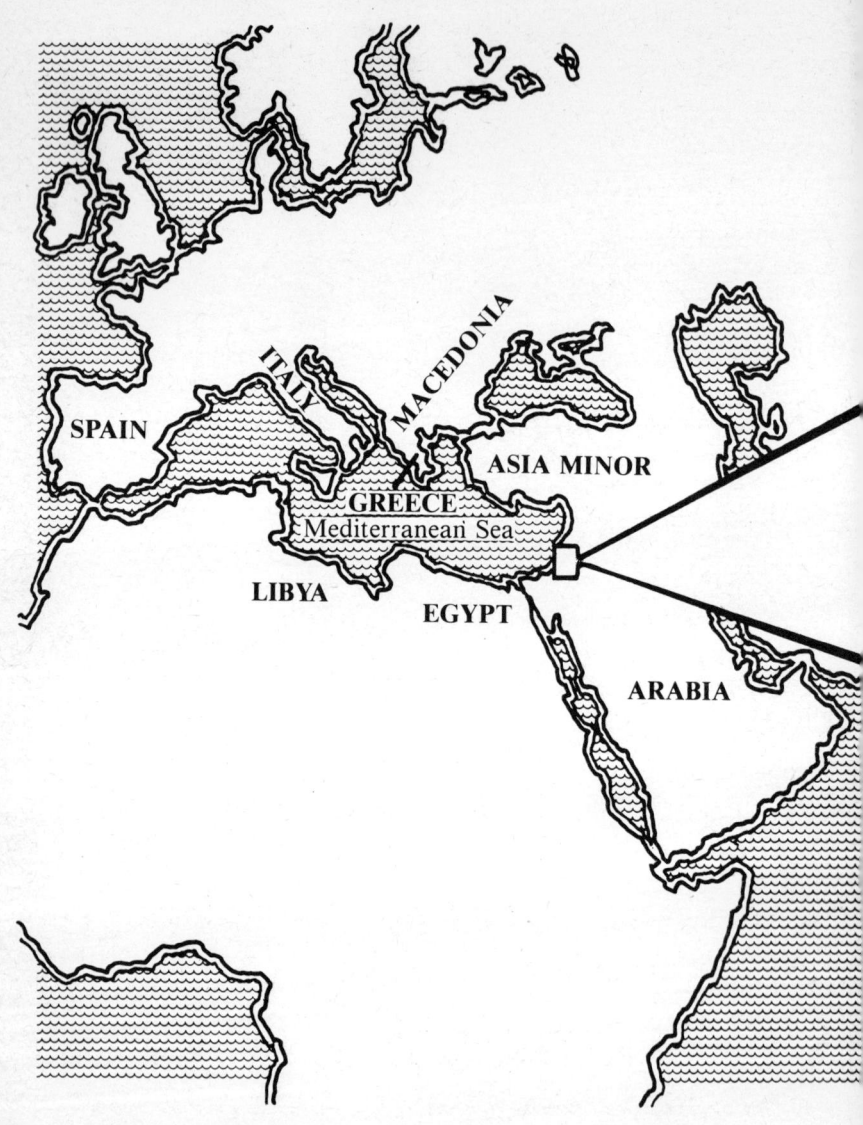

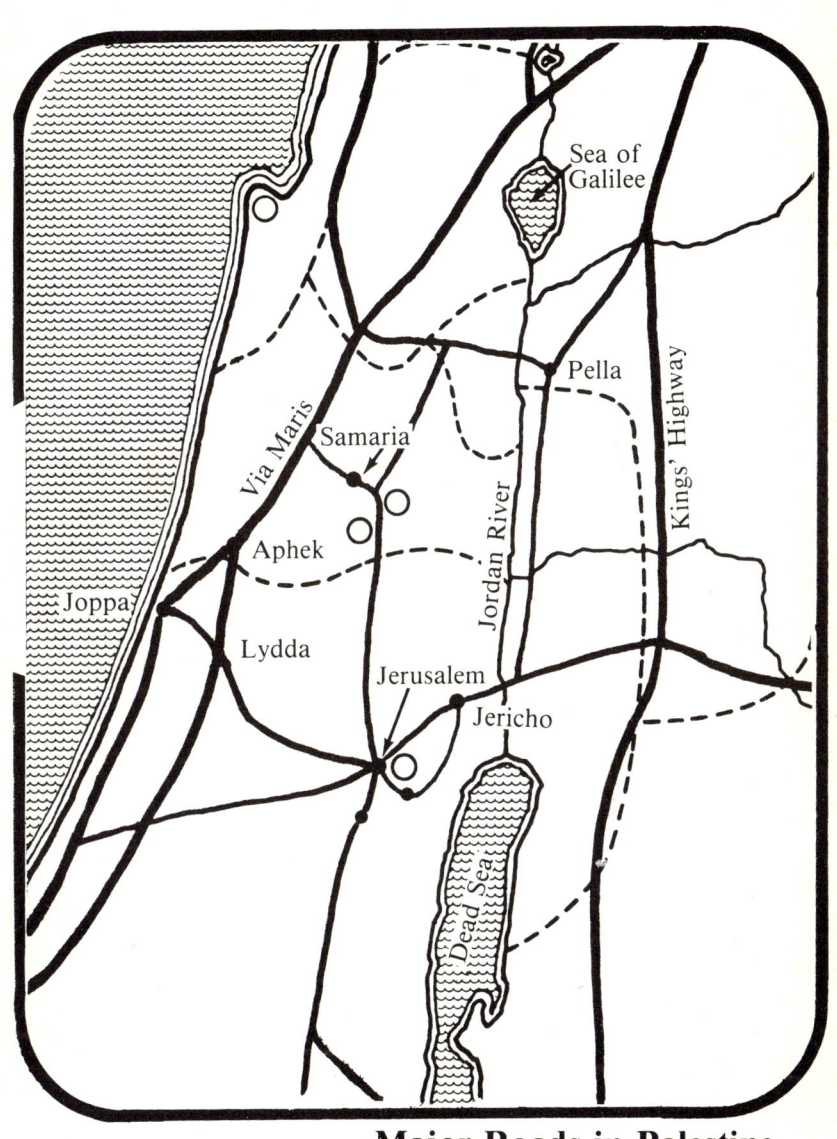
Major Roads in Palestine

Acts, as well. In all likelihood, it is for both, as he anticipates bringing his work up to the date of his writing. The purpose of his work is also stated: to bring certainty. This was a need in the first century, and it is no less a need today.

Professor Cadbury continued his remarks to the student in the Harvard library by explaining that he had been walking through those stacks just the week before with Albert Schweitzer, who was visiting the Harvard campus at the time. Schweitzer had asked Cadbury to point out the worthwhile recent books on Jesus. Cadbury confessed his embarrassment as he admitted, "I didn't have a single one to show him."

It is ironic that both these men had written books about Jesus in former years. Schweitzer wrote *The Quest for the Historical Jesus*,[1] in which he insisted that the historical Jesus passes us by in the twentieth century to return to the first century from which He came. Along a similar vein of thought, Cadbury entitled his book *The Peril of Modernizing Jesus*.[2] He gave due warning that one should not try to make Jesus into one's own ideal, whatever that might be—super salesman, revolutionary, or whatever line of interest an individual might have today. Although the warning is needed—to refrain from molding one's concept of Jesus to his own liking—Cadbury went too far in that he, too, limited Jesus to the first century.

Luke writes for today as well as for the first century. He presents a Jesus whose work continues. The Gospel tells of what Jesus "began to do and to teach," and the book of Acts tells of His continuing work, which He continues even today. In Luke's century, there was warning of those who would deny that Jesus came in the flesh (1 John 4:2ff.). They were saying He was really God, but He was not man. Today, some say that Jesus was really man but not divine. In some circles, it is popular to say that what happened is not important, but what the early church believed about Jesus is all one has to go on. Scholars in these circles make a distinction between the Jesus of history and the Christ who was preached in the early church. History is not important, they

---

[1] Albert Schweitzer, *The Quest for the Historical Jesus* (New York: Macmillan, 1948, from the German, 1906).

[2] H. J. Cadbury, *The Peril of Modernizing Jesus* (New York: Macmillan, 1937).

say; the experience one feels is the criterion. So in guarding against such undependable, subjective standards, Luke supplies a need. He gives historical grounds for the faith of a Christian. He proposes a work well-based in testimony and for a good purpose, to provide certainty. He was recommended in the past. He can still be recommended in the present.

The Silence Is Broken (5-17)

One of the last of the prophecies in the Old Testament, recorded in Malachi, concerned the coming of Elijah before the Day of the Lord (Malachi 4:5, 6). After this, a period of silence descended. Israel realized that no prophet was serving as a spokesman for God. The silence lasted for four hundred years. It was finally broken when Gabriel stood before Zechariah in the Holy Place of the temple and informed him that he and Elizabeth were to have a son who would come in the spirit and power of Elijah (Luke 1:17). The silence of the centuries had been broken with the announcement of the coming fulfillment of that very prophecy with which the silence had begun.

Without a doubt, this was the greatest day in Zechariah's life thus far. The day began with Zechariah's preparation to burn incense on the altar in the Holy Place. This could only happen once in a lifetime. The privileged priest was chosen by lot, but there were so many priests that no priest who had once served was ever eligible for lot again. Some of the priests served a whole lifetime and never had the opportunity. So this was the greatest day in Zechariah's life, but he had no idea just how great it would be: the appearance of an angel, the announcement of a son, and this son to be the fulfillment of well-known prophecies of the Scripture. It was too good to be true.

How Can I Be Sure? (18-25)

One can almost feel Gabriel bristle with indignation that Zechariah would question the word of the archangel who had the importance to stand in the presence of Almighty God. It is true that the miracle was great. Zechariah and Elizabeth had been praying for years for a child, but they had long since given up any hope. After all, this was not the age of miracles, and no one had heard of such a thing for centuries. But Gabriel was not to be placated. Indeed, he would give a sign. Not until the event occurred would Zechariah speak one word. This would keep him reminded of what was coming, and also of his doubt at the announcement from God. So the day the silence of the centuries was broken was the day that silence began for Zechariah.

How Will This Be? (26-34)

The scene shifts from Jerusalem to Nazareth some six months later. Gabriel again appeared to make an announcement, this time to a young woman still a virgin, unmarried but engaged. The news that she would have a son was as shocking to her as Zechariah's news had been to him. And she asked a similar question: "How will this be?" But her question was not accompanied by the same doubts that Zechariah had. Gabriel's explanation was patient and beautiful: the power of the Most High would overshadow her and the child will be the Son of God.

May It Be As You Have Said (35-45)

The words of Mary reflect the attitude God desires in all of His people. The gospel of Luke is filled with events that must come to pass in the plan of God. The mother of Jesus gives a moving example of willingness to fulfill her role. It was high honor to be chosen of God to bear His Son, but this was not without sacrifice to Mary. What would become of her betrothal? If a son was born without a visible father, what would happen to her reputation? How would she be able to rear Him? It might be not only a loss of honor, but a loss of life as well. Despite all this, she could say, "May it be to me as you have said."

One great comfort Mary had in her trying circumstances was the information that her relative, Elizabeth, was sharing her experience of having a miraculous type of birth in the near future. Mary made a journey of at least three days travel to visit this one related not only by blood but also as specially chosen by God. The words of joy expressed at their greeting scarcely measured up to the excited conversation that must have filled their days together.

The Magnificat (46-56)

Mary's song of praise has been called the Magnificat because this is the first word of the song in the Latin Vulgate translation of the Bible. This song is like the Psalms, but has special parallels with the song of Hannah (1 Samuel 2:1-10). Mary must have felt particularly close to Hannah as Hannah expressed herself to the Lord in the dedication of her son, Samuel, to his service to the Lord.

The message of this song fits well the interests of Luke. God has brought down the rulers from their thrones and has exalted the humble. He has filled the hungry and sent away the rich empty. These sections in the latter part of the first chapter and the second chapter of Luke are filled with Hebrew constructions, although Luke opened his Gospel with classical Greek. One questions what sources Luke is using in composing this portion of his Gospel. It is not beyond reason that he received the words of Mary from Mary herself. It is not necessary, however, that he have extensive Hebraistic written sources for the section. Luke is perfectly capable of adapting his style to the particular background he is describing.

His Name Is John (57-66)

Zechariah had learned his lesson about following instructions with belief and trust. When objection was raised concerning the name of his son, he was insistent. It is difficult to hold up one's end of the argument when a person cannot speak, and it becomes clear that Zechariah could not hear either; but he wrote down the answer: "His name is John." This name comes from the Greek but is derived from two Hebrew words meaning, "Lord" and "shows grace." Once again, one sees the fitting application to the coming age for which John was to prepare. At the birth and the naming of John, Zechariah could speak again. The words of Gabriel were confirmed on all counts. These were not matters that were done in a corner. People were asking all around, "What is this child going to be?" So Luke was making his rounds among the older generation, learning what he could about the birth of John.

The Benedictus (67-79)

Zechariah offered his praise to the Lord. This song, like Mary's, receives a name from the first word in the Latin version. *Benedictus* means "praise." Whereas Mary's song resembled the Psalms, Zechariah's praise was rather like the prophets in content. His son would be a prophet of the Most High and would go before the Lord to prepare the way for Him. The salvation He brings will rescue those who live in darkness. Luke's history of redemption is beginning to unfold.

Content Notes

The Prologue (1-4)

Although some modern translations divide Luke's opening sentence into shorter sentences, in the Greek, the first sentence is four verses long. A long sentence was not strange in antiquity for a formal beginning. In fact, it was expected. Luke's language and style are precisely what the classicists would have considered in the best of taste. But besides correctness, Luke has beauty; and besides beauty, Luke provides a rich amount of information. In contrast with Luke, Arrian, in his opening sentence to a history of Alexander the Great, shows how the form can be kept but the words contribute nothing to one's understanding: "If anyone wonders why, after so many historians this work of history occurred also to me, when such an one has both read through all their works and perused also this of ours, so let him wonder."

Luke's beginning not only satisfies the criteria of the ancients but of modern scholarship as well. Certain elements are expected in the opening paragraph. (1) The purpose for writing. Luke gives this in the closing statement, "That you may know the certainty of the things you have been taught." (2) Evidence of research. Luke is aware of the many who have undertaken narratives concerning the happenings of the gospel. (3) The need for something more. Luke gives the impression that these former attempts he refers to have lacked completeness. They do not begin at the beginning. They are fragmentary and lack order. Luke proposes to supply deficiencies in these numerous reports. (4) Sources of information. Luke specifies this also. They were eyewitnesses and servants of the Word. (5) Proposed methodology. Luke promises careful investigation from the beginning and orderly arrangement of all material. From the information given in this prologue, one comes to the conclusion that Luke could have written the textbook for form in scholarly works.

Many (1). These are distinguished from the eyewitnesses in verse two. Thus Matthew would not be included in the "many" and Mark may not have been written as yet. It is not likely that Luke had either of these in mind when he referred to the "many." The Greek for "narrative" could refer either to an oral report or to a written account. The word for "draw up" does seem to necessitate putting some episodes together rather than isolated sayings or events. Luke does not say whether these other attempts have resulted in a measure of success or not.

Fulfilled among us. This means the things happened in the same generation as the writing of this account. This may be an indication that Luke was intending this as the prologue for Acts as well as the Gospel. *Fulfilled* is the best translation because it associates the happenings with the Old Testament prophecies. The New King James Version, like its predecessor, has "most surely believed among us." It is true the verb sometimes denotes full conviction (Romans 4:21; 14:5), but what Luke is writing about here is not what was believed but what actually occurred. The belief may be identical to the actual happening, but it destroys the significance of Luke's purpose to interject belief in this context. The Revised Standard Version and the New American Standard Bible have "accomplished among us."

From the first were eyewitnesses (2). These would include the apostles and the charter members of the believers who had known Jesus and experienced some of the happenings of His lifetime. Luke did not include himself in this group. Matthew would have qualified.

Servants of the word. These are evangelists, teachers, and pastors—those who had personal experience in the power of the gospel for the salvation of souls. *Word* in this context means the gospel or the doctrine (Acts 6:4; 8:4; 14:25; 16:6; 17:11).

Carefully investigated. Luke traces the course of the matter back to the beginnings, even as he records the announcement of John's birth to Zechariah. (See Mark 1:1 for the beginning in John the Baptist.) He does this thoroughly, considering "everything."

An orderly account. In a person's life, one thing is always tied to another, but not necessarily in chronological order. Luke gives a careful report of Jesus' life in an orderly fashion so that each step follows upon the last step in a sequential way, but not necessarily chronologically.

Most excellent Theophilus (3). The Greek for the name means, "friend of God," but it probably refers to an individual and is not a symbolic usage referring to all those who love and are loved of God. Many conjectures and possibilities can be noted: (1) Some suggest he was a wealthy Christian in Antioch who had formerly freed Luke from slavery. (2) Others believe he was a Roman official who had begun his own investigation of

Christianity, and now Luke writes to add factual information to what Theophilus has learned thus far. (3) Some have suggested he was a Gentile who was not a Christian but a God-fearer, one who respected the one God but had neither accepted Judaism under the law of Moses nor Christ and His gospel. In this case, Luke would be writing to lead him to accept Jesus. (4) Perhaps he was a person high in Roman government who had become a Christian and Luke was writing to strengthen his foundation and encourage him in his growth. (5) Since the phrase "most excellent" is used, it would seem to indicate an individual of importance, either wealthy or in high government position. (See its use in Acts 24:3; 26:25). (6) Luke may have sought an individual of sufficient means to be his patron and provide the financing for the publication of his two-volume work. Note Theophilus is named in the second volume also: Acts 1:1. In this case, he probably was already a Christian. The last two of these suggestions seem most likely, although some elements in the others may be true as well.

Certainty (4). Because of the order of the words in this prologue, the word that gains the most emphasis is *certainty.* This is the bottom line. Luke wants to establish assurance from the historical facts of the Gospel. It was addressed to Theophilus, but it is meant for every individual, as long as the world continues, that each one might know the certainty of the way of redemption in the Lord.

About the Coming of John's Birth (5-25)

Herod (5). This was Herod the Great, who ruled over Judea (used of all Palestine here—see Luke 4:44; 23:5), including Samaria, Galilee, and much of Perea and Coela-Syria (37 B.C.—4 B.C.). He is not to be confused with his son Herod Antipas, who had John beheaded and held one of the trials of Jesus. Luke gives the ruler's name here in order to date this opening event. It was an effective way antiquity had of marking time. Luke is being faithful to his intention of setting the historical grounds for the coming action.

Observing the commandments blamelessly (6). This did not mean they were sinless-perfect but that their observance of the Old Convenant law was above reproach. Similar praise is given to Simeon (Luke 2:25) and Joseph (Matthew 1:19).

Chosen by lot (9). The priests were so numerous (about

18,000) that the services of highest honor were designated by lot each day. Four were chosen by lot in the morning to tend the golden lampstand; the table of the Presence; and the highest honor, the offering of incense on the altar in front of the Holy of Holies. In the evening, the lots were again drawn. This time only one—for the offering of incense. The chosen one would select two others to assist him, but they would complete their assignments and withdraw, leaving the priest alone to complete his offering of incense. It is not known whether Zechariah was there in the morning or the evening.[3]

Angel of the Lord (11). This is a title used to describe his function rather than specify one particular angel. (See Genesis 22:15; Exodus 3:2; 1 Kings 19:7; Acts 12:7.) In this case, however, it was Gabriel (Luke 1:19).

Do not be afraid (13). Fear is the immediate reaction commonly registered in the Old Testament as well as the New Testament at the appearance of an angel or when confronted by the miraculous (Judges 6:22; 13:22; Luke 1:30; 2:10; 5:10). This is understandable: the fear of the unknown, the higher power, the humbling admission, the realization of sin in the presence of righteousness, of man in the presence of God. Reassurance is frequently the opening statement of God's spokesman.

Your prayer has been heard. There was a time when Zechariah and Elizabeth's prayers had been fervent for a child. To be childless in Jewish circles was particularly tragic. Not only was the couple deprived of the personal joy of children in the home, but there was the fear of association with divine disfavor, and the added weight of reproach from society in general. But with the coming of old age, the prayers must have waned, and if they continued at all, they lacked faith behind them. Zechariah may have forgotten his prayer, but God had not.

Never to take wine (15). This is part of the Nazirite vow (Numbers 6:1-21). It would include the promise that his hair was not be cut, and he would be wholly dedicated to the Lord. Samson and Samuel (Judges 13:5-7; 1 Samuel 1:11) are Old Testament examples.

Filled with the Holy Spirit. Instead of influence from strong drink, he was to gain his true power from the Spirit. (See Ephe-

---

[3]Alfred Edersheim, *The Temple: Its Ministry and Services* (London: Religous Tract Society, 1908), pp. 129-142.

sians 5:18.) Although his is a special gift of the Spirit and one that is to remain constant throughout his life, not intermittent as in the Old Testament period, one does not read of John's working miracles. This is a contrast between his ministry and Jesus'.

In the spirit of Elijah (17). This is the identification of John with the prophecy of Malachi (4:5). He did not return as Elijah *redivivus* (John 1:21), but he was the spiritual embodiment of the great prophet, who preached repentance in the period of the divided kingdom. Jesus made the identification as well (Matthew 11:14; 17:10-13).

To turn the hearts of the fathers to their children. The preaching of John was to have not only an effect in announcing the coming of the Messiah, but to bring about a reformation in the lives of many. A reformation to the righteousness of God will be reflected in the state of the family as the basic residence of the wholesome and good. John would truly turn the hearts of the fathers to their children as the first step toward a new relationship with God. Some have suggested that this is a figurative passage referring to the patriarchs in Heaven as they rejoiced upon the return of the children of Israel on earth, but such a notion is difficult to accept.

Gabriel (19). The Scripture alludes to tens of thousands of angels, but only two are named. Gabriel means "mighty one" or "hero of God" (Daniel 8:16; 9:21-23) and Michael (Daniel 10:13, 21; 12:1) means "one who is like God." Gabriel seems to represent the ministering angels, and Michael, the warring angels in opposition to Satan. Gabriel is the angel of mercy and Michael the executor of judgment. Gabriel was the fitting one to deliver God's message both to Zechariah and to Mary (Luke 1:26-38). When Zechariah voiced his doubts about having a son, he reminded the angel, but "I am an old man." The reply was, Yes, but "I am Gabriel." One can have full assurance in what Gabriel has to say.

The people were waiting (21). While Zechariah was offering incense inside the Holy Place, where only the selected priests could go, the people were praying and worshiping outside the precincts of the building (Luke 1:10). The priests were careful not to tarry inside the Holy Place because the people outside would be anxious for their welfare lest some unpredictable event should take place so close to the Divine Presence. So on this occasion, the people had become concerned because Zechariah had taken more time than was ordinary. When Zechariah did appear, the crowd was sure their fears had been justified. By his looks, by his attempts to communicate through gestures what had happened, by the fact that he could not speak, the people were assured that Zechariah had seen a vision (something or someone of the supernatural, generally invisible to human eyes).

Service was completed (23). The length of public service in Jerusalem for the priest was one week (from one Sabbath to the next Sabbath) every six months. Zechariah completed this week and went to his home. It is not known where his residence was, other than in the hill country of Judah (Luke 1:39). Perhaps it is the town pointed out by tradition as a Levitical city, Juttah, a few miles south of Hebron.

Remained in seclusion (24). The reason for the withdrawal is not fully known. No such custom for pregnant women has been established for this particular time and place. Perhaps Elizabeth was reluctant to undergo the doubt and debate of her acquaintances early in her pregnancy. The following verse, however, would indicate that the basic reason was to give herself to a period of joy, devotion, and thanksgiving for the blessing the Lord had promised and was fulfilling. This, indeed, would take away the reproach the people had made against her in the past because she had no children. The fact that her pregnancy remained a secret explains why it was unknown to Mary, and Gabriel was able to make the announcement to Mary that her relative also was to have a child (Luke 1:36).

About the Coming of Jesus' Birth (26-45)

In the sixth month (26). From the time of John's conception and the next month after Elizabeth's period of seclusion (v. 24).

Nazareth in Galilee. The fuller identification of the town is given for the benefit of Luke's initial readers, probably Gentiles who had never been to Palestine. It would be very unlikely they knew of the location of so small and insignficant a town as Nazareth. It is not named in the Old Testament nor mentioned in Josephus. Even Nathanael made a contemptuous remark about it (John 1:46). To add the region of Galilee would be helpful for Luke's readers. It is in the southern part of Galilee, about twenty-five miles from the Mediterranean Sea and twenty from the Sea of Galilee.

To a virgin (27). The description of the birth of Christ is lined from beginning to end with an emphasis on the virginity of Mary when Jesus was born. No amount of comparison with other literature or variant manuscripts can erase all of the references and bridge the account without the vital truth that Mary was a virgin. (See page 58ff.) Her age is not indicated, but from the Jewish custom of early bethrothal and marriage, it is likely that she was quite young.

Pledged to be married. Engagement in the Jewish society of that time was tantamount to the marriage vows. No breaking of the engagement could be approved without a regular procedure of divorce.

A descendant of David. From the usage in the sentence, it is impossible to determine whether this refers to Joseph or Mary. From other passages, it is inferred that Mary and Joseph were both of the lineage of David (Luke 1:32; 2:5). Jesus' bloodline came through Mary, but his formal, paper lineage, through Joseph. But since both were of the line of David, this passage is not changed either way.

Kind of greeting (29). Whether in the home or some other private place (the tradition that the scene occurred at the town well seems highly unlikely), Gabriel's appearance would be an awesome experience for a young girl. But it was his greeting that seemed to trouble her most. She was highly favored of God. Why? What for? The words, "The Lord is with you," is an Old Testament greeting (Judges 6:12; Ruth 2:4) and seems to say, "The Lord will help you perform your divine service."

The name of Jesus (31). Mary was told she would conceive and bear a son and His name would be Jesus. (The meaning is "the Lord saves," the same as the Hebrew, Joshua. See Matthew 1:21.) Like the announcement of John's birth, the naming of the son was included. Gabriel did not specify when the conception and birth would transpire, but it is evident that Mary concluded the fulfillment would begin immediately. Joseph also was informed about the name of Jesus (Matthew 1:21).

The Son of the Most High (32). A title of God used in the Greek translation of the Old Testament (LXX) as well as Hellenistic circles (Galatians 14:18; see also Luke 1:35, 76; 6:35; 8:28; Acts 7:48; 16:17; Hebrews 7:1).

Throne of his father David. Possibly from 2 Samuel 7:12, 16 comes the allusion made here. The Messiah was expected from the line of David (Luke 20:41; 18:38).

House of Jacob (33). Jacob has his spiritual descendants (Galatians 3:7, 28, 29) and the kingdom is not of this world (John 18:36).

Forever. Christ's kingdom will be forever because it will be absorbed into the Father's (1 Corinthians 15:24-28) and thus will continue eternally (Daniel 2:44; 7:14; John 12:34; Revelation 11:15).

The Son of God (35). Jesus is the Son of God on more than one count: His eternal relationship with the Father, His birth into this world when He became flesh through the operation of the Spirit in miraculous conception, and upon the completion of His earthly task, He became the Son of God in the resurrection (Acts 13:33; Romans 1:4). Christ affirmed it of himself (John 10:36; Mark 14:61, 62), the voice from Heaven confirmed it (Luke 3:22; 9:35), Peter declared it in his confession (Matthew 16:16), the centurion chose those words (Mark 15:39), the devil used them (Luke 4:3, 9), and the demoniacs gave their witness (Mark 3:11; 5:7). Already Luke was building his case for the deity of Jesus. Even before Jesus was born, the angel of the Lord declared Him to be the Son of God. This claim did not come by chance, nor by afterthought, but in the unfolding of God's way of redemption.

Elizabeth your relative is going to have a child (36). Mary inquired how these things could possibly become reality. Gabriel patiently explained the role of God through the Holy Spirit, and then knowing this by no means could bring complete understanding, he gave news that served both as a sign and a deep comfort to Mary. Her relative (the word is not specific; so one cannot tell whether this is cousin, aunt, or more distant relative), whom Mary evidently knew well, was also going to have a baby; and since she was well advanced in years, this, too, must be of a miraculous nature. Zechariah's sign was his silence, but Mary's sign was her relative. Zechariah had inquired in doubt, but Mary had asked in trust.

Hurried to a town in the hill country of Judah (39). Why the hurry? Mary was eager to confirm her experience with the information from Gabriel by hearing of Elizabeth's experience. She also wanted to receive encouragement and counsel from an older woman, especially one who was having her first child, also.

Leaped for joy (44). The whole narrative is filled with the note of joy and rejoicing as the episodes occur one after the other.

Mary's Song (46-56)

God my Savior (47). In the later years of the Old Testament period, the title Savior was reserved for God himself. It is used that way here, but Luke also records it as a title for Christ. (See Luke 2:11.)

Humble state of his servant (48). Mary spoke as one who came from a little village in Galilee, betrothed to a carpenter, but chosen to be the mother of God's Son. In His mercy to those who fear Him, God had turned things around. He had exalted the humble and sent the rich and powerful away empty.

Stayed for about three months (56). Mary probably remained with Elizabeth until the birth of John and then left.

The Birth of John the Baptist (57-66)

Her neighbors and relatives (58). When John was born may have been the first that the neighbors knew about the pregnancy of Elizabeth. The note that followed his birth was joy.

To name him (59). It was not ordinary to wait until the eighth day when the baby was circumcised for naming the child. This may have occurred because the matter was kept a secret until the actual birth had taken place. Then they discussed the name. Zechariah's forced silence complicated communication.

Writing tablet (63). The writing tablet Zechariah requested was probably a small board with wax on it. Perhaps Elizabeth and Zechariah had communicated on the name already, but it may be that Elizabeth had also received divine instructions on the matter. (Both Joseph and Mary were informed independently of the name Jesus.) Zechariah wrote down the name he had been told by Gabriel, and with this act of obedience, his speech returned.

Zechariah's Song (67-80)

Filled with the Holy Spirit (67). The Gospel of Luke indicates the work of the Spirit in a variety of roles. Here He gives divine guidance in the deliverance of praise. This does not mean that Zechariah had no part in the choice of thoughts and expressions, but he spoke in complete harmony with the divine presence. The first part of his message praised God for the salvation He had brought to His people and joyful results (67-75). The second part turned directly to the role that John would have in this Messianic deliverance (76-79)

A horn of salvation (69). The most powerful part of an animal is his horn. The figure was used to denote God's power in deliverance. "A Mighty Savior" is the connotation as applied to Jesus.

The knowledge of salvation (77). Zechariah did not speak simply of national or political deliverance. This salvation would come through the forgiveness of their sins.

The rising sun (78). This is a beautiful figure depicting the light that came into the world when God visited man in His Son. To those living in darkness and death, He has brought light and peace.

Lived in the desert (80). It may well be that Zechariah and Elizabeth, being elderly already at John's birth, did not live to see John reach manhood. He preferred the uninhabited areas of Judea in the Dead Sea region. He may well have known of the Essenes in this district, but there is no evidence of association.

Faithful People

When one looks at the world just prior to Jesus' birth, he finds many discouraging notes. Gilbert Murray[4] describes the religious state of the Hellenistic world with the chapter title, "Failure of Nerve." The people had been so plagued by civil wars and political corruption, and the old beliefs in the gods and goddesses had brought such little relief, that the average person was desperate in his longing for security and peace. The Jews did not consider themselves much better off. In fact, some thought they were worse off. Many were subject people living in an occupied country. If they did not have Roman authorities to contend with, they had their own Idumean, Herod, who catered to Rome and made things still worse for the Jews. Their religious leaders were demanding. They charged exorbitant prices in the temple area both to change money and to sell sacrificial animals. The Pharisees and Sadducees were always fighting with one another, and the people suffered in between. The question was, "Where do you find hope in the world? Can you find any of the people of God there?"

---

[4]Gilbert Murray, *Five Stages of Greek Religion* (New York: Columbia University Press, 1925).

Just when the picture is darkest, Luke introduces us to people who brighten the outlook for all mankind. When God chose the people to occupy a role in His plan, He did not draw them from the senate in Rome or from the Areopagus in Athens or from Herod's palace in Tiberias or even from the high priest's chambers in Jerusalem; but He found two of His faithful people in an ordinary priest's home in the hill country of Judah. Zechariah was of the eighth section of priests that went under the name of Abijah. There were twenty-four sections in all. Each section went to the temple to serve for one week each six months. The dates they served were much the same each year, April 17-23 and October 3-9. It was preferable that a priest should marry a woman of the line of Aaron also, and Zechariah had done so. Here were two faithful people God could use.

Then there were a Mary and a Joseph in the little town of Nazareth in Galilee. Not many people had heard of Nazareth, but there were faithful people there. When Jesus was born, He was taken to the temple in observance of the law. And there were two more people of God waiting there, Simeon and Anna.

But that is not all. Years later, Jesus found brothers working in Galilee as fishermen. He called them from their nets, and they were willing to follow Him. Peter, Andrew, James, and John. They were all people of God, and Luke introduces us to them. We meet such men as Jairus and Joseph of Arimathea. The two disciples on their way to Emmaus move our hearts with their testimony about Jesus.

Because of Jesus, all these lives were changed. They were faithful people of God. And because Luke told us about them, they keep changing other lives who also see the sun rising to drive back the darkness of sin and death. Life and peace mark the paths of the faithful people.

CHAPTER TWO

The Reception
Luke 2

No more tragic words have been given than the statement of John the apostle concerning the Lord Jesus: "He came to that which was his own, but his own did not receive him" (John 1:11). Even in this, however, the plans and accomplishments of God were served. Paul put it this way: "Though he was rich, yet for your sakes he became poor, so that you through his poverty might become rich" (2 Corinthians 8:9).

But all was not gloom at His coming. Luke shows the brighter side. The angelic hosts in Heaven were celebrating, and they were seen and heard by men. The shepherds, not a group especially noted for worshipful response, were ready to give homage. When the baby was taken to the temple of God for the first time, a devout man and an elderly prophetess were waiting to give welcome to God's anointed one. Years later in the temple, Jesus' reception as a youth was not so clear. It portended of mounting contests to come. The Jewish experts in the law must have been impressed by the youth, but there is no indication of recognition or reception. Even the initial scene of Jesus' birth has its sad notes. The emperor Augustus was ignorant, he simply did not know; and the innkeeper was overcrowded, he simply did not care. And still the world today is filled with much the same kinds of reception.

Birth and Youth

In Bethlehem (1-7)

Caesar Augustus (1)

By using the name of Augustus, Luke achieved several purposes. (1) This lifted the narrative out of the provincial scene in Judea to the universal significance that Luke wanted. The gospel is not for the Jews alone, but the whole world is its field of concern. Caesar Augustus was the highest authority in the Roman empire, and this was the biggest part of the world known in that time and place. He was representative of the whole. (2) The use of his name separated the following narrative from the files of myth invented for some certain purpose. This birth was a real event, and the use of the emperor's name gave it a definite point in time. It was the historian's way of dating a happening. (3) Augustus supplied the reason that brought Joseph and Mary to Bethlehem. This is how it happened that the birthplace of Jesus was this town that had been prophesied (Micah 5:2). The home of Jesse, the father of David, was appropriate because of Jesus' lineage in the house of David. All this became associated with the decree of a Roman ruler. Although he was unaware of it, Augustus had an important role in the fulfillment of the prophecy of the God he did not know.

Augustus stood at the crossroads of the history of Rome. Over seven hundred years were behind her, and over four hundred lay ahead. Until his time, Rome had been a republic, but with the reign of Augustus, the empire began. Augustus was her first emperor, and probably her greatest. He was ruthless and cunning in the beginning, but mellowed as time went on. He wanted to establish law and order throughout the Roman world. He wanted peace and stability. On walls still standing in Ankara, Turkey, is inscribed a copy of his acts during his forty-five years of rule. Included in these is the detail that the doors of the temple of Janus were shut, signifying that peace was enjoyed within all the borders of Roman territory—for only the third time in all her history. Roman roads tied together the whole of the empire from the heart of Rome to the remotest provinces. It would not be long before Christian missionaries would be traveling these post roads attempting to take the gospel to all the people of the known world. Despite the official Latin of Rome, the Greek language was still more universal in use in all parts of the empire and beyond. Building programs were underway on the material side, but Augustus instituted moral reform as well, although his record was not the best in his own household. It was in the fulness of time, in the midst of the reign of Gaius Julius Caesar Octavianus, voted the title of Augustus in 27 B.C., that God sent forth His son. But He was not born in Rome or Alexandria or Antioch; He was born in Bethlehem of Judea.

City of David (4)

At the decree of Augustus that a census be taken throughout the provinces, Joseph with Mary went back to their ancestral home of Bethlehem. A thousand years before, David had grown up in this very town and watched his father's sheep on these very hills. It had been prophesied that from this small town, Bethlehem Ephrathah, would come the ruler of Israel (Micah 5:2), the successor of David, whose rule would be forever.

The village was located about six miles south of Jerusalem. It would be a good three days' journey from Nazareth to Bethlehem, perhaps longer because of the condition of Mary.

Some have denied that a Roman census would require individuals to return to their ancestral homes in order to enroll. Examples, however, of this very procedure have been found in Egypt. C. Vibius Maximus, Prefect of Egypt, gave such an order in A.D. 104. Others have pointed out that if property was still owned from their family ties, then it was a necessary trip, although it cannot be established that Joseph owned any land in the vicinity. He was simply a poor carpenter from Nazareth. Also there are some critics who dispute that it would have been necessary for Mary to come with him. Was she of the tribe of Judah, of the line of David? This is indicated. But did they enroll women as well? It seems they did. But even if it was not necessary by the census requirements, Joseph certainly would not have left her in Nazareth under the circumstances. She was about to have a child, and they were still in the betrothal arrangement or very early in their formal marriage contract although their marriage had not been consummated. All of this would lead to talk and accusations in their home community, so that Joseph would not want to leave Mary alone at this time. And so they arrived in the City of David.

A Manger (7)

When Mary and Joseph came into town, they looked for a place to stay. It was understandable that the inn was overcrowded. Other returned Jews from the line of David needed accommodations. Furthermore, officials and soldiers connected with keeping the census needed a place to stay; and since they were not Jews, no home could keep them. They had to have a place in public housing quarters. Whether this was a second floor with individual rooms intended for the guests, or whether this was one large reception room with individual stalls around the wall for the travelers, no one knows for sure. The first overflow areas would be above on the flat roof of the building or the courtyard below. The servants would be accustomed to these quarters. It was understandable that all these places were filled, and one does not know just how much to blame the innkeeper when he said there was no room.

To read that Joseph and Mary bedded down for the night in the stable is also understandable. At that time and place, the stable would have been on the first floor if the guests were in the upper room or the second floor. It might have been a building directly connected to the guest lodging or it may have been in the center of the large room with compartments for the human occupants on all sides. Or it may even have been an adjacent cave for the animals, as Justin Martyr affirms. Stables were not so remote and separated as they are in our culture, and it is understandable that Joseph and Mary sought shelter there.

What is most striking of all is that when Jesus was born, they laid him in a manger. The manger has come to be so identified with the crib for the baby Jesus that we tend to forget that a manger is simply the feeding trough for the animals. It is true the manger could be made thoroughly clean, and the manger could be made snug and comfortable with fresh straw, and the manger could be surrounded completely with love—but the manger could not be made suitable for a palace or, for that matter, even a middle-class home. Jesus was identified with the most humble, lowly beginning when they laid Him in a manger. Of all the details Luke could have told us about the birth of Christ, he chose this—the manger. He speaks volumes to his readers through the ages in just this one detail. What kind of reception was this for the Son of God? And the life that was begun in a manger ended on a cross!

The Angels (8-14)

Good News (10)

Luke does not dwell upon the somber thoughts of deprivation at the beginning of Jesus' life. Rather he presents the facts without comment and with a selection of detail not to inspire sympathy so much as to lay a basis for identification with the lowly throughout His ministry and throughout the centuries.

Abruptly, the scene changes. Luke shows the rejoicing in other quarters. As Jesus said to the Pharisees when they had told Him to quiet His disciples in the final week of His life, "I tell you, if they keep quiet, the stones will cry out" (Luke 19:40). In like manner, it could not be that the birth of the Christ should go unnoticed. If the inhabitants of Bethlehem did not provide a jubilant reception, the angels did. It is not the celebration in Heaven, however, that is described. Luke is recording history as viewed from the human side and investigated and verified by eyewitnesses and ministers of the Word. Only the angels' testimony that broke through to man is related.

Heavenly recognition of Christ's birth began with the appearance of one angel. He had an announcement to make—as to Zechariah (Luke 1:11) and to Mary (Luke 1:26) formerly. As with them, the angel began with reassurance: "Do not be afraid" (Luke 2:10). Every phrase he had to deliver was of prime importance. It was "good news." This was the Greek word for "proclaim the gospel." This is what the whole first volume of Luke is about. The town crier would make announcements in the public square. Sometimes it would be good, sometimes bad. But this was news of "great joy." This, too, is a theme that runs throughout the Gospel of Luke, as well as Acts. "For all the people" is also an important element in the announcement. Most often, what is good news for some people will be bad news for others. But this is good news to all the people of the world and for all time. The note of the universality of the gospel's invitation is seen at the outset in this Gospel in the message of the angel of the Lord. The good news is for the Gentiles as well as the Jews.

Savior (11)

The angel then summed up the good news in terms that are packed with meaning. He told where the event he announced was going to take place. Instead of naming Bethlehem, he designated it as the "town of David." This introduced the association with the place, King David, and the Son of David, a Messianic title. But then he used the title *Savior.* This is the only place in the Synoptic Gospels where this word is used in reference to Jesus. John uses it once (John 4:42), and the reference there is also to Jesus, as are Luke's two references in Acts (5:31; 13:23). It does not appear at all in Matthew or Mark, and Luke uses it only one other time—to record Mary's words in reference to God (Luke 1:47). Paul uses it sparingly in his early epistles

(Philippians 3:20; Ephesians 5:23) in reference to Christ; but in his later pastoral epistles, he uses it frequently of both God and Christ. The title is also used often by Peter in his second epistle to refer to Christ. The growing usage of the title in the later books of the New Testament can probably be explained by the increasing work among the Gentiles. The term *Savior* would be more meaningful to the Gentiles than the title *Christ* (the Greek word for the Hebrew, *Messiah*). But the angel used the word *Savior* from the very moment of Jesus' birth.

Although the word *Savior* was known and used constantly by the Gentile world, it was used in a different way than the angel intended it. The Gentiles used it often to refer to a savior of the body who, they hoped, would bring health and healing to their physical bodies. Esclepius was a pagan god from whom they sought help as a "savior." Another usage of the word was as "savior" of the Roman state. In his fourth Eclogue, Virgil spoke of a "savior" the world was looking for. But he wrote as poet laureate of the Roman government, and in all likelihood, he was referring to Augustus and the people's hope that their emperor would bring peace and prosperity to the Roman empire. When the term is applied to Jesus, it has another dimension. It was a title of the one, true, living God; so when applied to Jesus, it carried the dimension of deity. Of a truth, in Jesus' ministry, He healed physical bodies, but His was more than a ministry in a physical way. He was Savior of the soul. He brought redemption of the spirit that was eternal. He introduced a citizenship in the kingdom of God. All this could not be said in the announcement of the angel; but by using this word, the Gentile reader would have new interest in reading further about the Savior, and the Jewish reader would marvel that Jesus had been born as God, the Son (John 1:18).

The angel did not leave the Jewish audience in doubt. He used the term *Christ* to specify the Messiah whom the faithful Jew had long awaited. And with this term, he coupled still another title, *Lord*. This last title was meaningful to Jew and Gentile alike. When *Lord* was used in a context beyond respectful honor given to an important human person, it denoted the divine.

A Sign (12)

Just as Zechariah was given the sign of silence (Luke 1:20), and just as Mary was given the sign of Elizabeth's conception

(Luke 1:36), so the angel gave a sign to the shepherds to validate the truth of all he had announced. This sign would be recognized when they found a baby in a manger and wrapped in the usual strips of cloth upon cloth. Then they would know this was the child, and that what the angel had said was true. Notice again the significance of the manger. From the description of the angel, this baby was to be the most exalted kind of person ever heard of. How could a common ordinary person hope to get close enough even to see Him? But when it is added that He is in a feeding trough—this puts Him within the reach of all. If this were all, then one last thought may have come to the mind of the hearers. The baby has been deserted. He has been left to die. But the detail of the manger was coupled with the cloths. These cloths were the usual swaddling clothes in which the babies were lovingly wrapped. No doubt Mary had brought them with her just in case they were needed. It was the simplest kind of layette. Just as the manger represented a lowly association with a stable, so the cloths represented the tender, loving care of conscientious parents. This was a combination that served as a sign to all the world: the humble and loving care.

Glory and Peace (14)

And then the single angel was joined by a whole army of angels, praising God and presenting thoughts that gravitate around two words: *glory* and *peace*. They gave the glory to God, a glory that required the companions of respect, honor, submission, and obedience. They petitioned God for peace toward men. Different levels of peace must be remembered. Peace of body is the basic physical peace one cannot have without a healthy condition free of all serious ailments or handicaps. But this is just surface peace. This is the level where battles are fought and physical violence breaks out. But beyond this level of peace, there is also a peace of mind. One needs something to measure by here—something to provide order and certainty, something to drive back fear, something to establish goals to aim toward, some way to determine the course. But this is not all. Beyond these levels of peace, physical and mental, there is the peace of soul that cannot be present until there is forgiveness of sins. And this is Luke's concern—to lay down the way of redemption that brings peace to the soul, a peace with God. Luke found it in the message of the angels at the very birth of Jesus.

The Shepherds (15-20)

But who would be selected to receive this message from the angels? Who of all the people in Bethlehem would be informed as to the momentous happenings of that night? A group of shepherds was chosen. Were they the most Godly men in Bethlehem? One cannot be sure. The shepherds as a whole did not have that reputation. They were rather looked upon as a wandering lot who could not be trusted too far as they passed through other people's property. Of course, these may have been special shepherds keeping the flocks of the temple sheep ready for sacrifice. This is why it is impossible to say whether this was winter or summer—the rainy or the dry season—because the temple flocks might be found in the fields at night any time of the year. Certainly the shepherds were not chosen because they were the most important people in town, nor the most widely known either in business deals or political circles. In fact they did not count for much at all, and this may be the very reason they were chosen. They were from the lowly among the people, and Jesus from the beginning was receiving identity with the common folk. Luke was particularly interested in this, and when he found out about it, he wanted it known. Besides, the shepherds were at home with the animals in a stable. The shepherds would feel at home in those surroundings—much more so than in a palace.

Verification

When the shepherds had heard and seen the angels, they did just what Mary did following her visit from Gabriel. She went with haste to see Elizabeth and verify what she had been told. The shepherds went with haste to find what the angels had told them about. But how would they know where to look? If you were looking for a manger, why not in a stable? As to which stable, why not the one strangers would use when they came to town? It is unlikely that Bethlehem had more than one inn, and this would be the first stop for the shepherds. They found everything just as they had been told (Luke 2:20).

Publication

The shepherds took the next natural step. They wanted to spread the word about what they had seen and heard. They told it the rest of their lives. No doubt many took this as another shepherds' tale originating around the campfire. But the evidence was not just the appearance of the angels or just what the angels said about Jesus. The shepherds themselves saw the baby in the manger; they themselves met Mary and Joseph. Mary treasured in her heart what the shepherds told her that night. After all, she had a right to expect something special when her son was unique, the only Son of God.

One more important thought can be added to the testimony of the shepherds. If the baby the shepherds told about grew to be the man we read about in the Gospel of Luke, the Jesus who brought salvation, it is not difficult to believe the reception the shepherds gave Him. One wonders whether Luke was able to find one of those shepherds who had seen the baby Jesus and was still alive when Luke was researching for his Gospel. If Luke talked with Mary, she certainly would have told him about the shepherds. Perhaps that is why Luke records that Mary treasured these things in her heart—because he probed into these treasures years later and wrote them down in his Gospel. The publication of the shepherds had extended to that day and beyond.

Glorification

The example of the shepherds does not end with the publication of the good news. They returned to their duties in the field, but this time, they were glorifying God (Luke 2:20). Their lives, their tasks, everything had a new meaning now, and God was at the center. They anticipated each new day watching for the Messiah and His kingdom. As the angels glorified God at the birth of the Christ child, so did the shepherds. This must be counted as part of the reception of Jesus on the first night. God was glorified.

Welcome (21-40)

Presentation

Luke continues to include notes that tell about Jesus' humble beginnings. When He was taken to the temple for His presentation to the Lord, a sacrifice was given for the purification of the mother (Leviticus 12:2-8), and the firstborn of both man and animal were to be dedicated to the Lord. The animals were offered in sacrifice, but the human lives were to be dedicated in service. Since the Levites were the ones who actually devoted their time to the Lord's service, arrangements were made by which their service could be substituted for each of the other firstborn males. A sum of five shekels was the ordinary payment made for the Levitical substitution privilege (Exodus 13:12; Numbers 3:11-13; 8:17). In the case of Mary and Jesus, instead of the regular requirement of a lamb and a pigeon (or dove), two pigeons (or doves) were offered as was allowed when the individuals were too poor to provide the regular sacrifice. As for the five shekels, nothing is said. Some have interpreted this as another indication that the couple was too poor to afford the substitution payment. More likely, the substitution payment was not necessary because Jesus' dedication was complete in itself. No Levitical substitution was necessary because Jesus was to render a service greater than any other, and He could pay no one else to serve for Him. But the family was poor, and the option for the lowly was accepted in the purification sacrifice.

Simeon (25)

Not uncommon to the presentation of an infant in the temple area was the role of an older rabbi who would add his blessings and prayers for the baby.[5] In the case of Jesus, He was approached and taken into the arms of a man named Simeon. One is not told whether he was a rabbi or not, only that he was righteous and devout. Neither is one told he is old, but this may well be true since his words pronounced over the baby Jesus included his avowal that now he was ready to die—he had seen the one who would bring Messianic redemption to both the Gentiles and Israel. His words are known as the *Nunc Dimittis,* which are the opening words of the lines in the Latin translation. They signify that now Simeon was ready to be dismissed from this life upon the fulfillment of his duty, waiting for the coming of the Messiah. Now he had seen Him and been able to add his words of welcome to His reception.

Simeon's testimony informs the reader of three utterances where the Spirit led Simeon: a prediction to Simeon personally, a prayer of joy and fulfillment, and a prophecy of ominous import. His prediction to Simeon had been that he would not die until he had seen "the Lord's Christ." His prayer was given

---

[5]H. L. Strack and P. Billerback (1954-56), in E. Earle Ellis, *The Gospel of Luke* (Greenwood, SC: Attic Press, 1974), p. 83.

as he held Jesus in his arms. It gave thanks for the salvation personified in the person of Jesus and was destined for Gentile and Jew alike. His prophecy was given to the face of Mary. It was the first inkling of the opposition and tragedy to come with the way of redemption. It was almost as though he could see Mary standing before the cross at Jesus' death. Such sorrow she would have! "And a sword will pierce your own soul too," were his words to Mary (Luke 2:35).

Anna (36)

Another figure approached to add further word of welcome to the reception of Jesus. This time, it was a prophetess. Only seven women are listed in the Talmudic Megillah as having prophesied to Israel: Sarah, Miriam, Deborah, Hannah, Abigail, Huldah, and Esther. It was an honor to be counted as a prophetess. Anna was counted also as a widow for many years. Perhaps she belonged to a type of widows' guild and lived in the precincts of the temple area. At least, she was there each time the gates were open for prayer and fasting. Her welcome included thanks to God and identification of the child to those who were concerned about the redemption of Jerusalem.

His Father's House (41-52)

The Bottom Line

To discern the fullest meaning of a passage, it is well to determine the bottom line. What is the most important truth the author intends to teach? It is well to look at Jesus' journey to Jerusalem when He was twelve and try to decide, "What is the bottom line?"

The bottom line is not always the last line of a passage. The last line of this account has to do with Jesus' growth—"in wisdom and stature, and in favor with God and men" (Luke 2:52). No doubt, this truth was important to Luke's selection of this material. He presents Jesus as a baby, as a youth, and as a young man. This episode was needed as an example of His youth. But that is not the bottom line. Some remember most clearly from the event how precocious Jesus was. True, He amazed the scholars of the Jews in the temple, listening to them, answering their questions and asking still more. This is important, but still not the most important information from the episode. Then what about the fact he returned to Nazareth afterward and was subject to Joseph and Mary? This is important to understanding the whole of these developing years. But the bottom line appears when Jesus declares, "Didn't you know I had to be in my Father's house?" (Luke 2:49). By this, Jesus made self-claim in these early years to His relationship with His Heavenly Father. Mary was reprimanding Jesus for having caused worry by staying behind in Jerusalem after the Passover. Mary had said, "Your father and I have been anxiously searching for you" (Luke 2:48). In this context, Jesus reminded her that His true Father was God.

By this one incident, Luke informs his readers of a number of important answers. Yes, Jesus was conscious of His Sonship to God at an early age. No, He did not work miraculous signs to accelerate His divine calling in the period before His public ministry. Yes, He grew up in a home where He was subject to parental guidance as other children. His reception as a youth in Nazareth must have been mixed as was His reception in Jerusalem. All who heard Him were amazed at His understanding. When His parents saw Him, they were astonished, but they did not understand what He was saying to them. Nevertheless, His behavior in the home was marked by obedience (Luke 2:51).

Growth (52)

One reads in the Old Testament that "Samuel continued to grow in stature and in favor with the Lord and with men" (1 Samuel 2:26). Of John the Baptist, Luke tells that "the child grew and became strong in spirit" (1:80). Jesus' growth is traced in the second chapter of Luke—from a baby to a child to a youth to the man Jesus. His growth was physical (stature), intellectual (wisdom), spiritual (in favor with God), and practical (with men).

Content Notes

Jesus' Birth (1-7)

In those days (1). After telling of John the Baptist's growth to manhood, Luke returns to his narrative in the days of Herod the Great. (See Luke 1:5.) This was six months after the birth of John when Joseph and Mary came to Bethlehem, but it is not known when the decree was given.

The entire Roman world. "All of the world" was a designation used to denote Rome and all the territories under its control.

The first census (2). Some deny that Rome conducted a census at this time because other sources do not confirm it. Such an argument from silence is entirely inadequate to deny Luke's report and other sustaining indications: (1) Augustus was a ruler of such orderly procedure that a census would be likely. Information found in the acts of Augustus (*Res Gestae* 2:8) would be impossible except for some kind of census. The census was taken each time for the purpose of taxation and army enlistment. In the case of the Jews, however, men had exemption from military service, and taxation was the most likely motive. Relations in the later years of Herod's reign were so strained between him and Augustus that the emperor felt it necessary to require an oath of allegiance to himself as well as the regular oath to the client king (Herod). Suggestion is made that this enrollment may have been associated with this condition. That Herod should have conducted a census in his own kingdom may have been adjusted to meet a number of possibilities since Herod continually bent in order to stand well with Rome. Besides the likely censuses one has no record of, there are numerous censuses we do have record of.[6] (2) It can be established that censuses were ordinarily taken every fourteen years. These can be traced back from A.D. 230 to A.D. 20 (by indirect reference) every fourteen years. Fourteen more years would project a census in the year A.D. 6. Further evidence for this census comes from Josephus *(Jewish Wars* vii. 253; *Antiquities* xviii.1). This is when a rebellion under Judas occurred (Acts 5:37). This is, however, different from the census at Jesus' birth because Luke notes both of them and designates the earlier one as "first." Subtracting fourteen more years to conjecture the date for the earlier census would bring one to 8 B.C. But this date disagrees with other data concerning the date of the birth of Christ.[7] Allowance could be made for the first census' being somewhat late for need of time to set up the machinery and schedule for a program that had not been

---

[6]See William Ramsey, *Was Christ Born at Bethlehem?* (London: Hodder & Stroughton, 1898).

[7]See the discussion on "Lukan Chronology" at the end of chapter 3.

undertaken before. This was the first census. Thus the most likely date for Jesus' birth (6-4 B.C.) could still be maintained on the basis of a late original census. That the rebellion occurred at the second census (Acts 5:37) is understandable because the Jews had discovered how the results of the first census were used in taxation and resisted the second attempt. (3) There is evidence that a taxation census was held in Egypt in 9 or 8 B.C., which may have served as a forerunner of the decree for a universal census that soon followed. (4) The very credibility of Luke as an historian lends confidence in following him in a detail that has so many indications in its favor and only the lack of an explicit, external statement left to question it.

While Quirinius was governor of Syria. Quirinius is a name that occurs frequently in the annals of Syria between 12 B.C. and A.D. 16. He served in many capacities: military governor, commander-in-chief, and officer in charge of censuses. From 9-6 B.C., Sentius Saturninus was governor of Syria, and from 6-4 B.C., Quinctilius Varus. The next recorded governor was P. Sulpicius Quirinius in A.D. 6. In between it is uncertain. But since Quirinius is governor in A.D. 6, Luke is again accused of inaccuracy. It may be that while Quirinius was serving in Syria, he may have been governor more than once or even served as officer of the census-taking before he was governor. (The word in the Greek is a general word for *lead* or *leader*, and may refer to another position than the conventional head of the province.) Luke may have chosen to specify Quirinius because he was particularly well known for his place in government throughout this period in Syria and especially associated with censusing.

Her firstborn (7). Use of this term would indicate there was another child or children born to Mary at a later time, otherwise "only son" would have been used. (See Luke 7:12.) Luke may use the term also because of the significance in regard to the law (Luke 2:23).

Announcement (8-20)

Christ the Lord (11). This is the only use of this combination in the New Testament. It could mean: Messiah, the Lord; the/an anointed one, the/a Lord; Anointed Lord; the/an anointed one, the/a Lord. What would be understood by Jew and Gentile reader alike would be that this child is Anointed and Divine (not the same as 2:23).

Peace to men on whom his favor rests (14). This is the New International Version's translation. The New American Standard Bible translates it, "Peace among men with whom He is pleased." The New King James translates this (also the older King James) "Peace, good will toward men." The major difference comes from variant readings in the manuscripts. Some manuscripts have a ς (Greek sigma) to end the word meaning "favor, good will, good pleasure," and some do not have the ς. With the ς, the word is in the possessive case, which would signify that the men possess the good will or are the object of God's good will; and the other would signify the *good will* is the nominative case, the same as *peace,* and is another gift to man, parallel to *peace.* Looking at the passage as a whole, it presents a beautiful balance. God—in the highest—glory. Man—on earth—peace. This, however, leaves one word remaining, *eudokia(s),* the Greek word that has raised the question both in manuscript differences and in meaning: (1) "good will" given to men, parallel with *peace;* (2) peace given only to men who have good will; (3) peace given only to men who are under the favor (good will) of God. It seems that the second or third use of the word is required because in a realistic way, peace does not come to all men at the birth of Christ. Somehow, this is an indication that the number is limited. This means that *peace* and *good will* are not parallel in the passage, but *good will* is to be taken as differentiating which persons are intended. In choosing between the remaining possibilities—whether this describes the good will that man has or the favor that God shows, the latter is preferred. Then the word serves as a bridge that connects the two balanced parts: glory to God, peace to men, recipients of God's grace. This does not mean that God is arbitrary in His choice. Man is allowed freedom of the will and God's selection is made on the basis of man's response to God in faith and obedience. The manuscripts are divided in their readings with the majority favoring the King James, but the earlier manuscripts, as represented in different families of texts as well, favor the reading preferred here, "on whom his favor rests," rather than "good will toward men" or "men of good will."[8]

---

[8]See Bruce Metzger, *The Text of the New Testament* (New York: Oxford University Press, 1964), pp. 229, 230.

In the Temple (21-40)

On the eighth day (21). Circumcision was commanded in the law (Leviticus 12:3; see Genesis 17:12). This occasion, far from home for Joseph and Mary, was in contrast to the attendance of the neighbors and relatives in the case of John the Baptist (Luke 1:59).

Time of their purification (22). After the birth of a son, the mother would not be in attendance at the sanctuary for forty days. After this, offerings were made and she was returned to full communion with the assembly of worshipers. Since they were so close to Jerusalem, about six miles, they went personally to give the offerings. It is disputed whether it was necessary for Joseph to be included in this purification. It may be that through contact with Mary, it was necessary. Or it may be that since Joseph was responsible for seeing the law was carried out and providing the sacrifice, the language is used "their purification."

Consecrated to the Lord (23). The purification of the mother and the presentation of the son were combined in one trip to Jerusalem. Jesus' consecration was not accompanied by the redemption payment because Jesus' life was to be given wholly to the service of God, and He needed not appeal for Levitical assistance.

The consolation of Israel (25). Simeon was waiting for the Christ and salvation, which would bring consolation to God's people in the Messianic Age.

Moved by the Spirit (27). In this instance, the Spirit was to bring recognition, to deliver prophecy concerning Christ, and to bring praises to God.

Dismiss your servant (29). "Let me die."

The falling and rising of many in Israel (34). One interpretation of these words sees the truth expressed that the crucified Messiah was going to mean the fall of those who reject Him and the rise of those who accept Him. Another interpretation sees reflected here the truth that before a person can follow Jesus, he must first deny himself and in a sense experience a falling in humility before he is picked up in the strength and redemption of Christ. The former interpretation is preferred.

Sign ... spoken against. Those who reject Christ are opposing the greatest sign of God's love and work, and thereby they oppose God.

Thoughts ... will be revealed (35). What a person is thinking in his heart will be manifest in his treatment of Christ. No neutrality is possible.

Daughter of Phanuel, of the tribe of Asher (36). With utmost care, Luke sets down the historicity of Anna. She was no invented figure. Her father is named and even the tribe she was from. Since Asher is one of the ten tribes which lost its records in the Assyrian conquest, the only way knowledge of one's ancestry could be retained was through preservation from one generation to the next. This was done in some cases, as evidently in the example of Anna.

She was eighty-four (37). From the way this is expressed in the Greek, it is likely she was considerably older than eighty-four, having been a widow for eighty-four years. (See the NIV footnote.) She could have been quite young, possibly 14, when she married, and after seven years her husband had died. Her total age at the time recorded here would then be one hundred five. This is not unheard of. Judith is an example (Judith 8:4-8; 16:22f.).[9]

Required by the Law (39). It is noteworthy that Luke is eager to show that Jesus from His birth was reared as an obedient and conscientious observer of the law of Moses. He was not brought up in a household of rebellion.

Jesus at Twelve (41-52)

Feast of the Passover (41). Jews were commanded to attend three feasts during the year: Passover, Pentecost, and Tabernacles (Exodus 23:14-17; 34:23; Deuteronomy 16:16). Because of traveling distance for those in different parts of the country, it was customary to attempt at least one trip a year, and Passover was usually that one.

When he was twelve (42). The Jewish boy was introduced to the full responsibilities of adulthood at the age of thirteen. For the year prior to this, a Jewish father was busy preparing his son for the step that was coming. To take Jesus to the temple at the age of twelve was most appropriate.

Three days (46). One day had been spent traveling before Mary and Joseph learned that Jesus was not in their company.

---

[9]See I. Howard Marshall, *The Gospel of Luke* (Grand Rapids: Eerdmans, 1978), pp. 123, 124.

Then another day was spent in returning to Jerusalem, and still a third day in search for Him.

In my Father's house (49). The phrase in the Greek allows for still more significance. The word *house* does not appear in the Greek. It says simply, "I must be about the ... of my Father." Obviously something must be added to make it an intelligible sentence in English. It could be any neuter word: the *things* of my Father, my Father's *business,* the *affairs* of my Father, or even, my Father's *house.* Since the question Mary wanted answered, in reality, was, "Where have you been?" Jesus answered by telling a place. The temple was where they found Him, and by using the terminology of "my Father," He was reminding them of the most important truth of all: He is God's Son.

The Virgin Birth

One of today's most seriously questioned doctrines taught in Scripture is the virgin birth of Christ. The attack usually follows this line of approach: (1) A virgin birth is contrary to the natural laws of human birth. (2) Two of the Gospel writers do not mention it, nor is it confirmed by Paul (3) Belief in the virgin birth of Christ is not vital to the faith of the Christian nor the teaching of Jesus. (4) Such a birth account can be explained by stories of miraculous births in other religions of the world. (5) The value of the doctrine can be preserved in a figurative way without actually accepting a literal virgin birth.

Further examination of these objections to the virgin birth of Christ leads to a deeper conviction and appreciation of the truth of the place of the virgin birth in the life of Christ rather than the denial of the doctrine. Numerous books have been written on the subject. Two of the best are James Orr's *The Virgin Birth of Christ* (published in 1907 by Scribner's in New York) and another book of the same title by J. Gresham Machen (published in 1930 by Harper, also in New York).

To deny the virgin birth because it would necessitate a miracle involves one's belief in God and His power. If it is impossible, in one's thinking, for God to perform such a miracle, this simply reflects the skepticism and limitation imposed by the individual. His god is restricted, having the power to do some things but not others. In addition, the very basis for imposing this limitation is significant. Some refuse to accept any claim that lies beyond their own experience, and this leaves them with provincial limitations. Such an insistence confines what one believes to his own small sphere of observations and tests. If one is to confront the evidence for the virgin birth of Christ honestly, he must accept at least the possibility of its truth: that is, Jesus of Nazareth, who lived at a particular time and place in history, was born without human father, being conceived in the womb of the virgin Mary by the power of God through the Holy Spirit.

The following points corroborate the actuality of the miracle. (1) The miracle was predicted hundreds of years before its occurrence (Isaiah 7:14; cf. Matthew 1:22, 23). (2) The virgin birth was attested early and clearly (Matthew 1:18-25; Luke 1:26-38). (3) It was accepted early and fully (in creeds used by Irenaeus and Tertullian, and prior to this in Ignatius [Smyrna 1.1] and Justin Martyr).

The belief in the virgin birth is aided by the following observations. (1) The Christian faith is constantly associated with the miraculous in the life of Jesus (the incarnation, Jesus' power to work miracles, the atonement, the resurrection, the ascension). (2) When the descriptions of the virgin birth are accompanied by descriptions of the life of Jesus, who claimed to be the Son of God, and His claims are matched with His teaching and the miracles He performed, one is compelled to accept His miraculous beginning as commensurate with the whole. (3) If Jesus is the unique son of God, one would expect a beginning that would be more than ordinary. (4) Although one would acknowledge that God could have sent His Son in a number of different beginnings, as a matter of fact, the way that is described in Scripture is the virgin birth. (5) The fact of the virgin birth is more easily accepted than any of the alternatives suggested in denying it.

After dismissing the possibility of the miraculous, deniers of the virgin birth frequently go to a second objection, that the Gospels of Mark and John make no reference to the virgin birth and Paul does not refer to it. From this, some would like to conclude that it did not actually happen, but that the story was started and inserted at a later time. Several observations point up how unwarranted such a conclusion is. (1) Mark begins his Gospel narrative with the baptism of Jesus, and since he does not tell of the birth of Christ, he has no occasion to include the virgin birth. Likewise, the Gospel of John does not include a description of details associated with the birth of Christ. (2)

When John does refer to Christ's coming to earth, although he could have used language fitting a normal human conception if this had been the case, he employs language carefully appropriate to the virgin birth described by Matthew and Luke. "The Word became flesh . . ."(John 1:14). (3) The situation of Paul is similar. Nowhere in his writings does he describe the birth of Christ. In fact, he makes very few allusions to the events of Jesus' life apart from the death, burial, and resurrection (1 Corinthians 15:3, 4). Paul was writing his epistles to those who were already Christians and was not introducing individuals to the events of the life of Christ, let alone of His early life. Once again, however, when he does refer to Jesus' beginning in His earthly life, he uses language in no way contradictory to the virgin birth. "But when the time had fully come, God sent his Son, born of a woman . . ." (Galatians 4:4).

That the New Testament does not give more attention to the doctrine of the virgin birth is not sufficient grounds to deny it ever happened. Jesus did not choose to spend His time in teaching in this area, which would have led to further controversy and where He would be able to verify no more than what the participants had already borne witness to. On the other hand, the doctrine was not forgotten, but became a prominent item of the early creeds. It is evident that the virgin birth of Jesus became an essential doctrine very early; otherwise it would not have drawn such attention. It is likewise evident that Jesus was not the son of Joseph, or there would not have been occasion for the slander and criticism leveled at this point.

Modern attacks against the virgin birth attempt to suggest alternate explanations of the source of the account. In Greek myths, pagan gods, such as Zeus, in a union with mortal women were represented as having famous heroes as offspring. Even Harnack and Lobstein, who deny the virgin birth of Christ, nevertheless recognize that it would take long decades for such a myth to have developed from heathen sources, and this long period of time does not exist before this is doctrine among the Christians. Furthermore, the early sources, Matthew and Luke, are thoroughly Jewish in their accounts, not Gentile in background, and the Christians abhorred the very stories that some would suggest served as sources for the birth of Christ. There was no time for myths, there were no pagan Greek roots, and there were totally different elements in the birth accounts of

Christ. Some critics today would attempt to perpetuate ancient polemics against Christ, which maintained that His birth resulted from a relationship between Mary and a Roman soldier, Panthera. Such attacks have no more grounds than the slurs in Jesus' lifetime that He was born of a Samaritan (John 8:48) or related to Beelzebub (Matthew 12:24ff.). Whether malicious attacks, myths, or slanderous tales, all variant proposals fail to taint the tactful and factual records of Matthew and Luke as they give places, time, and names of historical figures to inform future generations of the virgin birth of Christ.

Finally there are those who would relegate the virgin birth to an optional area where one can interpret these two Gospel accounts either literally or figuratively. This is but a polite way to deny the testimony of Matthew and Luke. They have presented their material in a literal, historical way as part of the whole cloth of the Gospel. Neither textual differences nor labeling a passage as a later interpolation can remove the clear, intended presentation of the birth of Jesus of the virgin Mary. It is not repeated each step of the way through the New Testament, but it is consistent with the whole and vital to an understanding of the incarnation of Christ, when the Word became flesh and lived among mankind. The virgin birth of Jesus is so closely associated with other Biblical doctrines that invariably, when one denies it, other Scriptures are dismissed as well. When one acknowledges the power and the wisdom of God, the humble submission of the virgin Mary, the willing acceptance of the steady Joseph, and the baby Jesus in the manger—one opens his mind and his heart to an understanding of the good news God has delivered to those made in His own image.

CHAPTER THREE

Preface to Ministry
Luke 3:1—4:13

An important event deserves an important introduction. It was both proper and necessary that the coming Messiah have a forerunner who would make preparation for Him and His message. Not only was he commissioned to proclaim Christ's coming, but John the Baptist turned the people into the direction the Christ would be leading them. John stirred the hearts of Israel; and from all over the land, the people turned out to hear this voice crying out in the desert. John wanted to straighten the crooked paths of misunderstanding, to level down the pride of the lofty and fill in the valley of those in despair. He warned of coming judgment, and urged repentance. He introduced baptism for the remission of sins; he announced the coming of the One whose baptism was still greater. He was like a meteor flashing across the sky just prior to the rising of the sun. As Jesus appears in the Gospel ready to undertake His ministry, Jesus' baptism by John is the opening scene. Then follows the genealogy of Jesus, placed here because it is part of a preface for Jesus' ministry and His role of Messiah. Luke does not begin Jesus' line with David or even Abraham, but traces it from Adam. Jesus' mission is to all mankind. His temptations burgeoned as He stepped forth to begin His ministry. Luke completes the preface to Jesus' ministry with His victory over the devil.

John the Baptist and Jesus
Prepare the Way (3:1-20)

The Point in Time (1, 2)
Luke the historian stops to date the opening of Jesus' public activity in a way that no other writer of the New Testament does.

He dates the event with a thorough coverage. The common way of marking a definite date in antiquity was to designate the ruler at that point in time. Luke proceeds to indicate the Roman ruler, the local rulers of the Jewish parts of the empire, and religious rulers as well as the civil rulers.

The precise year is given from Tiberius's reign. This would be about A.D. 26. After A.D. 6, the successors of Herod the Great were no longer allowed to rule in Judea (until Agrippa, A.D. 40 to his death in 44), but instead, governors (prefects) were sent from Rome. In the very year being designated by Luke, Pilate had arrived to occupy the position for ten years. The local rulers, Herod Antipas (4 B.C.-A.D. 39), Philip (4 B.C.-A.D. 34), and Lysanius (discussed below) were enumerated not so much to clarify the dating as to provide political background. The same is true of the high priests. Luke lists two of them to show his awareness that the Romans had deposed Annas in A.D. 14, but the Jews continued to recognize him as their high priest, whereas the Romans recognized only Caiaphas. But despite the two, the singular form was used for the priesthood. This was the Annas-Caiaphas high priest.

A Voice in the Desert (2-9)

The preaching of John sounded a chord that drew crowds of people from all over the land. This chord had certain dominant notes. A warning of the judgment to come was given. A call for repentance was issued that each individual could not escape. A baptism was commanded to mark their turning. And immediate hope was given to fan the growing expectancy of the Messiah. John did not go to the city and preach from the steps of the temple. He did not go to the marketplace where the crowds had come to buy and to exchange news. He did not even stand at the gates and stop those who entered. John cried out in the desert, and they went out to hear him. He probably chose a place at the ford in the Jordan, a few miles north of the Dead Sea where the caravans from the East crossed into the land of Judea. He was heard, and the word spread that a prophet had risen again in Israel.

When Luke introduces John's ministry, he chooses his words carefully: "The word of God came to John" (Luke 3:2). Often this terminology had been used to describe the experience of the Old Testament prophets: "Then the word of the Lord came to

Isaiah" (Isaiah 38:4; see also Jeremiah 1:2, 4: 13:3; Ezekial 1:3). All four of the Gospel narratives tell of the ministry of John the Baptist and all three of the Synoptic Gospels use a quotation from Isaiah to show fulfillment in the work of John. But only Luke carries the quotation far enough to include the words, "And all mankind will see God's salvation" (Luke 3:6; Isaiah 40:5). This is important to Luke's theme as he records the Gospel, and in his independent way, he takes advantage of recording these words from Isaiah. The gospel will be for the Gentiles as well as the Jews.

What Should We Do? (10-14)

John's primary purpose was to prepare the way for the Messiah, but he saw the needs of the world and urged in no uncertain terms the unmistakable fruits of true repentance. No appeal to their Hebrew lineage could save them. The ax was ready to fell the tree of Israel if the tree failed to produce the proper fruit. To the sincere question for instructions for immediate action, John gave clear command. Particular temptations are associated with different walks of life, and John hit directly at the sins of the individuals who raised the questions. Selfishness is a universal failing. Fruits of repentance will be seen when you share your clothing and your food. Tax collectors had a strong temptation to collect enough to have extra left over for themselves. The Roman system contributed to this abuse because the actual taxes were contracted for and paid ahead of time to the government, and then the tax collectors were sent out to replenish the coffers of the company that had already advanced the sum of money to the government. The trouble was that at each level the funds passed through, the agents took out a cut for themselves. John told them not to collect more than was actually called for in their jobs. Soldiers, too, felt they were underpaid. Their temptation was to intimidate and threaten violence in order to extort from the people. To resist such temptations would be evidence of repentance. No doubt these were Jewish soldiers of the temple guard or specially assigned escorts to the tax collectors.

Who Is He? (15-18)

The excitement was running so high some were ready to identify John as the Messiah himself. The question as to John's identity had been raised from his birth (Luke 1:66). In no uncertain terms, John denied any Messianic claims and used the opportunity to contrast his role with that of the Messiah. The Messiah is stronger, He is more worthy, His baptism is superior, and His judgment is final.

The baptism in the Holy Spirit was fulfilled on the Day of Pentecost (see Acts 1:5; 2:4, 16, 38), and "in fire" is explained in the following verses as a fire of judgment that comes upon the lost. (For alternate interpretations of this term, see the "Content Notes" below.) The winnowing fork was a type of shovel used by the farmer to separate the grain from the chaff. The chaff was destroyed, but the grain was preserved.

Luke does not want to close his summary of John's preaching on a negative note. The people heard him gladly and responded (see Luke 20:6), but Matthew makes clear that those addressed as a brood of vipers (Matthew 3:7; cf. Luke 3:7) were the Pharisees and Sadducees who came to look on. To the people, from the outcasts such as the tax collectors to the fishermen who became Jesus' followers, John's message was good news.

Imprisonment of John (19, 20)

One of the characteristics of Luke is that he prefers to complete a subject while he is treating it rather than to wait for the chronological development of the matter. This is an example. Luke tells of the arrest of John the Baptist at this point even though it did not occur for at least another six months. But he wants to tell about it at this time to complete his report concerning John the Baptist. Herod Antipas was the son of Herod the Great, and his mother was Malthace. He had a half-brother, Philip, whom he stopped to visit on his way to Rome. The brother rewarded Philip's hospitality by leaving with his host's wife and making her, Herodias, his own wife. Besides becoming Herod's wife, she was also his niece. When John condemned Herod for this affair, Herod had him put in prison. Luke does not tell at this time of John's death at the order of Herod but alludes to it later on when Herod had misgivings over the deed during his worries about Jesus (Luke 9:7-9). By tradition, the prison where Herod confined John was Machaerus, a Herodian palace-fortress to the east of the Dead Sea at its northern end. Rather than repent, Herod added to his many evil deeds still another, the assignment of John to the misery of a dungeon.

Jesus' Baptism and Genealogy (3:21-38)

Jesus' Baptism (21, 22)

Although Luke's account of the baptism of Jesus is very brief, it includes independent details not found in the other Synoptic accounts. That Jesus was praying at His baptism is specifically noted in Luke alone (Luke 3:21). Prayer is a special theme in Luke. (See Luke 5:16; 6:12; 9:18, 28, 29; 11:1; 22:32, 41; 23:34, 46.) That the Holy Spirit descended as a dove is related in all the Gospel narratives, but Luke alone adds explicity "in bodily form" (Luke 3:22).

John's baptism was characterized by repentance. It was for the forgiveness of sins (Luke 3:3). Then why was Jesus baptized? He had no sin; there was no need for repentance, no place for forgiveness. Luke gives no explanation of this. Matthew includes the words of Jesus that it was done "to fulfill all righteousness" (Matthew 3:15). Luke describes Jesus' baptism as occurring when all the people were being baptized. This may reflect the role of Jesus as representing man and as an example to him. Certainly it gave evidence of His submission to the will of God as in the case of each individual's being baptized in order to follow the instruction of God. The baptism was particularly appropriate to mark the beginning of Jesus' public ministry. It was an act of consecration to the task ahead, to undertake the fulfillment of the purpose for which He had come. It was also the occasion that brought Jesus and John together. Baptism had been prominent in the ministry of John. The Gospel Jesus brought included baptism. It was fitting that the forerunner and the Messiah were linked together at baptism. It was done to fulfill all righteousness.

The Family Line (23-38)

The ancestral descent of an individual in ancient near eastern cultures was highly important. This becomes doubly true when one enters the circle of royalty and nobility. But when the Messiah comes into view, His lineage is absolutely essential: He is the Son of David. It is significant that the two Gospels that tell of the birth of Jesus also give His genealogy. Matthew associates it with His birth, but Luke gives it as a preface to His ministry. There are other differences as well. Matthew begins with Abraham, the father of the Hebrew nation, and traces the line to Jesus. Luke, however, begins with Jesus and goes back, not just to the origins of the Jews, but all the way to Adam and God, thus including the origins of all the people of the world. This is in keeping with Luke's emphasis that the gospel is for the Gentile as well as the Jew.

Another difference that has posed the major problem between the two genealogies is the variety of names that appear at a number of places. If Jesus is one person, then the line of descent should be identical, it would seem. From Abraham to Adam there is no problem because Luke alone has these names. And from David to Abraham the lists are practically the same. But from David to Christ the differences are greater than the parallels. Four major solutions have been offered,[10] but the best seems to be that Matthew gives Joseph's line of descent and Luke presents Mary's. Joseph was the legal father for the tracing of formal records, but he was not the actual father, and it was important to show that the bloodline through Mary could be traced to David as well. Both Mary and Joseph were of the line of David.

The major objection to this view, that the genealogy ordinarily proceeds through the father's side, is not conclusive because the virgin birth itself is not ordinary.

The Temptation of Jesus (4:1-13)

The temptations Satan leveled at Jesus were not confined to these three at the time of Jesus' fast. There must have been many times before and many afterward. But in the preface to Jesus' ministry, the devil made a concentrated effort to penetrate Jesus' defense.

When one chops wood, he always examines the chunk he is splitting. If it is hard wood and a big, tough piece, he will look for splits that have already shown in the log. Even if it is a small, hairline crack, this is the weakest spot and the axman proceeds to cut away at that place. This is the way Satan proceeds. He finds the weakness in a person's life and pounds temptation at that spot. In the case of Jesus, however, there was no prior sin, there were no hairline weaknesses to draw the probes of Satan. But there are other areas the devil concentrates on. Wherever an individual has a special interest, he is liable to carry that interest

---

[10]See the discussion under "Content Notes," below.

to an extent that he neglects responsibilities in another direction. He is tempted to concentrate wholly in one area to satisfy the fulfillment of his particular interests. What were Jesus' particular interests? What thoughts would be filling His mind in this period following His baptism as He fasted and prayed and communed with His Father? Undoubtedly, He would be thinking of the purposes for which He had come to live among men, to lay plans for how He could best accomplish these purposes. This may be a helpful reminder in viewing the temptations of Jesus—to see in the interests of Jesus the cause of Satan's selection of temptation. Rather than a superficial selection of thrusts from three different categories, the physical (make bread), the lust for power (receive the kingdoms of the world), and the craving for fame (jump from the pinnacle of the temple), Satan had more shrewd grounds for choosing the temptations he gave.

When the devil told Jesus to turn stone into bread, it was not simply the physical desperation of gnawing hunger from forty days of fasting that tempted Jesus. What if He should have gone too far in physical privation and died before He fulfilled His purpose in coming to earth? So this temptation may have gone beyond the physical hunger into the anxiety Jesus must have had about living to perform His tasks. Satan knew Jesus' highest desires and goals, and he suggested what could be done, but it was outside the will of God.

Another matter Jesus must have been thinking about was the program of His ministry. How was He going to gain the attention of the people so they would hear His message? The devil had a brilliant suggestion: just jump off the pinnacle of the temple. God would rescue Him, and He would have the attention of all the crowds. The real temptation here was not a desire for fame and show. It was a play to tempt Jesus at the very question of His heart: how could He cause the people to notice Him and listen to His message? To follow Satan's proposal would have been a sensational shortcut, contrary to the true ministry of Jesus. It was not a part of the plan and will of God. It would have been a presumptuous testing of what God would do in the face of an act of violation to His will and direction.

Still another focus of Jesus' thoughts in these hours and days of contemplation in the desert must have included the final end of it all. The final act was not the suffering and crucifixion, not even the initial stages of triumph in the resurrection, but the ultimate triumph of God when His Son will be glorified and acclaimed in His rightful place of honor and authority as every knee will bow before Him. So Satan had his suggestion. Jesus had been contemplating about the way ahead, and as usual, the devil tried to suggest a shortcut. When the devil offered Jesus all the kingdoms of the world if He would only bow down before him, the temptation was not a lust for power. Jesus had already known all power and authority. The temptation Satan was laying before Him was a shortcut to the ultimate glorification of Jesus without all of the pain and suffering associated with the arduous existence in the three years of ministry lying just ahead. Satan offered to deliver it to Him instead of combating Him all the way. But there were several things the matter with this. Satan did not actually possess what he claimed. He could not have produced what he said he would. Secondly, even if he could, he would not have done so. He is the father of liars. It was not right to defy the plan and will of God. It was not right to worship any but the divine. Especially it was blasphemous to bow before Satan.

Content Notes

The Dating (3:1, 2)

The fifteenth year of the reign of Tiberius Caesar (1). Different methods of counting a reign leave this precise date uncertain. (1) The Romans ordinarily started counting the beginning of rule from the death of the former ruler. Tiberius' accession date by this method would be August 19, A.D. 14, and thus the fifteenth year would be August 19, A.D. 28—August 18, A.D. 29. (2) The Jews had two methods of calculating a reign. (a) The Jewish ecclesiastical year began on Nisan 1 (in March or April) and was used to mark any non-Jewish rulers. The regnal year of the Jews, however, would be counted from the New Year's before the actual accession of the king. This would date the fifteenth year of Tiberius's reign about September A.D. 27. (3) The provinces were known to keep their own methods of marking the extent of reign. From Augustus to Nerva, in Syria, the regnal years of the emperor were calculated with the first year extending from the accession date (August 19, 14) to the first civil New Year (Tishri 1). Although this would be but a month or two in Tiberius' case, it would count for a whole year. Thus the

WHERE JESUS' MINISTRY TOOK PLACE

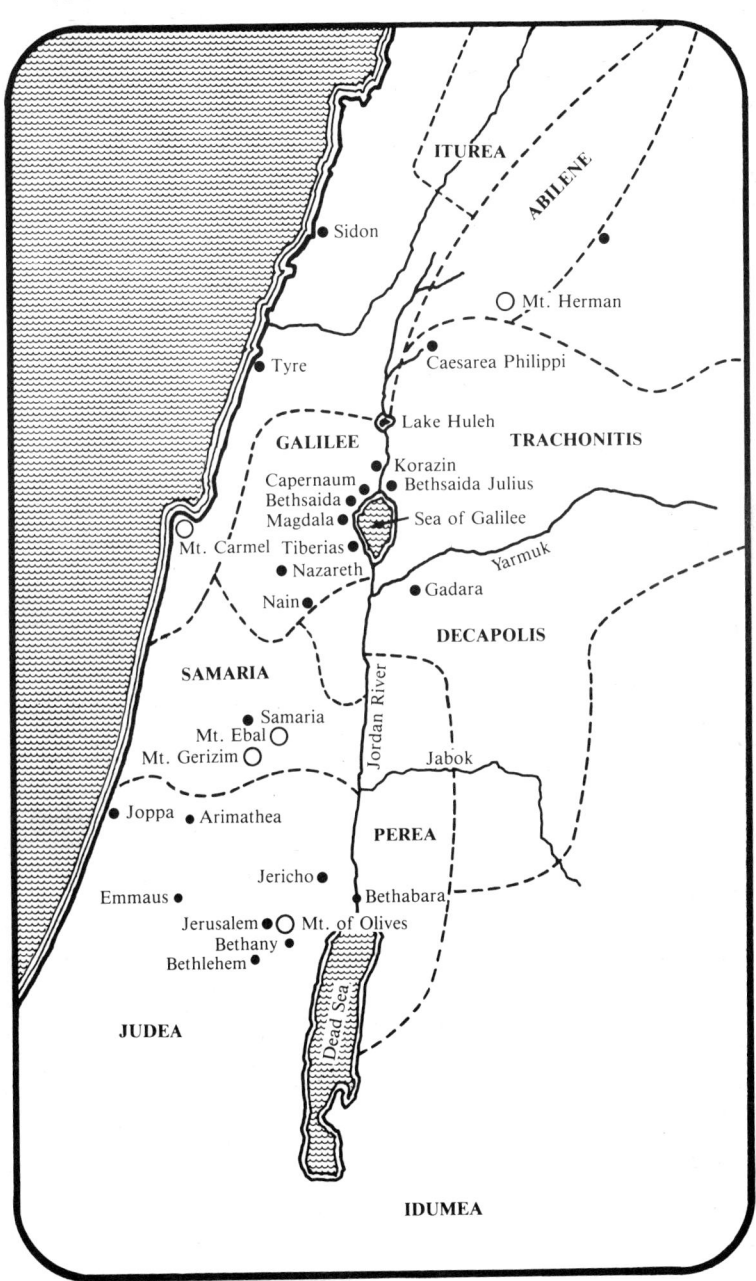

fifteenth year would be Autumn, 27, to Autumn, 28. (4) Another method dependent upon the conditions in the provinces notes the time of Tiberius' co-reign with Augustus, when Tiberius was given imperial authority in the provinces.[11] The year 11 is indicated for this designation of authority. The fifteenth year from the beginning of this provincial power would be 26. This last calculation of time best fits other data in the chronological notes in the life of Jesus. For this reason, the date A.D. 26 is preferred. That there is no coinage supporting this type of dating is not surprising because central Rome would see to it that a semblance of uniformity prevailed in Rome's approved dating of its emperors. That Luke pursues a method neither strictly Jewish nor strictly Roman, but adapted to the provinces, is also not surprising.

Pontius Pilate. Luke uses a general term for ruler (translated *governor).* The technical term for Pilate has been found in Caesarea, *praefectus.* From the time of Claudius (41-54), the ruler of Judea was *procurator* and after A.D. 70, a *legatus* was in charge.

Herod tetrarch of Galilee. This was Herod Antipas, the son of Herod the Great and Malthace. He later had John the Baptist beheaded (Matthew 14:1-12), and he figured in the trials of Jesus (Luke 23:8-11). The term *tetrarch* means literally the ruler of a fourth, but it is also used to denote a ruler of a part in general.

Philip. This was the son of Herod the Great and Cleopatra of Jerusalem. The realm of Iturea and Trachonitus was an area northeast of Galilee, with Caesarea Philippi as its capital.

Lysanius. An earlier Lysanius had been executed by Mark Antony (36 B.C.), and Luke has been accused of inaccurately putting his name at this point. Further information, however, has made clear there was more than one Lysanius who ruled in the area, and it is the younger Lysanius to whom Luke refers. He lived in the first century and died some time between A.D. 28-37. Josephus has a reference to him *(Antiquities* xix, 5, 1), and inscriptions have identified him as well. His tetrarchy was the mountainous territory around Abila, about eighteen miles northwest of Damascus. Probably his region is included in Luke's listing here because in A.D. 37, this land was added to

---

[11]Suetonius, *Tiberius,* 21; Tacitus, *Annals,* 1, 3, 3; Velleius Patercullus 2, 121.

the jurisdiction of Herod Agrippa I. Thus, by the time Luke was writing, it had more Jewish significance.

John's Preaching (3:3-9)

Baptism of repentance (3). John proclaimed openly the need for repentance—a change of heart, arising from sorrow for sin, and leading to reformation of life. This was also a major note in the preaching of Jesus (Luke 13:3). John's emphasis on baptism was noted by Josephus *(Antiquities* xviii, 5, 2) as well as later Christian references (Acts 13:24; 19:4). John's selection of the Jordan as a place for his ministry was probably associated with the need for water for immersion.[12] Baptism marked a person's willingness to break with the sins of the past.

For the forgiveness of sins. This was the purpose of being baptized—that the baptized might be assured of deliverance from the burden and penalty of sin (Luke 1:77; Acts 2:38). This remission was not fully effected until the death of Christ on the cross (Romans 3:25; Hebrews 9:27, 28).

Isaiah the prophet (4). Luke quotes a prophecy from Isaiah (40:3-5). Matthew (3:3), Mark (1:3), and John (1:23) use parts of the same prophecy, applying it to John. The first application of these words depicted God's leading the joyous procession of Jews through the deserts from Babylonia to their homeland in Palestine. The figure itself reflects the custom of improving the roads a king was about to travel when going to a distant land. The prophetic application to John's work is made by all the Gospel writers, and by Jesus himself (Matthew 11:10 [cf. Malachi 3:1]). John is the voice that prepares for the Lord. The way of the Lord is made easier by coming to a people whose hearts are repentant and ready to receive Him.

Abraham as our father (8). There were some who were insincere in their motives to come to hear John. There were some who thought they could depend on their Jewish lineage as the chosen of God and did not need repentance.

The ax is . . . at the root (9). God is ready to bring judgment upon those who do not know the fruits of repentance in their

---

[12]Alfred Plummer, *A Critical and Exegetical Commentary on the Gospel According to St. Luke* (Edinburgh: T. and T. Clark, Ltd., 1896; Fifth edition, 1922), p. 86.

lives. The ax is lying there at hand to be used in cutting down the trees that are not fruitful.

The Responses (3:10-14)

Two tunics (11). In response to the questions from individuals of different walks of life as to how these fruits could be shown, John gave specific examples. If a person was blessed in a material way with enough and to spare, he was to share his food and clothing with the one who did not have the very necessities. The tunic was like an extended undershirt. One could get along without an extra tunic (Luke 9:3; Matthew 10:10).

Don't collect any more than you are required (13). The tax collectors were not told to leave their jobs, but to be fair in their business. Their greatest temptation was to collect extra for their own pockets.

Don't accuse people falsely — be content with your pay (14). Neither were the soldiers told to leave their jobs, but to avoid the temptation to use the threat of their power to gain unjustly for themselves. To each one of these groups, John was saying, "Renounce your besetting sin."[13]

Is John the Christ? (3:15-18)

Baptize you with water (16). Again and again, John denied that he was the Messiah. He even enumerated specific differences. Baptism was so important in the message of John that he came to be designated John the Baptist. But even his baptism was not all that Christ's baptism would be. This was indeed a baptism from God, and new to the knowledge of the Jews. It was not the taurobolium or any baptism associated with the mystery religions of the Greeks;[14] it was not the repeated washings of the Essenes;[15] it was not the proselyte baptism of the Jews

---

[13]G. B. Caird, *The Gospel of Luke* (Baltimore: Penguin Books, 1963), p. 73.

[14]J. Gresham Machen, *The Origin of Paul's Religion* (New York: Macmillan, 1921).

[15]R. C. Foster, *Studies in the Life of Christ* (Grand Rapids: Baker, 1971).

(the historical testimony for this baptism does not go back as far as the time of John).[16] It was baptism of repentance in water for the remission of sins, and it was from God.

Baptize you with Holy Spirit. Luke records the words of Jesus delivered to His disciples as He prepares for His ascension. At this time, He compares the baptism of John in water with the baptism in the Spirit to come "in a few days." Then the day of Pentecost is described (ten days after the ascension), when the apostles were filled with the Holy Spirit and the indwelling gift of the Spirit came upon all those who were baptized (Acts 2:38). The name of Jesus and the role of the Holy Spirit were associated with Christ's baptism on Pentecost—and after—in a way not known to John (Acts 19:2 ff.; see 1 Corinthians 12:13).

Baptize ... with fire. Variant interpretations of this passage have been suggested. (1) The tongues of fire at Pentecost (Acts 2:3, but note that references to this occasion omit "with fire" from the wording, Acts 1:5; 11:16). (2) The testing of the works of a Christian (1 Corinthians 3:13). (3) The illumination of the Spirit (1 John 2:20). (4) The judgment of the condemned (Revelation 20:15). In view of verse 17, the last interpretation is preferred. There were those in John's audience who would be baptized in the Spirit, and there were others who would be baptized with the fire of punishment (2 Peter 3:7, 12; Malachi 3:2; 2 Thessalonians 1:7, 8).

Winnowing fork (17). A wide shovel was used to throw the loose grain heads into the air. The wind would scatter the chaff, but the heavier grain would fall in a pile. Then the chaff would be gathered to be destroyed.

Herod the Tetrarch (3:19, 20)

This was Herod Antipas, who, under his father's (Herod the Great) last will, received the tetrarchy of Galilee and Perea. According to Josephus *(Antiquities,* xviii, 5, 1), Herod feared that John's popularity with the people might lead to an uprising against him; so he had John put in prison. The Biblical account, however, brings out the direct condemnation John had made against his marriage with Herodias, who had been courted by

---

[16]H. H. Rowley, "Jewish Proselyte Baptism," *Hebrew Union College Annual,* 15 (1940), pp. 313-334.

Antipas while she was married to his brother, Philip. John's imprisonment probably lasted at least a year, and ended in his death (Matthew 14:3-12).

The Baptism of Jesus (3:21, 23)

When all the people were being baptized (21). The inference is that the baptism of Jesus occurred in the later stages of John's ministry, after the majority of the people had responded to his preaching.

In bodily form (22). Other accounts of the descent of the Holy Spirit (Matthew 3:16; Mark 1:10) might have been interpreted that the descent was gentle as a dove, but not necessarily in the physical form of a dove. Luke makes it clear, however, that it was indeed in the bodily form of a dove. John saw the dove and understood the sign of identification (John 1:32). The people probably saw the dove and heard the voice, but did not understand what was said or the significance. (See John 12:28, 29.)

You are my Son. This is one of three Gospel-recorded times Jesus was addressed by a voice from Heaven. (See also Luke 9:35; John 12:28.) This recalls the language of Psalm 2:7 and Isaiah 42:1. The phrase "whom I love" is not only a warm, personal note, but is a word in the Greek reserved for an only child. This is an assurance that there is no suggestion of an adoption at baptism, but a continuing relationship of Father and Son, and that the Father acknowledges this and the Son is aware of this fact. Jesus was more than the contemporary concept of the Messiah; He was the very Son of God.

About thirty years old (23). Luke has already given the historical note dating the beginning of John's ministry, and now, recording the events of perhaps six months later, he wants to locate the beginning of Jesus' ministry in relation to the years of Jesus' own life. At thirty years of age, the Levite began his service (Numbers 4:47); and at the same age, the contemporary culture considered a man to have begun his mature years.

The Genealogy of Jesus (3:23-38)

So it was thought (23). Luke is careful to insert a phrase remaining consistent with his earlier account of Jesus' birth. If Jesus was born of the virgin Mary and conceived through the Holy Spirit, then the genealogical line of Joseph would not reflect the bloodline of Jesus. The significance of the phrase may not only be Luke's way of saying that he knows this, but he may also be saying that he is not giving the genealogy of Joseph, but the line of Mary. The possibility of this is increased when one finds the differences between the genealogy of Jesus as recorded in the Gospel of Matthew and that given in Luke. Some of these differences are purely a matter of choice and arrangement, but some involve such differences in the list of names that it would seem impossible for both lists to be the ancestors of the same individual. There are four explanations suggested to explain the differences. (1) One suggestion notes that the difference in names begins after David where Matthew's list comes down from Solomon through the kings of Judah whereas Luke follows the line of Nathan, another son of David. This has led some to say that Matthew's genealogy gives the succession to the throne as known, and then follows a secret royal line for the remainder whereas Luke pursues the actual bloodline of Joseph. However, there is nothing to confirm this line of explanation. (2) Africanus very early (220) suggested that a levirate marriage may account for it. Other modern scholars have held the same thing (e.g., B. F. Westcot). Jacob (in Matthew's list just before Joseph) and Eli (in that position in Luke's list) may have been half-brothers and Eli died without children. Then Jacob may have married the widow in levirate marriage and Joseph was born to that pair; but his formal, legal line would be through Eli while his bloodline would be through Jacob. The main objection to this theory is that there is no single thread of evidence to confirm this. (3) M. D. Johnson more recently[17] has tried to explain the variation because of a type of poetic license enjoyed in Midrashic speculation where factual information is lacking. Although it is obvious that Matthew has arranged his genealogy in groups of fourteen, and that he frequently abbreviates by omitting some generations, and he includes the names of four women—all of this does not justify a free introduction of unrelated individuals simply to develop a mysterious meaning to it all. Luke is anxious to present reliable history, and it is incredible that he would simply conjure up names to serve his interest. This

---

[17]M. D. Johnson, *The Purposes of Biblical Geneologies* (London: Cambridge University Press, 1969).

is just the type of procedure he tries to avoid. (4) Since Matthew does show an interest in Joseph's side of the happenings at Jesus' birth and Luke deals more with Mary's side, and since it would seem that Mary also is of the lineage of David, and the variation of names from David to Joseph is where the lines differ, it would satisfy the date to find in Matthew's genealogy the legal line of Joseph, but in Mary the bloodline of Jesus. Annius of Viterbo (c.1490) seems to have introduced this thought and Luther followed the explanation. Godet gives a good treatment.[18]

The Temptations of Jesus (4:1-13)

Led by the Spirit (1). The role of the Holy Spirit is of special interest in the writings of Luke. All three Synoptic accounts draw attention to Jesus' going immediately from His baptism to His forty days of fasting in the desert, and the direction of the Spirit is specially noted. In Luke, however, the presence of the Spirit is noted in a double way, "full of the Spirit" and continually "led by the Spirit." It is impossible to say whether the temptations from the devil came only at the close of the forty days and were restricted to the three recorded ones or whether they extended throughout the period and the ones described in the Gospels are only representative. Probably the presence of the Spirit and the assaults of Satan continued throughout the forty-day period, but Matthew makes clear it was at the end of these days, when Jesus was most hungry, that Satan approached Him particularly (Matthew 4:2).

It is written (4). In reply to the devil's proposals, Jesus quoted Scripture. (See also verses 8 and 12.) It is disconcerting that Satan also uses (or rather abuses) Scripture. Jesus cites Deuteronomy continually and has no reluctance to use it as the very Word of God. His high regard for Scripture is seen consistently throughout His teaching. (See Luke 24:25-27, 44-47; John 5:39; 10:35).

All the kingdoms of the world (5). How could one see *all* the kingdoms in an instant? What high place could provide such a view? How long would it take to get there? Does this

---

[18]Frederic L. Godet, *A Commentary on the Gospel of Luke* (Grand Rapids: Kregel, 1981; reprint of 1878 edition), pp. 127-130.

mean just the kingdoms existing then, or did it include future ones as well? If it is literal in its meaning, it would take a miracle of considerable proportions to bring this scene to a reality—which, of course, is not an impossibility. If it were accomplished in a vision, it would not be without Scriptural precedent. Ezekiel was taken to a very high mountain, and it was plainly stated this was "in visions of God" (Ezekiel 40:2). John, too, was "carried ... away in the Spirit to a mountain great and high" (Revelation 21:10). A third type of interpretation would suggest that the whole experience be viewed as a figure of speech and not require any kind of action. The second view—the vision type—is particularly commended. Especially important is the recognition that these temptations were real, neither simply a figment of the mind nor a mechanical exercise that had no live option of falling into sin. Christ was tempted as we are, but He endured all and was without sin (Hebrews 4:15).

The highest point of the temple (9). One should not envisage an apex of a sloping roof. The temple structure in its entire complex had many high wings that would have flat areas accessible from inside ascent. One of them overlooked the Kedron Valley and presented a sheer drop of 450 feet. From such a place, James, the Lord's brother, is said to have been thrown to his death (Eusebius, *Ecclesiastical History* 2, 23). Josephus (*Antiquities* xv, 412) describes the effect of looking down from a rooftop into the valley: "He would become dizzy and his vision would be unable to reach the end of so measureless a depth."

Do not put the Lord your God to the test (12). The devil had quoted Psalm 91:11, 12. This passage reflects a simple, humble trust in God. What the devil suggested, that Jesus jump off the pinnacle, was far different. It was more like the defiant Israelites on their long trek out of Egypt. Dissatisfied with their lot, they made their demands of God regardless of His knowledge and His plans. Jesus wisely quoted a message from this context in His reply to Satan (Deuteronomy 6:16; Exodus 17:1-7).

An opportune time (13). Satan knew he had suffered defeat in his attempts to penetrate the perfection of Christ, but this did not mean that he made no further attempts during the ministry of Jesus. At every opportunity, he renewed his efforts to draw Jesus from the course God had put before Him.

Lukan Chronology

Luke's Purpose

Luke's primary purpose for writing his Gospel is to provide a historical foundation for the good news of salvation. This centers in the life and teaching of Jesus. One must not, however, equate history with the memorizing of dates, nor the order of Luke's report with an absolute chronological order. But it is entirely in keeping with Luke's interest that an individual strive to determine the dating and the chronological order of Jesus' life to appreciate what Luke is saying to us and to see how his report fits into the information from the other Gospel narratives.

Indeed, Luke is the one who gives us the definite statement on the year of the reign of a world ruler in order to date the action in the Gospel; John the Baptist began his public ministry in the fifteenth year that Tiberius Caesar was the Roman emperor (Luke 3:1). But since, as we have already seen, this can indicate years from A.D. 26-29, we are anxious to assemble other notices that might help with dating to see whether these years can be narrowed down, as well as to profit by dating other parts of Jesus' life.

Key Details

These are pieces of the puzzle that should be put together:

(1) Herod the Great died in April of 4 B.C. Since his death occurred after the Wise-men approached to honor the newborn babe in Bethlehem, then Jesus must have been born before Herod's death. When Herod heard of the recent birth of an alleged king, he gave the order for the slaughter of the male infants to two years of age in Bethlehem. To some, this would indicate that the birth of Jesus would have been two years prior to the order. Knowing the cruelty and barbarity of Herod, however, one is assured that he increased the number of years in order to make sure the soldiers not misjudge the age of a baby rather than that two years had actually elapsed since the birth of the child. Thus the most likely years for the birth of Jesus would be 4 or 5 B.C.[19]

---

[19] Jack Finegan, *Handbook of Biblical Chronology* (Princeton: Princeton University Press, 1964), pp. 215-255.

(2) Luke provides the detail that Jesus was about thirty years of age when He began His ministry (Luke 3:23). This may indicate a few months before thirty or even a year or two before or after. This would indicate about the year A.D. 26.

(3) When Jesus was disputing with the Jews in the temple area very early in His ministry, the affirmation was made that they had been working on the building of the temple for forty-six years (John 2:20). Since the building had been started in 19 B.C., this would indicate that Jesus was discoursing with the Jews at the time of the Passover in A.D. 27. In all probability Jesus' baptism and the beginning of His ministry had taken place several months before, sometime in the year 26. This would agree with His birth in 4 B.C. (He was about thirty years old), and the fifteenth year of Tiberius' authority in the provinces.[20]

---

[20] The length of Jesus' ministry and the date of the crucifixion will be considered later. For further details and sources for the study of chronology, see Lewis Foster, "The Chronology of the New Testament" in *The Expositor's Bible Commentary,* vol. 1, Frank Gaebelein, ed. (Grand Rapids: Zondervan, 1979), pp. 593-607; cf. Harold W. Hoechner, *Chronological Aspects of the Life of Christ* (Grand Rapids: Zondervan, 1976).

Part Two

Ministry in Galilee

Luke 4:14—9:50

CHAPTER FOUR

The Recruitment

Luke 4:14-6:16

A young girl went around her neighborhood and invited all her little friends to a birthday party. They accepted gladly and showed up at the appointed time. A major difficulty resulted, however. The parents of the young child were totally unaware of any such invitations, and all the children were politely sent back to their homes. This was a sad disappointment, but the invitations had been given with no real authority behind them. No party took place.

Invitation and Resistance

When Jesus gave an invitation, there was authority behind the promises. He came preaching—with authority (Luke 4:32, 36). The people felt it, and they followed Him in throngs. Jesus kept on preaching (Luke 4:44). He preached with love, healing the sick and driving out the evil spirits (Luke 4:40, 41). He preached with understanding, knowing their needs and providing the answers (Luke 5:22-25). He preached with challenge, calling people to repentance and urging disciples to follow Him (Luke 5:32; 5:11, 27). He preached a new message, not to be confused with the old (Luke 5:38; 6:5). All were amazed at the new authority of Jesus' word.

As goodness gained a more popular hearing, evil mounted to resist it. When the people flocked to see Jesus and praised Him, those in His own hometown were disbelieving and rejected Him. The Pharisees, jealous and suspicious, tried to stop Him. The teachers of the law found ways to criticize Him. Although these men must have had something good in their teaching, evil won out in them as they raised opposition to Jesus. They would not give place to Jesus, even though He had the truth. He had the power. He had the authority. To resist Him simply sent a person deeper into the depths of sin and error. This was true then, and it is true now.

Between the baptism and temptations of Jesus (Luke 4:13) and Jesus' return to Galilee (4:14), a year may have gone by. The events recorded in John 1:19—4:42 occurred in this period. If Jesus' visit to Nazareth (Luke 4:16ff.) is the same as that recorded in Matthew 13:54 and Mark 6:1, another year may have passed by the time Jesus made this trip to Nazareth. In this case, Luke departs from chronological order as he describes the visit at the opening of Jesus' Galilean ministry. He may well have done so for a number of reasons. This incident provides an example of synagogue preaching, which characterized this period of Jesus' ministry. It also sets the stage for resistance to Jesus in the midst of general popularity. Finally, it also indicates the type of self-claim to the Messiahship that Jesus was making in this period.

Content Notes

Ministry in the Synagogues (4:14-30)

Return to Galilee (14, 15)

In order to avoid further head-on confrontation with the Jewish authorities in Jerusalem, Jesus returned to the region of His earlier years. This would give Him time to deliver His message to wide audiences in Galilee, and He must avert reaching His crisis in Jerusalem too soon. The people of Galilee had a need, and Jesus was prepared to fulfill His ministry there.

In the power of the Spirit (14). This might indicate the guidance of the Spirit, but from the wording (power), and from the context (the news that spread about Jesus), and from usage of the term elsewhere (Matthew 12:28; Luke 5:17; 6:19), this may have particular reference to the working of miracles, which was an important part of Jesus' ministry. The power of the Spirit is linked also with the coming apostolic witness (Luke 24:49; Acts 1:8; 10:38), and may have particular reference here to the authority of Jesus' teaching.[21]

---

[21]See Marshall, *Gospel of Luke,* p. 176.

Taught in their synagogues (15). In this period of Jesus' ministry, He went from town to town and did His teaching in the religious meeting places of the Jews, the synagogues. Later, the crowds became so large the synagogues would not hold the throngs, but for now, this was the ideal center of His activity. The synagogue was used for worship, instruction, and Jewish community meetings. The main service was on the Sabbath. It consisted of the recitation of the *Shema* (Deuteronomy 6:4-9; 11:13-21), a prayer, a reading from the law, and one from the prophets, and a benediction. The reading of Scripture included an original reading of the Hebrew (one verse from the law or three from the prophets), then a translation into the Aramaic (the dialect understood and used by the Jews of Palestine at that time), and then an exposition on the passage if the reader desired to give one. Priests and Levites frequently served as the readers, but any man of the congregation might be designated to give the reading of the day, or a visiting rabbi or distinguished guest might be the invited reader.[22]

And everyone praised Him. The news that spread through the whole land (Luke 4:37) had to do with Jesus' miracles of healing and casting out of evil spirits, His teaching and preaching as well as His ministry of love and understanding. Could this be the Messiah?

Spurned at Home (16-30)

The outline of a mountain in New Hampshire resembles the features of a man's face. The likeness gave the decided impression that the man was kindly and helpful, yet strong and determined. It carried the assurance of virtue and integrity. The local people kept watching the tourists who came to see the extraordinary sight in hopes that one of them would answer the description of the man in the mountain. An extensive search was made to find such a man and to satisfy the feeling that the stone likeness would be identified with a living person. After years had passed and a young local boy, Ernest, had grown old watching

---

[22]See G. F. Moore, *Judaism,* Vol. 1 (Cambridge, MA: Harvard University Press, 1927), pp. 300ff. and E. Schurer, *The History of the Jewish People in the Age of Jesus Christ,* Vol. 2, revised and edited by G. Vermos and F. Millar. (Edinburgh: T. & T. Clark, 1973), pp. 52ff.

for the right individual to come along, finally a famous poet came to visit. As he talked to Ernest and studied the features of the mountain cleft, the poet suddenly threw his arms aloft and shouted—"'Behold! Behold! Ernest is himself the likeness of the Great Stone Face!' Then all the people looked and saw that what the deep-sighted poet said was true." It became apparent that the personification of the great stone face had been in their midst all along, and they had not recognized him.[23] This was similar to the case in Nazareth when Jesus returned, except He identified himself and they continued to refuse recognition even after He announced himself as the Messiah.

And on the Sabbath day he went into the synagogue, as was his custom (16). The synagogue worship was a vital part of every good Jew's life-style. The observance was a part of Jesus' regular practice as well. He had grown up in Nazareth. These people knew how long He had been doing this. He had a custom of continued attendance, but now He was accustomed to speaking as well as worshiping. Furthermore, Luke was making note of the custom Jesus had of regular worship to God. This speaks to our lives as well.

And he stood up to read. This reflects the custom of standing to read the Scripture and being seated to give the exposition (Luke 4:20). Paul, however, stood to give his exhortation (Acts 13:16) after the reading of the law and the prophets.

The Spirit of the Lord is on me (18). This Scripture may have been designated for Him to read as the passage chosen for that day (Luke 4:17), or Jesus may have turned to this particular prophecy from Isaiah (61:1, 2; cf. 58:6) because of the announcement He wanted to make. In any event, this was the passage He wanted to present. The Messiah is pictured as speaking and telling of His work.

He has anointed me. In the Old Testament, the prophets (1 Kings 19:16), priests (Exodus 28:41), and kings (2 Kings 9:6) all were anointed for their tasks, representing the authority from God and serving as spokesman of God. Especially this was true of the Messiah. The very name means "anointed" (Hebrew, *Messiah;* Greek, *Christ*).

---

[23]Nathaniel Hawthorne, *The Great Stone Face and Other Tales of the White Mountains* (Boston: Houghton, Mifflin and Co., 1935).

Good news to the poor ... freedom for the prisoners ... sight for the blind ... release to the oppressed. A prediction of the work of the Messiah, this was a description of the actual ministry of Christ. The "poor" could be meaningful to those struggling in deep poverty, but it reaches to all those poor in spirit; the "prisoners" could be applied to those returning from exile, but it has significance for all those in the bonds of sin and living under the fate of the eternally condemned; Jesus healed the physically "blind," but this passage goes still further to include the spiritually blind; and the "oppressed" would be quickly identified with a people living under the yoke of a foreign power, but this, too, would extend to all individuals who must bear the burdens of the soul brought by the circumstances of life, sometimes because of one's own sin and sometimes through hardships outside one's own fault. The Messiah, the servant of God, would bring relief. (See Matthew 11:28-30.)

The year of the Lord's favor (19). This is not to be considered as one year of calendar days, but is a reference to a period of time when salvation would be proclaimed—the Messianic Age. Some would see in Isaiah's original utterance a reference to the year of Jubilee, which returned every fifty years (Leviticus 25:8ff.)[24] This was the year when slaves were freed, debts canceled, and ancestral property returned to the original family. This provides another possible backdrop to the fulfillment Jesus affirms in this His hometown.

Today this scripture is fulfilled (21). Without using the very words, Jesus was saying, "I am the Messiah, and this describes what I am doing." The reaction of the people is a warning to all of us. They heard His words, and they could not help but admire His message and His person, but their skepticism won out. Their hearts could not agree with their ears. They had known Jesus as a boy. He had lived among them as simply Joseph's son. How could He rise to the heights He was claiming and His works attested? Luke has not forgotten the virgin birth account he has written of Jesus' earthly beginning, but here he faithfully records the expressions of unbelievers as they attempted to undermine the appeal of Jesus.

"Physician, heal yourself!" (23). Whether jealousy or

---

[24]Godet, *Luke,* pp. 150,151.

stubbornness or materialism or love of the world was basic in their opposition to Jesus, He put His finger on the complaint uppermost in their minds just now. He was not putting on the demonstration for them that He had been doing in Capernaum. In this sense, He was not doing for himself and His own hometown what He had been doing for others in other places by way of the miraculous. They did not recognize that faith and commitment were present among those coming to Him out of their need in those other places. But here unbelief, hostility, and rejection were uppermost.

In Elijah's time . . . in the time of Elisha . . . (25, 27). Jesus' reply was to give two examples from the lives of outstanding prophets, Elijah (1 Kings 17:1) and Elisha (2 Kings 5:1). They could have worked miracles for the people at home, too, but instead Elijah was sent to the widow of Zaraphath, a Gentile, in Sidon; and Elisha's illustration was the cleansing of leprosy for another Gentile, Naaman, who lived far from home, in Syria.

The people . . . were furious (28). The course the inhabitants of Nazareth took is a lesson to each of us. They began with hostile curiosity and moved to amazed admiration upon hearing the reading of Scripture and the exposition following. The next step, however, was determined disbelief and scornful rejection. This soon turned into adamant hatred. If they could not answer Him or discredit Him, and would not accept Him, they must destroy Him.

To throw him down the cliff (29). Sites are pointed out today that would satisfy the description here. All are outside the town of Nazareth. In any case, the resolute rush to take the life of Jesus is appalling and would necessitate a considerable violent march to transport Him to the cliff.

Went on his way (30). Jesus did not do works of healing here in Nazareth because of their unbelief, but His power and authority were not diminished. He could, and apparently did, make use of miraculous power as He walked away from this situation.

Concluding Notes.

From Jesus' visit to Nazareth the following points are basic. (1) Jesus claimed to be the Messiah. This was not introduced years later and read back into the life of Christ. Luke wants us to see the heart of Jesus' purpose and the fulfillment of prophecy in His life and work. He records this at this early time so that the reader will be conscious of the Messiahship of Jesus from the beginning. (2) Jesus was rejected in the town where He had grown up. One might get the impression from the crowds that followed Jesus that everyone was in His favor. This was not so, and Luke tries to avoid such a misconception by recording this scene early in the ministry.

Verisimilitude[25] is seen in the record. Jesus returned to the place where He had grown up. One would expect this. Jesus was traveling from town to town, and surely He would return to the familiar scene of His boyhood. Also, He went to the synagogue. This, too, would be expected. He had done so as a youth, and He continued now to do so with a dual purpose, not only to worship God, but to have the opportunity to proclaim His message. Another element of verisimilitude was the immediate reaction of the people as they marveled at His gracious manner.

Besides the expected of verisimilitude, the account is combined with the unexpected. One would not expect a public announcement with such clarity that Jesus claimed to be the Messiah—not at this period of His ministry, not at His visit to His hometown. Another unexpected element is Jesus' reply to their resistance to His announcement. Instead of working miracles to substantiate His claim as they were anticipating, He introduced the inclusion of the Gentiles in God's suppling needs of the past. This, indeed, was in keeping with the interests of Luke, the inclusion of the Gentiles, and was of import to foreshadowing the mission of the coming church to include Gentiles as well as Jews; but to interject the subject of the Gentiles at this particular time is unexpected. Finally, the very fact that the people of His own hometown tried to kill Jesus is shocking. How could they think of such a thing, let alone attempt to do it?

To return to the purposes of Luke helps to gain the import of the happenings and to see how they fit into the account. Luke wanted to emphasize Jesus' ministry to the lowly. From Mary's song before the birth of Jesus ("He has scattered those who are proud ... but has lifted up the humble. He has filled the hungry with good things"—Luke 1:51-53), from the manger in a stable and the presence of the shepherds to welcome Jesus' birth, to

---

[25]True-to-life situations; true to the customs of the time and place being described and, often, true to life today.

this moment in the synagogue at Nazareth and the words of Isaiah describing the Messiah, and Jesus' application of this to himself—all this serves to justify Luke's interest in ministry to the poor, the blind, the oppressed (Luke 4:18, 19). This set the course for the ministry of Jesus to follow. The expressed purpose of Luke, however, was to give certainty that these things really happened and the message was true. The very combination of verisimilitude and the unexpected lends credence to the actuality of the occurrence. Even if one would attempt to make a fictitious description match the time and place being described, he would not be so bold as to invent the unexpected that might foil his deception. That is why the combination helps Luke achieve his purpose of assuring the reader of certainty about the things recorded of Jesus here. Luke puts it down in a way that helps the reader believe. The fact that people tried to kill Jesus in Nazareth prepares us to see how it was fulfilled in Jerusalem two years later.

Fame Throughout the Land (31-44)

He went down to Capernaum (31). For his Gentile, non-Palestine readers, Luke adds the description, "a town in Galilee." In fact, it was considered the capital of Galilee for the Jews, as Tiberias, the center of Herod's power, was the Gentile hub in Galilee. Jesus continued teaching the people, again on the Sabbath, and again in the synagogue.

His message had authority (32). The characteristic most noted about Jesus' message was the authority of the messenger. He did not teach like the Pharisees and the teachers of the law, who continually quoted the rabbinic sayings of the past to establish their positions. Jesus needed no greater authority than His own word. He had authority in His preaching, and authority in healing. He even had authority to forgive sin. His gospel was a new message, but He had authority to inaugurate it. When He used the expression, "I tell you the truth" (verily, I say to you), it was more than a means of getting attention or declaring importance; it was an affirmation of authority.[26]

---

[26]In Luke, this expression is used six times: Luke 4:24; 12:37; 18:17, 29; 21:32; 23:43. See Joachim Jeremias, *Abba* (Gottingen: Vandenhoeck & Ruprecht,1966); cited in Marshall, *Gospel of Luke,* p. 187.

Possessed by a demon, an evil spirit (33). Of all the [miracles] Jesus and His disciples accomplished, casting out demo[ns was] considered among the greatest. When the seventy-two dis[ciples] returned from an evangelistic campaign and reported on [what] had been accomplished, they climaxed their joy with the words, "Lord, even the demons submit to us in your name" (Luke 10:17). On one occasion, the disciples were desperate because they were unable to perform the cure (Mark 9:14-29). Evil spirits were the servants of Satan. They brought different results and possessed people to different degrees and for different reasons. Their presence in a life was not necessarily the fault of the person. They might bring physical ailment, such as blindness and loss of speech (Matthew 12:22), or epilepsy (Matthew 17:15).[27] The condition might be one of complete control (Mark 5:1-5) or in the case of this man in the synagogue at Capernaum, a possession that broke through intermittently. At the approach of Jesus, the demon felt threatened by His power and cried out in objection: "Ha" (Luke 4:34), translation of the Greek for "Let go."

Holy One of God (34). The title was used as a designation of the Messiah. (See Psalm 16:10.) It signified a special one dedicated to God. The demon did not identify Jesus this way in order to assist Him or to submit to Him, but rather to embarrass Him by offering his evil source of information or else to thwart Jesus in any plans He might have to delay further identification of His Messiahship.

With authority and power (36). Jesus silenced the demon and ordered him out of the man. The fact that the man was thrown down showed the struggle the demon put up and the severity of the matter, but the man's unharmed condition assured the completeness of the miracle. Although the restoration of this person to a normal condition was of great benefit in itself, the record of this episode is given to note the reaction from the people. They were amazed at an authority that extended to the unseen world of the spirits. By the question, "What is this teaching?" they did not ask what magic words He used, but they recognized that this

---

[27]Here, as in Matthew 4:24, the NIV originally read "epileptic." As of the 1984 revisions, however, it has used the more general expression, "has [having] seizures."

new gospel had power behind it. Luke's choice of this miracle, as the first of a series worked in Capernaum, is significant.

Simon's mother-in-law (38). This scene is as true to life as one could imagine: Jesus left the synagogue and accompanied Peter to his home for the meal to follow. Perhaps Jesus was staying at the home of Peter and Andrew (Mark 1:29). Jesus had already moved with His mother and His brothers and His disciples from Nazareth to Capernaum (John 2:12; Matthew 4:13); so it is more likely that it was a visit for the day. That the tax collector approached Peter later about Jesus' temple tax does not prove He was living in his house, although this might be a slight indication in that direction (Matthew 17:24ff.) Obviously Peter was married, as is evident from other references as well (1 Corinthians 9:5).

High fever. Of the three Synoptic writers, Luke alone describes this illness with a "high" fever. Some see in this evidence that Luke was a physician. Although this is not sufficient to establish his medical background, this does fit his profession, since Paul tells us he was a doctor (Colossians 4:14). The completeness of the cure is evident by the mother's immediate return to the kitchen and help with the meal.

When the sun was setting (40). By the time evening had come, word had spread about the two miracles already performed that Sabbath day. Not until the Sabbath was over, in the evening time, were the townsmen free to come by droves, bringing all kinds of sick individuals.

Son of God (41). The sick included those who were plagued with demons. As did another demon earlier in the day (see Luke 4:34), these were crying out an identification of Jesus. Although the people were quick to associate the Messiah with the son of David, He had not yet been identified so clearly as the very Son of God. The demons knew Jesus was the Messiah (Christ), and they addressed Him as divine. Jesus did not allow their testimony to continue. (1) The servants of the devil were not the right source of recommendation. This would be more liability than asset. (2) This was not the right time for the announcement. Jesus had much instruction to give and training to complete before His time would come for the final confrontation. (3) The demons were not the right ones to be left in control, or even the appearance of control, by their presumptuous announcements, true or false.

Solitary place (42). Luke reminds us that despite what the conditions were, Jesus took time out to seek refreshment from being alone with God, His Father. Mark adds at this point, "where he prayed" (Mark 1:35). Luke includes this also when he repeats the scene (Luke 5:16). Whether He had opposition as at Nazareth or was at the height of popularity as with the crowds at Capernaum, whether He was restraining untimely testimony or calling followers, He took time to commune with His Father.

Good news of the kingdom of God (43). Jesus was under a divine imperative. He must preach the gospel. This was the purpose of His coming: to prepare for God's kingdom. This was not a kingdom with an earthly palace or a visible boundary. The kingship and authority of God transcends the material and the spiritual. That kingdom is present today in the church and will be triumphant in eternity, but it was present in the person of the King, Jesus, as He went from town to town heralding its coming.

In the synagogues of Galilee (44, New King James Version and NIV footnote). This is a summary of Jesus' first general evangelistic campaign in Galilee. An interesting textual difference occurs at this passage. Some early manuscripts read "in the synagogues of Judea." This reading would not have been taken seriously except for the high respect granted the five principal Greek manuscripts that carry it. In favor of the reading "in the synagogues of Galilee" are the following factors: (1) The land of Palestine had four major areas: Judea, Samaria, Galilee, and Perea. In this section of Luke's Gospel, Luke has told of Jesus' return to Galilee (4:14), Jesus' recorded activity seems to be confined to Galilee, and in a passage close to this one (Luke 5:17), Luke uses the terms Galilee and Judea (in conjunction with Jerusalem) as two different areas. One would expect this summary at 4:44 to refer to the area of Galilee and not the southern section of Palestine, Judea. (2) In passages parallel to this one in Luke, both Matthew (4:23) and Mark (1:39) support the reference to Galilee. (3) Although the testimony of five major manuscripts is impressive for *Judea,* nevertheless they represent, for the most part, one single family, whereas the reading for *Galilee* is supported by two early families and the vast majority of later manuscripts. In support of the rendering *synagogues of Judea* are the following: (1) Five early, major manuscripts have this reading. (2) The more difficult reading to understand is

Judea; but in textual criticism this makes it the preferred reading if it can be established that the variant is a deliberate change made by the scribe. He would not introduce a reading that would make the passage more difficult but one that would help explain. Thus, one might introduce *Galilee* to be relieved of explaining the *Judea* reading, but *Judea* would not be introduced at all if the passage read *Galilee* in the beginning. Also, there is a scribal tendency toward harmonistic renderings when a scribe is familiar with a parallel passage in another part of Scripture, and he is liable, consciously or unconsciously, to make it like the other rather than its being like the other in the beginning. In this case, the original would have had *Judea,* but a scribe who knew of the Matthew and Mark passages' having *Galilee* made the Lukan passage read *Galilee* also. The weakness with both of these arguments (the "more difficult reading is preferred" and the "harmonistic tendency") is they presume the scribe is making a deliberate change (unless it is an unconscious harmonistic change). This is what cannot be established, and if it is an accidental, unconscious change that introduced the variant reading in the first place, it may have been a slip to *Judea* from *Galilee,* the original, as easily as vice versa. (3) *Judea* does have the meaning of the land of the Jews in general, including Galilee also, and Luke uses the word this way at times (Luke 1:5; 6:17; 7:17; 23:5; Acts 1:8; 10:37; 11:1, 29). Jesus did have Judean ministries in the south which John records, but the Synoptics do not cover. Perhaps this is Luke's way of referring indirectly to the larger ministry of Jesus not included in his Gospel. Pliny, the Roman historian, uses *Judea* in the general inclusive way for the land of the Jews.[28]

Still another reading suggests the rendering "[the land] of the Jews." When all of the arguments are in, it is apparent that no vital doctrines are at stake and that Luke is telling us of Jesus' ministry in Galilee, although this is a possible reference to His wider ministry as well.[29]

---

[28]*Natural History,* 5.15 (70).

[29]Bruce M. Metzger, *A Textual Commentary on the Greek New Testament* (New York: United Bible Societies, 1971), pp. 137f. Godet, *Luke,* pp. 29-31, 162. William Hendriksen, *Luke* (Grand Rapids: Baker, 1978), pp. 272ff.

Ministry of Recruitment, Part One:
Calling the First Disciples (5:1-11)

Jesus' ministry had three sides. His teaching and preaching communicated the Word of God, His healing and works of compassion demonstrated the power and love of God, and His selection and training of disciples paved the way for the founding of the church and the spread of the gospel of salvation. Luke now joins all three of these into the following section. First he tells of a miracle, then the recruitment of disciples, after this two more miracles, another recruitment, questions and answers in teaching, and finally the selection of His twelve special disciples.

The independence of the Gospel accounts is seen more clearly in this period of the life of Christ than in any other. Sometimes the independence is seen because one Gospel alone carries an episode. But this is an example of when all three Synoptic narratives tell of the same general section, the early period in Jesus' Galilean ministry. The order of events is different at times and agrees at times; the episodes described are the same at times and are different other times, and even when the same episodes are recounted, the details vary but are not contradictory. In the wealth of detail, one finds the most vivid and clear picture of what happened by putting the accounts together.

Jesus' major speeches in the Gospel of Matthew are special marks in the progression of Matthew's record. His first major discourse is the Sermon on the Mount. In Matthew, the calling of the first disciples, Simon Peter and Andrew, precedes the sermon. After the sermon, Matthew tells of healing the man of leprosy and then the centurion's servant (Matthew 8:1-13), followed by the cure of Peter's mother-in-law. In Mark, the calling of the first disciples (Mark includes James and John as well as Simon and Andrew) was the first event recorded after Jesus' return to Galilee (as in Matthew). Mark, however, puts the leprosy cleansing after the Capernaum Sabbath of many miracles, including the cure of Simon's mother-in-law (Mark 1:29-45). Luke, however, does not record the call of Simon, James, and John (Andrew is not named) until after the Sabbath of miracles in Capernaum (Luke 4:31—5:11), and the leprosy occasion follows still after this (Luke 5:12-14). Thus, for the leprosy occasion alone, one finds three different orders of events in Matthew, Mark, and Luke. One cannot say that Matthew and Luke agree against Mark, but neither can one say that either Matthew or Luke always agrees with Mark. They do not do so here. They do not copy from one another but are independent accounts. Which one is chronological is difficult to say. Mark is probably the nearest, for the other two show signs of giving arrangements other than chronological at places. But a work can give other than chronological order and still be dependable historically. Besides the difference in order, and the difference in detail, one must take into account the possibility that descriptions may reflect similarities, but in fact be from different incidents. The calling described in Matthew and Mark may have been earlier than the one given in Luke. The earlier one did not include the miraculous catch of fish and did not end with so decisive a statement as, "[They] left everything and followed him" (Luke 5:11).[30]

Put out a little from shore (3). Capernaum was on the northern shore of the Sea of Galilee. Luke always uses the term *lake* to describe this body of water. In the Old Testament, it is referred to as a sea (Numbers 34:11), and the other Gospel writers so designate it. Since its size was about seven by twelve miles, the term *lake* suits it well for the readers outside of Palestine. Gennesaret is the designation for the land just south of Capernaum. Its shores were occupied by a number of flourishing towns and villages. Many fishing vessels made their way daily to favorite spots to gain a livelihood from the catches of fish. The most common type of boat for this purpose was an open vessel about twenty to thirty feet long. Jesus had returned from His traveling from place to place and preaching. He was on the shore one morning close to the place where Simon Peter pursued his work of fishing. Jesus climbed into Simon's boat and told him to shove out a little way in the water. Crowds had already been pressing Jesus to hear Him speak. This represents a second stage in the ministry of Jesus. At first, the synagogue had been a center of Jesus' teaching and healing activity. Now, however, the crowds had grown to such proportions that the synagogue would not hold them. The sea shore, the hillside, the whole out-of-doors became His auditorium. Jesus was already well acquainted with Simon, for he had met him in Judea (John 1:41,

---

[30] J. Norval Geldenhuys, *Commentary on Luke* (Grand Rapids: Eerdmans, 1951), pp. 180, 183f.

JESUS IN GALILEE

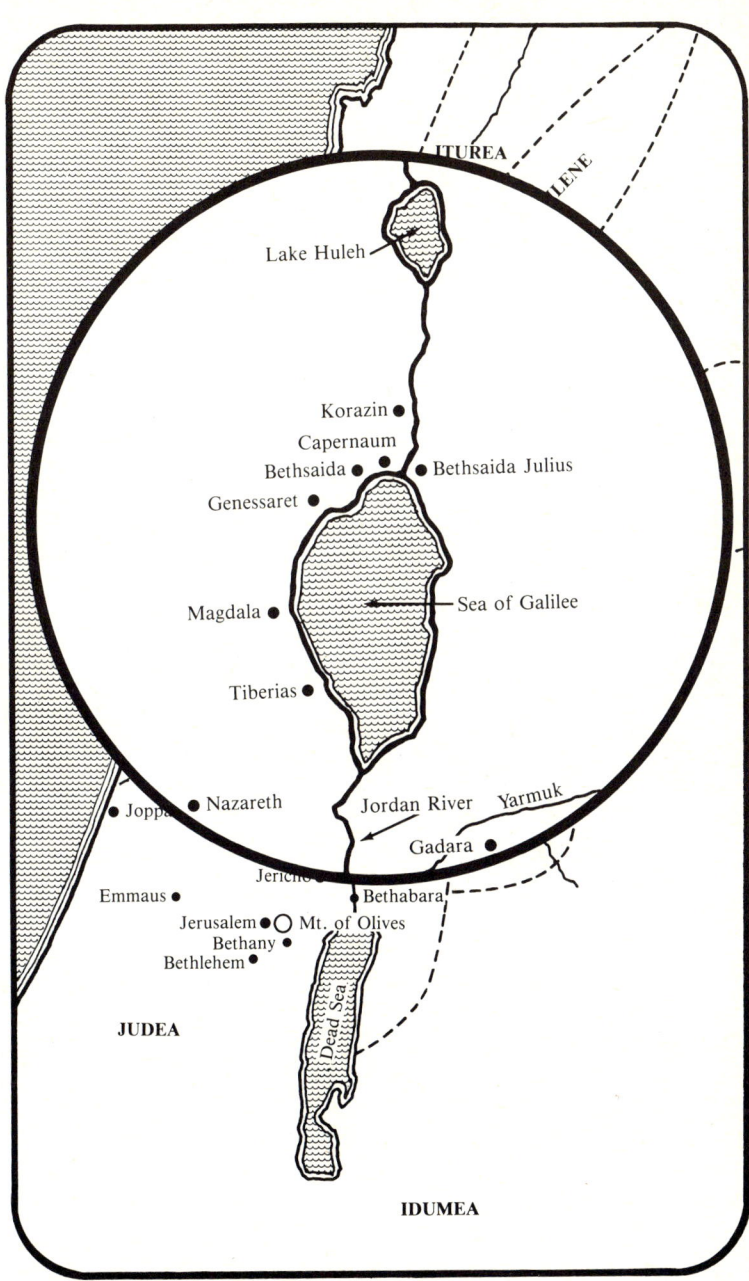

42), He had been in his home and healed his mother-in-law (Luke 4:38f.), and perhaps He had talked with Simon on former occasions along this very spot on the shores of the lake (Mark 1:16, 17). Simon readily complied with Jesus' request, and Jesus was supplied with an ideal arrangement where the people could see and hear Him, but could not crowd Him so that He could not be heard.

Let down the nets (4). The purpose of Luke's recording this incident was not the teaching of Jesus at this point, or he would have told us what Jesus preached. The most important part was to follow. Jesus told Peter to put out into the lake and spread his nets for a catch of fish. Peter was sure this would be futile because he had just tried everything he, as a fisherman, knew could be done, and they had not caught anything all night long.

Master. . . . because you say so . . . (5). Luke is the only Gospel writer who uses this word in describing address to Jesus. It carries more respect and authority than the word *rabbi*. Despite Peter's doubt about Jesus' knowledge and control in this field of fishing, Simon was willing to try. It was not faith, but a willingness to follow Jesus' direction.

Go away from me, Lord (8). When the nets were filled beyond their capacity, Simon could find no limitation to the power of Jesus. He exchanged his doubts about Jesus for doubts about himself. His reaction at first is unexpected, but then it becomes understandable. Why would Simon beg for Jesus to depart from him and bring up Simon's own sinfulness? A Chinese proverb says: "Bright lights cast dark shadows." When Simon recognized the divine person and power of Jesus, he was struck with his own sin and limitations. He was not worthy to be in the presence of such an individual. This same feeling came upon Abraham (Genesis 18:27), Job (Job 42:6), and especially Isaiah (Isaiah 6:5) in the presence of the Lord.

You will catch men (10). The miraculous catch of fish answered any doubts Simon had about the power of Jesus. Then Jesus answered the misgivings Simon had about his own life by a call beyond his highest ambitions. He must exchange catching fish for saving people. By this time, Simon had been joined by James and John, the sons of Zebedee, Simon's partners. The bottom line of this passage is not in the teaching of Jesus on the shores of Galilee nor in the miraculous power of Jesus to bring about a catch of fish, but in the fruits of his recruitment ministry. In the words of Luke: "So they pulled their boats up on shore, left everything and followed him" (Luke 5:11).

Ministry of Healing (5:12-26)

Leprosy (12-16)

In Jesus' country and times, leprosy was a dreaded disease, incurable in advanced stages, and requiring separation from normal society. Because of fear of spreading this disease to others, the afflicted were required to cry the warning, "Unclean," to those who approached. The Old Testament Law laid down the requirements for the treatment of those who had leprosy (Leviticus 13:1—14:57).

Covered with leprosy (12). Although *leprosy* designates a variety of skin diseases, it includes the dreaded condition that disfigures and is fatal. Literally, the phrase here means "full of leprosy." Only Luke uses the phrase, and this may have relationship to his being a physician. Medical writers in antiquity used the descriptive word, but not in connection with leprosy.

Don't tell anyone (14). The simple faith of the one who had leprosy was rewarded, and he was healed. But Jesus gave an unexpected command not to tell anyone about it. The Gospel of Mark gives more detail in reporting that the man disregarded the instruction (Mark 1:45). The result was that Jesus could no longer enter a town openly, but retired to more isolated places until the excitement subsided.

Show yourself to the priest Several purposes were served by giving this command: He was (1) urging the man to keep the law *(that Moses commanded,* Leviticus 14:1-32), (2) convincing the authorities that the man was cured, (3) establishing further proof for the future that the man was actually cured, and (4) providing the best way the man could be reinstated to his normal place in society. This was an example of healing especially significant to the expectations of the Messiah (Luke 7:18-22).

Jesus often withdrew . . . and prayed (16). Jesus was not only pacing himself in withdrawing from the enthusiasm of the crowds, but He was seeking the necessary refreshment of time alone with His Father.

Paralytic (17-26)

From the Gospel of Mark, one learns that the following episode took place in Capernaum after Jesus had returned from His preaching campaign (Mark 2:1-12). The scene is used not only to describe another miracle of healing but also to show the criticism of the Pharisees and the teachers of the law. In fact, in the next five paragraphs of Luke's account, criticisms are introduced to the actions of Jesus or His disciples.

Pharisees and teachers of the law (17). Opposition to Jesus arose in Galilee from the religious leaders. For the first time, Luke here refers to the Pharisees and their resistance to Jesus. This was a group of the Jews known as "the separated ones," numbering about six thousand and spread over the whole of Palestine.[31] They were the teachers in the synagogues, the religious examples in the eyes of the people, and the self-appointed guardians of the law and its observance. They had shared in raising a hedge around the law by adding the oral interpretations and regulations handed down by tradition as though they were part of the doctrine of God (Matthew 15:1-9). Already Jesus had experienced bitter confrontations with the religious leaders in Jerusalem (John 2:13-20; 5:16ff). Now they were on a front row among the spectators waiting to hear and see what would transpire in this home in Capernaum. The teachers of the law were the same as the scribes, those whose vocation was to study the law (both written and oral) to expound and teach it. The majority of these scribes belonged to the Pharisaic party, although the Sadducees had their scribes as well.

Power of the Lord . . . to heal. Luke alone of the three Synoptic Gospels makes this editorial affirmation. It is in keeping with Luke's particular interest in the work of the Holy Spirit, and the power to heal is closely akin. That this power was manifest to all is not clear. That other works had preceded the miraculous cure of the paralytic is not stated. Mark specifies only that Jesus had preached the word to them (Mark 2:2). In any event, the situation is in contrast to the unbelief at Nazareth. The people had crowded the house to see and hear; the Pharisees and teachers of the law were there to check out the teachings, claims, and works of Jesus.

Lowered him on his mat through the tiles (19). An example of the faith present is seen in the fact that the man who was paralyzed, unable to walk, and the four men who carried him would

---

[31] Josephus, *Antiquities,* xvii, 2, 4.

not be stopped by the crowded condition. They wanted to get to Jesus; so they tore up a section in the roof large enough to let down a stretcher-mat holding the sick individual. This was not as destructive as it might sound since the roof was flat, probably tile, and easily relaid. The plan was successful.

Your sins are forgiven (20). These were the first words of Jesus to the man. But why bring up his sins when he was there to be healed, not to talk about his personal life? Does this mean that Jesus was associating sin with all physical ailment? Not necessarily. The sin of Adam and the fall of man ultimately has its bearing on the presence of pain, suffering, and physical sickness, but this is not the whole of the answer as was seen in the case of Job. We are not told further about the sinfulness of this particular man in the Capernaum home. What ensues has more to do with the right of Jesus to forgive sin than it does with the life of the one who is being healed. The ministry of Jesus had more to do with their spiritual needs than their physical plight. But man is more conscious of the physical, which he can see and keenly feel, but the spiritual consequences are eternal. The very purpose of miraculous healing is involved here. It was a sign of God's approval on the one who had His power to heal. His message was endorsed. Although the alleviation of suffering and sickness was kind, the individuals died in the end anyway. The lasting value was salvation to the soul. In this particular case, Jesus wanted to bring out the spiritual import of His work as well as the physical assistance He had the power to give. That Jesus chose this time to do so may have been because of the Pharisees on the front row rather than because of the particular sins of this man who was being healed. Or more relevant still, Jesus said it for your benefit and mine.

Speaks blasphemy (21). Sure enough, the statement of Jesus drew fire from the Pharisees, not from the man. They accused Jesus of blasphemy, the worst sin they could find to condemn. This was the accusation made at the trials before Jesus' crucifixion. One type of blasphemy was a railing attack upon God or some impious statement concerning Him. Another type, however, was claiming to be or to do what was a prerogative of God alone. This latter type was intended here. If Jesus claimed to forgive sin and only God could forgive sin, then this was blasphemy. If the question stopped there, then it would indeed have been blasphemy, but the Pharisees failed to take into account the true person of Jesus. He was God's Son. He himself was divine and could claim the peculiar rights of God; so for Him, it was not blasphemy.

Which is easier? (23). In this context, the question of Jesus gains more import. It was easier to say, "Your sins are forgiven," because there was no visible proof as to whether this was carried out or not. But in the case of telling a paralytic to get up and walk, one could see when this was accomplished. Jesus then proposed to give assurance that He indeed forgave his sins by demonstrating the other—enabling the man to walk. One might question whether this meant that since the disciples could work miraculous cures, they could also forgive sins. This does not follow because the disciples did not claim to forgive sins. The role of the miraculous gave endorsement to the message proclaimed, and the significance of Jesus' claim here is tremendous. The Pharisees recognized this and rejected Him. In a true sense, it was still more difficult to pronounce a man's sins forgiven effectively, for God alone could do so; but Jesus was divine.

Filled with awe (26). The miracle was accomplished and the exclamations of wonder that the people gave had to do, not just with what was seen, but with the import of who Jesus was and what He claimed to be.

Ministry of Recruitment, Part Two: Calling of Levi (5:27-32)

After the example of healing and controversy with the Pharisees, Luke (as well as Matthew [9.9ff] and Mark [2:13ff]) proceeds to describe a second example of recruitment. His first example was that of the fisherman, Peter (Luke 5:10), along with James and John. Now he tells of the invitation to a tax collector, Levi (called Matthew in his Gospel, Matthew 9:9). Tax collectors were generally thrice-hated in Palestine. They took the hard-earned money of the people to satisfy the needs of the rulers. They were collecting money for the Gentile, foreign power Rome. Finally, they were often dishonest individuals who robbed the people to become rich themselves. The tax collectors were so despised they were regularly ostracized from all common social and religious gatherings.

Follow me (27). Taxes were of different kinds. Poll taxes were exacted from the individuals in their own locale. Toll taxes were gathered as they traveled from one place to another or as they were transporting goods. Probably, Levi was collecting toll tax along the Great West Road that led from Damascus to the Mediterranean and passed along the lake through Capernaum. Taxes collected here were for Herod rather than directly for the Roman emperor. Jesus spoke to Levi as he sat outside by his tollhouse. Whether they had previous contact with one another is not known, but certainly Levi must have known considerably about Jesus by reputation. Luke adds to Matthew's account that he "left *everything* and followed him" (Luke 5:28). This was something different from Peter and the fishermen. They could come back and pick up where they left off; but this was not true of Levi. There was no turning back when he rose to follow Jesus.

Not come to call the righteous, but sinners to repentance (32). Another commendable aspect of Levi's decision to follow Jesus was that he wanted to make his change known to all his old circle of friends and to introduce Jesus to them, also. He gave a big banquet. Luke is particularly interested in meals. (See Luke 7:36; 9:12ff; 10:38ff; 11:37; 14:1; 19:7; 22:14; 24:30, 41ff.) This must have been a considerable collection of the outcasts from society, such as the tax collectors. The Pharisees came, also, not as honored guests—they would not have entered the house—but as disgruntled demonstrators who gathered around the door and sent criticisms in to Jesus. "How could He associate with such people?" they complained to His disciples. Jesus used the analogy of the doctor in reply. The doctor had come to treat the sick, not the healthy, and so had He. Jesus was not saying that the Pharisees were the healthy, and therefore needed no doctor; but a person must recognize he is a sinner before Jesus can help him. Jesus had come to help the sinner and to urge him to repent. The existentialist of today emphasizes how Jesus can reach the lowest sinner, farthest from God. What is frequently omitted, however, is that Jesus will not allow him to remain as he is without striving to become what he ought to be. Repentance is another favorite theme of Luke (See Luke 3:3, 8; 10:13; 11:32; 13:3, 5; 15:7, 10; 16:30; 17:3, 4; 24:47.)

Questions and Answers (5:33—6:11)
About Fasting (5:33-35)

The criticisms continue, probably on another day. This time it seems as though the disciples of John join in asking questions about fasting. From Mark, it would seem to be that questions were asked on one of the fasting days observed by both the disciples of John and the Pharisees. (See Mark 2:18.)

John's disciples often fast and pray (33). For a contrast, John's regular diet was meager—locusts and wild honey (Matthew 3:4). His message was sober, and his spiritual concentration was rigid. The Old Testament did not have many required fastings. It was observed on the Day of Atonement (Leviticus 16:29-31). It was associated with times of mourning and disaster (1 Samuel 1:7, 8, 18; Nehemiah 1:4). Unfortunately it became associated in the minds of many with meritorious works, and they made a show of it (Matthew 6:16). The Pharisees had insistent schedules. They designated Mondays and Thursdays as fast days and sometimes added extra fasting days. Many Jews fasted twice a week (Luke 18:12). Jesus fasted himself and permitted its use voluntarily for spiritual gain (Matthew 4:2; 6:17, 18; see Acts 9:9; 13:2, 3; 14:23). Jesus condemned it for meritorious work or display, and gave no place for its use as compulsory practice.

While [the bridegroom] is with them. (34). Jesus made His point by an analogy. A wedding is a joyous occasion, and the guests do not fast at the time of celebration. Jesus, while He was with the disciples, was the cause of gladness, and the time should have been like the hours when the bridegroom is present. When He was not there, possibly referring to the coming days following the crucifixion, would be the time for fasting.

Parable (36). A parable can be a proverb as well as a story. The lesson Jesus conveys is that the new and the old are not to be mixed. In patching an old garment, you should not ruin a new one by cutting a piece out of it to put on the old. It does not match, and will probably cause another tear since the weaker old cloth will simply rend further. Since Jesus is preaching a new gospel, people should not expect to impose the old law and its form upon the new. The same is true of wineskins. The old wineskin loses its elasticity, the stretch necessary to expand with the fermentation of new wine. If it cannot stretch, it will burst. Jesus was indicating a real difference between the old law, with its regulation and rules, and His new teaching. The New Covenant cannot be forced into the framework of the Old.

The old is better (39). Jesus is not recommending the old over over the new. He is simply drawing attention to the natural preference people have for the old. This is a source of the trouble: they are reluctant to change from the old ways.

About the Sabbath Day (6:1-11)

Luke records five criticisms in a row that the Pharisees have made. They considered Jesus blasphemous when He declared the forgiveness of the paralytic's sins (5:21). They complained about Jesus' eating with tax collectors and sinners (5:30). Jesus needed to fast more (5:33), and now, on two occasions, violation of the Sabbath is claimed.

Why are you doing what is unlawful on the Sabbath? (2). As they walked along, Jesus' disciples had been picking heads of grains, rubbing them in their hands, blowing away the chaff, and eating the kernels. This was tantamount to threshing, was therefore work, and was unlawful on the Sabbath. So declared the Pharisees.

The Son of Man is Lord of the Sabbath (5). First Jesus gave David as an example of one for whom the law was violated under particular circumstances. When he was hungry and fleeing from Saul, he ate bread consecrated for use in the Holy Place of the tabernacle (1 Samuel 21:1ff). Were the Pharisees ready to condemn David? In the second place, the Sabbath was not Lord, but the Son of Man was the controller of the day. He has the authority to override rules of the law concerning the Sabbath. *Son of Man* is the term Jesus regularly used to apply to himself.

On another Sabbath (6). On this occasion in the synagogue, Jesus took the initiative and put the question to the people before He worked the miracle on the Sabbath. "Which is lawful on the Sabbath: to do good or to do evil, to save life or to destroy it?" (Luke 6:9). Although the Pharisees were there and waiting to accuse Him if he worked a miracle on the Sabbath, they did not dare to reply to the way He had put the question.

They were furious (11). After Jesus healed the man with the withered hand, the Pharisees and teachers of the law were bitterly angry and frustrated. They deliberated together about how they could stop Jesus.

Ministry of Recruitment, Part Three:
Choosing the Twelve (6:12-16)

He called his disciples (13). By this time, Jesus was being followed by large numbers of people. Some would seek Him for just the day when He was in their vicinity. Others would stay with the group as they went from place to place on a particular trip. Still others were determined to follow Jesus wherever He went. This group included women as well as men (Luke 8:1-3). From this wider group of disciples, Jesus here chose twelve as special leaders. Characteristic of Jesus, He spent the night in prayer before making this important selection (Luke 6:12).

Designated apostles. The term means a person sent with special commission. Lists of these twelve apostles are found in several passages (Matthew 10:2-4; Mark 3:16-19; Acts 1:13.) The names vary somewhat, but by comparing the lists, one is able to determine which are the likely names for the same individuals. Nathaniel in the Gospel of John and Bartholomew in the Synoptics seem to be the same person. Matthew and Levi are identified as one; and Judas the son of James (Luke 6:16; Acts 1:13) and Thaddaeus (Matthew 10:3; Mark 3:18) are the same. All of the Twelve seem to have come from Galilee except Judas Iscariot. His designation, Iscariot, indicates a man of Kerioth (Joshua 15:25) in Judea. The names appear in different orders in the lists, but they are all consistent in putting Peter first and Judas Iscariot last.

"Follow Me"

When a missionary returned from China some years ago, he brought with him a leaf from an ancient manuscript. The page was from the New Testament and from the writing was dated as fifth century. After the proud possessor of the manuscript page showed it to a friend in the United States, the question was raised, "Was there Christianity in China in the fifth century?" The answer had to be "Yes," because of the Scripture manuscript page in front of them. Certainly the Nestorian Christians are known to have been there. The next question was, "But now you are having to take Christianity to China today. Whatever happened to it along the way?"

"I don't know," said the missionary, "except that one generation failed to pass it on to the next."

You can see the importance of a recruitment program in the example of Jesus' ministry. He was eager, not simply for the salvation of one soul, or of one generation—but He wanted to ensure the proclamation of the gospel through the centuries to the end of time. He began in the early period of His ministry, for it was marked by teaching, healing, and recruitment. Disciples must be called, they must be trained, they must carry on the work when Jesus was no longer here in person to continue as He did for three-and-a-half years. He began recruitment immediately after His baptism, as He talked with two who were apprentices under John the Baptist (John 1:35-39). Of these two, Andrew found his brother, and then there were three. The next day Jesus said to another, "Follow me" (John 1:43), and he came, bringing another with him. And then there were five. When Jesus attended the wedding feast of Cana, He was already accompanied by disciples (John 2:2). He moved to Capernaum, and disciples went with Him (John 2:12). Then He returned to Judea, and again His disciples were with Him (John 3:22). After John the Baptist was put in prison, Jesus went back to Galilee (Mark 1:14). This must have been a time when some of the faithful disciples were given an opportunity to return home and set things in order after their absence. Jesus did not want them to follow Him without counting the cost (Luke 14:26ff). He invited many who did not come (Luke 14:16ff; 9:62). Then Jesus came again to talk with the earlier followers as they worked along the shore (Mark 1:16ff). Finally, He said, "Follow me," and they left everything and followed Him (Luke 5:11). Another left his booth where he was collecting taxes (Luke 6:27). One left a life in a Jewish nationalistic party ready to rebel against Rome, and followed Jesus (Simon the Zealot; Matthew 10:4). Finally, there were twelve, backed by scores who traveled with Jesus to be molded by His words, His deeds, and His life.

Four centuries before Jesus, an elderly man walked a street in Athens. He put out his staff to stop a young man hurrying by. "Can you tell me where you can buy bridles and saddles? Equipment for horses?" asked the old man.

"Yes, right down this street. Then turn to the left at the cross street. They sell all things there," replied the youth.

The old man continued, "Can you tell me where I can find beans and vegetables for sale?"

"Yes, that's straight ahead and to the right."

Finally the elderly man looked the young man in the eye and asked, "Now, can you tell me where the fair and noble are to be found in this place?"

The youngster looked puzzled and admitted, "I don't know."

A challenge was given, "Come, follow me, and I will teach you of the fair and noble." From that day, young Xenophon became a disciple of the elderly philosopher, Socrates.

Jesus is truly a paradox. So humble as to identify with the lowliest on the face of the earth, and yet He remains King of kings. His self-claims of Messiahship and divinity are reflected in His unabashed invitation to leave everything and follow Him. He taught also of the fair and noble in life, but more. He told of God's kingdom, of forgiveness of sins, the need of repentance, and the way to eternal salvation. He had a new teaching, the gospel. He established it with divine authority, authenticated by His miraculous works. He taught it with divine wisdom, through the power of His word. He passed it on with a recruitment emphasis to be kept alive through every generation. The whole of the Christian message can be summed up in two words: "Follow Jesus."

CHAPTER FIVE

Sermons to Live By

Luke 6:17—7:50

The sermons of Jesus teach us how to live, and these sermons are not confined to His words. He taught us by His deeds and by His example. Even His words need not be in formal discourses to teach us. Sometimes He worked a miracle and then made a point from the action. Luke may give a description of Jesus that preaches a sermon to us. Sometimes Jesus gave instruction one to one, other times to multitudes. Sometimes He addressed friends, sometimes foes. But everywhere you turn, you find Jesus preaching sermons. Plutarch, as he introduces his life of Alexander the Great, draws attention to the fact that an individual can be judged better by his spontaneous exclamations, his side remarks and little stories, than by his carefully prepared speeches to an army before a battle or to citizens in the political arena. Jesus excelled in all the avenues of communication. Furthermore, the messages He gave were consistent, whether in what He said, in what He did, or in the very emotions He showed.

Preaching in Action

In this section, Luke gives examples of Jesus' formal discourse in His sermon on the plain (Luke 6:20-49). Luke continues to record another type of sermon through the remarks of Jesus upon the healing of the centurion's servant and the raising of the widow of Nain's son (7:1-17). In each instance, it is not the cure or even the resurrected individual who is important to the record; but the focus is the message left in Jesus' bottom line to the episodes. Jesus preached another sermon in answer to the doubts of John the Baptist (7:18-35). Today, we live in a world of questions and skepticism. We need Jesus' sermon of assurance.

At a dinner in the house of a Pharisee, Jesus continued to preach—first to his host (7:40-47), then to the sinful woman (7:48-50), first with a parable (7:41-43), then with a comparison (7:44-47). In all of this, each of us finds his own name written there, and Jesus gives us truths to live by.

Content Notes

The Sermon on the Plain (6:17-19)

The sermon recorded here in Luke closely parallels the Sermon on the Mount (Matthew 5—7). Luke's is shorter, but they both begin with Beatitudes and end with the figure of the wise and foolish builders. In fact, every part of the Sermon on the Plain has a counterpart in the Sermon on the Mount (except 6:39, 40, 45, and these have parallels elsewhere in Matthew). There is considerably more material in Matthew's record of Jesus' sermon, but much of this is given in different settings in various places in Luke.[32] Only a small portion of Matthew's Sermon on the Mount does not appear some place in Luke.[33]

Went down ... stood on a level place (17). Jesus and His newly appointed apostles descended from the higher slopes of a mountain to a level place which, no doubt, formed a natural amphitheatre. A vast number of people from all over the land of the Jews and Phoenicia were waiting there. His disciples who traveled with Him regularly formed a considerable crowd themselves, and the Twelve were closest to Him. This is the time and place in Luke's record of Jesus' Sermon on the Plain.

Possibly it represents the same message recorded in Matthew as the Sermon on the Mount. Although the places are described differently—one a plain, the other a mountain—it might be a plateau in the foothills, which would fit both descriptions, the

---

[32]Mt. 5:13/Lk. 14:34; Mt. 5:15/Lk. 11:33; Mt. 5:18/Lk. 16:17; Mt. 5:25, 26/Lk. 12:58, 59; Mt. 5:32/Lk. 16:18; Mt. 6:9-13/Lk. 11:2-4; Mt. 6:19-21/Lk. 12:33, 34; Mt. 6:22, 23/Lk. 11:34,35; Mt. 6:24/Lk. 16:13; Mt. 6:25-33/Lk. 12:22-31; Mt. 7:7-11/Lk. 11:9-13; Mt. 7:13, 14/Lk. 13:24. Cf. John Martin Creed, *The Gospel According to St. Luke* (London: Macmillan, 1969), p. 90.

[33]Instruction about almsgiving, prayer, and fasting: Matthew 6:1-8, 16-18.

mount or the plain. Matthew reports the sermon early in Jesus' ministry as the keynote message, but Luke puts it later in the out-of-doors period of His ministry. Here, too, Matthew need not be chronological, nor Luke either for that matter; so Matthew may have wanted to give early an example of Jesus' preaching, which told people the principles of the life He was urging. The standard He brought was entirely different from what the world used. Although both the sermon in Matthew and the one in Luke sound so similar as to be one, it is possible that Jesus presented much the same material more than once. In fact, it may be that Matthew has made a collection of parts of different sermons and arranged them into a composite message typical of the presentations Jesus made. The fact that Luke has much of the material found in Matthew's Sermon on the Mount distributed in other parts of his Gospel may reflect the original setting of the saying at times. In any event, whether one sermon or two or many, Jesus has given us the truths to live by, both timely and timeless.

Blessed . . . (20). Three dimensions are clearly discernible in what Jesus had to say to this multitude and to us through them. In the Beatitudes, this is particularly evident. Jesus wanted to help those who were weighed down with the tragic problems of extreme poverty, lack of food, and being outcasts from society. Still, He was not ready to give a blanket blessing upon all physical poorness. Some of this may be the fault of choice, foolishness, laziness, or sin. A second dimension to this condition of deprivation comes into view when we see the promises—the kingdom of God, satisfaction, joy, a Savior. The spiritual realm is always present, but just out of sight physically. To make sure one does not miss this, Matthew explicitly includes, poor *in spirit* (Matthew 5:3). The satisfaction that is promised is more than enough to eat; there is a satisfaction of mind and soul as well. This leads to the third dimension in not only the Beatitudes but the whole of these sermons, both in Matthew and in Luke. This dimension is directly related to the Son of Man. Not just anyone who is hated, insulted, and rejected of men is talked about in Luke's fourth Beatitude, but the significant phrase that ends the sentence is "because of the Son of Man." When hardship comes because we follow Jesus—this is the qualifying part of the sermon and to its promises. But this dimension is more than qualifying. The Son of Man is our hope. Many have taken the Sermon on the Mount and the Sermon on the Plain as being statements on the subject of ethics (how to live) and neglect to see the necessity of faith and a Savior in their message. The ethics are so high, however, this is where we learn of our need for a Savior.[34] Jesus promises us help when we are poor and hungry, physically and spiritually, and we endure opposition and rejection because of Him. Then hardships become a blessing.

Woe to . . . (24). To make sure the points are not missed, Jesus gave the opposite side of the picture. Once again, the truths are not restricted to one dimension. The rich and the well-fed have to do with worldly possessions, the physical level. Having them is not wrong, but the attitude toward these material things is where the danger lies: "A man's life does not consist in the abundance of his possessions" (Luke 12:15). When a person's *regard* for riches is weighed also, the spiritual, or the lack of the spiritual, is necessarily involved. If the standards of the world are used and material wealth is put at the top of the list, covetousness enters the heart; service to God and love for others suffer. The only enjoyment is in the physical dimension, and this is short-lived (James 5:1-6). Laughing is not wrong, but it depends on what you are laughing about. The blessings given to the followers of Jesus include rejoicing and leaping for joy. Certainly this includes laughter, but this is a laughter that penetrates the second dimension and includes the spiritual, rather than excludes it.

A scientist once said that he could never take up a single item in the universe and study it, isolated and alone. He found it was always tied to something else, and its connections must be studied also. Man cannot live on the physical level alone and ignore his moorings in the spiritual. He may be well-fed physically, but hungry for spiritual food. He may be popular with the crowd, but if it is the wrong crowd, this only indicates his own compromise of that which is right. Jesus came to comfort the afflicted and to afflict those who had found false comfort.

Love your enemies (27). Of all the commands of Jesus, this is the most extraordinary, the most contrary to the inclination of the world, the hardest to justify logically. The only way it becomes reasonable is to use God as our starting point, His love

---

[34]R. C. Foster, *Life of Christ,* pp. 462-487.

and mercy and unselfishness as our compass. To strive to soften the passage by the study of the Greek word (a love that can be commanded of an individual although it may not rise from natural affection) or to maintain the stark impossibility of fulfilling such an injunction may help our understanding, but Jesus' own illustrations still stand: turn the other cheek (here the Greek may well indicate, rather than a slap on the cheek, a full blow to the jaw), let both your cloak (outer garment) and tunic (undershirt) be taken by the robber and do not expect it back. The bottom line to the whole passage has come down through the ages as the bottom line to the whole of the Christian ethic: the Golden Rule. *Do to others as you would have them do to you* (Luke 6:31).

Jesus emphasized in this passage, as in the whole of the sermon, how you are to treat your enemies, the ones with whom you do not get along. If you are loving, merciful, and unselfish with these, certainly you will treat your friends properly and even those you are not personally involved with. God himself is given as our example. But who can be as merciful as God? None will ever match His example, or even come close. This does not cause Jesus to lower our goal. To compare ourselves with one another is no comfort. God is our challenge, and Jesus is our only hope to supply what we lack.

Do not judge (37). This passage has been twisted to serve devious purposes. Some, in sin and realizing it, would like for this passage to mean, "I won't condemn you if you won't condemn me." Others would like to be relieved of the responsibility of discerning right and wrong and quote the words with the conclusion, "I'm not going to decide in any matter of judgment." Neither of these uses of the passage is faithful to the context. Jesus is speaking of our treatment of others. We should not condemn the other person by a stricter measurement than we are willing to use on ourselves (Luke 6:38; Matthew 7:2). Furthermore some matters are explicitly condemned in Scripture. These we will condemn with the authority of the Word. If, however, it is not explicit or is a matter of disputed interpretation, a matter of opinion or discernment of motives, Jesus says, "Treat others the way you would like to be treated." This does not relieve us from all judgments. Soon after these words, He told us to mark the good man by his good fruit and the evil man by his evil fruit (Luke 6:43-45). This requires judgment. What Jesus condemned was unjust judging of others and exacting more from their lives than we would expect of ourselves. By a generous outlook in life, we will find generosity returned. "A good measure ... will be poured into your lap" (Luke 6:38). This probably has reference to a measure of wheat. The customary outer garment was worn in such a way as to leave a fold over the belt that could be used as a large pocket to receive a measure of wheat.

A blind man (39). Jesus' sermons were filled with illustrations. The next two (Luke 6:39, 40) are not included in Matthew's Sermon on the Mount, but they do appear in other places in Matthew (10:24; 15:14). They had the immediate application to the Pharisees and the teachers of the law. They attempted to go beyond the teaching of the Scripture and insist upon condemning all others who would not follow their traditions. They were the blind, the presumptuous student dictating to the teacher. The application is equally true today of those who teach their opinions as tantamount to the Word of God. The third illustration (Luke 6:41, 42) is related to the other two. It has an additional condemnation for the individual who has serious vision problems but tries to improve an individual with a minor difficulty. The hypocrite needs to clear up his own problem before starting on someone else.

A good tree (43). You can recognize the kind of life a person has by the kind of fruit he produces. This figure is followed by another: "Out of the overflow of his heart his mouth speaks." Musonius Rufus was a Stoic philosopher in Rome in the time of Paul. In one of his sermons, he concluded that the man who grew unashamed of thinking evil thoughts would not wait long before he would be saying evil words; and if he grew unashamed of saying those evil words, it would not be long before he would be doing those evil things. Solomon wrote: "Above all else, guard your heart, for it is the wellspring of life. Put away perversity from your mouth; keep corrupt talk far from your lips" (Proverbs 4:23, 24).

The builders (46-49). Jesus' sermon on how His followers should look at life concluded with a tragic warning. To hear His words and nod your head in agreement to His wisdom and love is not enough. Even to call him "Lord, Lord," with seeming respect and acceptance, is not enough. You must give up the world's standard of measurement and change your attitude toward others. You must put God and the inner life first, the spiritual values in the place that the Son of Man teaches and enables you. If you do as He says, you will dig deep and build on the rock, and you will weather all the storms life can bring. If you try to build with only the surface dimension in mind, no foundation, no depth in the spiritual, no help from the dimension of the Son of Man, the house with no foundation will be swept to destruction. You must do what He says as well as hear His sermons.

A Message of Faith: the Centurion (7:1-10)

Capernaum (1). Following His message on the plain, Jesus returned to His home base, Capernaum. Not far from Capernaum, a few miles to the west, a grassy slope rises gently to the higher hills where the appointment of the Twelve may have taken place. This site, west of Tabgha and known today as the Hill of the Beatitudes, is a more likely site for Jesus' sermon than the mountain called Kurn Hattin (the horns of Hattin), some six miles from the Sea of Galilee.

Centurion's servant (2). Although Capernaum was not garrisoned by Roman soldiers, the forces of Herod Antipas were there, and these in turn were disciplined by Roman authority. A Gentile centurion occupied a position of considerable weight in the community. Ordinarily, he controlled a hundred men, but this number might vary considerably. Besides the soldiers under his command, the centurion had his own personal slaves. On this occasion, one of these slaves had become seriously ill and was expected to die. This centurion was an exceptional man on several counts. First, he had already won the favor of the Jewish people of the vicinity. He had a genuine love for them and had built a synagogue for their worship. Second, he had a love and concern that extended to his slave, and he wanted to do everything he could to bring him through his illness. Third, he had heard about Jesus and His power. Perhaps he had personally heard Him preach and had seen Him work miracles of healing. He had faith that Jesus could help his servant. Fourth, he was well aware that a deep chasm separated Jews and Gentiles, but he was willing to submit and ask for assistance from Jesus. But he wanted to ask in the best way. He decided to appeal for representatives from the Jews to approach Jesus on his behalf. This was done for a deeper reason than simply looking for the most likely way to gain the approval of Jesus. He later explained he did not feel worthy to speak for himself to Jesus. Fifth, he changed his mind. He had sent asking that Jesus come and heal his slave; but when he heard Jesus was coming, he sent his friends to tell Jesus He need not come because He could say the word wherever He was and that would heal his slave. This, indeed, was an exceptional centurion.

Elders of the Jews (3). Note who it was who was willing to recommend the centurion to Jesus. These were not the Pharisees or teachers of the law. They had been on the front rows in the synagogue criticizing the work of Jesus. They would not be the ones to carry a request for Him to work a miracle for the centurion. The rulers of the synagogue might go to Jesus with a question (Luke 18:18), but to request something of Jesus, and on behalf of a Gentile, would be too much. The men who came were not Pharisees, not teachers of the law, not rulers, but elders—highly respected Jews of the community who could fairly represent the feeling of the people.

This man deserves (4). The centurions in the Roman empire had earned a high reputation for themselves in general. They were men to be admired for their dependability and strength of character more so than individuals in any other part of the Roman system. But this centurion had won particular respect from the very people he policed and protected. Today, the major remains left on the ancient site of Capernaum is a synagogue. It probably dates from the second or third century, but it is held that the synagogue from the time of Christ may have stood on the same location. It was paid for by this centurion. Could this have been a political move on his part simply to gain favor with the people? The elders added the words, "He loves our nation." This was established by more than one act. The pattern of his life and consistent treatment of the people convinced them of that love. He deserved Jesus' help. They wanted Jesus to heal his slave.

Say the word (7). In Matthew's description of this scene, the centurion speaks with Jesus directly, but in the Lukan passage, his friends deliver the message. The full picture may be seen in that the friends began the delivery of the revised request by the centurion—that Jesus not come into his house, as the centurion knew His entering a Gentile's quarters would cause some misgivings to many Jews—but that the centurion was close enough to witness the interchange and he could not refrain from making

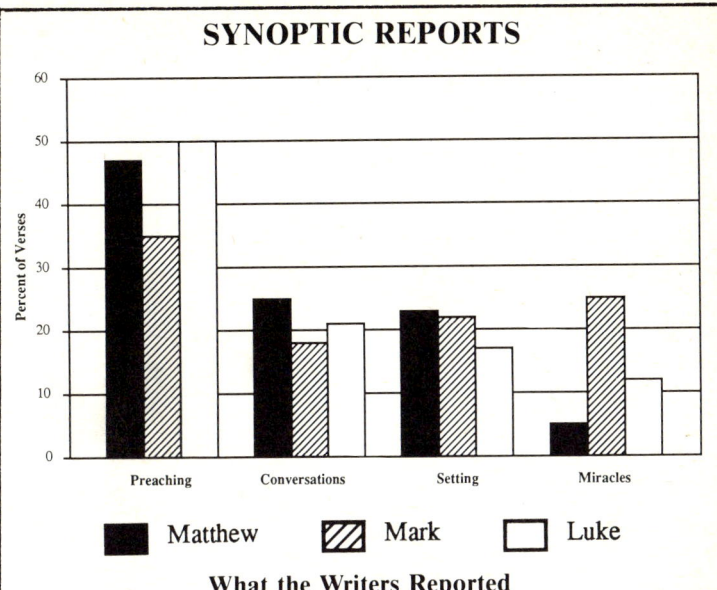

What the Writers Reported

Explanation

To formulate this chart, each Gospel was studied to determine how many verses were devoted to report (a) the preaching of Jesus, (b) His conversations, (c) the transition from one scene to another and the setting or action of an episode, and (d) the description of a miracle.

The numbers to the left of the chart indicate the percentage of verses found in each Gospel devoted to each of the four categories listed above. Added together, the numbers of the four categories for each Gospel will total 100%.

Observation

Despite the longer discourses found in Matthew, more of Luke's report is preaching (50%) than is Matthew's (47%). In Luke, the sermonic material is distributed among more different scenes.

Jesus gave much instruction in His conversations with people. Matthew has the highest percentage in this category (25%).

Matthew is noted for giving editorial comment on the episodes, especially the indication of fulfillment of prophecy; therefore, it is no surprise to see that Matthew spent more of his space on setting material (23%) than Mark or Luke.

Mark devoted much more space to the recording of miracles in the ministry of Jesus (25%) than did Luke (12%) or Matthew (4%). But even Mark gave more of his space to recording Jesus' preaching (35%) than to His miracles.

The importance all the writers attached to Jesus' preaching can be seen at a glance.

direct contact with Jesus himself. The centurion had faith that Jesus could as easily heal at a distance as he could with His very presence.

Such great faith (9). This was the sermon Jesus preached on the occasion of this miracle. Three points come through with emphatic clarity. (1) The centurion had great faith. He had complete trust in the power and love of Jesus. Luke registers the reaction of Jesus as "amazement" at his faith. Mark registers Jesus' reaction of "amazement" on another occasion—the unbelief in Nazareth (Mark 6:6). (2) The centurion showed much humility. His approach to Christ was a deep feeling of unworthiness. Although he had considerable authority himself, he acknowledged the supreme authority of Christ. (3) The centurion was a Gentile. How do you think the Twelve felt on this occasion—to be told this Gentile soldier had more faith than they did? How do you think the Jews of Capernaum felt, or the whole of Israel? Jesus had not found faith like this anywhere in His own nation. Matthew gives further words of Jesus at this point: "I say to you that many will come from the east and the west, and will take their places at the feast with Abraham, Isaac and Jacob in the kingdom of heaven. But the subjects of the kingdom will be thrown outside, into the darkness, where there will be weeping and gnashing of teeth" (Matthew 8:11, 12). One wonders that these words are not included in Luke—but he does have the statement in another setting (Luke 13:28).

Found the servant well (10). We do not know the name of the centurion nor are we introduced to the slave who was made well, but we hear the sermon of Jesus.

Grounds for Hope: The Widow of Nain (7:11-17)

Nain (11). This was a town (modern Nein) on the northern slope of Little Hermon, a mountain twenty-five miles southwest of Capernaum and seven miles south of Mt. Tabor. The town was large enough to have a wall, but small enough to have but one gate (Luke 7:12). "Soon afterward" is an indefinite period of time, leaving the exact chronology uncertain. Luke is the only Gospel writer who records this miracle of a raising from the dead at Nain. It may be that Luke is eager to give an example of a resurrection since in his next section, Jesus makes special reference to raisings (Luke 7:22), but until now, no specific instance had been given.

Only son. (12). As Jesus approached the town, He was accompanied by His disciples and a large crowd. They were met by another large crowd coming from the city—a funeral procession. In very few words, Luke explains the pathetic situation. The person who had died was an only son. This meant that with his death, the family name and inheritance would no longer be carried on. The Greek word for *only (or only begotten)* is the same word used to describe Jesus (John 3:16).

A widow. Not only was the dead person an only son, but his mother was a widow. She had already lost her husband and now her son. He was a young man (learned from the words of Jesus, Luke 7:14), and would not only be the object of great affection, but the practical need for the care and provision he would be responsible for in the uncertain years ahead for a widow. All of this would be apparent with just these few details, no doubt repeated by the mourners who walked beside the body. But the Lord could know without being told.

Don't cry (13). The compassion of Jesus is an important part of His teaching and preaching. No one was in grief but Jesus grieved with him. According to custom, the mother would be leading the way to the burial place. Most likely, it was the very day of the death. Jesus spoke this simple word of encouragement.

Touched the coffin (14). The word *coffin* may be misleading to those of us who are accustomed to its being a type of box with a lid on it. This evidently was not the case. It was a portable, open frame on which the body was carried, more like a stretcher.[35]

By touching the bier, Jesus would become unclean according to the ceremonial law. He, however, was both above the rule and not to be restricted in providing the good to come. His gesture effectively stopped those who carried the body and the progress of the whole crowd.

Get up. This is a miracle where no request for help was given, no evidence of faith recorded. Jesus simply went forward and raised the young man from the dead. Other occasions when Jesus volunteered His services were to the lame man at the Pool of Bethesda (John 5) and to the man born blind (John 9). In each of these instances, Jesus took time to build faith before the

---

[35]Hendrikson, *Luke,* p. 390.

miracle was accomplished. The high emotional element in this scene is felt in the concluding statement: "And Jesus gave him back to his mother."

Great prophet (16). Luke gives the sermon left from this occasion by relating the reaction of the people who witnessed the miracle. Although the young man and his mother must have been favorites with the people (otherwise the crowd in the funeral procession would not have been so great), nevertheless the rejoicing was not so much for the son or the mother as in the very praise of God. They were in awe because a great prophet was in their midst. Old Testament prophets had raised people from the dead. In fact, Elijah had raised an only son of a widow (1 Kings 17:17ff), and Elisha had raised a son of the Shunammite woman (2 Kings 4:18ff) not far from Jesus' miracle. (Nain was located just between Shunem and Endor.)

God has come to help his people. Although their words do not include the explicit identification of the Messiah, this has Messianic overtones. (See Isaiah 7:14; Matthew 1:23.) As Elijah gave the resurrected son to his mother, she exclaimed to him, "Now I know that you are a man of God and that the word of the Lord from your mouth is the truth (1 Kings 17:24). These were the conclusions in the town of Nain concerning Jesus almost nine hundred years after Elijah, and now over nineteen hundred years after that day in Nain, the same message is heard.

This news about Jesus (17). Raising the dead was a miracle that climaxed the curing of leprosy or the casting out of demons. News of this spread throughout Judea. Luke may have used this term to indicate the whole of the land of the Jews or he may have intended southern Palestine, for his next section takes us to the setting of a prison cell in a castle off the coast of the Dead Sea.

Questions to Be Expected: John the Baptist (7:18-35)

After Herod Antipas had arrested John the Baptist, Jesus returned to Galilee and began His first evangelistic campaign from His new quarters in Capernaum (Matthew 4:12; Mark 1:14). According to tradition, John was put in prison in the fortress of Machaerus, near the northeastern shore of the Dead Sea. At least a year had gone by and John was still kept in his dungeon cell. Herod had John brought before him periodically and listened to him preach. If we know anything about John, we know that John did not preach to please him, but forthrightly condemned him for his sin. He was living with his brother Philip's wife (Mark 6:18). This makes all the more surprising Mark's report that Herod liked to listen to John (Mark 6:20). John was stimulating and disturbing to him, but Herod was by no means ready to make a change in his life. John's own lot in prison must have been miserable indeed. Not that John was about to give up, but a number of frustrating factors are evident. Whereas he was suffering in prison each day and the plight of his followers was daily growing worse, the popularity of Jesus continued to grow in Galilee. Whereas John had predicted of the One who would come after him, "His winnowing fork is in his hand, and he will clear his threshing floor, gathering the wheat into his barn and burning up the chaff with unquenchable fire" (Matthew 3:12), this was not happening. Still the same sinful power was on the throne in Galilee, the same oppressive force claimed supreme authority in Rome, and the same hostile religious leaders controlled the temple and Jerusalem. Where were the changes? When would they come? With such bright promises for the coming kingdom, was it not fair that John expect a better lot than he was receiving? Is it any wonder that John wanted to ask Jesus some questions? Still variant suggestions are made about his motives. (1) Some say that John asked these questions in order to settle the questions in his disciples' minds, not his own. (2) Some say John asked the questions to spur Jesus on to a more aggressive program. (3) Some maintain that John's persecution in prison had brought him to the brink of despair and he was pleading to Jesus for help. (4) Some maintain he was indeed puzzled and wanted to know Jesus' role and where it was leading. If it was not to be what John expected, what should he expect? Perhaps the true situation was not any one of these reasons alone, but a combination.

[John] sent them (19). Even though John was in prison, he somehow maintained contact with his followers, who kept him informed not only about his own group but concerning the work of Jesus. Disappointment must have plagued John and his followers because of the deep contrast between the freedom and success of Jesus compared with the plight of John and those identified with him. Could it be that Jesus had forgotten about His forerunner? It could not hurt to send a message of reminder and at the same time inquire about what to expect. Luke alone

(compare Matthew 11:2ff) tells that two were sent. John proceeded wisely and carefully in his instructions.

Should we expect someone else? (20). John's misgivings were put in the form of a question. The question was phrased so it was not in disagreement or even necessarily doubt, but it was, in fact, a challenge. "If you are the one who is coming, then prove it." Then too, the question was asked in public. Had John specified this? It put Jesus on the spot. He could not give private reassurance and encouragement to John. He could not say He would come and talk it over with him personally. Jesus had to give an answer for the whole audience, and this is what John wanted. If Jesus would make a public, positive affirmation as to who He was, this, John thought, would lead to the type of program the Messiah should be pursuing.

Go . . . report to John (22). Jesus could easily have replied in indignation at such a question. But in respect and patience, He replied in a way that was so natural one cannot think of a more simple or convincing response. He pointed to what He was doing. The blind, the lame, those who had leprosy, the deaf, even the dead, had been restored to normal life. Three conclusions can be reached from this: these are good fruits; so the tree must be good (Luke 6:43); these are miraculous works; so they must be evidence of God's approval on the message of the worker (Hebrews 2:4); they are works prophesied of the Messiah (Isaiah 29:18; 35:5f); He must be the One who comes. Jesus replied to John in effect, "You need proof? I have been proving it every day." John wanted and expected the final judgment he had predicted of Jesus, but it was not yet time. For the present, Jesus said nothing more than He had been saying; He did nothing more than He had been doing. John could not force Him into a program more to his liking nor into a revised time table to help his situation temporarily.

Good news is preached to the poor. When Jesus gave a report on His work, which established who He was, He used an ascending scale toward the climax. He noted even the raising of the dead, but this was not the summit—the gospel for the poor was the climax of all. This was used in Nazareth as a Messianic identification (Luke 4:18; Isaiah 61:1). It was a subject especially close to the heart of Luke.

Who does not fall away on account of me (23). Jesus was eager to include a word of encouragement, and at the same time a warning, to John the Baptist. He should not allow anything that Jesus said or did to offend him, that is trigger a trap, that would separate him from Jesus or cause him to fall away from the will of God. Even though John's expectations and methods may have been different from those of Jesus, he could only trust and press on in full commitment.

Why does Luke stop to tell us of this episode? To hear John ask this question is unexpected and disappointing. Luke does not dwell on the imprisonment of John. He recorded it earlier (Luke 3:19, 20), but here he does not even mention that John was in prison. Luke has a deeper purpose than to arouse sympathy for John. Neither does he stop to make excuses for John or suggest his motives, as well he could have. This was not his purpose. The underlying purpose Luke expressed in his prologue was to establish the certainty of these things the Christians were being instructed in Luke 1:4. To establish this certainty, Luke records the unexpected and the unpleasant along with the setting of the natural and expected. The reality of this kind of picture is the most convincing record.[36]

More than for realism and an understanding of the situation Jesus faced, Luke records this answer to John because of the importance for us to hear Jesus cope with the questions that recur in lives in every generation. Is Jesus the One we are looking for? Can we expect another? Jesus' answer rings true. (1) See My ministry. Examine My life and My teaching. They fulfill the prophecies made centuries before. I am the one God promised. (2) Keep faith despite adversity, despite your own expectations, do not give up. (3) Do not allow My words or ways to cause you to turn away from the Son of Man. This was another sermon Jesus gave for us to live by.

Reed swayed by the wind (24). Jesus gave His first message to John's representatives. Upon their departure, He gave another message to the crowd that had been listening. This was the real proof of the stature of Jesus. Instead of being irate at John, He delivered a sermon praising John's greatness. John was no weak individual, bending with the pressure of powers in high places. He was not a specimen softened by the luxuries of the palace.

---

[36]Marshall, *Gospel of Luke,* p. 287.

More than a prophet (26). He was indeed a prophet, but because he was the forerunner of the Messiah, he was still more than a prophet. Jesus gave him the highest praise of being excelled by no man who had ever lived.

Least in the kingdom ... greater than he (28). This was the way Jesus could praise John and at the same time point out the superiority of the New Covenant and the coming kingdom with Jesus as King and Savior. John was still under the Old Covenant prior to the kingdom.

Pharisees ... rejected God's purpose (30). Some consider verses 29, 30 as a parenthetical comment by Luke, but this is unlikely. Jesus seems to have made the observation himself. The common people of the land had recognized the message of John as from God. They had shown their acknowledgement by being baptized by John. The Pharisees and law experts had rejected God's plan when they refused to be baptized by John.

Like children sitting in the marketplace (32). Fickle people of Jesus' generation had joined the rejection of both John and Jesus, but for different reasons. Some said John was too austere with strictest of rules, and others said Jesus was too free, associating with sinners and eating with them. Note it was the enemies who accused Jesus of being a glutton and a drunkard and John of having a demon. These critics are like children in the marketplace who refuse to be joyful to play a wedding game or to be mournful to play a funeral game. Whichever it is, they are against it. They are determined to reject both John and Jesus in like fashion.

But wisdom is proved right (35). True children of God are not like the fickle children in the marketplace. The true children can see that wisdom is right in recognizing both the ministries of John and Jesus although they had different roles and methods.

The Proud and the Pentitent:
The Pharisee and the Sinful Woman (7:36-50)

One of the Pharisees [Simon (v. 40)] invited Jesus to have dinner (36). Jesus was constantly in contact with the Pharisees and teachers of the law, usually under hostile circumstances. Although an invitation to dinner was an unexpected occasion, it happened other times as well (Luke 11:37; 14:1). The town is not specified, but because of the location of the associated events, Galilee is most likely, and Capernaum the city. The Pharisee's motives are not told. They could have included a mixture: curiosity, desire to test Jesus, expectation to learn, hope to find common grounds, more likely discovery of grounds to accuse Him. Whatever the motives, Jesus' reception was not warm.

Woman who had lived a sinful life. (37). This description probably indicates she had been a prostitute. The understanding of the occasion is helped by filling in the probable circumstances. A formal meal of this kind would be eaten with a door open to the street or an inner court, and outsiders could come and observe the table and the guests. Some might presume to come in the dining room and seat themselves around the walls to watch and listen. They were even known to engage in the table conversation on occasion. This particular woman must have heard Jesus preach, perhaps in personal interview as well. As a result, she had changed her life. She now had such relief from her sins, such joy and gratitude in her new life, she wanted to do something special for Jesus to honor Him herself. She learned of Jesus' formal invitation to Simon's house for dinner, perhaps on the Sabbath day following the services, and of Jesus' acceptance. This was her opportunity.

Alabaster jar of perfume. The woman came to the Pharisee's house and brought a costly, long-necked bottle with expensive, perfumed ointment, not cheap olive oil. She was determined to anoint Jesus to express her gratitude for Jesus' restoring for her, not physical health, but a cleansed soul. This was not a case of her passing by in the street and on the impulse deciding to go in. She knew Jesus would be there, and she brought the jar of ointment with her.

Stood behind him (38). A guest at a formal meal would not be seated in a chair, but reclining on a couch. His face would be close to the table as he leaned on his left elbow and ate with his right hand. His feet would be extended behind him on the couch. This is how Jesus could go on with his conversation with Simon and pay no attention to what was happening at His feet and behind Him. It may be that the woman had planned to anoint His head, but found it too difficult to reach that far. It was far less ordinary to use precious ointment on the feet, but there are recorded cases, especially for the teaching of rabbis and in gratitude. She may in humility have planned originally to anoint His feet. What she had not planned was to be so emotionally moved that her tears had covered Jesus' feet before she could anoint them. This necessitated her drying the tears with her hair. This in turn would necessitate her letting her hair down in public, another act extremely humiliating in the proper society. But this woman was oblivious to customs in expressing her gratitude to Jesus.

If this man were a prophet (39). From this happening, Simon drew the conclusion that Jesus was no prophet. If He were, He would have been able to discern what kind of reputation this woman had; and knowing this, He would not have let her touch Him. The Pharisees were strict in their rules to avoid all contact with unclean persons. He thought this to himself and said nothing to Jesus.

Simon, I have something to tell you (40). Jesus still had given no sign to Simon that He was aware of what was transpiring at His feet. But He told Simon of the two men who owed different sums to a moneylender.

One owed five hundred denarii, and the other fifty (41). A denarius was equivalent to one day's pay, but whatever amount is put on it, one man owed ten times more than the other. The moneylender canceled the debts of both. To Jesus' question, Simon reluctantly had to answer that the one who had the greater debt canceled would be the one expected to have the more love.

You did not . . . but she has . . . (44-46). Now Jesus gives in no uncertain terms a contrast between Simon and the woman, a contrast between the proud and the penitent. Simon had not even provided water for the customary foot-washing on arrival, but the woman had wet His feet with her tears. Simon had given no welcome kiss, but she had kissed His feet. He had not even used oil on Jesus' head, but she had perfumed His feet.

For she loved much (47). The conclusion is that her sins, which were many, have been forgiven—this is seen in her love. The unfortunate understanding that some have reached from this passage is that the woman was forgiven because she had great love. To the contrary, the one whose debts were canceled loved more *as a result* of having his debt canceled, not *because* he loved more. The woman's love became a proof of her penitent life and her forgiven sins. In the case of the Pharisee, his little love is an evidence that he has been forgiven little as well.

Your sins are forgiven (48). These words were spoken as much for Simon and those in the room as for the woman. This gave testimony to the changed character of the woman, it gave testimony to Jesus' power to forgive. It was a sermon to live by for all generations to come. This sermon was preached not so much in words as in the life of a penitent woman.

Your faith has saved you; go in peace (50). Jesus made it clear that she was not saved by the merit of her love, but in the response of her faith. Her love had come as a result of her forgiveness. Her faith was her belief, trust, and commitment to Jesus, who was the epitome of God's grace. This sermon in the life of this woman proclaims these elements. Gratitude overflowed from her great love, which rose up because she had been forgiven her sins, that followed her repentance and reformation of life that accompanied her faith in Jesus Christ and commitment to Him. What followed it all was a peace this world cannot know—a peace of body, mind, and soul.

With Mind, With Heart, With Soul

A Dutch professor was living through days of near starvation in the Netherlands following the end of World War II. He wrote to a colleague in America telling about the difficult time he was having applying his mind to his studies. His wife and daughter were gone for the afternoon, and he was alone. All they had left to eat were some bread and a tulip bulb. He knew that he must wait for the wife and daughter to return before the food could be divided and eaten. But he was so hungry and wanted so much to eat it right then, he was unable to concentrate on his studies. The physical condition of the body is so closely joined to the mind that one cannot function best without the cooperation of the other.

Even so, a person might be in perfect health physically but so torn in his mind as to the direction of his life, the uncertainty of its end, or the criteria to measure right and wrong, that he can have no peace of mind despite an ample supply of food and health for his physical needs. Likewise, a troubled relationship with God, a realization of guilt in sin, may cause the soul to cry out in need. If his mental and spiritual conditions remain in turmoil, it will not be long before his physical condition will be suffering, also. This is the reason one finds in Jesus' healing and preaching that the whole man is His concern. In His Sermon on the Plain (Luke 6:17-49), He addressed the poor, the outcasts, and the needy, but their physical state or social standing was not the end of Jesus' treatment; He included dimensions of our lives that many would like to leave untouched. But once Jesus has awakened our realization of needs in all areas of life, to the depths of the spirit, our souls cry out for a Savior. The Son of Man offers himself as the answer. The decision to follow Him begins with what Jesus designated the greatest commandment: "Love the Lord your God with all your heart and with all your soul and with all your mind and with all your strength" (Mark 12:30). Jesus alone can bring peace of body, peace of mind, peace of soul. The people Jesus healed were not simply cured physically; they were made whole.

CHAPTER SIX

Establishing Identity

Luke 8:1—9:50

When a stranger moves into a new community, the neighborhood immediately begins to ask some questions. "What's his name?" "Where did he come from?" "Do we know his family?" "What does he do?" "Who are his friends?" "What are his plans for the future?" In order to establish identity, these questions must be answered satisfactorily. When Jesus moved to Capernaum, you can be sure the neighbors asked these things about Him.

Who Is This?

His name was Jesus of Nazareth, but He referred to himself as the Son of Man. The people of Nazareth said that Joseph, the carpenter, was His father, but Jesus said His Father was in Heaven. Jesus' mother and brothers were known in Capernaum, but Jesus said His family was made up of all those who heard the Word of God and practiced it. He did not support himself by carpentry any longer, as He had at Nazareth, but He traveled about teaching and preaching of the kingdom of God and repentance. He had many friends, especially twelve disciples. Most of them had been laboring men from Galilee. They, too, traveled around, sometimes with Jesus and sometimes on their own, preaching the same good news Jesus preached and trying to establish Jesus' identity. Jesus had many enemies, too; and they were important men, religious leaders: Pharisees, teachers of the law, and some of the rulers of the synagogue, not to mention the top men in Jerusalem: the Sadducees, the chief priests, and the high priest. Herod Antipas was having Him watched, and Herod had his own ideas about Jesus' identity (Luke 9:7-9). The common people were reaching different conclusions. The miracles

He worked were the part that no one could deny. He must be someone special to have such power. But His teaching matched His incredible deeds. They were new teachings not found in the law, but not disregarding the law. They were presented in a way that all people could understand. He did not appeal to the rabbis, ancient or recent, for authority. He had not trained in the schools of the Jewish teachers, yet he could debate with the most highly educated. He could use their language, apply their forms of discussion, and they were unable to best Him or even embarrass Him.

Who was this man? Whoever He was, those who had been healed by Him felt constrained to help Him in His work (Luke 8:2). Whoever He was, many who felt threatened by His power and popularity were determined to stop Him. Others wanted to use His power for profit to themselves.

The question still remained, who was this man? The Jews had been taught all their lives about the Old Testament prophets. These men of God had worked miracles. Could He be one like them or one of them returned? But they had not known a prophet in Israel for centuries now, unless John the Baptist had been a prophet. But John had not worked miracles, and now he had been beheaded by Herod. But John had predicted one greater than he was coming. Was Jesus the one? Everyone was expecting that this one would be the Messiah. Was Jesus the Messiah? With His works and His teachings, all He needed to do was to make public the claim. His disciples reached the conclusion that He was the Messiah, Peter affirmed it. Jesus himself confirmed it, but He ordered the disciples not to make that identification public. Then God himself identified Jesus. "This is my Son" (Luke 9:35). Again the identification was accompanied by an injunction not to make this scene known to others until the rising from the dead (Luke 9:36; cf. Mark 9:10).

This was the dilemma in this period of Jesus' ministry. He was establishing His identity, but in such a way that His hearers had to put the evidence together to draw their own conclusions. He taught in parables, easily remembered, easily understood on the surface, but difficult in the depths. It was almost as though He was building a case that would not be understood along the way. After the matter was complete, then the miracles, the action, and the sermons could be put together to establish identity. Meanwhile, the people asked, "Who is He?"

Content Notes

The Supporting Group (8:1-3)

Jesus traveled about (1). This seems to mark a new phase in Jesus' ministry. He had already undertaken speaking campaigns that introduced the good news in numerous towns (Luke 4:43, 44), but His activity had brought Him back regularly to Capernaum. Now, however, the itinerant life became the norm. Literally, He had no regular place to lay His head (Luke 9:58).

Good news of the kingdom of God. This kingdom phrase is used at least thirty times in Luke (e.g. Luke 4:43). In different contexts, it has different connotations: the eternal kingship of God, from everlasting to everlasting; the presence of the kingdom in the person of Jesus, the King (Luke 11:20); the immediate coming kingdom, the church; the future kingdom of the new heaven and earth.

These women were helping support them (3). To keep a group of thirteen men supplied was no small task. Luke stops to tell of one type of assistance they had. A group of women were helping from their own money and, no doubt, in a practical everyday way, with such things as cooking and sewing when they were camping along the way. This group of women had something in common. They were grateful, for each had been cured by Jesus.

Mary (called Magdalene) (2). Called after the town of her origin, Magdala—on the west shore of the Sea of Galilee, three miles north of Tiberias. She was the first to see Jesus after His resurrection (John 20:1f). She is not to be confused with the Mary of Bethany (John 11:1) or the sinful woman of Luke 7:37. There are no grounds for associating immorality with her former state of demon possession.

Joanna. She was among the women who came to Jesus' tomb on resurrection day (Luke 24:10). Her husband, Chuza, was probably a man of wealth, being manager of Herod Antipas' properties, or at least steward as a political appointee.

Susanna. This is our only reference to her in the Scripture.

The Seed and the Soil (8:4-15)

He told this parable (4). Luke not only marks a beginning of Jesus' itinerant ministry at this time, but he also notes the first of Jesus' major parables. Although Luke rather reserves Jesus' teachings and His parables to the next section of His Gospel record, He does give the important parable of the sower at this point. Only three parables are found in all three Synoptic Gospels: the sower (Matthew 13:1-23, Mark 4:1-20; Luke 8:4-15), the mustard seed (Matthew 13:31, 32; Mark 4:30-32; Luke 13:18, 19), and the vineyard (Matthew 21:33-46; Mark 12:1-12; Luke 20:9-19). Luke does not specify where Jesus was when He gave this parable, but Matthew and Mark note the seaside—probably at Capernaum—as the place. The scene serves as a bridge between Jesus' teaching in Capernaum and the incidents happening along the campaign from town to town. Jesus used parables to good advantage. They were stories thrown alongside a lesson He wanted to teach. The stories were about something familiar to the hearers and were both easy to understand and easy to remember. But this was just the beginning of the advantages. At times, the lesson to be learned was easily discerned, and at times, there was meaning beyond their grasp unless an explanation was given or the passage of time made clear the significance of relevant events. This was precisely the combination Jesus wanted. He was not ready to announce His Messiahship so that the selfish would twist it to their own purposes or the religious leaders use it to force their final measures. He could not teach the kingdom in its full significance as the coming church or its final Heavenly state. He needed a teaching with a surface that was clear and a depth that went beyond their sight.

A farmer went out to sow his seed (5). Perhaps Jesus pointed to a sower who was within view, doing his work on a distant hill.

Along the path. Often the footpaths would lead directly through the fields. The sower broadcast his seed over the whole field, and he could not keep the seed from falling on the paths as well. The pathway had a hard crust on top, and the seed would be trampled underfoot or eaten by birds before it had a chance to grow.

Some fell on rock (6). This was not a soil filled with rocks, but a thin covering of dirt on a solid rock area. The seed started to grow, but soon dried up and died.

Fell among thorns (7). The thorns grew up with the seed and choked it out.

Good soil (8). The yield of over a hundred grains for one grain is not unheard-of in some fields in Palestine. In this parable, the sower is the same and the seed is the same, only the soil is different.

Let him hear. All were in agreement with what was said thus far, but what was the significance? Jesus gave a challenge to come within the understanding distance to hear the rest.

His disciples (9). Mark makes clear this included more than the Twelve (Mark 4:10). To the ones who had a deep enough interest to wait and hear more, the explanation was given.

Though seeing, they may not see (10). This quotation from Isaiah (6:9, 10) and the thought are used frequently in the New Testament (besides in the parallel sower passages in Matthew and Mark, John 12:40; Acts 28:26, 27; Romans 11:8; 2 Corinthians 3:14). These words do not mean that God desires that some will not understand, but it expresses the sad truth that those who are not willing to dig for the treasure will never find it. Their disinterest in spiritual truths and their concentration on the things of this world keep from pursuing the deeper lessons of the parable.

The word of God (11). This message tells about God, but more specifically, it comes from God.

The soils (12-15). The different soils represent different types of individuals: the hardened do not receive the Word at all; the ephemeral have a joyful response lasting but a short time; the choked allow the worries, the riches, and the pleasures of this world to crowd out God's kingdom; but the one with an honest and good heart hears the Word, and his life matures and bears fruit. The message of the parable cuts two ways. It brings encouragement to the proclaimers of God's Word. When disappointment strikes as people reject the gospel, the one who has delivered the good news tends to blame himself for the lack of reception. The disciples were going to have this experience time and again in the years ahead. Through the ages, Christ's followers have identified with this feeling of disillusionment. We know the power of the gospel. Why does it not bring the same success at each occasion? Jesus gives this reassuring reminder. The difference is not in the seed or the sower; the difference is in the soil that receives the seed. But just when we are lifted up by the recognition of this truth, we see the second way this parable thrusts. The disciples, along with all the readers of this parable, cannot escape the inevitable question, "What kind of soil am I?"

Use the Light (8:16-18)

That those who come in can see the light (16). Jesus used three shorter parables pursuing the theme of light. The first emphasizes the responsibility of the one who has the light to put it into use and share it. This relates to the seed parable in that the sower has a responsibility to sow the seed even though the response is different, dependent on the soil. Once you have received the teaching of Jesus, you must pass it on and make it known to others who are entering. The sayings of these three lessons (Luke 8:16-18) are found individually in other parts of Luke. This first doublet teaching appears again in Luke 11:33.

Nothing concealed (17). The second lesson from light introduces another use. Light brings into view our lacks and our faults. The emphasis here is our sins we would like to keep a secret, but in the judgment, all will be brought to light. The doublet to this teaching is given in Luke 12:2.

What he thinks he has will be taken from him (18). The third lesson has less to do with light, but ties together lessons from the sower and the light. The one who has ears to hear must listen further to gain the explanation. The next step is to act upon it and to heed what he has heard. But the following step is to share what he has heard. We must become the sower, we must use the light; and if we do not, what we thought we had becomes nothing in our lives—like the first bite of cotton candy. We will be back to the rocky soil, or the thorns of life will choke the growth. Only if we share the good news will we be the good soil and the good listener. This will bring fruit for our lives and for the growth of the kingdom. This last lesson is found in its doublet in Luke 19:26. All three of these teachings (Luke 8:16-18) are found in Matthew as well (5:15; 10:26; 13:12).

Heed the Word (8:19-21)

Jesus' mother and brothers came to see him (19). Four of Jesus' brothers are named in Scripture: James, Joseph, Simon, and Judas (Jude) (Matthew 13:55; Mark 6:3). To protect a later belief that Mary remained a virgin throughout her life, several interpretations of this passage arose. Epiphanius held they were sons of Joseph by a previous marriage. Jerome, despite the regular use of the word (*brothers*) maintained they were cousins. Helvidius, however, supported the usual use of the word and rightly considered them the sons of Joseph and Mary after Jesus had been the firstborn of the virgin Mary.[37] There are no actual grounds for denying that Jesus had brothers and sisters.

The attitude of the brothers during the ministry of Jesus was disbelief (John 7:3-5), but following a resurrection appearance (1 Corinthians 15:7), James became a leader in the church (Acts 12:17; Galatians 2:9) and wrote an epistle included in the New Testament. The epistle of his brother, Jude, also has a place in the canonical writings. Just now, as they tried to approach Jesus, but could not get to Him because of the crowd, their frame of mind remains uncertain to us. Mark gives further information (3:21, 31-35). Since Mary accompanied them, it is unlikely that their motives were entirely hostile. If He persisted in maintaining the killing schedule He had been keeping in the past, His health would break. He must be out of His mind to try it, His brothers concluded, and His mother was equally concerned for His sake that He gain some kind of relief from the rigors of each day. They wanted to bring Him home. Jesus understood the intent of their visit. He was not receptive to outside coercion either to hasten His ministry or deter His plans. His answer to them was made in public rather than resorting to an unpleasant scene in private.

My mother and brothers are those who hear God's word and put it into practice (21). Jesus did not renounce His family ties, but pointed to a larger family with whom His relationship was on a still higher plane, and His responsibility to them directly related to His being here. He may have made these words still more personal with a sweeping gesture to indicate this was His family—these believers who pressed around Him. Those who heeded His word were the ones most closely related to Him.

See the Power (8:22-56)

Power Over the Wind and the Waves (22-25)

Luke gives a series of miracles showing the power of Jesus. The first is an example of His authority over nature. Luke does not make clear the day of this happening, but Mark records the

---

[37]J. B. Lightfoot, *St. Paul's Epistle to the Galatians,* sixth English ed. (Andover: Draper, 1899), pp. 88-128. Although he argues for Epiphanius' position, Lightfoot gives a good explanation of all three of these fourth-century positions.

occasion as the same day the sermon of parables was preached. It has earned the title of "the busy day." To escape the press of the crowd and find relief from His constant ministry to the people, Jesus climbed into a boat. Some suppose this would be one of Simon's former fishing boats kept ready for Jesus' use. The disciples were instructed to sail for the opposite shore, about six miles away. The Sea of Galilee is six hundred feet below sea level and surrounded by hills and ravines that funnel the wind to the surface of the water in such a way to churn up great waves in a short time. Mount Hermon, almost 10,000 feet in height and just thirty miles away, is responsible for frequent chilling air currents and unpredictable, violent storms. Such a storm hit the boat as Jesus was sleeping in the stern (Mark 4:38).

The boat was being swamped (23). The disciples were near panic. They were particularly disturbed because Jesus was still sleeping peacefully despite the danger of drowning. That Jesus slept through the raging storm shows a trust in God's care and the exhausted state He was in. This is the only time in the Gospels He is described as sleeping.

Rebuked the wind and the raging water (24). When the disciples desperately awakened Jesus, He got up and quieted the wind and the sea with a word (Mark 4:39). The fact that Jesus "rebuked" them need not indicate Jesus personified these forces, but that evil powers or Satan himself was using these forces of nature in an attempt to destroy Jesus and His disciples. Jesus' control was complete. Not only the immediate subsidence of the wind but the instant change from the high waves to a calm sea would have been most impressive to the disciples.

Where is your faith? (25). This question is unexpected in more than one way. First, we would not expect that Jesus should ask it just at this time of recent peril; and second we are surprised that the Synoptics should all record this uncomplimentary reflection from the fear of the disciples (cf. Matthew 8:26; Mark 4:40). These are kinds of notes that give credence to the historicity of the incident. The disciples lacked confidence, and the only reason it was put in the description is to record the truth of what happened. Faith is based on belief, leads to trust, and demands commitment. Which of these were the disciples lacking? They lacked a full belief in the deity of Christ or they could not be so frightened under these circumstances. Most lacking, however, was their trust.

Who is this? Luke records this question to continue to build the case for making the identity of Jesus the crux of the Gospel. Even the strongest forces of nature heed His commands. As the disciples came to full conviction, Luke tells it in such a way that Theophilus, or whoever the reader might be through the ages to our own day, will come to a certainty as to who Jesus is. You have to decide as you view His life, see His deeds, and hear His teaching. Those who deny the possibility of miracles involving the laws of nature fail to give God His rightful place, or the Son of God His true power and authority. The laws of nature are simply the way God usually works. He made the laws, and He can transcend them if He chooses. This is not violating law and order, but recognizing an ultimate law of a higher order, which can override the ordinary procedure. Even if Satan is allowed some use of natural forces, his control is temporary and limited (Job 1:12ff, 2:6ff). If, on this occasion, Satan attempted a specific attack, Jesus showed His power to rescue himself and His disciples from the elements, to thwart the plans of Satan, and to provide evidence of His power to His disciples and to posterity.

Power Over the Demons (26-39)

On the eastern side of the Sea of Galilee, much of the population was Gentile. The crowds and excitement were not as great as among the Jews. Jesus had cast out unclean spirits on many occasions (Luke 4:35, 41), but now Luke records an incident that had singular significance. (1) All three Synoptic writers tell about it: Matthew 8:28; Mark 5:1. (2) The demons were many (*legion* [a full Roman legion was 6000, but the number varied considerably]). (3) The demons were allowed to go into other bodies (the pigs). (4) Jesus was asked to leave the area because the people were afraid, and probably because of the loss of the pigs suffered by the inhabitants. (5) The cured man was told to stay home rather than follow Jesus. (6) The one formerly possessed by demons was told to make known what Jesus had done for him rather than remain silent.

Region of the Gerasenes (26). A great many manuscript differences occur in all three Gospel narratives at this point.[38]

---

[38] See Metzger, *Textual Commentary,* pp. 23f, 145.

Probably the original reading of Matthew (8:28) was Gadarenes because of the town of Gadara (modern Um Qeia) about six miles from the likely site along the lake where the happening took place. Josephus calls Gadara a Greek city. Mark (5:1) and Luke probably had the reading Gerasenes in the original because Gerasa (modern Jerash) is a larger city forty miles to the southeast, but it may have had holdings on the sea shore district which gave its name to the area. Pliny numbers Gerasa among the cities of the Decapolis. Luke may have preferred the name of this city to designate the area because he wrote for a Greek audience, and they were more likely to be acquainted with this name than other names of the locale. A third reading for the narrative in the three Gospels is Gergasenes, which may have come from a little town of Gergsa (possibly modern Kersa). This last suggestion was made by Origen to solve the problem from the other two names, but it may actually be a word introduced for the first time by Origen. All three of the passages have all three of the readings in different manuscripts. This is a good example of scribes' being influenced by the readings found in the other Gospels and trying to make them the same. It also is a good example of the Gospel writers' telling the same episode, but each in an independent way.

Jesus, Son of the Most High God (28). When Jesus landed, He was met by a man (Matthew speaks of two men [8:28]) who was demon-possessed. He was without clothes and lived in the tombs. When Jesus commanded the evil spirit to come out, he cried out addressing Jesus as "Son of the Most High God." Since Jesus is in the Greek territory of the Decapolis and Luke is writing particularly to Greek readers, the title used here is especially meaningful as a Hellenistic phrase denoting deity. The expression is used frequently, however, in the Septuagint, the Greek translation of the Old Testament, so it has considerable Semitic background as well.[39] It is different from the address recorded of the demons in Capernaum (Luke 4:34, 41), but the same as used by the angel (Luke 1:35) and Zechariah (1:76). It may be a slight indication that the possessed man was a Greek.

What is your name? (30). This question was used in order to draw a rational answer from the man, but the reply concerned

---

[39]See Marshall, *Gospel of Luke,* pp. 67f, 338.

the demons who were in control. The answer, "Legion," given by the demons because they were so many, might indicate a number in the thousands if taken literally. Some associate the number of pigs (Mark specifies two thousand, 5:13) with the number of demons, but this need not be directly proportionate. All that is clear is they were many and exerted tremendous strength and violence.

The Abyss (31). The great fear the demons had was to be sent to the place of imprisonment either waiting punishment or where the punishment has already begun (Revelation 9:11; 17:8; 20:1, 3; cf. 2 Peter 2:4).

They went into the pigs (33). At this point, some have attacked Jesus' action because, they maintain, He caused the destruction of other people's property without justification. The first issue to clarify is that Jesus did not directly destroy the swine, but only permitted the action of the demons, who caused the pigs to run down the steep place and to drown in the deep water. Next, we must remember the pigs involved were in large herds. We might question who the owners were, and for what purpose were they keeping swine? Jews were forbidden to eat unclean meat, and the pig was unclean by the definition (Leviticus 11:7, 8). We do not know whether this had a bearing on the decision of Jesus to allow this destruction or not. This was a predominately Gentile territory, and perhaps the demon-possessed man himself was a Gentile. Would the Gentiles have a responsibility to observe Jewish dietary laws?

Many factors remain unknown to us, and we are in no condition to declare to Jesus what is just and what is not just. He was able to compare properly the worth of one man's life compared with a large herd of pigs. He also was able to weigh in the evidential value of having this indication of something going out of the man and entering the pigs. This was not a psychological quirk. The demons were real, though not seen. They caused the destruction.

Return home (38). In this case, Jesus left instruction for the miracle to be made known. The people of these regions were not flocking to hear Jesus. No danger of Jesus' ministry getting out of hand was anticipated here. In fact, the people asked Him to leave; but Jesus left a constant reminder in the person who had lived in the tombs but now was free from the demons. This was what God had done for him.

Power Over Every Ailment (40-48)

When Jesus returned (40). Jesus came back to Capernaum or its vicinity, probably in the morning or the early afternoon, and the people were watching for Him. This expectation may have been increased because a man, Jairus, was searching desperately for Him. His child was ill and would die unless he was able to find Jesus. The crowd was growing. They wanted to know how this was going to turn out. Note the contrast between the Decapolis, the Greek area, where Jesus was asked to leave, and the environs of Capernaum, the Jewish district, where a multitude was waiting for Him.

A ruler of the synagogue (41). This was the "Head of the Synagogue," probably chosen from the elders of one particular synagogue. His responsibility included oversight of the synagogue services, inviting visitors to address the assembly (Acts 13:15), and maintaining order in all the functions (Luke 13:14).[40]

His only daughter (42). Luke includes this personal detail, which Matthew and Mark omit: she was his only daughter, and this made his pleading on her behalf all the more desperate as he asked for Jesus to come and make her well. Jesus gave a measure of assurance by starting out for Jairus' home.

A woman ... subject to bleeding (43). In the throngs of people who pressed in on Jesus as He passed through the streets, a woman reached out to touch the "edge" (border, hem) or more probably the "tassel" of His outer garment. This woman had been plagued for twelve years with a continual hemorrhage. This would not only take its toll physically, but would erect social and religious barriers as well. According to the Mosaic law, she would be unclean and must abide by all the restrictions associated with this condition (Leviticus 15:19ff). But the burdens did not stop here, for Mark makes clear (and many manuscripts in Luke as well), "She had suffered a great deal under the care of many doctors and had spent all she had, yet instead of getting better she grew worse" (Mark 5:26). The purpose of this detail is not given to inform us of the unfair doctors' fees or of the malpractice of the physicians, but to establish the incurable nature of her physical condition and the exhaustion of all her

---

[40]See Moore, *Judaism,* Vol. 1, p. 289.

resources. This woman was at low ebb from every aspect, but one. She had faith in Jesus. And when she touched the tassel of His garment, she felt herself cured.

"Who touched me?" (45). Jesus asked this question for several reasons. He did not want anyone to have the mistaken notion this was some kind of magic. Power was not automatically applied because of some inanimate object, such as Jesus' robe. The faith of the woman in Jesus' power to help her was crucial. Another factor was the very purpose of the miraculous to provide testimony to God's approval upon the person and message of the healer. Then, too, it must be made known that the woman was healed before she could regain her normal place in society. She was no longer under the severe prohibitions she had endured for years. All these factors, an acknowledgement of her faith, a testimony to the power possessed by God's representative, Jesus, and the assurance that she had been cured, were taken care of when she answered Jesus' demand to give a public admission of what had happened.

"Daughter, your faith has healed you" (48). This is a tender address, the only place recorded where Jesus used it of an individual. (Compare Luke 23:28.) She had complete trust that if she somehow reached Jesus, all would be well, and she was not disappointed.

Power Over Death (49-56)

Your daughter is dead (49). One can imagine the feelings of Jairus while all of these interruptions were causing delay. The synagogue ruler had been looking for Jesus for a period of time before he found Him. Then he had to persuade Him to come. Then the streets were so jammed with people the progress must have been very slow. On top of all this, to have this further delay of an additional healing along the way, plus the ensuing conversation, must have been agonizing to Jairus. On the other hand, Jesus never seemed to be disturbed by interruptions. He always took them in stride, never in a hurry, always in control—whether wakened from His sleep in a storm (Luke 8:22ff), questioned by a man in the audience (Luke 12:13), or interrupted by His disciples while in prayer (Mark 1:35-39). But now Jairus' worst fears had become a reality: his daughter had died. Too much time had been taken along the way. To add heartless sting to the reality, the messenger advised, "Don't bother the teacher anymore."

Don't be afraid, just believe (50). In contrast to the message of despair, Jesus gave assurance that this was no time for faith to lessen.

She is not dead but asleep (52). These are the words of Jesus addressed to the mourners, many of them hired according to custom to wail for the occasion. They laughed at Jesus. They would not be there, not if the child were not dead. Jesus had chosen to interject something startling that would give pause to their irrational vent to noise and emotions. In the statement, He was declaring that the girl was only in a temporary state of death, in appearance like sleep, because He knew she would have life again. He used a similar description about Lazarus (John 11:11-14).

He did not let anyone go in with him except Peter, John and James, and the child's father and mother (51). Jesus did not want to provide a spectacle for the sensation-hungry multitude. This would only arouse their excitement all the more. He did, however, want dependable witnesses of what took place. The five were enough to provide witnesses and not too many to excite the crowds beyond control.

Her spirit returned (55). The true mark of death was not simply when the breathing stopped or when the heart stopped beating or when the brain stopped functioning, but when the spirit left the body. In like manner, the renewal of life is accompanied by the reunion of body and spirit.

To give her something to eat. This order from Jesus served several purposes. The weakened body of the resurrected girl needed physical sustenance. But feeding the physical body was another indication the body had returned to its normal needs and treatment. Jesus had power over death to bring a person to his former state, alive and well. He could do this for the body and also the spirit.

Not to tell (56). This is another occasion when Jesus gave strict instructions for the miracle to be kept private for the time being. (See the notes on Luke 5:14, above). Of course, the presence of the girl in the future, the record in the Gospel narratives, and the preaching of the eyewitnesses would not allow the scene to die, but a public announcement at this time would jeopardize the planned tempo of Jesus' ministry. The witnesses remained silent at this time, but the significance of the power to renew life grew with the passage of time.

Urgent Mission: Commission to the Twelve (9:1-6)
(Matthew 10:1-42; Mark 6:7-13.)

Jesus had been leading His disciples on evangelistic campaigns into all parts of Galilee. He had been healing the sick, driving out evil spirits, and preaching the kingdom of God. Now had come the time for the Twelve (the apostles, Luke 6:13)[41] to be sent out on their own and to do the same things they had been watching Jesus do. They would gain valuable experience and increase the number of people reached at the same time. This was the final thrust of Jesus' ministry in Galilee.

Take nothing for the journey (3). They were to travel as light as they could: no extra clothing, no luggage, not even extra money for supplies. They should be dependent on the places they were visiting to take care of them.

Whatever house you enter, stay there (4). As they came into a village two by two (Mark 6:7), they should find a place to stay and remain in that place for the duration of their visit. Several advantages are evident. They would not be tempted to move from one house to another as they discovered better accommodations. They would be kept on the move from one village to another because they would not be able to stay overly long in one place.

Shake the dust off your feet (5). This was a customary way to express one's desire to be separated from a place or people who had renounced him and his message—even wanting to leave every particle of dust associated with a place. It was a gesture of disgust and disappointment. Jesus gave this word so they would be forewarned that every place would not be ready to welcome them. It may be significant that Luke, who is writing especially for a Gentile audience, does not include the injunction of Jesus to fulfill this mission in the villages of the lost sheep of Israel alone; but Matthew gives this information. Jesus explicitly commanded at this time not to go to the Gentiles (Matthew 10:5).

Mistaken Identity (9:7-9)

Some were saying that John had been raised from the dead

---

[41]For a note on the *Apostles* and the *Twelve*, see Ellis, *The Gospel of Luke*, pp. 132-135

(7). At this point Luke interjects a note about Herod Antipas in relationship to identifications being made about Jesus. References made to Herod in Luke provide a good indication of the author's procedure in arranging his material. Luke tells us beforehand of John's coming arrest because he does not want to interrupt his narrative to introduce Herod at the particular time when the arrest occurred. (See Luke 3:19, 20.) Likewise, the death of John the Baptist is not recounted in Luke in a sequence of time, but it is alluded to in this Lukan note about Herod. As a matter of fact, here just before the feeding of the five thousand is the precise time when Matthew records the arrival of the news that Herod had beheaded John (Matthew 14:3-12). Luke informs his reader of John's death at this point in his narrative, not as the time of the happening—but it *is* the time, just before the feeding of the five thousand—but in order to give an example of a false identification of who Jesus was. Herod's conscience, as hardened as it must have been, was troubling him after giving the order to behead John the Baptist. Now that John was dead and Jesus' ministry had gained such fame, Herod was fearful lest John had returned to haunt him. Luke chose to weave this into his report as one more mistaken identity about Jesus. Herod's interest in seeing Jesus was not one of faith or even of self-conviction, but mainly of curiosity. Such people today are legion. They have just enough interest in Christianity to make them miserable but not enough to do anything about it.

Elijah had appeared (8). Another mistaken identity was to consider Jesus as Elijah. People associated the coming of Elijah with the coming of the Messiah (Malachi 4:5). They did not realize that John the Baptist had already fulfilled this prophecy (Matthew 11:14; 17:11-13).

Popular Pursuit (9:10-17)

Bethsaida (10). When the twelve had returned from their evangelistic campaign, they were in high spirits, but exhausted. They needed a period of retirement from the crowds (Mark 6:31). Just at this time, it seems the news of John the Baptist's death reached Jesus and His disciples. This tragic report added still more burden to the demands of the day. So Jesus and His disciples embarked in a boat, going along the northern shores of the Sea of Galilee. But the people saw the direction they were going and started running along the shore route trying to keep up with Jesus' progress by sea (Matthew 14:13). When Jesus and His disciples disembarked at what was ordinarily a solitary place, a vast crowd of people were already awaiting them. Luke designates the site as Bethsaida,[42] but it is evident that a city was not intended by the account for they were seeking retirement, not a populated place. Rather, this probably has reference to an isolated shore area which had as its closest town, Bethsaida Julius (not the same Bethsaida mentioned in John 1:44 or Luke 10:13), newly developed by Herod Philip and located to the north of the Sea of Galilee, about an eighth of a mile east of the Jordan.[43]

In locating the scene, Luke gave the name of Bethsaida simply as the nearest well-known town. Another possible significance is the meaning of *Bethsaida*, "fishing place," which might be identified with a number of sites along the sea.

Find food and lodging (12). The feeding of the five thousand is the only miracle, other than the resurrection of Jesus, that is recorded in all four Gospel narratives. This says something about the importance of the event and perhaps indicates a type of turning point in the course of Jesus' ministry. From the Gospel of John, one learns that the gathering occurred near the Passover season (John 6:4). This would be spring, and since Jesus' crucifixion took place during another Passover Week, this feeding of the five thousand, in all likelihood, would be about one year before the close of Jesus' ministry. Although Jesus had come to this place seeking a period of privacy with His disciples, He welcomed the pursuit of the crowd. After all, the trip across the lake had provided some time alone with the Twelve. So He followed His general practice of preaching about the kingdom of God and healing the sick. Afterwards, the question was raised about food and lodging because this was an isolated spot. Jesus may have introduced the question himself and left the disciples to puzzle over the difficulty of feeding such a multitude (John 6:5).

---

[42]A number of variant readings are found in the manuscripts at this place. See Godet, *Luke,* pp. 256f.

[43]See Josephus, *Antiquities* (xvii, 2, 1), *Wars* (ii, 9, 1; iv, 7, 2), *Life* (72).

Sit down in groups of about fifty (14). When the sum of all the known food in the crowd was found to be five loaves of bread and two fish, Jesus gave the order to seat the people in groups of fifty (Mark describes hundreds and fifties, Mark 6:40, which would give the same result if each hundred had a double fifty). This arrangement provided an orderly basis for both counting the men and serving them. (The women and children were in addition to the 5000 number.) But where was the food? It took considerable faith to go through the motions of preparing for a meal—in fact similar to Moses' instruction to divide the people of Israel for the appointment of officials (Exodus 18:21)—but to have no more food at hand than the few loaves and fish, supplied by a little boy who was willing to give all he had (John 6:8, 9). Those who deny the possibility of the miraculous resort to all kinds of fantastic suggestions at this point. Maybe half the people had their food with them and Jesus just caused them to share with one another. This is stark denial of the record. No mention of additional food is made, the event was viewed as a miraculous sign by those who were present (John 6:26), and twelve baskets of fragments were taken up after everyone had eaten to his satisfaction. No amount of sharing would have resulted in leftovers as well. Other claims of exaggerations and myths are equally unfounded,[44] while the climactic place this episode occupies in the popularity with the people then as well as the prominence of the loaves and fish in early Christian art show the continuing role this real happening occupied.

He gave thanks and broke them (16). The Jews were accustomed to beginning a meal with a recognition and address to the Lord, who was blessed and thanked for the food. While the prayer was being said, the bread might be broken. Whether the multiplication came at the hands of Jesus in the breaking of bread, in the words of the blessing, or in the distribution act itself is of no importance to the report. It was a miracle that filled their physical needs and inflamed their enthusiastic support of Jesus. Unfortunately, with many, it did not help their understanding of the kingdom and an acceptance of the true identity of the Teacher.

---

[44]William F. Arndt, *The Gospel According to St. Luke* (St. Louis: Concordia, 1956), p. 256.

Twelve basketfuls of broken pieces that were left over (17). By collecting the remnant, Jesus taught a lesson against waste and at the same time gave clear evidence that each person had been fed to his satisfaction.

Identity Affirmed (9:18-36)

Expressed by Peter (18-20)

As one traces the thread of inquiry in Luke's arrangement of material, in this section it focuses on one question—the identity of Jesus. From the question expressed at the stilling of the storm, "Who is this? He commands even the winds and the water, and they obey him" (Luke 8:25), to the mistaken identity Herod made when he considered Jesus as John the Baptist returned, then to the discussions that must have accompanied His high point of acceptance at the feeding of the five thousand. Now He put the question directly to His disciples, first, "Who do the crowds say I am?" and then, "Who do you say I am?" In reporting this episode, Luke does not stop to tell where the scene occurred. Both Matthew and Mark make explicit the location, Caesarea Philippi (Matthew 16:13; Mark 8:27). Since this was a Gentile setting and Luke is constantly anxious to give the precise location of happenings, his omission of the site is doubly surprising. Another mystery comes to the surface when one notes that Matthew and Mark tell of a number of happenings, including a trip to Phoenicia and the circuit in Gentile Decapolis area before this confession of Peter at Caesarea Philippi (Matthew 14:22—16:12; Mark 6:45—8:26). But Luke does not include any of these reports. Why? Perhaps he wants his reader to be so absorbed with this question of identifying Jesus that he wants to relate the feeding of the five thousand immediately with the report of Peter as to what the people were saying. They were saying the same things that had reached the ears of Herod (Luke 9:7, 8): John the Baptist, Elijah, or one of the ancient prophets returned to life.

Peter answered, "The Christ of God" (20). This whole section of Luke has been building up to this time. The way Jesus asked the question put a special emphasis on *you*. So when we read it, the question no longer appears academic; it becomes personal. "Who do *you* say I am?" The *Christ* is from the Greek word for the Hebrew *Messiah*. He had been predicted and expected for centuries.

Confirmed by Jesus (21-27)

Jesus strictly warned them not to tell (21). Jesus added His confirmation to their conclusions, both from His teachings and from His works. But He also included an injunction not to make this identification explicit as yet. His time had not yet come.

The Son of Man must suffer (22). At this very occasion when the disciples had reached a great climax in giving evidence they had learned well the teachings they had been receiving for over two years now, Jesus began to prepare them for His coming death. This is the first of a long series of predictions concerning the suffering of the Messiah.[45]

Rejected by the elders, chief priests and teachers of the law. This combination of Jewish officials made up the Sanhedrin, the highest official authority of the Jews.

He must be killed and on the third day be raised. This prediction could not have been given in plainer language. Thus it is difficult to see how the disciples could have failed to see what was in store for Jesus in that final period of His life. After the events had transpired, then it was clear what was indicated. Until then, however, so many possible fulfillments could be seen. The dullness of the disciples in ascertaining what Jesus intended for them to know is one of the truly unexpected elements in the Gospel narratives. But this is a factor that contributes to our assurance that these things really happened and in the way recorded for us. For who would ever create such an element in the earlier lives of these very men who were heroes when these things were being written down?

If anyone would come after me (23). Jesus was just beginning His recruitment when He won the Twelve. This was a continuing program, and Jesus did not want followers to join Him without knowing the cost. "He must deny himself." This is the direct opposite of the selfish demands in popular thought of every generation. This is not an asceticism where suffering is deliberately sought in order to gain spiritual value. If one stands for the right and is willing to extend himself on behalf of others, he will not need to seek suffering, it will come to him. "And take up his cross daily." This would paint a familiar picture to the reader of

---

[45]See later references: Luke 9:44; 12:50; 17:25; 18:31-33. Compare Luke 24:6, 7, 25-27.

the first century. In Palestine itself, hundreds had died each year on the crosses along the roads where travel was heaviest, and the tragic sight of the dying figure remained indelibly implanted on the mind of the passerby. Each had carried his own cross to the execution. What a promise! This was no catchy campaign slogan. This was no promise of a high place in wealth and honor in the coming kingdom. This was heavy reality. But the word that strikes hardest is "daily." One spectacular catch does not make the all-star ball player. One all-night effort to help in an emergency does not prove full dedication. The Christian way demands a daily life-style consistent with that of Jesus Christ. "And follow me." This is what separates the philosophies and religions of the world from what Jesus was offering. To be involved, regardless of the cause, to be suffering for just anything, was not enough. There must be dedication to Christ and obedience to His will every step of the way. Furthermore, to follow Jesus is significant in another way. He does not ask anyone to do what He has not been willing to endure himself. He goes before us. As Jesus spoke to His disciples and used the figure of the cross, it was doubly significant both in His own coming suffering and in warning of the sacrifice the disciples must also expect.

Whoever loses his life for me (24). The one who selfishly tries to get ahead for himself will in the end lose out, but the one who gives his all for Christ will find a new life, full and eternal. This process of losing and gaining is part of the unexpected in the Gospel. Christopher Columbus shocked the people of his time by trying to reach the East by sailing west, and he discovered a new continent. So it is with the one who denies self and follows Jesus. One marvels how Jesus could make such uncompromising demands for first place in everyone's life and yet maintain the image of the ideal in humility and service. His deity shows through when He, in an unassuming and natural way, commands complete commitment and at the same time tells of His willingness to give His life in sacrifice for others. No other saying of Jesus has been given more emphasis than this one (Luke 9:24). It is found, with some variation in wording, in all four Gospels, and in Matthew and Luke, it is given more than once.[46]

---

[46]Matthew 10:38, 39; 16:24, 25; Mark 8:34, 35; Luke 9:24, 25; 14:26, 27; 17:33; John 12:25

When he comes in his glory (26). Jesus' suffering was followed by glorification. But if an individual spurns Jesus, denies the words of His teaching, is ashamed of Jesus in the period of His suffering, so the individual himself will be spurned in Christ's glorious return.

Will not taste death before they see the kingdom of God (27). Whatever is referred to here must occur within the lifetime of some of those who were then in the presence of Jesus. The question is, "What does the *kingdom of God* indicate in this passage?" Plummer[47] lists seven interpretations of the saying: (1) the transfiguration, (2) the resurrection and ascension, (3) Pentecost, (4) the spread of Christianity, (5) the internal development of the gospel, (6) the destruction of Jerusalem, (7) the second advent. If Jesus intended to apply the term *kingdom* to His second advent, then He was mistaken, for all these have long since died and He has not returned. To those who trust the knowledge of Jesus, this is not a live possibility, and since there are so many viable options, it is impudent to insist on such an interpretation, knowing this would claim Jesus was wrong. Since the kingdom is frequently equated with the church, and since the church was started on the day of Pentecost only a year after this, the preferable meaning would look upon this as the beginning of fulfillment to the glory of Christ in the establishment of the church on the day of Pentecost.

Attested by God (28-36)

About eight days after (28). This was an ordinary way of saying a week had passed. The Jews counted the first and last days of an interval as whole days. Thus the time between the confession and the transfiguration may have been expressed so that it included the first and last days as whole days. It is proper to understand the phrase "after six days" in Matthew's and Mark's records (Matthew 17:1; Mark 9:2) and the week indicated by Luke as denoting the same period of time but expressed in independent ways. So a week passed between the confession of Peter at Caesarea Philippi and the transfiguration scene on a "high mountain."

---

[47]Plummer, *Critical and Exegetical Commentary ... Luke,* pp. 249, 250.

Peter, John and James. On two other occasions, note is given of these particular three in the company of Jesus (the raising of Jairus' daughter, Luke 8:51, and in Gethsemane, Mark 14:33.)

Onto a mountain to pray. Again Luke emphasizes prayer. He alone of the Synoptics tells this purpose for going up the mountain. The exact mountain is uncertain. Early tradition, as far back as Helena (by the time of A.D. 326), the mother of Constantine, has designated Mt. Tabor as the location. This lies ten miles southwest of the Sea of Galilee, but rises only 1,843 feet above sea level. A more likely location would be Mt. Hermon, on the northern boundary of the promised land (Deuteronomy 3:8). This is indeed a "high mountain" (Matthew 17:1; Mark 9:2), the highest in Syria, rising to an altitude of almost 10,000 feet. Caesarea Philippi is situated in its foothills and would be near at hand as the site of the last mentioned episode (Matthew 16:13). This would have been a convenient starting point for the ascent of the four men.

Two men, Moses and Elijah, appeared in glorious splendor (30, 31). The transfigured Jesus, changed to dazzling appearance in face and clothing, was joined by two men of God from long ago. The question immediately rises, "Why these two?" Are they the most important figures from the Old Testament period? This may be. Does one represent the law as the lawgiver and the other represent the prophets as the outstanding example? This may be. Or could it be that these two at death went to Heaven, but their bodies were not found to be buried by men, and this has something to do with their coming back at this transfiguration scene? We cannot say the precise reason for the choice, but we can trust God's wisdom and see ample grounds for His selection.

They spoke about his departure. The subject of their conversation was bound to be of the utmost importance. They would not be wasting time talking about the weather. The main topic was the coming death of Christ in Jerusalem. The word for "departure" in the Greek is frequently used to denote "death." Jesus obviously had more knowledge on the subject than they did, but these men of God could still give words of encouragement and exhortation.

Let us put up three shelters—one for you, one for Moses and one for Elijah (33). Luke gives an editorial note following this suggestion from Peter: "He did not know what he was saying."

Jesus could not stay in this company and in this place. He must return to the valley and proceed to fulfill the purpose for which He had come. But we must give Peter credit for the kind of dreams he had. He was expressing what he considered the ideal. A place in a palace with power, wealth, and fame was not his dream. He could not think of anything better than to be in the presence of Jesus, Moses, and Elijah, and to see they had accommodations they deserved while they had fellowship was the best Peter could imagine. Although it was an unreal suggestion, it opens before us the purity and wholehearted dedication of this zealous leader of the apostles.

This is my Son (35). This is the attestation of God. Peter had affirmed the identity of Jesus, but who can begin to match the value of the testimony from God himself? This is the ultimate identification Luke has to offer. Given on a mountain, given in the presence of the most venerated spokesmen of God from the Old Covenant period, given before the witnesses of three apostles, this word was spoken by God the Father himself to establish Jesus' identity.

Discouraging Obstacles (9:37-50)

Power Failure (37-43)

I begged your disciples to drive it out, but they could not (40). When Jesus and His three disciples descended from the mountain the next day, they found that the rest of the disciples had been undergoing a disappointing experience. They had been unable to help a father and his boy, who was plagued by an evil spirit. These spirits could bring different types of woe upon an individual. In this case, the spirit was responsible for causing convulsions (Luke 9:39) and a condition that left the boy speechless (Mark 9:17). But the disciples found they were ineffective in ridding the lad of his torment. This was not so much a failure of power as it was a failure to keep contact with the source of power through faith. This was particularly difficult in the face of the hostile and skeptical attacks from the teachers of the law (Mark 9:14f).

O unbelieving and perverse generation (41). Jesus condemned the attitude of the generation in general and not just the failure of His disciples. (See Matthew 17:20.) He healed the boy upon the father's expression of faith, which also carried an admission of a lack of the amount of faith he should have. The father expressed the sentiments of all believers when he pled: "I do believe; help me overcome my unbelief" (Mark 9:24). Jesus healed the boy and the impact on the people reflected the identification the people were making. Although they argued about the person of Jesus, they identified His works and His words with God. "And they were all amazed at the greatness of God" (Luke 9:43).

Imminent Betrayal (44-45)

The Son of Man is going to be betrayed into the hands of men (44). This is another prediction of Jesus' coming death. In every way, Jesus was attempting to prepare His disciples for the pending tragic tests both to His own life and to the lives of His followers. In addition to helping His disciples in their particular needs, He was giving aid to all posterity to understand that He was not taken unawares in the events of the final week of His ministry. His power did not fail, but He willingly gave up His life to fulfill the very purpose of His coming to mankind. Even though the disciples were unable to see what was going to happen or even have the nerve to ask further about it, nevertheless when it came to pass, it was a help. They could look back and see that Jesus knew what He was doing all along. His identity was never uncertain with His own understanding. His determined course was never shaken despite His knowledge of coming betrayal.

Self-centered Ambition (46-50)

An argument started among the disciples as to which of them would be the greatest (46). Still another obstacle had to be faced before Jesus could gain victory in the lives of His disciples then, and likewise now. Certain faults are universal, such as selfishness, jealousy, stubbornness, and a self-centered focus that keeps us from seeing the predicament of others. Even in the growing strain of uncertainty, mounting opposition from the enemies of Jesus, and concern for the future, the disciples still had selfish thoughts of their position in this coming kingdom. In fact, this subject reared its head on more than one occasion. (See Mark 9:33-37; 10:33ff; Luke 22:24.)

Whoever welcomes this little child (48). At times, Jesus said a follower must become like a little child (Luke 18:16, 17), and on another occasion He warned against endangering their safety, but here He said you must receive them gladly. To think we do not have time, or to feel the children are not important enough, are danger signals that we have our priorities confused. The least becomes great as he looks away from himself and sees the true value of a child. In this, he thinks with the mind of Christ and honors Him. Finally, when he follows Christ, he reveres God. He finds how small he really is in relationship to God, to Christ, to others, even to a little child. As he grows in realization of leastness, his greatness grows in the kingdom.

We tried to stop him, because he is not one of us (49). Luke records another mark against the attitude of the disciples. Here they are again taking a wrong direction. John reports that a man was driving out demons in Jesus' name, but the Twelve were not acquainted with him. He had not been traveling in their company. He could not be considered a brother and must be stopped from claiming any power from Jesus. They demanded he stop his work. The answer Jesus gave was direct. "Do not stop him." For one thing, John could not say that he knew for sure that he could identify everyone who was a disciple of Jesus. Just because he had not shared in the same experiences that John had was not enough basis to condemn him. Jesus may have implied this when he changed John's pronoun from "he is not one of *us,*" to Jesus' statement, "for whoever is not against *you* is for *you.*" In other words, Jesus may have been telling John, "Don't talk about *us;* you really mean he is not one of *you.* And even in this case you should not write him off the list as long as he is not opposing what you are doing." The most difficult side to this saying is relating it to the later passage where Jesus states, "He who is not with me is against me" (Luke 11:23). This is a good example of the importance of context. In the case that John brought to Jesus, the unknown worker of miracles was doing so in Jesus' name and was not opposing Jesus' work in any way that John knew. Evidently, from John's knowledge, no specific invitation had been given to join the group. Therefore, he was to be considered as supporting them as long as he did not oppose Jesus. In the later passage, however, the context is just as opposite as it can be. There are those who say that Jesus was driving out demons by Beelzebub. Others were asking for a sign from Heaven. In this context, when an individual is confronted with a decision either to accept Christ or put Him in the camp of Satan, then to fail to declare oneself for Him is tantamount to a rejection. To keep these two contexts clear in our minds today is important in our efforts for unity among all Christians, recognized or unknown to one another, in contrast with the identification of those who deny the authority of Christ and the Word of God. The same principle accrues here as in the previous passage: welcome the children, follow Christ, revere God.

How Do You Refer to Jesus?

When you think about Jesus or talk about Him, how do you refer to Him? When you worship Him, how do you address Him? When you use a title, do you realize the significance of what you are saying? Should you be using other titles because you are neglecting to appreciate the role Jesus fills in your life? A good way to check this out is to examine the way He is referred to in Scripture. To note who is addressing Him and at what time in His ministry is important as well. How did Jesus refer to himself? Did the time and place make a difference? The following are titles for Jesus recorded by Luke, or are descriptive of the work Jesus was doing, in this phase of His ministry.

Christ. This means the "anointed" and was the Greek form of the Hebrew "Messiah." At Nazareth, Jesus claimed to be the one God had anointed (Luke 4:18), the one prophesied by Isaiah, but Jesus as yet did not use the term itself—as far as the record goes.

Son of Man. This is the term used most often by Jesus to designate himself, but no one else uses it of Him in the Gospel records, only Jesus. (Later, Stephen does in Acts 7:56.) The term was particularly appropriate for Him to use of himself because it emphasized His identification with man. Also, the term could refer to Him not only as a representative of man in general, but as the ideal man, man in perfection. Most significant was its possible application as a Messianic title coming from Daniel (7:13). This means that Jesus could possibly be making Messianic claims each time, but the people would hesitate to identify Him as such because of their preconceived notions they had about the Messiah.

Master. Simon addressed Jesus this way (Luke 5:5). The title was used to designate special teachers. It not only indicated one's willingness to follow them for instruction, but to acknowledge their control in his life.

Lord. The term was used in the Hellenistic world to address honored individuals, but it was a title in the Old Testament to designate God. The address was directed to Jesus constantly (Luke 5:8, 12; 6:46; 7:6), and at Luke 7:13, Luke uses the term in his own designation of Jesus. This was a favorite Lukan address that the other Gospel writers do not use in the same way.

Son of God. The demons made this affirmation about Jesus (Luke 4:41). Jesus did not deny the fact, but He silenced their testimony because the time was not right and the source of acknowledgment was detrimental.

Redeemer. Although this term was not used at this period in the record, Jesus time and again claimed to forgive sin, the work vital to the role of Redeemer. This incensed the Pharisees (Luke 5:21) and even shocked the people (Luke 7:49).

Savior. This title was not used of Jesus in this period of the record, but His work has to do with the saving of people (Luke 7:50), and the very word *Jesus* means "Savior." (See Matthew 1:21; also Luke 2:11.)

Prophet. In this period of Jesus' Galilean ministry, this was the term most often applied to Him (Luke 7:16). Its basic meaning was a spokesman from God. This might include miraculous knowledge of the future, or special discernment in present events or the hearts of people, or the power to work miracles, but the basic responsibility was the delivery of truth from God. Jesus was indeed the prophet like Moses that had been prophesied (Deuteronomy 18:18), but Jesus was more than the ordinary conception people had of a prophet. To see how the understanding of the people grows and how the testimony mounts is a part of the purpose for which Luke writes. The certainty of the gospel and the understanding of each of us grow apace. Our appreciation and understanding of who Jesus is, what He has done for us, and what role He has are reflected in the way we address Him.

Part Three
The Way to Jerusalem
Luke 9:51—19:27

CHAPTER SEVEN

Traveling With the Teacher
Luke 9:51—12:59

The moment of truth was coming. Imagine a mountain climber who, after years of training, months of planning, weeks of preparation, and days of laborious climbing, comes at last to the beginning of the final effort to gain triumph on the peak. The moment of truth has come. Or imagine the marathon runner who has trained and run for years to get ready for the Boston race, and now it has begun. He has completed long grueling miles and just ahead is Heart Break Hill. Beyond this lies the moment of truth and completion. Think of the doctor who has spent years of study in the classroom, months of internship, weeks upon weeks of demanding practice, now he stands beside the operating table and a life is at stake. The moment of truth has come. The feeling that comes over these is but infinitesimally small compared with the impact and consequences of Jesus' final trip to Jerusalem before His death. This was a momentous turn that Jesus took when He began to travel the road to Jerusalem. There He was to fulfill His purpose for being here. The moment of truth for all mankind was approaching as Jesus "steadfastly set His face to go to Jerusalem" (Luke 9:51, NKJV).

The Long Way Around
The Route He Took
Two main routes were used to go to Jerusalem from Galilee. One was the fast and short way through Samaria; but this meant crossing territory hostile to the Jews. The other route crossed the Jordan south of the Sea of Galilee, came down through Perea, recrossed the Jordan at a ford near Jericho, and approached Jerusalem from the east. The strange thing about Jesus' trip to

ROUTES TO JERUSALEM

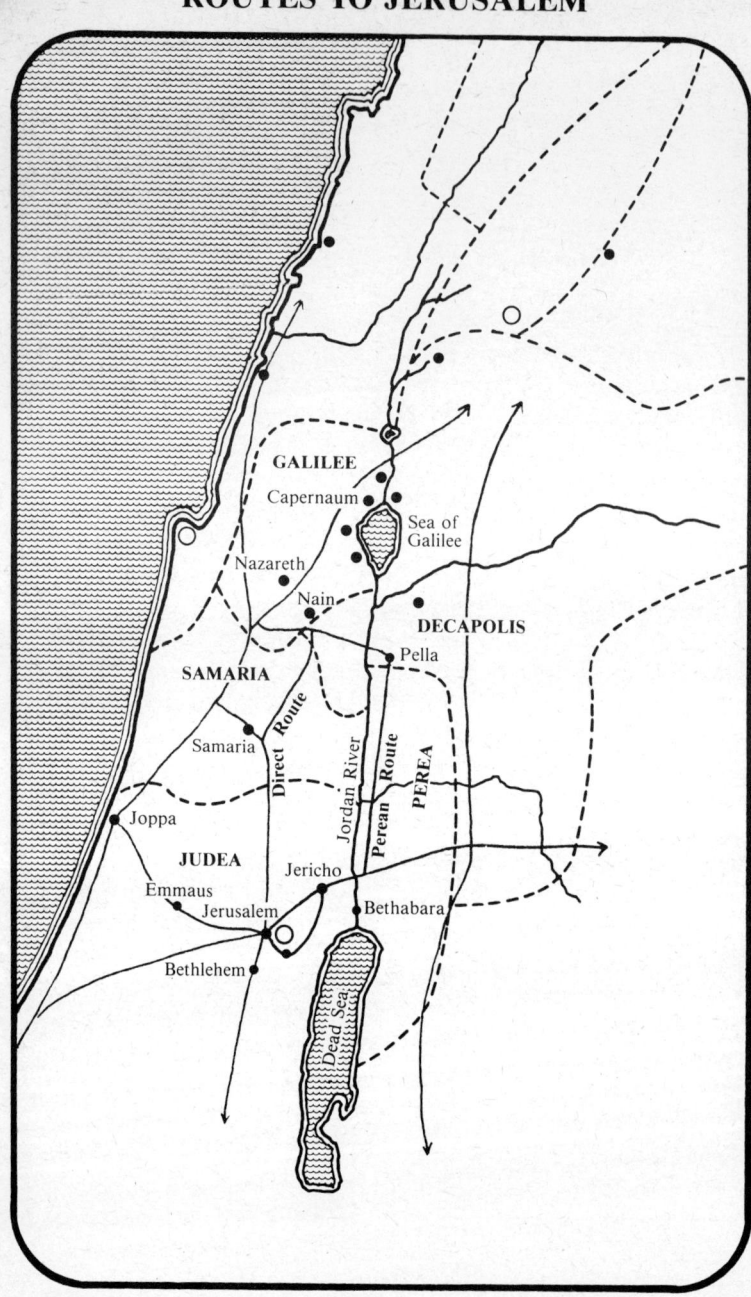

Jerusalem, begun in the ninth chapter of Luke and not completed until the nineteenth chapter, is that it included both routes. He started out going through Samaria and ended up entering Jerusalem via Jericho.

The puzzle is increased when one realizes that in the chapter after Jesus is reported to have begun His journey, He is found in the home of Martha and Mary (Luke 10:38ff). This is less than a mile from Jerusalem. One might conclude that all the rest of the material before His entrance to the city would take place in the territory close to Jerusalem. Not so. In chapter 17, Jesus was up along the borders of Galilee and Samaria (Luke 17:11). But later He approached Jerusalem from Jericho (Luke 19:1). Throughout these chapters, Luke reminds us that Jesus all this time is on His way to Jerusalem (Luke 9:51, 53; 13:22, 33; 17:11; 18:31; 19:11, 28; see also Luke 9:57; 10:1, 38; 14:25).

Several explanations have been given. (1) Perhaps Jesus went back and forth in a delaying movement because He did not want to confront the Jewish leaders in Jerusalem until the Passover season. By His unpredictable itinerary, it would be impossible for the enemies to anticipate where He would be in order to plot His arrest. This answer would maintain that all the incidents recorded in this section occurred at this time and much in the sequence given. (2) Perhaps Luke grouped together incidents that occurred in different times in Jesus' years of ministry, but these examples of His teaching are reserved for this section of the Gospel. Luke tells them in this order that the reader might be able to understand better how the final week in Jerusalem came to reality. By this division of material, Luke gave more importance to the final week in Jerusalem. This is an importance it rightly deserves. (3) Perhaps Luke groups together incidents from different trips Jesus made to Jerusalem and around Judea. John tells of some of these (John 2:13; 3:22; 5:1; 7:10; 10:22; 11:7; 12:1). But Luke tells of only one trip to Jerusalem during these ministry years of Jesus.[48] If Luke wanted to tell of teachings Jesus gave on any of these trips, He may have put them together with other teachings along the way on this final trip. (4) In any event, the way Luke has divided his material indicates the

---

[48]See Luke 4:44 for a possible reference to Judea, but see the author's notes on that verse (above) for reasons it may *not* refer to Judea.

importance he wants to put on this final trip, which preceded the death, burial, and resurrection of Jesus. This more evenly divides his material between Galilee and Jerusalem, even though it is not in Jerusalem but on Jesus' way to the climax of his life. The suspense mounts as you read these chapters (9:51—19:27) approaching the end.

The Teaching He Gave

Not only was the route He traveled a circuitous one, but Jesus' teaching of necessity was a kind that began with illustration, wove in personal experience, and ended in a definite point that the hearer would never have listened to except that Jesus brought him the route He did. Jesus led the expert in the law to declare that the Samaritan in Jesus' parable was the good neighbor (Luke 10:37). If an annoyed friend will get out of bed to do you a favor so you will not bother him any longer, you know God will do more than that in answering persistent prayer (Luke 11:5-8). After Jesus had worked so many miracles, the people still asked for more signs. Instead of giving them more miracles, Jesus gave them the sign of Jonah. What would they make of that? He was identifying himself as one greater than Jonah, and they had better listen to His preaching even as the Ninevites had repented and been spared (Luke 11:29-32). Jesus condemned the Pharisees themselves. But they were the religious leaders. Jesus was a religious teacher. This was an unexpected route to take—to condemn the ones the people recognized as the most righteous among them (Luke 11:37ff). And the rich man—he was a fool. He died just when he thought he had years of leisure and wealth ahead (Luke 12:13ff).

The Plan He Fulfilled

Not only the geographical route Luke records, not only the teaching methods Jesus employed, but the very plan Jesus unfolded is one hard to follow and beyond our comprehension. The disciples knew by this period of time that when they went to Jerusalem, death was imminent (John 11:16). But Jesus could go the other direction and avoid it. In fact, the disciples had faith Jesus could use His power and overcome His enemies. But instead, He went resolutely to His death—in order to bring life. The wise and learned do not understand, but the children do (Luke 10:21). Even the prophets did not know just how these things would be fulfilled (Luke 10:24), but He was bringing the truth to the disciples. This is our challenge, to travel with the Teacher that we can see those things we miss in the assessment of life (Luke 12:56).

Content Notes

Barriers in Samaria (9:51-56)

As the time approached (51). When one follows Jesus throughout His ministry, he becomes increasingly conscious that Jesus was keeping a strict timetable. Some things He could not do because it was not yet time (John 7:6). Other events were to occur because the time had come (Matthew 26:18). Now Luke notes the approach of the culmination to Jesus' time on earth. Jesus was determined to fulfill His purpose of living at the time and in the way God directed.

For him to be taken up to heaven. Luke does not choose to mark Jesus' start for Jerusalem by the negative note of His death at the end of the journey. Rather, the peal of victory is struck when He refers to the ascension of Jesus.

Sent messengers on ahead (52). They would make known the coming of Jesus. They would also make arrangements for overnight accommodations, and this was no small task when at least a dozen men were traveling with Jesus. Then, too, the messengers would be able to report the kind of reception they would anticipate from that community.

A Samaritan village. This shows that Jesus was taking the direct route to Jerusalem through Samaria. It also indicates that Jesus was going through a territory ordinarily hostile to all Jews. The Samaritan people were descendants of intermarriages between Gentile settlers and Israelite inhabitants following Assyrian conquest in the eighth century B.C. Not only were the mixed marriages despised by the Jews in the following centuries, but the Samaritans added to this an apostasy in religion. They set up a rival to the Jerusalem temple in locating a sanctuary on Mt. Gerizim (John 4:20). They only accepted the law, the five books of Moses, as their Scriptures.[49] The remaining books of the Old Testament—history, devotions, and prophets—were not

---

[49]Moore, *Judaism,* Vol. 1, p. 27.

accepted. The Jews hated the Samaritans and the Samaritans hated the Jews.

Did not welcome (53). This was a time when Jesus was refused entrance to a town and denied a place to stay overnight. He had been driven out of his hometown, Nazareth (Luke 4:29), was asked to leave the Gentile Gerasa (Luke 8:37), and here suffered a Samaritan rejection—all from different motives. This time, the reason is given that He was on His way to Jerusalem. The Samaritans would not help a person, especially when a festal season was approaching such as Passover, when he was on his way to worship in the Jewish holy city.

Call fire down from heaven (54). James and John spoke up from the group and suggested the possibility of retaliation on the Samaritan village by destruction. The use of fire was specified, probably with Elijah's bout with the priests of Baal in mind. (Some manuscripts include "as Elijah did" in verse 54.) They were probably walking along as they spoke, and Jesus turned to silence even the thought of such action in this case. His kingdom was not coming in this manner; His Messiahship was not accompanied by revenge, violence, and destruction. The "sons of thunder" (Mark 3:17) had earned their title in other ways than by this suggestion, and Jesus would not allow their records to be marred by pursuing the thought further. He rebuked them (Luke 9:55).

Went to another village (56). Whether they found another village in Samaritan territory which did receive them or whether they retreated outside Samaria for the night is not clear. Some maintain that this is the point where Jesus changed the route He was formerly taking through Samaria and now reverts to the Perean route reflected much later in His arrival at Jericho (18:35).[50] This is unlikely.

Conditional Offers (9:57-62)

I will follow you (57). Three offers are recorded here concerning following Jesus. Two of them were made by individuals, and Jesus put conditions on His acceptance. The other was made by Jesus, and the individual put his condition on this one. Two of these conversations appear also in the Gospel of Matthew (8:18-

---

[50]Godet, *Luke,* pp. 284ff.

22) in the Galilean portion of his narrative. In Luke, the place is not specified where the scenes occur. Jesus warned His would-be followers that life with Him would not be easy. They would have no place they could really call home. But Jesus asked no more of them than He had experienced himself for some time. We are not told whether the individuals accepted the conditions or not.

Let me go and bury my father (59). This sounds like a respectful and loving request, but Jesus was able to read the heart and the motives lying behind a person's words. If the father had already died, the funeral procedures would have been underway right then; for the dead were buried on the same day or just the next two following days in exceptional circumstances. If it was a request to return and wait for the time of the father's death, this might take years. Nothing can be put ahead of proclaiming the kingdom of God. Leave the burial of the dead and the numerous observances of the ceremonial traditions to those who are spiritually dead and have no realization of the urgent need to preach the gospel *now*.

Let me go back and say good-by (61). This, too, may have involved much more than putting things in order and bidding a word of farewell. The request may include days and weeks of parties and pleas for reconsideration of commitments to Jesus. Again, the cost of discipleship does not allow anything else to be put ahead of Jesus' call or, for that matter, to look back longingly at what is being given up.

No one who puts his hand to the plow and looks back is fit (62). If you have cultivated corn for the last time before it becomes too tall for the tractor to pass over the top of the stalks, you know the importance of looking ahead as you plow. When you hear the *plop* that indicates a stalk has been hit and has fallen, the temptation is to look back to see what has happened. When you look back, however, then you hear a sickening *plop, plop, plop* because looking back will cause you to leave the straight furrow and bring all kinds of damage. Although they did not have tractors in Jesus' day, the plowmen had similar difficulties when they looked back. And the follower of Jesus today has the same danger of losing direction when he looks back to former days of aimless and sinful life. Jesus himself fully complied to all of the demands made to His followers. He is the highest example to those who commit themselves to full, wholehearted service.

Seventy-two on Tour (10:1-23)

At first Jesus had traveled from town to town with His disciples and led His own tours (Luke 4:43, 44). Then He sent out the Twelve to conduct similar campaigns (Luke 9:1, 2). Finally, He sent out seventy-two for a still larger undertaking (Luke 10:1). The tempo of His ministry was building up. His time was growing short, and He had much territory yet to cover. The disciples were sent two by two to give encouragement to one another and more strength to their witness. Mark told that the Twelve had been sent out that way as well (Mark 6:7), and the early church followed the practice also (Acts 13:2, 3; 15:27, 39, 40; 17:14; 19:22). Jesus himself, probably with the Twelve, would be following the routes of the seventy-two, and this would necessitate much zig-zag progression toward Jerusalem. Such an itinerary would help account for the length of time indicated for this last trip to Jerusalem before His death. Many refer to this period as Jesus' Perean ministry. This term comes from the Greek meaning "on the other side," and is used to indicate the land on the eastern side of the Jordan River. To this point in Jesus' ministry, we have been told of His extensive work in Galilee, and John tells us of His trips to Jerusalem for periodic ministry there. Following Jesus' trip to Tyre and Sidon, He visited the Decapolis area, which was mainly beyond the Jordan. But the Perean area was generally neglected in Jewish affairs compared with the attention given to Judea and Galilee. Up until now, this seems to have been true of the amount of time Jesus had spent there as well. His only visits there seem to have been when He had only been passing through rather rapidly. This, then, may be the time when He did a concentrated work in the area. Although there is no positive identification, this may rightfully be called the Perean ministry.

The sending out of the seventy-two is recorded only in Luke. Some old reliable manuscripts have the number seventy, and other equally-respected manuscripts have seventy-two. This is a manuscript variation that runs through Old Testament passages as well as in the New Testament. The number denotes the nations of the earth (Genesis 10) and those elders appointed by Moses (Numbers 11:16ff). The number is used to describe the group of men who translated the Hebrew Old Testament into Greek (about 280 B.C.) and was the usual number of the ruling body of the Jews in Jerusalem (Sanhedrin). Perhaps this had some

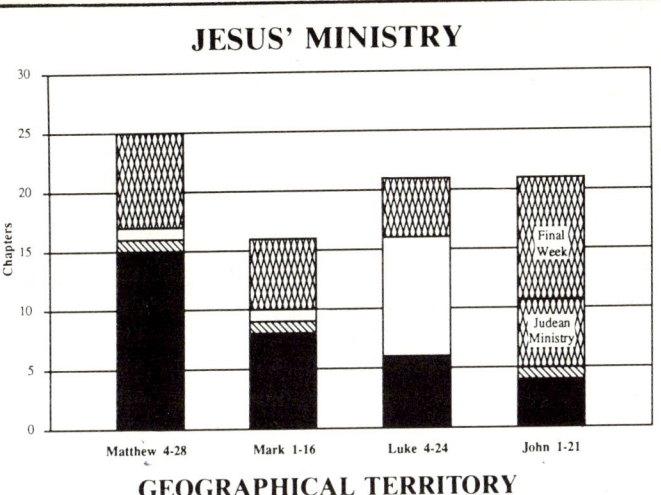

GEOGRAPHICAL TERRITORY

■ In Galilee   □ Final Trip to Jerusalem
▨ Non-Jewish Areas   ▩ Jerusalem

Where Jesus Ministered

Explanation

The Synoptics and John stand in contrast to one another in a number of ways. The Synoptics confine their reports of Jesus' ministry to the northern part of Palestine. John includes an early Judean ministry and extra trips to Jerusalem during Jesus' three years of ministry. The Synoptics describe Jesus' final week in Jerusalem but no other incidents there during His ministry. The black areas of the graph indicate the number of chapters devoted to Jesus' ministry in Galilee. Jesus spent time in non-Jewish areas as well, such as Samaria, Phoenicia, and the Decapolis district. These are represented by the diagonal lines on the chart. The solid white areas denote the final trip to Jerusalem at Passover time, and the checkered areas show the number of chapters devoted to Jesus' time in Jerusalem. One third of John's Jerusalem chapters describe Jesus' early Judean ministry and feast days there, but two thirds describe the final week.

Questions

Why did Luke devote such a long section to Jesus' final trip to Jerusalem (Luke 9:51—19:27)?

Why do the Synoptics confine their attention to Jesus' Galilean ministry?

Why did Luke, who was probably a Gentile and interested in Jesus' ministry to non-Jews, omit His trip to Phoenicia and the Decapolis?

Why do all four Gospels emphasize the final week?

meaning to Jesus' choice of the number for this major evangelistic campaign.

The description of this commission is given in three parts: (1) instructions for the trip (verses 1-12), very similar to those given to the Twelve in Luke 9:1-5, (2) warning of the judgment to be expected by towns that had opportunity to accept but still rejected Jesus (verses 13-16), and (3) joy and significance concerning the results (verses 17-20).

Do not greet anyone on the road (4). Eastern salutations in antiquity were long and drawn out. The need was so great and the time so short, nothing like this could be allowed to interfere with the important mission.

The worker deserves his wages (7). Paul quotes this passage from Luke in 1 Timothy 5:18, and it may be his reference for 1 Corinthians 9:14 as well. Although the rabbis had a principle, not always practiced, that Scripture should be taught gratuitously, Jesus made clear that His followers should receive a living by the preaching of the gospel.

The Kingdom of God is near you (9). The heart of Jesus' message concerned the kingdom, its nature, its coming, and its future. The evangelist had this emphasis as well. The kingdom was near in more than one way. Jesus was the King, and in His presence, the kingdom was in their midst. With the death, burial, and resurrection, the full gospel would soon be preached and the church established. The kingdom in this way is also near.

More bearable on that day for Sodom (12). This refers to the Judgment Day. Jesus was warning that the cities where He did the most of His work will bear greater responsibility, thus receiving a heavier weight of judgment, than those cities that did not have as much opportunity to hear Him and respond to His message. Sodom had not heard Jesus preaching in her streets, and although the city was destroyed for its iniquity (Genesis 19:24), in the time of final judgment, its condemnation will not be as severe as that upon those cities where Jesus had lived and worked continually, but still had been rejected.

Woe to you Korazin . . . Bethsaida (13). These are towns in the vicinity of Capernaum.[51] They had constant opportunity to see

---

[51]Korazin (Chorazin) is mentioned only here and in the parallel passage of Matthew 11:21. Its site was probably about two miles north of

and hear Jesus. This was different in the cases of Tyre and Sidon, cities of Phoenicia to the north, thirty-five and fifty miles respectively from Capernaum. These cities were notoriously wicked, and Gentile cities at that. But although Jesus had made a short visit to the region of Tyre and Sidon (Matthew 15:21; Mark 7:24, 31), they did not have the privilege Capernaum had enjoyed since Jesus lived there. The cities the seventy-two would be entering now would also be cities which had not enjoyed the constant presence of Jesus, but although their opportunity would be brief, they must not reject Jesus.

And you, Capernaum, will you be lifted up to the skies? (15). Simply the fact that Jesus had spent much time in Capernaum did not assure her a place in glory. Rather, for this city to reject Jesus would bring all the more condemnation upon a place that had such rich opportunity. "You will go down to the depths." The word used in the Greek for "depths" is *Hades.* It is used only one other time in the Gospel of Luke, and that usage indicates a place of torment (16:23).[52] Here in Luke 10:15, the usage parallels the wording "on that day" in Luke 10:12 and "at the judgment" in 10:14. In all three of these cases, condemnation is demanded. But there will be degrees of condemnation, dependent on the opportunity.

He who rejects me rejects him who sent me (16). Jesus delivered strong words of self-claim here. He was assuring His disciples that a rejection of their message in the towns they were going to would really be a rejection of himself, Jesus; and a rejection of Jesus is really a rejection of God.

Returned with joy (17). Some appointed place must have been designated beforehand where they would meet following the completion of their various itineraries. How long this tour would take is unknown. Perhaps two months would be a conservative suggestion. Where they met is equally uncertain. Many questions are involved. Was Jesus actually on His way to Jerusalem all this time? What season of the year was it? If He arrived

---

Capernaum. Bethsaida was on the Sea of Galilee between Capernaum and Tiberias, the home of Philip and Peter and Andrew (John 1:44). It is not Bethsaida Julius.

[52]In Acts 2:27 *Hades* means simply the "grave," whether of the saved or of the lost, as does the Hebrew *Sheol.*

for the Passover in A.D. 30, this would be about April 7. But this would put the campaign's beginning in January or February, a rather unlikely time to plan a tour. Winters in Palestine vary considerably with the locale and elevation. But even in a district that rarely had snow, at least the winter rains made travel miserable. (See Matthew 24:19, 20.) In spite of this, it would seem that Jesus' temptation period in the deserts of Judea was in the winter and that His travel through Sychar was in the winter (four months until the harvest, John 4:35).[53]

Another suggestion attempts to relate this period with the Gospel of John. In John 7, Jesus is present at the Feast of Tabernacles, early in October. In John 10:22, He was present again in Jerusalem at the Feast of Dedication, which fell about December 10. Perhaps between these two feasts are the months for the tour of the seventy-two.[54]

In that event, these chapters in Luke (9:51—19:27) would reflect an extended trip indeed, including trips to more than one feast in Jerusalem. This would allow still more time during the winter months for the teachings of Luke 10:21—19:27 to be given. Some of these, however, may have been occasions that took place as Jesus traveled with the Twelve following the courses laid out in the travels of the seventy-two.

When they did get together—Jesus and the Twelve along with the seventy-two—the reports were mingled with great joy and excitement. The height of the experiences seems to have been the feeling of victory when the very demons were driven out in the name of Jesus.

I saw Satan fall like lightning (18). In Jesus' reply to their enthusiasm, He added His own word of confirmation. He could assure them that He had seen the very fall of Satan himself, not just his emissaries, the demons. As to when this fall took place, one is left uncertain. Some insist that the pre-existent Christ was present as God cast out Satan when he rebelled in Heaven, and this foreshadowed the defeat of the demons even now. Others hold that the incarnation of Christ and His victory over Satan in the temptation bout is the occasion. Others see this very tour and

---

[53] See R.C. Foster, *Life of Christ,* "The Influence of the Weather Upon the Ministry of Jesus," pp. 51-58.

[54] Arndt, *Gospel According to Luke,* pp. 284f.

its consequences as triggering a decisive defeat in Satan's plans and another graphic fall from his heights. Or what Christ saw may have been like the visions of John in the book of Revelation, which enabled him to report proleptically events that still lay in the future. This could then have been a reference to the vanquishing of Satan's power by the cross, still in the future to the time Jesus was speaking to His disciples in this scene. Or still further in the future, Jesus may have been referring to Satan's final, ultimate defeat and his assignment to his place in Hell (Revelation 20:10). Of these various possibilities, one is fully justified in preferring to look on this as a picture of what Jesus saw happening on these very occasions when His disciples were subduing the demons in the name of Jesus. What Jesus described has probably recurred on numerous occasions throughout the history of man, and this was one of the times.[55]

Nothing will harm you (19). Jesus used this moment of triumph as an opportunity to give encouragement for the future. The power they had seen at work on their mission would be with them, and they did not need to fear the poison and sting of evil in the future. Their authority would win out in the end. Jesus described Satan's fall in symbolic language of lightning, and then He used further figurative language of scorpions and snakes as the symbolic equivalent of the devil and his demons. Jesus frequently used figurative language in this way, although there have always been some who have tried to make them literal (Matthew 18:9; 19:24; 16:6-12; Luke 8:52; John 2:19-21; 6:51).

Rejoice that your names are recorded in heaven (20). Jesus reminded them that their greatest gift was the redemption of their souls for eternity. This was greater than any victory they had seen in healing or driving out demons, any power or authority they had been able to use—nothing was more important than their lives' being counted with God's people.

Hidden these things from the wise and learned (21). Jesus teaches us by His example. He did not want to share this joy of accomplishment with His disciples without stopping to give thanks to the Father. In this thanksgiving, He included thanks for these simple, trusting, dedicated disciples who were willing

---

[55] See Hendrikson, *Luke,* pp. 580f.

to go out under such severe orders and meager supplies to travel unknown places and speak to strangers on behalf of their Lord. They were like children, but they understood what Jesus was saying needed to be done for the kingdom. In contrast with this, not too long before, Jesus had been engaging the religious leaders in Jerusalem in heated debate (John 7:1—10:39). They were the wise and learned, but they did not accept the truths Jesus offered to them. They were "wise in their own conceits" (Romans 11:25, KJV; cf. 12:16; 1 Corinthians 1:18ff). See Matthew 11:25-27 for a comparable thanksgiving. Jesus was thankful for His faithful band of followers who were willing to begin the conquest of the world in His name.

No one knows who the Son is except the Father (22). No one completely understood Jesus except God. His enemies, who rejected Him, certainly did not have the slightest notion of what He was attempting to do. Most of the world was ignorant of His existence. Even those who thronged to see Him came more to see His miraculous works than to learn from Him. When they did listen to His words, they failed to see the real import of them. Even those who loved Him and had given up all to follow Him did not understand what He must do and the kind of kingdom He was setting up. How lonely Jesus must have been when He spoke to His Father from a world that did not know Him.

No one knows who the Father is except the Son. This passage is memorable in the Synoptics because it enunciates in unmistakable terms the sonship of Jesus. John's Gospel is noted for such teaching: John 3:35; 6:46; 8:19; 10:15, 29; 14:9; 16:15; 17:6, 10. In the Synoptics, the same Sonship is asserted, but the passages are not as many: see Luke 3:21f; 9:28-36; Matthew 11:27; cf. Mark 13:32; Matthew 26:63f; Mark 14:61f; Luke 22:70. The Son alone knows the Father. This affirms His unique relationship with the Father, and He is enabled to reveal the Father to whomever He chooses.

Blessed are the eyes that see what you see (23). This is one of the additional beatitudes given outside the Sermon on the Mount collection. (See Luke 7:23; 11:28; 12:37; Acts 20:35.) An interval of time may have elapsed between Jesus' affirmation of v. 22 and this statement given privately to His disciples. Here He emphasized their privilege, but equally well affirmed again the Messiahship they had been able to see.

Questions of Eternal Life and One's Neighbor (10:25-37)

The conversation began with a question. "What must I do to inherit eternal life?" This was a good question, but put in such a way that it arouses our suspicion that the inquirer expected some special work by which he could earn salvation. He was an expert, well-schooled in the law,[56] no doubt a scribe, and the question was one frequently raised for discussion. Probably Nicodemus had that question in mind when Jesus answered him (John 3:3). The rich ruler also asked it (Luke 18:18).[57]

Another doubtful element is the spirit in which the question was asked. The expert wanted to test Jesus (Luke 10:25). He was not so interested in Jesus' answer as he was in debating with Jesus, or at least in having an extended dialogue.

Love the Lord your God ... and love your neighbor (27). Jesus answered the lawyer's question with what has come to be called the Socratic method—answering a question with another question. The reply from the lawyer was a good one, quoting a combination of Deuteronomy 6:5 and Leviticus 19:18. In fact, Jesus used this same answer on the day of questions in Jerusalem in the temple area during the final week of His ministry (Matthew 22:34-40; Mark 12:28-31). Perhaps He had used it earlier in His ministry, and the lawyer was using something he had heard from Jesus on a former occasion. Or it may be that this dialogue was longer than Luke's record, and Jesus drew this answer from him in an extended series of questions. Or it may be this was the independent conclusion of the law expert. At any rate, Jesus declared his answer correct but added the important corollary, "Do this and you will live" (Luke 10:28).

Who is my neighbor? (29). The lawyer was left with the unpleasant feeling he had been bested. He could not debate the answer because he had given it himself, but he had been left with the admonition to do precisely what the law had commanded, and this was too great for any man to undertake in its fulness. So to keep the dialogue going, the lawyer came up with a question

---

[56]This term for lawyer is used by Luke in several places and in the other Gospels only by Matthew, once (Matthew 22:35).

[57]Later Jewish tradition includes the question as well. See Walter Liefield, "Luke," *The Expositor's Bible Commentary,* Vol. 8, Frank Gaebelien, ed. (Grand Rapids: Zondervan, 1984), p. 942.

of his own. He could have asked, "How can I show my love for God?" or, "What can I do for my neighbor?" or, "What is eternal life?" Instead, he selfishly tried to narrow the responsibilities he would have by attempting to limit the meaning of *neighbor*.

Going down from Jerusalem to Jericho (30). Jesus replied with a parable—at least it appears to be one. This passage is another example of the true-to-life combined with the unexpected to produce the strongest assurance that this was the very way it was told. The stretch of road from Jerusalem to Jericho was about seventeen miles, very desolate, infested with robbers, and steep and curving in a descent from 2600 feet above sea level to below sea level at the destination. Jesus' audience knew well the likelihood of what Jesus described when a man traveling that road was beaten, robbed, and left nearly dead.

A priest . . . a Levite . . . a Samaritan (31-33). The true-to-life situation continued with the passing of the priest and the Levite one by one. They would be on that road returning to Jericho from their services in the temple. Half of them made their permanent residence in Jericho when they were not filling their duties in Jerusalem. Their first reaction in seeing the body along the road would be their own dangerous predicament. Perhaps the robbers would strike at them next. Secondly, they were particularly anxious about ceremonial rules of the clean and unclean. If the man was already dead, there was nothing they could do, and it would be undesirable for their priestly concerns—better keep going and not risk problems. But then the unexpected appeared. The people who listened to Jesus' story for the first time may well have anticipated someone's lending assistance, a Jewish "layman," perhaps, but never a Samaritan. In one stroke, Jesus uncovered selfishness, legalism, and the shock of the hearer's racial prejudice whereas He taught the lesson of love, mercy, and service as the Samaritan "bandaged his wounds," used his wine for disinfectant, his oil for soothing lotion, and his donkey for transportation to convey him to an inn.

Look after him (35). This was not a mother caring for her child, nor a friend watching out for a loved one, nor a patriotic national protecting a fellow countryman, nor even a broadminded international assisting a foreigner. This was a despised Samaritan helping what must have been a Jewish victim along the road—to the extent that he even left enough money for about two months' accommodations for a time of recovery.

Which ... was a neighbor? (36). This is another mark of the unexpected. Jesus changed the question of the lawyer from, "Who is my neighbor?" to, "Who acted as a neighbor to the one in need?" This again put the lawyer in the place of responsibility. The circle of neighbors had not been narrowed to his own countrymen, but he was obliged to prove his willingness to be neighbor to whoever needed his help. Once again, the lawyer gave the answer. He did not use the name of "Samaritan," but he said honestly, "The one who had mercy on him"—this was the neighbor. The bottom line of the episode is that speaking of the love of God is not enough, nor even affirming a belief, but showing the love of God and love of neighbor in what we do is necessary. *"Go and do likewise."*

Take Your Choice (10:38-41)

Martha opened her home to him (38). This domestic scene continues the note of the unexpected. The village where Martha and Mary lived was Bethany, about two miles southeast of Jerusalem. This is geographically and chronologically unexpected to have this incident described at this point. It seems strange that Jesus would be so close to Jerusalem and yet a considerable time and distance left before His arrival at Jerusalem in Luke 19:28. (See the above discussion about Jesus' trip to Jerusalem.) If this is not in chronological order, there must be some other reason for its placement here. Any topical link between the question from the lawyer before it (Luke 10:25ff) or the teaching on prayer after it (Luke 11:1ff) is difficult to discern. It may be a combination of reasons: (1) an interest in giving a snapshot scene of a visit to a home as Luke gave a picture of Jesus' visit to a synagogue (Luke 4:16); (2) an interest in showing that a woman could sit at Jesus' feet learning from Him as well as a man (cf. Acts 22:3); (3) a concern that the message of the parable about the Good Samaritan not be interpreted as salvation by service, but that learning from the words of Jesus is a better choice than the service of Martha—under those circumstances.

Tell her to help me! (40). The unexpected in the appearance of this episode is matched by its true-to-life aspects. The bustling Martha, driven to despair by all the final details in preparing a meal for such an important guest as Jesus, and probably a band of disciples as well, was unable to contain her exasperation at the behavior of Mary. She was sitting enthralled at the teaching of Jesus instead of helping in the kitchen.

Mary has chosen what is better (42). The bottom line of this passage has to do with priorities. Only one thing is needful, the presence of Jesus and His teaching. Martha is not to be driven from her zeal for service, but she must keep it in a proper place beneath the hours spent at the feet of Jesus. This is not a recommendation of the contemplative life over the life of service, nor worship over active Christian work, but it is the insistence that to be a close follower of Jesus is more important than being an elaborate host.

How to Pray (11:1-13)

The Lord's prayer is recorded in John 17:1-26, but the Lord's Model Prayer is found here, in Luke, and in Matthew 6:9-13. In Matthew, the example-prayer is included as part of the Sermon on the Mount, but in Luke, it is given on an occasion when one of Jesus' disciples explicitly asked Him to teach them to pray. They had observed how Jesus spent long periods of time in prayer, both before important events and as a regular practice (Luke 6:12; 5:16). They also recognized their own inadequacy and wanted help. Their reference to John the Baptist's offering instruction in prayer gives indication that the disciples had not forgotten him. It also demonstrates that we know little about John's teaching, for we have no information about what he said on the subject of prayer.

Differences between the prayers in Matthew and in Luke are obvious, but not great. Seven petitions are included in Matthew, but only five in Luke. That the prayer was given on more than one occasion is to be expected and that the wording would vary somewhat is understandable.

Father (2). The address to God is not as the "Lord God of Israel" but in the universal and tender approach of "Father."[58]

Hallowed. Although this, as well as the prayer for the kingdom, is given in the form of a petition—"Let your name be regarded as holy"—it is more an act of worship than an actual request.

---

[58]Joachim Jeremias, *The Lord's Prayer* (Philadelphia: Fortress Press, 1964), pp. 17-21.

Kingdom. In this context, the kingdom does not indicate the present church, but looks forward to the time of the triumphant kingdom in Heaven when earthly resistance will have ceased.

Daily (3). This is a rare word in the Greek, yet it appears in both Matthew's and Luke's versions of the Model Prayer. The translation is uncertain, but the most likely meaning is, "Give us today our bread that continues day by day."

Some maintain this has reference to receiving today a portion of tomorrow's bread with an association to spiritual food of the kingdom. Such an interpretation falls short of certitude. Jesus may have been giving a simple reminder that we need to pray for those daily physical necessities that keep us alive.

Forgive (4). The Christian has indeed received forgiveness, but this does not remove him from the constant failures to live a perfect life. For these sins, he must continue to pray for forgiveness in true repentance. But this recognition that we need continued repentance and forgiveness is combined with the forgiving attitude that we need toward others. Not that we earn forgiveness, nor even that God's forgiveness is dependent on our forgiving others, but if we do not have a forgiving attitude, it is doubtful that we can accept forgiveness ourselves. (See Matthew 18:21f.)

Temptation. The word in the Greek may denote trials from hardships as well as temptations toward sin. Our prayers for help in this regard should not reflect a misconception that God brings these temptations upon us, but that He is in control and can help us in providing a way of escape (1 Corinthians 10:13). Matthew's version of the prayer has the additional line, "But deliver us from the evil one" (Matthew 6:13). This identifies the source as Satan and explains further the help that we need.

Suppose one of you has a friend (5). Jesus continued His lessons on prayer by giving a parable. The bottom line to this story is that the man, though a friend, answers a request from his neighbor, not because of friendship, but because of the strength of the neighbor's request.

Because of the man's boldness he will get up and give him as much as he needs (8). The time is the middle of the night, the setting is the whole family finally quieted down in peaceful sleep, and the clatter at the door endangers the whole night's rest. But the neighbor needs some provision for an unexpected guest, and he continues his request for bread. This parable's application is a good example of the necessity of determining the specific point that is being made rather than trying to find allegorical application to all details. If man, because of impatience, inconvenience, and looking for the easiest way to be relieved of an unpleasant situation, as well as being ashamed of not doing what the occasion demanded, is finally compelled to answer this petition; how much more is God, above all these petty reasons, but full of grace and love, already prepared to honor the needs of a petitioner. (See a similar lesson in Luke 18:1-8.) God is unlike the man who simply responds out of "importunity" (KJV). It makes understandable how man is sometimes coerced to do good things by the circumstances, but if it is good and honorable, God will be doing it without the selfish motives involved with man. God, then, is not like the man, but in contrast to the man who provides the bread.[59] God provides the bread, but more readily and graciously than in the way of the irritated, reluctant man of the parable.

Ask, and it will be given (9). In contrast with the foregoing picture, God can be approached at any time, under any circumstances, repeatedly or otherwise, and He will provide. But man must take the initiative—ask, seek, and knock. This is prayer. It extends from simple petition to a search and finally to action. God responds in each instance.

If your son asks for a fish (11). The series of lessons on prayer is concluded with this additional illustration. First, a model prayer was given. Then a parable on answered prayer showed how even a poorly motivated individual provided for needs (how much more will God do so). Next the challenge was given to undertake the request: ask, seek, and knock. And in this last section, assurance was given that God will certainly answer your prayers in the way that will be best for you. Even you fathers, as imperfect as you are, would not give a snake to your son when he asks for a fish, or a scorpion with its poisoned sting instead of an egg. Some manuscripts include another pair, a stone for bread. (This pair is found in the parallel passage of Matthew 7:9.) The lesson is obvious. If earthly fathers will do all they can for their children, how much more will our Heavenly Father do for us.

---

[59]See Liefield, "Luke," *Expositor's Bible Commentary,* Vol. 8, pp. 746f.

Give the Holy Spirit to those who seek him (13). This is the unexpected. Who has been speaking about the Holy Spirit? He has not entered into these lessons on prayer. Actually, however, He is our advocate and our helper, and is associated with our prayers (Romans 8:26f). This may be the reason for introducing Him at this time. Or it may be that Jesus introduced something of what we are to pray for as well as how we are to pray. Matthew concludes this section with the words, "How much more will your Father in heaven give good gifts to those who ask him!" (Matthew 7:11). Perhaps the Holy Spirit was specified here as the best of gifts one could pray for.

God or Beelzebub? (11:14-24)

By what power? Again Jesus worked a miracle, and its record, as was customary, was accompanied by a significant message. No positive note of time is given to indicate when the event occurred. Similar scenes are recorded in Matthew and Mark earlier in their accounts during Jesus' Galilean ministry. They, too, have to do with the accusation that Jesus was performing His miraculous works by the power of Beelzebub. On the other hand, John records deeds and sermons of Jesus that occurred in Jerusalem where similar accusations were made especially late in Jesus' ministry. At the Feast of Tabernacles, His enemies said, "You are demon-possessed" (John 7:20); "You are a Samaritan and demon-possessed" (John 8:48). At the Feast of Dedication, they said: "He is demon-possessed and raving mad" (John 10:20). Since the attacks against Jesus were so frequent and in different parts of the country, it is not possible to say with certainty that Luke's account is the same as the occasion recorded earlier in Mark (3:20-30) and Matthew (12:22-37). However, the occasions are similar: Matthew and Luke describe a demon-possessed man stricken with dumbness, but Matthew notes he was blind as well. The accusation was made, as noted in all three Synoptics, that Jesus was able to drive out the demons by the power of Beelzebub. Jesus replied with the argument that a kingdom cannot use its own power to drive out its own forces—so Satan could not use his power to drive out his own demonic forces. In all three accounts, this argument was followed by the parable of the strong man who guards his house, but he is overpowered by one stronger than he is. In Matthew and Luke, this section is introduced by the same description, "Jesus knew their thoughts and said to them...." If these are indeed the same event, reasons can be seen for Luke's recording it in this part of his narrative. (1) This is Luke's section on Jesus' teaching (chapters 10-21). (2) This is Luke's block of material where he shows the growing opposition from Jesus' enemies. (3) This is the section in which Luke notes the building suspense on Jesus' way to Jerusalem for the final conflict. (Mark notes these scribes who introduced the accusation against Jesus were from Jerusalem, and Luke's purposes could be served by using this episode at this time.) Luke does not affirm that his Gospel is in chronological order. Luke writes in orderly fashion that he may inform his readers in the best way to lead them to understand the significance of the happenings and teachings. Thus Luke may have chosen to place this event and teaching at the unfolding of His trip to Jerusalem as an example of experiences often repeated and giving a proper grasp of conditions at that period.

By Beelzebub (14). This is a term used to designate Satan (see v. 18). The word appears in different places and with different spellings. In 2 Kings 1:2, 3, 6 it is used to designate the Baal worshiped at Ekron and is spelled Baal-zebub (literally, "lord of the flies"). Another form was Baalzebul (literally, "lord of the temple"). The Aramaic for Baal is Beel, and the Jews showed contempt for pagan gods by substituting zibbul for zebul—resulting in the word, Beelzibbul (meaning, "lord of dung"). This seemed to be an appropriate epithet for Satan and was so used (spelled either Beelzebub or Beelzebul).

When Jesus cured the man possessed by a demon, he was enabled to speak, and the crowd marveled. But hostility and skepticism were growing. Some (Pharisees [Matthew 12:24]) insisted that Jesus was in league with Beelzebub. Others asked for a bigger miracle—from Heaven (Luke 11:16).

A house divided against itself will fall (17). Jesus replied by giving two parables to show the absurdity of their accusation. Satan could not afford to give power to Jesus as He contended against Satan's own emissaries, the demons. He would be destroying himself.

By whom do your followers drive them out? (19). Evidently, Jesus was speaking to Pharisees, and they had followers who made a practice of going about attempting to drive out demons. (See, for example, the sons of a priest, Acts 19:13, 14.) Jesus did not say they were successful in what they were doing, but they claimed to be driving out demons and doing it in the name of God—not Satan. This made them stand as judges condemning the Pharisees for their accusation against Jesus, because Jesus was successful in just what they were claiming to do, and God, not Satan, was the authority for such a warfare.

The kingdom of God has come to you (20). The finger of God is manifest in the victories over the Satanic powers, and Jesus takes this occasion to make this Messianic affirmation.

A strong man ... someone stronger (21, 22). The strong man was Satan, watching and controlling where he could; but Jesus came, and He was stronger. Satan will be defeated, and what he counts as his own will be divided among others.

He who is not with me is against me (23). The context here pictures individuals who rejected Jesus and accused Him of Satanic powers. Alongside them were those who would not commit themselves. They wanted more miracles. Although Jesus had been working signs on all sides, they refused to heed. Jesus warned them this was tantamount to a rejection. This is a different context than found in Luke 9:50. (See the notes on that verse, above). The results from such a life are not only one's own loss, but he contributes to the confusion in other lives. He scatters when Jesus is attempting to bring people back to God. No one can read these lines without examining himself to see where he stands. Are you with Christ, or are you scattering against Him—and yourself?

A Life Left Vacant (11:24-28)

When an evil spirit comes out of a man (24). Jesus told this as a hypothetical case. The parable was told for its lesson and cannot be pressed for the particulars. Was the evil spirit driven out or did he just leave? Is the connection with the preceding section that this is an example of a demon driven out by the followers of the Pharisees? These questions are left unanswered in the text. This is not the point as yet.

Takes seven other spirits (26). Although the details of the parable are not the lesson, the traits of the demons are consistent with other instances. They dreaded to be without a body to occupy, and they dreaded the confinement in the abyss (Luke 8:31). We have no reason to question the real danger of the demon's returning to the same body or for that matter, of bringing other demons with him.

Final condition ... worse than the first. This is the bottom line. What went wrong? He cleaned up his life. This was good. But he left it vacant, he did not follow through to fill his life with the good. The life had been reformed; but without the presence of Jesus, a life is open to being occupied again—by evil. With the coming establishment of the church and the indwelling of the Holy Spirit, added significance is seen to Jesus' warning to lives left vacant.

Blessed is the mother (27). A woman spoke up in the crowd of people. This evidence of audience participation is exciting. Never a dull moment when Jesus was there. Not just His enemies broke into what He was saying. His admirers, too, had something to say. This time, it was a woman. It is just like Luke to take note of the woman's part. She was so carried away by the person of Jesus, His love, His wisdom, and His power that she could not refrain from exclaiming about the deserved pride His mother must have for His life. She deserved blessings in appreciation.

Blessed rather are those who hear the word of God and obey it (28). Jesus did not seek to treat lightly the praise of Mary—she had realized that generations would call her blessed (Luke 1:48), but this was not worship given to her, and only because of her Son was this exclamation uttered. But neither did Jesus turn the praise to himself. Jesus never neglected an opportunity to remind His hearers of their own responsibilities. This was not a veneration of Mary He sought, nor even a moment of recognition for himself, but He pointed beyond himself to God the Father, His Word, and obedience to it. This was where the man who had left his life vacant had failed.

Greater Than Jonah ... Greater Than Solomon (11:29-32)

A continuity is seen in the series of episodes recorded here. They probably occurred on the same day. The demon had been driven out of the man stricken with dumbness, the demand for a sign was made, and Jesus gave answer to the accusation that He was in league with Satan. Then He gave parables of the strong man overpowered and the man repossessed by evil spirits, and the woman spoke up from the crowd, giving praise to Jesus. As the crowds grew in number and excitement, as the tension and opposition grew in intensity, Jesus returned to the demand that had been made for a sign. What the people were looking for was a voice from Heaven or bolt of fire, but Jesus was not here to comply to the demands of the objectors. They had already witnessed enough of the miracles of Jesus to have abundant evidence of His power. They needed repentance, not more signs. Jesus claimed Jonah and Solomon as His signs: Jonah, because he preached and even the Gentile, pagan Ninevites repented at his message; and Solomon, because even the Queen of Sheba, from a foreign country (southwest Arabia, modern Yemen), recognized the wisdom of Solomom and came to give him honor (1 Kings 10:1-10).

The men of Ninevah will ... condemn it (32). In the Last Judgment, former generations who responded to the warnings from God will stand as witnesses against those who rejected Jesus in the days of His preaching and His miracles. Greater things than Jonah or Solomon were here then, but they did not heed. Because of their opportunity, their responsibility was the greater. By the same token, because of the added testimony of the completed gospel message we have today, and the inspired record of the New Testament, plus the centuries of witness to the power of Christ and His church, our own responsibility to respond wholeheartedly to the challenge of Jesus reaches awesome proportions.

One [something][60] greater than Solomon is here (31). Because Jesus referred not only to His person, but also to His teachings and His miracles, to His coming death and resurrection, He referred to "some*thing* " (neuter gender in the Greek) greater than Solomon, rather than "some*one* ." (This would be masculine gender.)

The Light Within You (11:33-36)

Jesus was accustomed to using the figure of light (Matthew 5:15; 6:22; Mark 4:21; Luke 8:16-18; John 3:19-21). He applied it here to a setting when people were demanding more signs. Jesus was, in effect, telling them they did not need more light, they needed good eyes. If their lives were filled with the recognition of God and His work and they were single in their vision, not double-minded or two-faced in their allegiance, then they would have light, not darkness in their whole lives. But another

---

[60]See the footnote at Luke 11:31 in the NIV.

important aspect must be given account. Light was not to be hidden under a bowl (container holding about a peck), but used to help those who were entering to see the way. If your life is not used to light the way for others to see Jesus and His message, then this is an indication that your own life is not full of light, for you would not be hiding it. Jesus was appealing to those in His audience to commit themselves wholeheartedly to Him and not remain in the darkness of those rejecting Him.

See Where You Fail (11:37-54)

Another indication that the former sections have been a part of an extended discourse is Luke's description, "When Jesus had finished speaking, a Pharisee invited him to [lunch]" (Luke 11:37). It was a noon meal, not an evening dinner.[61] Perhaps it was the Sabbath day, and Jesus had been speaking near a synagogue. This was not the only time He accepted such an invitation. (See Luke 7:36.) Other Pharisees and teachers of the law were present (Luke 11:45, 53). Their intent was not made explicit, but the denunciation Jesus delivered, and the consequences, indicates this occasion was but another step in the growing opposition to Jesus' ministry. Matthew records a similar denunciation at a later occasion (Matthew 23:1-39).

Jesus did not first wash (38). This was not the neglect of physical cleanliness, but a denial of the practice of the Pharisees with their ritual washings. (See Mark 7:1-5.) Although nothing was said about the failure to observe the Pharisees' customary ritual washings before the meal, Jesus noted their shocked reaction and opened His direct assault upon this basis.

You Pharisees clean the outside (39). Can you imagine washing the outside of your cups and dishes and leaving the inside, used and dirty parts, untouched? This is the picture Jesus gave of the individual who takes care of his physical cleanliness but does not clean up his heart and its desires, his mind and its motives, his will and its goals. (See Proverbs 4:23ff.)

You neglect justice and the love of God (42). The Pharisees were extremely insistent upon tithing to the degree that they sliced a tenth from the vegetables of their gardens, but when the opportunity came to take advantage of the poor or to ignore the

---

[61] See Plummer, *Critical and Exegetical Commentary ... Luke,* p. 309.

needs of their neighboring Gentiles or even their fellow Jews, they defied both justice and love. Jesus told them to straighten up their lives in justice and love, and the tithing would be observed as a natural companion.

You love the most important seats (43). They liked to occupy the places that held the most attention, the greatest honor, and the most power. Their feasts were observed with a seating arrangement carefully worked out, clearly marking the most important all the way down to the least.

You are like unmarked graves (44). If a Jew touched a tomb containing a dead body, he would be unclean for seven days (Numbers 19:16). For this reason, graves were kept whitewashed so that no one would come upon them unaware and become defiled by contact. Jesus accused the Pharisees of deliberately hiding the kind of persons they were inside, and when people came into contact with them, they were not simply in danger of ceremonial uncleanness, but moral corruption.

You load people down with burdens (46). The experts in the law (the scribes) complained that Jesus was not only attacking the Pharisees, but He was incriminating them as well. Jesus added this word aimed directly at these scholars in the law of Moses. They were adding on so many additional rules and regulations that no ordinary individual with a job could possibly observe them. They did not have the time and the money required. The scribes gave no assistance in helping the people of the land, but did invent ways of circumventing the rules for themselves.

You build tombs for the prophets (47). Outwardly, the religious leaders of Jesus' time seemed to honor the prophets by building or rebuilding tombs as monuments to the ones their forefathers had rejected and killed. In their rejection of Christ, however, and of the coming apostles and prophets, they would become responsible not only for the persecution in that generation, but would share in the rejection of God's spokesmen down through the ages.

To the blood of Zechariah (51). Abel was the first to suffer violent death (Genesis 4:8) and the last victim recounted in the closing book of the Old Testament (Hebrew order) was Zechariah (2 Chronicles 24:20-22). In the action of the religious leaders of Jesus' generation, they were entering the procession of such rejections back through the annals of time.

You have taken away the key to knowledge (52). People of the land were being given opportunity to accept Jesus and His kingdom, but the Pharisees and scribes were trying to take away this opening to true understanding of God and His will. They were not only missing the entrance themselves, but they were taking the key away from the people as well.

Began to oppose him fiercely (53). Even as Jesus set His face with determination to go to Jerusalem to fulfill His purpose (Luke 9:51), even so the Jewish leaders mounted in their determined opposition to Him. Luke is careful to point this out throughout the Gospel (Luke 6:11; 11:53, 54; 19:47, 48; 20:19, 20; 22:2).

Assurance in the Face of Peril (12:1-12)

They were trampling on one another (1). The crowds had become so large the people were in danger of getting out of control. The Greek expression, however, means a result that might have developed but did not actually occur. Jesus spoke first to His disciples, but the crowds listened to hear His warnings and challenges.

Be on your guard against the yeast of the Pharisees (1). Jesus' main condemnation of the Pharisees was against their hypocrisy—pretending to be better than they were. They tried to gain credit and power through deceit. They were like yeast, which permeates through the whole dough before you know how it got there. *Yeast* was generally used to illustrate the progress of evil (Matthew 16:6, 12; Mark 8:15; 1 Corinthians 5:6-8; but it was also a figure used to describe the spread of good (Luke 13:20, 21; Matthew 13:33). To this, Jesus added a double-edged warning. The secrets and furtive plans of the Pharisees (see Luke 11:53, 54 above) would be made known (Luke 12:2, 3); but the other cutting edge is that this is true of all of us. What sins have been committed in the dark because it was thought they would not be seen! But all will be brought to the light of day. The most private words whispered in secret will be announced to all the world in the name of the ones who thought they would never be heard beyond the strictest privacy.

Fear him who ... has power to throw you into hell (5). The Greek word for *Hell* is *Gehenna,* not to be confused with *Hades,* the general name for the place of the dead. Gehenna is related to the Valley of Hinnom, south of Jerusalem (see 2 Kings 23:10;

Jeremiah 7:31ff; 19:6) and is associated with fire and judgment. In the New Testament, the word is used only in Matthew and Mark, Luke at this passage, and James 3:6. Only God has this power to cast into Hell, and we should not be afraid of the threats of men who would try to pressure us into wrong or bring physical persecution to our bodies. As long as we stand right with the One who holds our eternal destiny in His hands, our souls are safe. Once we do respect and honor Him, we can also trust Him as our friend. God does not forget the cheapest little sparrow, nor does He fail to note any harm that comes to the slightest parts of our bodies. The accounts are not settled immediately, but when they are, the Son of Man will recognize us as His followers for the life in Heaven just as we acknowledge Jesus as our leader during our earthly days.

Anyone who blasphemes against the Holy Spirit will not be forgiven (10). Jesus was speaking to a group of people mixed in their attitudes. Some rejected Him, some were indifferent, some were favorable. But Jesus wanted to bring hope to all. Even if they were speaking out against Him now, even this could be forgiven. If this insistence to rebel against God's representative continued, however, there would be no forgiveness. Jesus does not say that the sin is "unpardonable," but that it will remain unforgiven as long as he continues to blaspheme against the Holy Spirit or "crucify the Son of God all over again" (cf. Hebrews 6:6). After Jesus had completed His death, burial, resurrection, and ascension, the Holy Spirit would continue God's ministry. He would "convict the world of guilt in regard to sin and righteousness and judgment" (John 16:8). To refuse the testimony of the Holy Spirit is tantamount to blaspheming God. Not that the Holy Spirit is more important than the Son of Man, but that the Holy Spirit follows the Son of Man in His testimony is what makes so grave the continued resistance to the Word of God.

Do not worry about how you will defend yourselves ... for the Holy Spirit will teach you (11, 12). The book of Acts describes just such scenes as Jesus predicted would take place (Acts 6:9ff; 4:5ff; 25:23ff). He encouraged His disciples to remain true in the face of persecution, to acknowledge the Son of Man, and to receive the help of the Spirit in defending the truth. This is one of the pronouncements of Jesus that relates to the inspiration of the Scriptures (cf. John 16:13). The testimony of the

Holy Spirit is heard as the Scriptures, which He inspired, are read (2 Peter 1:21).

On Your Guard Against Greed (12:13-34)

Even Jesus had people in the audience who were not listening to what He was saying. This time a man was so disturbed about his inheritance, he called out from the audience asking Jesus to be the arbiter in dividing his family inheritance. Probably this was a younger son, and he was incensed because the elder brother received twice as much as he did (Deuteronomy 21:17). Jesus declined his urgent appeal but went on to preach a sermon on covetousness. It is logical to conclude that the sermon was the answer to the man's actual need. His real problem was not for help to gain a bigger inheritance, but to overcome selfishness and materialism. One cannot calculate the worth of a life by adding up the things that he owns (Luke 12:15).

Jesus gave a parable to make His point. Picture a man who had been fortunate with good crops, bigger barns, enough to provide plenty for years. He could "take life easy; eat, drink and be merry" (Luke 12:19). *"You fool!"* This is a strong word. (See Luke 11:40; Ephesians 5:17.) God called for the end of the rich man's earthly days in the very night he felt he had arrived at ease and security. Better to count your riches in God. He is the true security. He is in control.

Do Not Worry (22)

The mere fact that you are not in control should not cause you to worry about it. Since God is such a God who provides for the ravens and clothes the lilies so beautifully, you can be sure that the special part of creation made in the image of God will not be forgotten. You cannot add one single unit to life—whether eighteen inches to your height or another hour to your life span (Luke 12:25, and notice the NIV footnote). So why worry about it? Better that God is in control. Put Him first in your life and, being a good subject in His kingdom, you will find that all the essentials of life will be given you (Luke 12:31).

Give to the poor (33). The possession of earthly wealth is not sin, but it is dangerous. Our focus of life may be diverted away from God and directed toward riches. To give to the poor is a good way to prevent this. This warning recurs repeatedly in Jesus' teaching and Luke's record of it (Luke 3:11; 6:30; 7:5;

11:41; 14:13, 14; 16:9; 18:22; 19:8). In giving to others, you not only help their need, but you help keep the values of life in their proper places for yourself.

For where you treasure is, there your heart will be also (34). Portions of Jesus' Sermon on the Mount, as recorded in Matthew 5—7, are found in different parts of Luke's Gospel. The largest section appears in Luke 6:17-49. Another major parallel is recorded here, in Luke 12:22-34.[62] The main thrust at this point is to trust in God, and He will take care of you. But this trust is not an inconsequential afterthought; it only comes when we have put God first in our lives. If this is where our treasure is, our riches will be eternal, untouched by moths or thieves.

Be Ready (12:35-53)

Ready for service (35). Although this parable is about a master, friend of the bridegroom, it is similar to another parable about the coming of the bridegroom (Matthew 25:1-13). This teaching of Jesus emphasizes watchfulness, service, and faithfulness. Jesus was preparing His disciples for a period of time between His going away and His coming again. In His coming again, the time will be delayed and the arrival unexpected. But regardless of the time, the servant must be ready. In a way, Jesus was preparing His disciples for the coming ordeal following His death and burial, and the long hours before the resurrection. In a fuller way, however, He was preparing them for their service after Jesus' ascension, and the continued faithful service they had to render as they awaited the Lord's second coming. In a third way, this Scripture is significant to each succeeding generation until Jesus comes again. All Christ's followers are under

---

[62]Luke 12 records sayings of Jesus that appear in other parts of Matthew (besides the Sermon on the Mount). For example, the charge to the Twelve (Matthew 10:5-42) and the prophecy of the last days (Matthew 24:4-51). Plummer *(Critical and Exegetical Commentary . . . Luke,* p. 316) notes the following parallels between Luke 12 and Matthew: Luke 12:2-9 = Matthew 10:26-33; Luke 12:22-32 = Matthew 6:25-34; Luke 12:33, 34 = Matthew 6:19-21; Luke 12:39-47 = Matthew 24:43-51; Luke 12:51-53 = Matthew 10:34-36; Luke 12:54-56 = Matthew 16:2, 3; Luke 12:57-59 = Matthew 5:25, 26. See footnote 32 above for parallels between Matthew 5 and Luke.

responsibility to be in service and ready, despite the Lord's delay and the unexpected moment of His coming.

Even ... in the second or third watch (38). The Romans divided the night into four watches (see Mark 13:35; Acts 12:4) but the Jews into three watches (Judges 7:19). What is probable here is the Jewish last two periods of the night. The feast was still underway in the first watch.

The Son of Man will come at an hour when you do not expect him (40). Just when you doubt He will return or when you neglect to remember His teaching about His return, Jesus will come. He deliberately left unknown the time of His coming (Matthew 24:36; Luke 17:30ff). Not only will the time of His coming be unexpected, but also the rewards. The master will serve the servants as they recline to eat (Luke 12:37).

Faithful and wise manager (42). To Peter's question whether this teaching was for everyone or just the disciples, Jesus answered with another parable. The key message is found in the conclusion: "From everyone who has been given much, much will be demanded" (Luke 12:48). All are included, great and small. When the master was away, he left a steward in charge. He was responsible for the work and welfare of all the personnel of his master. When the manager became selfish and cruel in his decisions, when he became pleasure-loving and duty-shirking, he was no longer faithful or wise.

Beaten with many blows ... beaten with few blows (47, 48). The teaching of this parable clearly indicates degrees of punishment in Hell, even as other parables indicate degrees of reward in Heaven (Matthew 25:21ff; Luke 19:17, 19). One category will include those who deliberately violated God's will and His laws in flagrant defiance (Luke 12:46). Another category will include those who neglected to do what they knew to be the will of God, deliberate omission (Luke 12:47). The third category will be those who in ignorance did wrong deserving punishment (Luke 12:48). If one questions the justice of the last category's receiving any punishment at all, the element of opportunity to know must be weighed in the kind of ignorance indicated here.

Come to bring fire (49). In bringing salvation to man, Jesus had to confront evil and Satan directly. This fire was a fire of judgment, division, strife, and suffering, but there was no other way.

And how I wish it were already kindled. This can be interpreted different ways (1) The Greek can be translated to indicate the kindling had already begun and was evident in the opposition of the Pharisees (Luke 11:53) (2) The phrase may denote Jesus' anticipation of the culmination of the conflict by His death on the cross and His desire that that moment had already arrived. (3) Jesus could have been expressing His recognition that this was the purpose of His coming. He wanted to kindle the fire and fulfill His purpose.

Do you think I came to bring peace? (51). Although Jesus is the Prince of Peace, this is a peace with God, a peace that is righteous and just. One cannot maintain such a peace and have a peace with Satan at the same time. (See James 4:4.) The enmity against sin, against wrong, and against error of necessity demands conflict. Unfortunately, families feel this division, and the differences become most bitter between those who are closest in home ties. When a decision is made for Christ, it arouses separation on other fronts. Jesus pointed directly to the separations that hurt the most.

Find the Meaning (12:54-59)

How is it that you don't know how to interpret this present time? (56) Times have not changed. They talked about the weather then, and we talk about it now. Different locales had different ways of predicting what kind of day it was going to be—rainy, cloudy, or hot and dry. But they failed to see the deceit of man and where it led, the judgment of God and the certainty with which it comes, the truth of God's Word and the correct understanding of its message.

Judge ... what is right (57). The Romans were the political overlords in the land. The Hellenists carried the day in cultural matters of the Mediterranean world. The Jewish leaders dictated to the Jews what should be their religious practices. But Jesus challenged the people to make up their own minds as to what was right—between them and God. For God is the judge and each one must make his peace with Him. One must settle with Him along the way in life because once He arrives at the bar of judgment, every penalty must be paid.

Final Thoughts

What does a man talk about when he knows he is going to die?

What did Jesus teach as He traveled on His last trip to Jerusalem? Words became more precious and more memorable as the countdown approached. This is the setting of the whole remainder of the Gospel of Luke after 9:51. "Jesus resolutely set out for Jerusalem."

The subject matter of chapters 10, 11, and 12 gives some indication of Jesus' choice of thoughts in the final stages of His instruction. Luke's selection of material gives an idea of the emphases important to be preserved for posterity. What it costs to follow Jesus (9:57-62) must be weighed. Jesus refused to win followers by painting a rosy picture with no realistic sacrifices. Jesus sent out seventy-two on an evangelistic campaign. The time was short, the territory vast, the walls awesome. He needed to use more followers for evangelism. The enemies of Jesus played a role in determining some of the things Jesus talked about. The Good Samaritan was a parable introduced in answer to the expert in the law's question: "Who is my neighbor?" In fact, much of His teaching was in direct opposition to the Pharisees' attacks. Warnings, encouragements, and challenges were given to disciples, friends, and foes. They were life-changing, and they are just as vital now.

A wealthy man lay on his deathbed. He was surrounded by his relatives, who had given him little respect and no love in life. Now, however, the time of dividing the inheritance was near, and they were definitely at hand. Quarrels broke out among them as they surrounded the bed of the dying man. He raised up and in a weak, exasperated voice said, "Oh God, that a man should die like this." Yet think of the Son of God, coming to His own creation and being rejected! He listened to their attacks, to their misunderstandings, to their selfishness and pride. The key message in all of this is Christ's plea for the proper priorities: "Seek [the Father's] kingdom, and these things will be given to you as well" (Luke 12:31).

CHAPTER EIGHT

Answer to Every Lament
Luke 13:1—15:32

Every person feels he has a special need. Some needs are obvious. A little boy in Calcutta, India, scooted across the pavement in front of the airport. He was seated on the concrete and pushed himself along with his hands. He had no legs. When he reached the large window extending to the floor in the front of the building, he tapped on the glass window pane and pitifully stretched out his hands. He did not ask for legs; he only begged for money.

A man stood on a subway platform in a busy section of London. He was waiting for the next train, but not to board it. He wanted to throw himself on the tracks and be run over. A Jamaican evangelist was watching him because this was the subway stop where more suicides occurred each week than any other place in the city. The despairing individual was stopped in his attempt, and he explained to his rescuer, "My wife is gone, my children are gone, my house has been sold, all my money has been withdrawn from our joint account. I haven't got anything to live on and nothing to live for."

Meanwhile, on the other side of the world, a banquet was taking place in a fine hotel in Pusan, Korea. Professors, doctors, lawyers, and professional men were present. Seats had not been assigned, however, and the scene was chaotic. Each was trying to determine how important a seat he could gain in the long dining area. Most felt a compelling need to win as much recognition as possible.

In Dallas, Texas, another crisis developed in a suburban home. The father had season football tickets for the family, the wife had season symphony concert tickets, and the children were faithful attenders in the church youth group. One Sunday afternoon, the church youth gave a special program, and the parents

195

allow us more opportunity to choose the right; but there comes the time when the chance to repent and produce good fruit will run out.

Some Were Angry; Some Were Delighted (13:10-17)

Crippled by a spirit (11). Evil spirits could cause various ailments and afflictions, although such conditions were not all caused by demons. In this case, however, it was, and Jesus was not only loosening the fused bones in her back, but He was freeing her from the bondage of the evil spirit.

Indignant because Jesus had healed on the Sabbath (14). The synagogue ruler registered his complaint with the woman whom Jesus had healed and not directly to Jesus. But Jesus replied to him, "You hypocrites!" (plural because Jesus was including other religious leaders standing alongside the ruler of the synagogue). In other words, "You are pretending to be something you are not. Wouldn't you take an ox or a donkey to water on the Sabbath? Then why can't I help this daughter of Abraham—one of the chosen race?" They pretended zeal from the law, but they were trying to attack Jesus.

All his opponents were humiliated (17). They were put to shame by the logic, by the emotional appeal, and by the obvious manifestation of power to heal. This is the last notice of Jesus' being in a synagogue. The ruler was the one responsible for the service and activity associated with the synagogue, and may have banned Him from the synagogue.

[All] the people were delighted. Throughout these chapters of Luke, the Pharisees and the rest of the Jewish people are in deep contrast. The people rejoiced at the preaching and the miracles of Jesus. The Pharisees and religious leaders had a burning hostility.

The Kingdom and Its Entrance (13:18-30)

It is like a mustard seed. . . . It is like yeast (18-21). Whether or not these parables Jesus gave followed in the same synagogue setting one does not know. Teaching of the kingdom was a major theme in His preaching. These two parables emphasize two lessons about the kingdom: (1) The kingdom will grow big from a very small beginning, and it will prove useful. (2) It will permeate to all corners of the world.

As he made his way to Jerusalem (22). One is reminded that

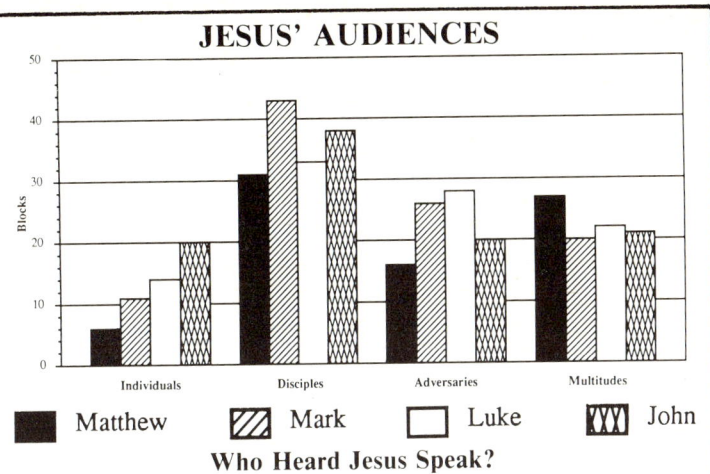

Who Heard Jesus Speak?

Information

Jesus had four distinguishable types of audiences: (a) individuals, with whom He had personal interviews to answer particular needs, (b) disciples, whom He was training for leadership in the coming church, (c) adversaries, who were trying to stop His work, and (d) the multitudes, who eagerly sought to hear Him teach and preach.

The column of numbers at the left denotes the number of blocks— as divided in the NIV— of material each Gospel writer used to describe Jesus' words to each of these audiences.

Investigation

Why does the Gospel of John have more than three times as many personal interviews as Matthew? Could Mark's emphasis on Jesus' instruction to His disciples be a reflection of Mark's association with Peter in writing his Gospel? Did Luke have a particular interest in the resistance of those hostile to Jesus? Is that the reason he included more blocks of the controversy than any of the others?

Did Jesus teach the multitudes in the same way as He did individuals, especially His disciples? Matthew has more blocks of teaching the multitudes than any of the others and the fewest blocks in all three of the other categories. The chart, however, is not entirely clear on this point because much of the controversy and the instruction given to the disciples was heard by the multitudes as well. On the chart, however, only the material that was specifically addressed to the people at large was included in the multitudes category.

Application

Jesus' example and the emphases of the Gospel writers have lessons for us. Jesus did not neglect the one-on-one method of instruction; He devoted much time to the development of leadership; He did not run from controversy; and He did not allow any of these audiences to take the place of public instruction given to large numbers of people.

Jesus was continuing His journey to the holy city. Whether these events happened one after the other is not important, but these represent the questions asked about the events experienced and the lessons taught in this period of Jesus' ministry.

Are only a few people going to be saved? (23). This is a sobering question. Consistently, the saved are few compared with the many lost (Matthew 7:13, 14). Are these a few Jews in contrast with the whole of the Jews? Or is this all the Jews but only a few compared with all the others of the world? Or is this the wealthy few who will be saved? Or only the prominent ones in the community? Will there be room in the kingdom for poor, struggling strangers?

I don't know you (25). Jesus did not answer the question directly. Any number He would have given would have had to be figurative (Revelation 7:4, 9) and would have been relative, depending upon what it was compared with. Instead, He made two points: (1) You make every effort to enter the door—and it is narrow. (2) Many will want to enter after it is too late.

Weeping ... gnashing of teeth (28). The plight of the lost is not left in a passive tranquility. Extreme and constant agony is described.

You yourselves thrown out. To the Jewish audience Jesus was addressing, His remark was doubly appalling. Abraham, Isaac, and Jacob, their revered ancestors, would be inside enjoying the feast, which is a common term used to describe the Messianic kingdom (Luke 14:15; Revelation 19:9). But (1) "you yourselves [with all your Jewish heritage] will be thrown out," and (2) "people will come from east and west and north and south [i.e., people from all over the world, including the Gentiles], and will come to take their places at the feast in the kingdom of God." To say that you knew Christ in the flesh, that He taught in your street, is not enough. You must belong to Him. Then it does not matter where you come from or what your lineage is, how much money you have or how high you rate on the social register. In fact, from man's point of view, the first will be bringing up the rear, and those who are last here will be given a leading place. (See Matthew 19:30; Mark 10:31; Matthew 20:16).

Threats and Laments (13:31-35)

Leave this place (31). Herod had already killed John the Baptist (Matthew 14:1-12); so Jesus would have grounds to accept a warning that Herod wanted to kill Him, too. But the fact that they were Pharisees who warned Jesus to leave the territory rather than fall into Herod's hands makes one suspicious. Perhaps they were more interested in getting Jesus out of their territory than they were in saving Jesus' life. Since Herod ruled in Galilee and Perea, Jesus was probably in His travels through Perea at this time. The Pharisees may have been anxious for Jesus to get closer to Jerusalem where the power of the religious leaders was stronger. So by convincing Him of threats in the Herodian territory, they thought they could drive Jesus into the lion's den in Judea.

Tell that fox (32). The fox was considered a crafty animal, but without the power of the lion. Jesus chose a fitting figure to describe Herod—sly, but secondary in a Roman world.

On the third day I will reach my goal. Jesus replied that He had a ministry to continue (drive out demons and heal people), and He would indeed go to Jerusalem—not because of Herod's threats but in His own calculated time. The third day is variously understood as three actual days, three years of Jesus' ministry, or simply denoting a definite period of time in a figurative way. The last is most likely.

No prophet can die outside Jerusalem (33). Jesus knew He was to die and that Jerusalem would be the place, but not until the time had come. The threats of Herod or the plots of the Pharisees were no cause of fright to Jesus.

As a hen gathers her chicks (34). This lament over Jerusalem is described in Matthew with a different setting (Matthew 23:37-39). It could have been given more than once, or Luke may have included it here because it fits the point he wanted to emphasize. At least, it reflects the fact that Jesus made a number of trips to Jerusalem and spent more time there than the Synoptics tell about.

Your house is left to you desolate (35). Jesus was looking ahead forty years to the time when Rome would destroy the city of Jerusalem. Later, the Jews could not even enter the city. It was left desolate, forsaken, empty.

Not see me again until.... This is something more than the triumphal entry (Luke 19:37f), more than a widespread acceptance of Jesus from among the Jews. It best fits the second coming of the Lord when "every eye will see him" (Revelation 1:7; cf. Philippians 2:10; Romans 14:11).

When Jesus Ate With a Pharisee (14:1-14)

Jesus was no doubt often invited to eat in the home of townspeople. Since the Pharisees were men of considerable means, they would logically be the ones who could entertain Jesus and His disciples. But the hostility between Jesus and the Pharisees was well known. If a Pharisee did invite Jesus to his home, he would expect criticism from his fellow Pharisees—unless he had invited Jesus there for the purpose of entrapping Him in a situation embarrassing to Jesus. We have no way of knowing how many times Jesus ate with the Pharisees, but in the three times recorded in Luke, all of them led to unpleasant exchanges (Luke 7:36; 11:37; 14:1). A number of teachings resulted from this one: a healing on the Sabbath, a parable illustrating the need for humility, the importance of motive in hospitality, and a parable on answering God's invitation to His banquet.

Miracles on the Sabbath (3). The times that Jesus worked miracles on the Sabbath[64] seemed to draw attacks from the Pharisees more than anything else. Perhaps the frequency with which it occurred and the explicit violation of the oral tradition accounted for this. No Scriptural rule forbade it, but the rabbinic regulations allowed healing on the Sabbath only if life was in danger. By asking whether it was lawful before working the miracle, Jesus put the Pharisees in a difficult position. The rule was not in the law of Moses and by forbidding it, the suffering of an individual was going to be prolonged. So the opposition remained silent. One wonders whether the man suffering from dropsy had been deliberately located in front of Jesus just to incite the incident. He was healed and sent on his way.

If one of you (5). Jesus pursued the matter by asking whether each one of them would not pull an animal out of a well when he fell in, even on the Sabbath. In fact, the question may go further. Some manuscripts have *son* and some have *donkey.* Since Deuteronomy 5:14 has a law about work on the Sabbath, and one category is introduced by *son* and the other by *ox,* it may be that Jesus was introducing these emergency measures by categories

---

[64]Peter's mother-in-law (Luke 4:38, 39); the man with a withered hand (Luke 6:6-10); the crippled woman (Luke 13:10-14); the man with dropsy (Luke 14:1-4); the demoniac at Capernaum (Mark 1:21-26); the paralytic at Bethesda (John 5:1-10); the man born blind (John 9:14).

of both man and beast: *a son or an ox.* The Pharisees had nothing to say (Luke 14:6).

Places of honor at the table (7). The most honored position at a banquet was the host's, in the middle. The places on the left and the right of the host were the next in importance, and the ranking continued in that fashion on to the least, the farthest from the host. The seating arrangement is still of great importance in the East. But Jesus was not simply giving a lesson in etiquette. Their behavior in the seating process was an indication of something more serious. He was unmasking the selfishness and egotism of those who were trying to push themselves forward. Furthermore, He was supporting humility as a truly good quality. The biggest surprise of all is that the one who has true humility will end up being exalted.[65] Certainly there was no questioning the humiliation of those who had been pushing and shoving for a higher place when Jesus pointed His finger at them and affirmed, "Everyone who exalts himself will be humbled" (Luke 14:11).

Invite the poor, the crippled, the lame (13). Another lesson that goes beneath the surface has to do with your invitation list. If you only invite people who can invite you back, your motives are suspect. You are expecting repayment. If, however, you are generous to those from whom you have no hope or thought of repayment, this is true hospitality, true concern and love. The bottom line here is another surprise. You will be repaid.

The resurrection of the righteous (14). The repayment comes at the final day when the accounts are settled. There will be a general resurrection of all (Acts 17:32; 24:15; 1 Corinthians 15:12, 21; Hebrews 6:2), and a resurrection of the righteous is specifically referred to (1 Corinthians 15:23; 1 Thessalonians 4:16; Revelation 20:5, 6). The language "repayment" does not mean they will earn the recognition by their actions, but they will be blessed through their putting into action the faith that responds to the grace of God.

The Feast You Do Not Want to Miss (14:15-24)

Blessed is the man (15). To have someone in the audience so

---

[65] 1 Kings 3:11-14; 2 Chronicles 7:14, 15; Proverbs 3:34; 25:6, 7; Matthew 18:4; 23:12; Luke 11:43; 18:14; 20:46; James 4:10; 1 Peter 5:6.

carried away by the discussion that he bursts out with an exclamation is always exciting. They had been talking about feasts, seating arrangements, invitations, and now one introduced the thought of the best feast of all—in the kingdom of God. One can tell that this man expects to be there. But Jesus interjects a note of warning. Will he be ready to accept the invitation, putting aside all other interests that might interfere?

Field ... oxen ... married (18-20). The Jewish custom included two invitations to a formal banquet. The first was answered by an agreement to come, and the second was the final summons sent at the time the preparations were ready. Jesus pictured three individuals who had accepted the first invitation, but declined to come when the final announcement was made. Each of the excuses is significant. The first represented a craving for land, property, and material possessions. The oxen meant doing some work, having bigger crops, making more profit—materialistic gain. But what about, "I just got married"? This indicated the importance of a wife, a home. Yes, these are important, but they will mean all the more if you put your commitment to God first. This is what is at stake in filling your place at this banquet. In all of these excuses, it was not a matter of renouncing the other things, but rather of not letting the other things keep a person away from the great banquet commitment.

The poor, the crippled, the people from the roads and country lanes are all the people of the world who are invited to the feast now that Israel has rejected Jesus, who was there inviting them. This is similar to the king's preparing a wedding banquet for his son (Matthew 22:1-14), but there are enough differences to be assured they are two accounts and two occasions.

How Much Are You Willing to Pay? (14:25-35)

The narrative moves on with large crowds following Jesus, but the same subject continues—what does it cost to follow Jesus? He did not want to be followed by people expecting great rewards and no sacrifices. In fact, Jesus put it in the boldest, most difficult terms.

Hate his father and mother, his wife and children (26). To appreciate the meaning of a passage like this, one needs to exercise common sense, an understanding of the full scope of Jesus' teaching, and an understanding from the heart. Common sense tells us that this could not mean that Jesus wants us to have a feeling of bitter hatred for those who are closest to our lives—our very families. An understanding of the scope of Jesus' teaching instructs us to love even our enemies and pray for those who persecute us (Matthew 5:44). This, then, could not mean we are to have an actual hate for our loved ones. What it could mean, however, is that our love for Christ must be so great that by comparison, the love we have for those we hold dearest in this world appears by comparison to be so much less.

Carry his cross (27). Not only does Jesus ask to be put ahead of all others in your life, but He asks to be put ahead of yourself. A willingness to sacrifice all is what He asks. It does not take a great person to follow Jesus, but it takes all there is of him, whoever he is. When a person carried a cross in that ancient world, it was his own cross carried to his own death. Jesus warned that this is what is expected. Notice, however, even in this, we are following Jesus; and in His case, it was not simply in a figurative way, but this is just what He did for us. (See Matthew 10:38; Luke 9:23.)

Began to build and was not able to finish (30). Jesus wants a person to realize what he is doing when he commits his life to follow Him. The danger is not that he will run out of supplies with which to build, but that he may run out of the will to build. Having counted the cost will help him to keep building later on.

A king is about to go to war against another king (31). This figure is a bit different from the previous one. In the tower figure, the man must decide whether to build or not. In the second, his land is being invaded, and he has no choice but to settle with the other king. But he has two alternatives: fight with the odds against him, or make a settlement. In both figures, he has to make up his mind and follow through, having recognized what is at stake. The cost is great, but can he afford not to?

Salt . . . loses its saltiness (34). Obviously, such salt is good for nothing. A follower of Christ without complete commitment to Him is no follower at all and is unable to perform his service to God or to man.

He who has ears to hear, let him hear (35). He who is standing within hearing distance, be sure to listen to these teachings.

Rejoice For the Saved (15:1-32)

The fifteenth chapter of Luke has thrilled readers through the centuries. It tells of the lost sheep, the lost coin, and the lost boy.

From its lesson, one has to be impressed with the importance of the salvation of each individual and of the love of God. Salvation brings such joy when it comes, and God goes to such measures to save the lost, that we can not help but see the importance of salvation.

Tax collectors and "sinners" (1). The tax collectors were despised because they worked to support the foreign occupation force, the Romans, and grew wealthy doing it. The "sinners" were outcasts because their lives were given over to gross sins of immorality, or they followed occupations making more difficult the keeping of the law. Jesus saw their needs, the same needs as anyone else's. He gave these parables to show God's love and concern for their souls. Another special reason for the parables was to combat the attitude of the Pharisees. They particularly condemned Jesus for associating with the "sinners" and even eating with them. By giving these parables, Jesus was not only emphasizing the love of God, but also combating the barrier of exclusion the Pharisees tried to build around the religion of God so they could keep out any they felt were undesirables.

One Sheep (3-7)

Although the shepherd has a hundred sheep under his care, he will leave the ninety-nine to go after the one that is lost. Furthermore, when he finds it, he carries it home with special treatment. Still not satisfied, he wants to share his joy with his friends and neighbors, a mark of the importance he attaches to the recovery of one sheep. To cap the climax, the rejoicing extends into the realms of Heaven when one sinner repents of his ways and is brought back to the fold. The ninety-nine are still safe, but the special rejoicing is over the lost one restored. The shepherd motif had been common for centuries: Jeremiah 31:10-20; Ezekiel 34:11-16; Psalm 23.

One Coin (8-10)

This coin was a drachma, worth at some time about a day's wage. Perhaps particular sentimental value was added to this certain ten. In any event, nine were not enough when there should have been ten. This is different from sheep. A sheep had wandered off on his own. But the coin had been dropped or somehow neglected. Through no fault of its own, the coin was lost. The lamp, the sweeping, the diligent search are described, just true to life. Especially this was true to the houses then, ordinarily dark with few or no windows, often earthen floors and limited furniture. But when it was found, what rejoicing! The neighbors are called in to help celebrate. They may not have known the coin was even lost, but now they do. So the angels in Heaven will rejoice at the recovery of a soul. They, too, are excited to keep up with the progress of redemption (1 Peter 1:12).

Two Sons (11-31)

The parable of the prodigal son has captivated the attention of non-Christians and Christians alike through the ages. Most would identify with the boy who leaves home and wastes his inheritance in wild living. But there are two sons in the parable. The publicans and "sinners" are no doubt represented by the son who loses his way, but the son who stays at home can probably be identified as representing the Pharisees, considering themselves the important mainstays, critical and exclusive from those who have separated themselves by wandering away.

Give me my share (12). The younger son requested his division of the inheritance he would receive upon the death of the father. It was not unheard of for the division to be made ahead of time. In such cases, however, the father commonly retained control of the estate, receiving the interest and income from the holdings but not touching the capital of the possessions. It seems in this case, however, that the younger son converted his capital into cash and left home. No doubt, this was his plan from the beginning and was the basis for the request to receive his inheritance early. The younger son received one-half the portion allotted to the older son. From this first episode in the parable, the love and generosity of the father for his young son is evident.

Squandered his wealth (13). Scripture speaks volumes in few words. The reader is free to fill in the meaning of "in wild living" in whatever sin and excesses come to the thoughts of the individual. Nothing is said here of prostitutes, but his brother later makes the accusation (Luke 15:30); nothing is said of drunkenness or gambling, but these may well have been included. There are hundreds of ways a fortune can be wasted in riotous living. The trip down was so easy and quick, but when he hit bottom, it was devastating.

Began to be in need (14). The kind of friends he made when he had plenty were not there when he had nothing left and famine struck.

To feed pigs (15). To the Jew, nothing was lower than feeding hogs. According to the law, the pig was unclean meat, not suitable for eating (Leviticus 11:7, 8). According to ordinary observation, the hog was unclean to keep. This prodigal (meaning wasteful, extravagant spender) hit bottom when he accepted a job feeding pigs. In fact, he was so hungry, he was anxious to eat the pods (seeds of the carob tree) used for the hog food.

Came to his senses (17). When a person facing bad conditions has a change of mind, this is the beginning of repentance. The change of mind arose from a sorrow for sin. ("I have sinned against heaven and against you," verse 18.) It had been a rebellion against God and a desertion of his earthly father. A reformation of life must come. ("I will ... go back to my father.") This is the completion of repentance.

His father saw him (20). Even from a distance, the father saw him. He must have been watching for his son, remote as the possibility was that he would be returning. The father ran to his son, threw his arms around him and kissed him. There was no holding back, no restrained acceptance. All was forgiven. All was joy. What a message to the tax collector and "sinner"! What a message to the Pharisee! What a message to each one of us!

Best robe ... ring ... sandals ... feast (22, 23). Each term here has significance. The long robe denoted esteem and position. Not just any robe would do: it must be the best in the house. The ring probably was a signet ring carrying the authority of the owner. The slaves would be barefoot, but the master's family would have sandals. The feast marked a special occasion.

The older brother became angry (28). The older brother raised a complaint on the basis of fairness. He had stayed home and done his work. He had been obedient all these years, but the father had not killed even a young goat (let alone the fattened calf) for him in celebrating with his friends. So he refused to join in the reception for his brother.

My son, ... everything I have is yours (31). The father's love included both sons. Now the older son must come to the point of repentance. He might plead on the basis of fairness to explain his attitude of exclusion, but the elements of jealousy and self-seeking cannot be dismissed. The father does not take away from the one son in welcoming the other, but to rejoice over this salvation of the lost is an absolute necessity.

The application of the older brother's role to the attitude and place of the Pharisees and teachers of the law cannot be missed. Neither can the application of the prodigal son to the plight of the tax collector and "sinners" be ignored. Neither can we miss the application of both sons to our own lives.

The One Answer

A little lady quietly lived out her days helping others and witnessing of Christ's love for all. No great attention was given to her. She sat in the same place at all the church services. She always complimented other people's work. She never held an official place in the offices of the church. But she never missed an opportunity to talk to her friends and neighbors about knowing Jesus as Savior. At her funeral, the minister asked for those who had come to accept Christ because of this little lady to stand. One by one, individuals rose from all parts of the audience. Her mailman was the first, then the meat cutter at the grocery store, the whole family from two doors down her street, an insurance man and his family, and the man who mowed her lawn. More than a score was standing when the last one arose, a little girl whom she had made a point of speaking to each Sunday morning. The minister quietly observed, "It is easy to see how in the kingdom to come, the last will be first" (Luke 13:30). This little lady had been doing what she could to supply the biggest need of all, the salvation of souls, with the one answer, Jesus as Savior.

Luke records the complaint of the Pharisees and the ruler of the synagogue (13:14; 15:2), the observations of the crowd (13:1, 23; 14:15), and the laments of Jesus (13:34, 35) in this section of Jesus' last trip to Jerusalem. What emerges from the variety of subject matter is the prime importance of repentance for sin (13:3, 5; 15:7, 10), of response to the invitation of Jesus (14:16-24, 27), and of rejoicing at the salvation of each sinner (15:6, 7, 9, 10, 32). No matter what lament was heard, whether physical or spiritual, Jesus had the same answer: "And anyone who does not carry his cross and follow me cannot be my disciple" (14:27). And to follow Jesus brings the answer to every lament.

CHAPTER NINE

The Unexpected

Luke 16:1—19:27

In the bombing of Pearl Harbor, one of the largest of the U.S. ships to go down took hundreds of sailors to the bottom with her. In one section of the ship, there was only one exit. As the vessel sank, a corpulent man lunged for the one way out, became wedged in the hatch and blocked the way of escape for all the men behind him. Not only was he unable to save himself, but he caused others to lose their lives as well. Tragic as this was in regard to the loss of physical life, the consequence is still more dire when the eternal state of souls is at stake. This is what Jesus referred to as He warned those who would cause a little one to sin (17:1, 2). Jesus was on His way to Jerusalem in order to make possible, not the temptation and sin leading to destruction, but the way of salvation. He was going to die that others might live eternally. He was opening the door to life.

Where God Leads

These are the closing chapters of Jesus' trip to Jerusalem. Since Jesus knew He was going to His death, one is particularly eager to study the subjects Jesus chose to talk about, and what He laid on the hearts of His hearers, whether by what He did or what He said. Some of these subjects we would expect, but there are other admonitions we would not expect. If the gospel is from God, however, one might look for something beyond the ordinary anticipation of man. God's thoughts are as high above ours as the heavens are above the earth (Isaiah 55:9). So actually, one might expect the unexpected from God.

Who would expect the kingdom of God to belong to such as the children? (See Luke 18:16.) Why were the tax collector and the beggar exalted (Luke 18:14; 16:23) while the Pharisee and the wealthy were not justified (Luke 18:14, 25; 16:22, 23)?

On the other hand, all the unexpected does not have its source in God. Why were the disciples unable to understand Jesus' prediction of His death? (See Luke 18:34.) This is unexpected, but understandable, because man's wishful thinking often overrides his realization of reality and must be guided by the wisdom of God. But the reality may turn out to be superior to his highest dreams.

Content Notes

Parables and Footnotes (16:1-31)

Two major parables are given at this point. When a parable is interpreted, the central lesson must be determined. The details of the parable may be helpful to fill in the background and color of the story, but may be misleading if included literally in the application. For example, in the parable of the unjust judge (Luke 18:1-8), although the action of the judge to answer persistent petition is an illustration of how much more we can depend on God's answering fervent, continued prayer, it does not mean that God is an unjust judge. The parallel extends only to the intended lesson. Therefore, to understand the central thrust of the parable is important at the outset. In the first parable of Luke 16 (the dishonest steward), Jesus was emphasizing that the believer must be wise in planning ahead and using what he has available in the best possible way for the greatest good. Even though the manager is dishonest in his ways, we should be challenged by his shrewdness, but not emulate his dishonesty. For fear someone might carry the parable too far, Jesus included, rather as a footnote, an additional admonition about honesty and dishonesty (Luke 16:10-12). Then Jesus added another footnote about money. We might get the idea that money is the main thing used to measure success, but just because money figures in the parable does not give it prominence. Still another footnote is added to put matters in perspective. This time, it concerned the law and the gospel (Luke 16:16-18). The law was another special interest of the Pharisees, and Jesus added a footnote both about an abiding aspect to the law and a replacement aspect at the arrival of the good news (the gospel).

You cannot be manager any longer (2). The full-fledged

steward in antiquity was one in whose hands the business of the master was entrusted. The manager in this parable occupied this important position; but he had wasted the holdings of the rich owner. We are not told how this was done—through dishonesty, foolishness, neglect, or adverse circumstances. At any rate, the manager had no defense, and he knew he would immediately be without a job and without prospects for getting one. What could he do?

People will welcome me into their houses (4). He devised a scheme that would obligate people to him in such a way he felt confident he could stay in their households for long periods of time. How could he do this without money of his own?

How much do you owe my master? (5). The shrewd manager called in people who had borrowed from his master. It may be that olive oil and wheat were only used as specifics to represent cash which would have been equivalent to eight hundred gallons of olive oil or a thousand bushels of wheat. The manager lowered the amount of the debt in each case and brought considerable rejoicing in the lives of the debtors. But this transaction included also a new indebtedness to the shrewd manager. So now, in the future, he could visit their homes indefinitely and know that he would be welcome. His future was assured.

The master commended the dishonest manager (8). This is the most unexpected element of all. Some have been disturbed by the appearance of urging Christians to follow the example of the dishonest manager and fear that this would include the inference that dishonesty was thus being condoned. For that reason, many attempts have been made to explain the manager's scheme as being morally justified. Some say each of the sums taken from the oil and the wheat debts would just equal the interest that might ordinarily be expected from the transaction. This was a matter of charging interest, and the rules in the law against charging exorbitant interest then become involved (Exodus 22:25; Leviticus 25:36, 37; Deuteronomy 15:7, 8; 23:19, 20). Thus the manager is excused on the basis that he should not have collected that interest anyway. Others maintain that the steward was accustomed to marking up a loan to include his own cut in the transaction and that the percent of lowering the debt was his own personal mark-up on the debt.

Yet after various possibilities are given to insist this was not a matter of writing off money that belonged to the master and was in his right to lesson the debt, then this statement comes from the master commending the steward for what he had done, but explicitly calling the manager *dishonest*. Until now, we might have suspected that he was, but here Jesus confirms our suspicions. Another reminder needs to be made. The master's commending the manager for his action is not the same as God's putting His approval on the ethics of the procedure. The master is part of the parable as well as the manager.[66] He may be commending the steward for at least collecting as much as he did of the debt, for if he had not collected anything, the master may have lost that sum as well. But all of this conjecture has wandered from the first principle of parables—determine the central truth to be illustrated. The world plans ahead to gain what it wants—so the believer should use his wisdom and his talents to gain advantage in the work of the Lord.

Following the second World War, as Japan was again opened to the business of the United States, the business circles in the U.S. prepared to send fifty businessmen to Japan for every one businessman who was there before the war. One did not, however, hear of fifty missionaries who were planning to go to Japan for every one missionary there before the war. The church should be as zealous, ingenious, and ambitious in carrying out the Great Commission as the world is in covering new economic frontiers.

Be welcomed into eternal dwellings (9). The follower of Jesus has the ultimate security in his vision—eternal life in Heaven. Earthly wealth, which is temporary, is not important and lasting. But our friend, Jesus, and those of like precious faith will welcome us into everlasting dwellings.

Whoever is dishonest (10). Here is the footnote (the word of explanation, the safeguard against misunderstanding, the source of information) that disallows any condoning of dishonesty seen in the parable above. In fact, unless we are honest and can be trusted with material things, how can God trust to our care true, eternal riches of the Spirit? As we serve as God's servant-

---

[66]Some, however, hold that the reference to "the master" in Luke 16:8 is a reference to the Lord Jesus instead of the master in the parable. See Liefield, "Luke," *Expositor's Bible Commentary,* Vol. 8, pp. 986-988 for an extended discussion.

managers with the temporary material things He intrusts to us, we are demonstrating whether God can trust us to enjoy the full possession of our own souls in eternity.

You cannot serve both God and Money (13). Here is another note. We have been talking so much about material things, about debts for oil and wheat and about money and payments, one might get the mistaken notion that money holds the world together. Wrong. Money is involved in the world, but God is in control. We worship Him and look to Him for guidance and sustenance. Money is not sinful in itself, but the desire for it is the root of all kinds of evil. And you cannot look to both God and money as your masters. Top allegiance goes to either one or the other.

The Pharisees ... loved money (14). The Pharisees were wealthy men in each community. They were guilty of just what Jesus was talking about (the tactics of the dishonest manager), but they sneered at His teaching. And Jesus deliberately warned them, "Your list of values is wrong. It is detestable in God's sight (Luke 16:15). The treasure of your heart is in money and not in God's law, as you want it to appear."

The Law and the Prophets were proclaimed until John (16). Another note is interjected. Since the Pharisees made much of observance of God's law, Jesus wanted to leave a word on this as well as honesty, money, and values. "The Law" refers to the Law of Moses as written in the Pentateuch, the five books of Genesis to Deuteronomy. "And the Prophets" refers to all the rest of the Old Testament books. They were proclaimed "until John," which seems to designate the termination of a period and the beginning of the preaching of the good news of the kingdom of God. (See Matthew 11:12, 13; Luke 7:28.)

And everyone is forcing his way into it. The message here seems to denote that men are trying to make what they desire out of the King and the kingdom (John 6:15; cf. Matthew 11:12).

The least stroke of a pen to drop out of the Law (17). The Hebrew alphabet has small marks as a letter and as horns on the ends of letters to distinguish one from another. This would be comparable to the dotting of the *i* and crossing the *t* in English. Jesus emphasized the endurance of the law, it would not allow the loss of the least part of the record.

The man who marries a divorced woman commits adultery (18). The introduction of this subject at this particular context seems to be in relationship to the Pharisees and their interpretation of the law. Not only were they more interested in money than the law, but they were interpreting the law in a way that missed the teaching (Deuteronomy 24:1-4). For example, Hillel had maintained that a man might divorce his wife for cooking a poor dinner. Here Jesus emphasized the sanctity of marriage and the warning against the looseness of divorce held among the Pharisees of that day. In a fuller treatment of the subject, Jesus noted that there was one exception giving grounds for divorce, marital unfaithfulness (Matthew 5:32; 19:3-12; see also Mark 10:11, 12).

There was a rich man (19). Since no break occurs between the last parable and this one, the context would seem to remain the same. Jesus was speaking to His disciples, but the Pharisees were listening in and reacting to His teaching (Luke 16:14). The key message to the whole of the parable of the rich man and Lazarus is the reversal of conditions between this life and the world to come. The rich man had enjoyment and luxury in this life, but the beggar had hunger and pain. After death, the rich man had thirst and agony while Lazarus had care and comfort.

A beggar named Lazarus (20). The text does not say explicitly that this is a parable. Some hold it is not a parable but describes real individuals and actual happenings. That the name of the beggar is given is cited as indicating he was an actual person. True, names are not ordinarily given to characters in Jesus' parables, but this may have been done in this case to give more recognition to the beggar than to the rich man. Lazarus is a common name, being the Greek form of the Hebrew, Eleazar, which means "whom God has helped." (Tradition has added the name Dives, which is Latin for "rich," for the rich man.) But even if it is a parable, this does not give excuse of denying the truth of the conditions described after death in this story. To say that Jesus simply concocted suffering after death or contentment in Abraham's presence as useful to the story but untrue to fact makes Jesus deceitful in an area beyond human experience. Better one trust the affirmations of Jesus than deny their place in the very lesson He was teaching. In the former parable, Jesus recommended wise use of what we have, and in this parable, He showed the dire consequences resulting from selfish use of wealth and the omission of opportunities to be helpful.

The angels carried him to Abraham's side (22). For the beggar, it was not important to note that he was buried, but that he received care from the angels and was welcomed beside Abraham. "Abraham's side" is a way of describing Paradise, where Jesus went at death (Luke 23:43).

The rich man also died and was buried ... was in torment (22, 23). The word for the place where the rich man was suffering in thirst and fire is *Hades.* Some find difficulty with the passage because they believe the lost will be annihilated at death and will not go on suffering. This passage denies such a doctrine. Others have difficulty with the passage because of chronology. In Revelation 20:13, the Judgment is held before death and Hades are thrown into the lake of fire. How can the rich man already be in agony before the Judgment? This can be understood if one sees the Judgment Day as a public recognition of what one realizes immediately upon death—whether he is in Paradise among the saved, or whether he is in that part of Hades that will be cast into Hell after the Judgment. That torment has already begun in Hades for the lost is the teaching of this parable. Another teaching essential to the parable is that the saved and lost are already separated by an impassible chasm (Luke 16:26). From the rich man's request that his brothers be warned (Luke 16:27, 28) one also learns there is no communication between those who have died and those who are still living on earth (Luke 16:29).[67]

They will not be convinced even if someone rises from the dead (31). In this parable, Lazarus is being requested to go in a resurrection (implied), but one sees that Jesus spoke, too, of His own resurrection. If one refuses to accept the testimony of Scripture, his mind is closed and no evidence from a resurrection will change him, either.

Watch Out for These! (17:1-10)

Causing to sin (1, 2). Jesus continued teaching His disciples, perhaps on the same day as in the last chapter (16), but perhaps

---

[67]The word *Hades* is used in the Old Testament to translate the Hebrew *Sheol,* the grave or the place of the dead. It is used ten times in the New Testament: Matthew 11:23; 16:18; Luke 10:15; 16:23; Acts 2:27, 31; Revelation 1:18; 6:8; 20:13, 14. In some translations, it is unfortunately translated *hell,* losing the distinction made in the Greek between *Gehenna (Hell)* and *Hades.*

on another day. Probably more than the Twelve were present. (Seventy-two had participated in a campaign previously—Luke 10:1—and could be considered a larger nucleus of His disciples.) Jesus said that you must expect temptations to come, but watch out, do not allow yourself to be the one that brings temptation to the life of another. Do not be the trigger on a trap that brings trouble to others. Your influence, your example, or your advice must not lead another into sin in false living, error in false doctrine, or indifference in false peace. *A millstone* is a heavy stone used for grinding grain. Better for you to have one tied around your neck and be thrown into the depths of the ocean than to lead a little one—either new in the faith or young in age—to sin.

Refusing to forgive (3, 4). Do not fail to forgive. When a fellow believer has sinned against you and comes later in the day, having repented, and asks forgiveness—even if he should do this seven times—forgive him each time (forgiveness without end; Matthew 18:21, 22). Musonius Rufus, a Stoic philosopher of the first century, said, "Better to be wronged than to wrong others in return."

Lacking faith (5, 6). The next subject of instruction was introduced by a request from the apostles, the Twelve in contrast to the general disciples. Whether the present petition for more faith is connected with the last subject of forgiving one's brother is not clear. Certainly, one recognizes his inadequacy when he faces up to the difficulty of possessing a fully loving and forgiving attitude. But is it more faith the apostles would have asked for in that case? Perhaps, for it takes faith and trust in God, who alone can work in human hearts, to make new creatures able to cope with the temptations and trials of life and with the right attitude towards others. In Jesus' reply, He did not tell them how to increase their faith, but emphasized what unbelievable things can result from just a small measure of genuine faith (a belief, trust, and commitment to God).

Expecting payment (7-10). Once again, the question rises whether this section of teaching is related to the others or whether it is an isolated link in a chain of thoughts. The former lesson was on faith, and this warning concerns grace. Although the word for grace is used only once in Luke (2:40) and none at all in Matthew and Mark, nevertheless the doctrine is clearly present. The key message of this passage is that a servant is not thanked for his service when he has simply performed what it was his duty to do. In other words, Christ's followers should not expect salvation as payment for doing what was expected of them already. Do not cause another to stumble in sin, be forgiving to your brother time and again, exercise your faith; but recognize that this is not meritorious work. It is the expected duty of the believer. His salvation is granted as the gift of God by grace. This is the truth reflected in Jesus' teaching in Luke 12:35-37. There the Master does have the servants recline at the table and waits on them. This symbolizes God's grace, also. But in the present instance (Luke 17:7-10), the picture is given of the normal expectation of the servant and the attitude expected from him, which is the true picture of all of Christ's obedient followers. Although the NIV translation "unworthy" is more meaningful than the KJV's more literal "unprofitable," the passage could be still better rendered as follows: "We are undeserving servants; we have only done our duty" (17:10).

Only One Returned in Gratitude (17:11-19)

Now on his way to Jerusalem (11). Here again, Luke reminds his readers that the teaching sessions and the action of Luke 9:51—19:27 are all depicted as occurring on a long, long trip to Jerusalem.

Along the border between Samaria and Galilee. Perhaps Jesus was actually traveling in a northerly direction from Ephraim in northern Judea (John 11:18) and this was the reason for the order: Samaria first, then Galilee. After this, Jesus may have crossed over into Perea and journeyed southward, recrossing the Jordan and entering Jericho on His way to Jerusalem (Luke 19:1).

Ten men who had leprosy (12). These men had become companions in their tragic condition. Excluded from society, with a dread disease bringing slow death, and sharing the worst kind of living conditions, these men huddled together in their struggle to survive. Most likely, they were Jews, but one of them was a Samaritan (Luke 17:16). This in itself would be a phenomenal combination; but such misery overwhelmed conventional barriers (cf. John 4:9).

Jesus, Master, have pity on us (13). They called from a distance because they were not allowed to approach. "Master" is a term used only in Luke. They dared ask for no more than pity.

Go, show yourselves to the priests (14). Several reasons can be seen for such a command: (1) This was the proper procedure after a person has been rid of leprosy (Leviticus 13:2, 3; 14:2-32). (2) This was a means of testing their faith because they normally would not go to the priests until *after* they had been cured from leprosy. To start out for such an assignment while they still had leprosy showed their trust. (3) It was the surest and quickest method of establishing their full cure and being restored to their normal places in society. (4) It was an impressive way to establish the validity of Jesus' cure by the testimony of the priests themselves in Jerusalem.

One of them . . . came back, praising God . . . and thanked him—and he was a Samaritan (15, 16). The sin of ingratitude is universal. The lesson of this occasion highlights the gratitude of the Samaritan. The other nine no doubt had their excuses, perhaps along these lines: (1) "We're doing what Jesus commanded us—going to the priests." (2) "We can look Jesus up later and thank Him." (3) "God knows we are grateful in our hearts—that's what counts." (4) "We have to hurry to get back to our families and into society again."

The Samaritan, however, reflected better reasoning about gratitude: (1) the thanks must be expressed, (2) the expression should be immediate, and (3) putting thanks into words adds to appreciation.

Your faith has made you well (19). For his gratitude, the Samaritan may well have received rich, additional benefits. The nine were cleansed, but the Samaritan "was made well [whole]," or it could be translated, "saved." The blessing declared here can indicate a physical healing, but it could also indicate a spiritual depth to the cure. This may have been received by the one in addition to the gift to the nine. The same phrase is used in Matthew 9:22 and Luke 18:42 (cf. Luke 7:50; 8:48, 50).

About the Kingdom of God and the Son of Man (17:20-37)

The Pharisees were accustomed to discussing at length the coming of the Messianic age and the kingdom of God. Jesus had emphasized the kingdom in His preaching. So on this occasion, the Pharisees asked explicitly when this kingdom would come.

The kingdom of God is among you (21, NIV footnote). The Greek can be translated in different ways and one must be dependent on the context for the preferred rendering. (1) "Among you" would mean that the kingdom was already present in their midst because Jesus was there, and He was king. Therefore, in a sense, the kingdom was present in the person of Jesus. (2) "Within you" would mean the kingdom is spiritual, "within" instead of a physical, material kingdom with its capital and geographical boundaries. It is unlikely that Jesus would have used this phraseology as He addressed an answer to the Pharisees. (3) "In your control" is a third possibility. Here, too, it is unlikely that the context would allow this interpretation.

You will long to see one of the days of the Son of Man (22). Now the instruction turns to the disciples. The words reflect a time of trouble, when His disciples would yearn for Jesus to return. But they were not to listen to the frequent forecasts of His coming, because His genuine coming will be so sudden there will be no time for rumor or debate.

First he must suffer (25). Jesus repeatedly predicted His coming death. This rejection in His present generation had to take place before His return. (See Luke 5:35; 9:22, 43-45; 12:50; 13:32f; 18:31, 32; 24:7).

Days of Noah ... days of Lot (26-28). These were days when business and pleasure were going on as usual. They were days notorious for their iniquity (Genesis 6:5-8; 7:6-24; 18:16—19:29). The interruption of life is abrupt and final for all involved except the chosen of God, who are spared.

The day the Son of Man is revealed (30). The second coming is marked by the appearance of Jesus (1 Corinthians 1:7; 2 Thessalonians 1:7; 1 Peter 1:7, 13; 4:13).

No one who is on the roof of his house (31). Flat rooftops in the ancient near east were used like porches in our country today as a place to relax. They frequently had outside steps to ascend. The appearance of Jesus will be so sudden that no thought should be given to re-entering the house to retrieve material objects. A similar description is given in describing conditions at the fall of Jerusalem (Matthew 24:17, 18: Mark 13:15; see also Luke 21:21), but they are joined with further details about the flight that will follow. Here there is no flight, the Lord has come. "Whoever tries to keep his life will lose it...."[68]

One ... taken and the other left (34). Since 1 Thessalonians

---

[68] See the notes on Luke 9:24, above.

4:17 describes a taking to be with Jesus, this reference is assumed to be a taking into the kingdom and not a taking into destruction. Whichever the one taken refers to, the significance is that two who have been close in life have no guarantee of going to the same eternal destination. One goes and one does not, one to judgment of condemnation and the other to salvation. (See also Matthew 24:40, 41.) It may be that both those in bed and those grinding grain are depicted because the entire earth will be involved at once; and it will be night on one side of the world and day on the other.

There the vultures will gather (37). To the question where the gathering will take place, Jesus does not point in a certain direction, but gives the mysterious answer that just as sure as the vultures will find a dead body, so sure you can be of the gathering at the Judgment of the condemned. Although it is tempting to translate the birds as eagles and find here a reference to Rome, there seems to be insufficient justification of such an interpretation (cf. Matthew 24:28).

Faithfulness, Humility, and Like a Little Child (18:1-17)

Jesus told His disciples still another parable. Whether on the same occasion or not, one would expect a relationship with the subject that has just been presented. He had delivered teaching about the coming of the kingdom and the coming of the days of the Son of Man. When events do not develop as one expects, he tends to become discouraged and impatient. So Jesus followed with an admonition to pray always and not give up (Luke 18:1).

A judge who neither feared God nor cared about men (2). He was a worldly man, neither concerned about standing right with God nor about the plight of man. He cared little about their needs or what they had to say about him.

There was a widow . . . who kept coming to him (3). A widow represents a figure in that society who had little help. She had no family to support her, and there were adversaries who were taking advantage of her. She had only the justice of her cause and the persistence of her plea to the judge in her favor.

Because this widow keeps bothering me, I will see that she gets justice (5). Although this judge was not eager to bring justice, she was wearing him out with her constant pleas. The Greek word means literally "to beat black and blue." The judge finally answered her petition simply to be relieved from this pounding.

And will not God bring about justice for his chosen ones? (7). The argument is convincing, that if the unjust judge will answer the woman because of her persistent approaches, how much more will a loving and righteous God take care of our petitions. Although this is introduced in connection with the coming of the Lord, the principle is applied to prayer in general.

When the Son of Man comes, will he find faith on the earth? (8). Now we return to the point from which we started—the coming of the Lord. Although Jesus has delayed His coming, will His followers remain faithful in their belief and trust in Him and continue their prayers until the Son comes again? Luke has in an unusual way put the key message at the beginning of the parable rather than at the end—we "should always pray and not give up" (Luke 18:1). Even though God seems to put off those who cry out to Him about justice for His chosen ones, in His patience He allows opportunity for repentance to the guilty. But when God acts, He does so swiftly (Luke 18:8).

We understand so little about all that is involved in God's answering our prayers. Perhaps we have prayed for the wrong thing. "You don't know what you are asking" (Matthew 20:22). Or, "When you ask, you do not receive, because you ask with wrong motives, that you may spend what you get on your pleasures" (James 4:3). Too often, our lives are fruitless because we simply do not pray enough. "You do not have, because you do not ask God" (James 4:2). Finally, we share the feeling of the disciples, "Lord, teach us to pray" (Luke 11:1). The companion always required with prayer is faith. The answer to the question, "Will the Son of Man find faith on the earth when he comes?" is, "Yes." The loyal followers of Christ must be patient and trusting.

To some who were confident of their own righteousness and looked down on everybody else (9). Once again, Luke explains Jesus' parable before he gives it. Actually, the parable needs no explanation, only honest application in each person's life.

Two men went up to the temple to pray (10). This lesson may have been taught on another day or the same day, but is related here because it treats the same subject as the previous parable, prayer.

One a Pharisee . . . prayed about himself (10, 11). Jesus spoke volumes by this simple description introducing the action of the proud, pious-appearing individual. He did not pray to God, but he wanted to tell God about himself, what a meritorious individual he was. The phrase could equally well be translated "prayed *to* himself," not to God, but simply from one part of his mind to the other, to himself. He thanked God that he was not like other evil men—or even like this tax collector. (He could see him in a nearby part of the Court of Israel.) He himself fasted twice a week (not commanded in the Mosaic law but usually done by the Jews, who observed them on Monday and Thursday. See Luke 5:33; Matthew 6:16; 9:14; Mark 2:18; Acts 27:9). He tithed his income, not all that he possessed.

God, have mercy on me, a sinner (13). The Pharisee had spoken as though he expected a reward that he had earned. The publican, a hated tax collector for the foreign power of Rome, admitted his sins and prayed for forgiveness by the mercy of God. He was made right, justified, in the sight of God rather than the Pharisee.

For everyone who exalts himself will be humbled, and he who humbles himself will be exalted (14). Beware lest you read this parable and heave a sigh of relief, saying to yourself, "Thank, God, I am not like that Pharisee." The moment you do that, you become the Pharisee.

People were also bringing babies to Jesus (15). The disciples tried to stop the parents and children. They were jealous to protect Jesus from any unnecessary interruption to His busy schedule and important works.

Let the little children come to me . . . for the kingdom of God belongs to such as these (16). Jesus did not consider the children unimportant. They were brought to Him so He would lay His hands on them and pray for God's blessings (Matthew 19:13). Mark describes Jesus' taking the children in His arms (Mark 10:16).[69]

The age of the children is not the object of praise. The kingdom did not belong to the children themselves but to all those, old and young, who had the qualities of the ideal child: loving, trusting, open, sincere, simple, teachable, devoted, obedient,

---

[69] At this point, Luke joins the reports found in Matthew and Mark. The long section from Luke 9:51 to this point is found only in Luke. There are parallels through these chapters, but the setting in Luke is Jesus' trip to Jerusalem.

dependent on the strength of another, and having wholehearted faith. One must become like a little child to enter the kingdom of God.

Not only the example from the children should be remembered in this teaching, but the attention Jesus gave to the children. In the work of the church, the ministration to adults occupies by far the major portion of time and money. But the importance of spiritual guidance and nurture for the children must be recognized. Thoroughly trained Sunday-school teachers, regular and meaningful services for the children, ample supplies for instruction—all these must be included in the hope for the lives of these children and the health of the congregation in the future. Nothing is said of baptism in this passage, but the responsibility remains to lead the child until he reaches the age when faith and obedience prompt a commitment to Christ, even as a child leads us to understand the qualities we should retain while we follow Jesus as citizens in His kingdom.

An Anxious Seeker, but Not Enough (18:18-30)

A certain ruler (18). He must have occupied a role of leadership among the Jews, but probably not as a member of the Sanhedrin in Jerusalem. More likely, he was a ruler in a local synagogue. Matthew calls him "young" (Matthew 19:20, 22) and all three accounts (Mark 10:17-22) make clear that he was rich.

Good teacher, what must I do to inherit eternal life? This is an important question, but Jesus could discern the depths of the man's heart. Evidently, He found there that the man was using terms and treating subjects too lightly, not weighing all that was involved. So Jesus stopped him in his tracks by asking a counter question: "Why do you call me good? No one is good—except God alone" (Luke 18:19). In other words, if you call Me good, and only God is good in an absolute sense, then you are calling Me God—are you ready to do this? Some interpret this to mean that Jesus was saying, "I am not God; don't call me good." But on the contrary, it is more likely that Jesus was testing the ruler to confront the decision. Was he ready to recognize the very deity of Christ in the language he was using?

You know the commandments (20). The ruler was like a student who wanted to be sure of making a good grade in a course. So he went to the teacher and asked what special assignment he could do to get a top grade. The teacher might well reply, "What have you done with the assignments I have already made?" In this case, Jesus said to inherit eternal life, you should begin by keeping the Ten Commandments. Then He gave examples, ending with "honor your father and mother."

All these I have kept since I was a boy (21). This is another evidence of the shallowness of the young man's thinking. He may have been an exemplary boy as he grew up, but to say glibly that he had fulfilled all of this—here is a big claim. Consider for instance, all that is involved in full honor to father and mother at all times, in no way bringing disappointment to their expectations, ever. But Jesus did not stop to complain about any exceptions He could well have pointed out. On the other hand, the teacher was being told by his student, "Oh, I've done all your regular assignments, I want something extra." The young ruler, in asking what to do, was probably thinking shallowly at the beginning. He probably thought Jesus would give him some additional pious works to accomplish. Perhaps Jesus would assign him additional prayers each day, or one more day of fasting each week, or more study of the Scriptures.

You still lack one thing. Sell everything you have and give to the poor. . . . come, follow me (22). Jesus did give him something extra to do, but it was nothing he expected. Sell everything and give it away! He was not willing to do that. In fact, how many of us are ready to meet that requirement? Since Jesus did not ask this of every follower, one must conclude this was a particular need of this particular person. But why? Not simply because he asked the question the way he did.

He became very sad, because he was a man of great wealth (23). There it is. This was what was separating him from God, and it needed to be taken out of the way. This message is not for the young ruler alone. All must face the same admonition. Whatever one puts on his list of values above God himself must be taken from that place. With some, money has the exalted place. With another, it may be fame or top recognition in work or sport or even family. But God must be first of all.

It is easier for a camel to go through the eye of a needle than for a rich man to enter the kingdom of God (25). Some manuscripts try to lessen the stark incongruity of a camel and the eye of a needle by substituting a similar Greek word for cable instead of camel. Others try to explain the eye of a needle as a narrow gateway in Jerusalem—for which there is no early evidence at all. Neither one of these explanations is adequate. Jesus affirms something that is impossible with man, but is possible with God.

We have left all we had to follow you (28). Peter utters these moving words to remind Jesus they had left their boats, their fishing, their families, their all to do just what He had been talking about. Jesus assured him that "no one who has left home or wife or brothers or parents or children for the sake of the kingdom of God will fail to receive many times as much . . . and . . . eternal life" (Luke 18:29, 30).

The Third Prediction of Death (18:31-34)

Jesus gave another warning to the Twelve that He was going to die in Jerusalem. He took them aside to do this, for these words were not for the ears of the crowd. This was the third prediction, recorded in Matthew and Mark as well.[70] In this prediction, Matthew and Mark include seven points of information: (1) The Son of Man would be betrayed into the hands of the chief priests and scribes. (2) He would be condemned to death. (3) He would be handed over to the Gentiles. (4) He would be mocked and spit upon. (5) He would be scourged. (6) He would be killed ("crucified," Matthew). (7) On the third day ("three days later," Mark), He would rise again. Luke does not include all of these, but begins with the third, He would be handed over to the Gentiles, and proceeds to cover the remaining points.

This is the most detailed prediction Jesus had given, and reflects the intensity of feeling as they drew near Jerusalem. Some critics simply deny it is prophecy, but maintain it was later written into the records as an account of the events after they happened. This denial of the truth of prophecy by these individuals is dictated by a denial of all predictive prophecy and, for that matter, the possibility of God's working at all in a miraculous manner. This is the same Jesus, however, who told a Samaritan

---

[70]First prediction: Matthew 16:21-28; Mark 8:31—9:1; Luke 9:22. Second prediction: Matthew 17:22, 23; Mark 9:30-32; Luke 9:44. Third prediction: Matthew 20:17-19; Mark 10:32-34; Luke 18:31-33. Other references to Jesus' death made to this point in Luke are at 5:35; 12:50; 13:32; 17:25.

woman upon their first meeting how many times she had been married (John 4:18), who told Peter where a fish would be found swimming with a gold stater in his mouth (Matthew 17:27), and who told His disciples forty years in advance how Jerusalem would fall (Luke 19:41-44). There are countless other examples of His possessing knowledge beyond the power of human intelligence alone. When so many prophetic details are woven into the warp and woof of such trustworthy accounts, one is constrained to accept these predictions as the predictions they claim to be and not as inventions of some later time.

The disciples did not understand any of this (34). Once the prediction is heard, the lack of understanding among the disciples is difficult for us to comprehend. The information of the prophecy is so clear, how could they have failed to grasp it? These factors should be considered: (1) The disciples did not want to believe that such tragic events lay ahead. (2) They believed in Jesus' power to avoid such dreadful happenings. (3) They wished to take the teaching in some figurative way. (4) God may have clouded their comprehension to hide the reality of the coming trials until they had already been accomplished.

Jericho at Last (18:35—19:27)

Bartimaeus (35-43)

As Jesus approached Jericho (35). A traveler coming from Galilee through Perea (on the east side of the Jordan River) would recross the Jordan at a ford and come to Jericho along the road to Jerusalem. The town was situated seventeen miles northeast of Jerusalem and ten miles northwest of the point where the Jordan empties into the Dead Sea. Luke records that Jesus was approaching Jericho when a blind man called out to Him. Matthew and Mark, however, describe the subsequent action as taking place when Jesus was leaving Jericho. The seeming contradiction has been resolved in several ways. Two Jerichos were identifiable in Jesus' time—the one an old rebuilt town on the site of the Jericho from Old Testament times, and the other, the Roman Jericho built by Herod the Great and occupied in Jesus' time. Perhaps Jesus was leaving the one and entering the other as He passed the blind man. Another explanation suggests that the blind man heard the crowd and learned of Jesus only after He had passed him, but that he managed to anticipate Jesus' departure from town. Then he hurried to take his position on that side of Jericho where the road left the town. This is where the healing occurred according to this view. There is always the possibility that a scribal change may have caused the difference, but there are ample possibilities to gain a picture of the happening without an appeal to scribal differences.

Jesus, Son of David, have mercy on me (38). Although the crowd told the blind man, "Jesus of Nazareth is passing by" (Luke 18:37), the blind man called Him, "Jesus, Son of David." This was a Messianic title. (See Matthew 22:41ff; Mark 12:35; John 7:42; also 2 Samuel 7:12, 13; Psalm 78:68-72; 89:3ff; Amos 9:11; Micah 5:2; Matthew 12:23; 21:15, 16.) Mark tells us the blind man's name was Bartimaeus (Mark 10:46). Matthew states there were two blind men (Matthew 20:30), but Mark and Luke tell of only one. Probably this is because Bartimaeus was the more forceful of the two and acted as the spokesman.

He received his sight and followed Jesus, praising God (43). This tells it all, and becomes a fitting epitaph for every Christian. But in this case, literal sight was restored and the rejoicing Bartimaeus followed Jesus with the crowds going to Jerusalem. One can imagine the enthusiasm in his voice as he praised God and exclaimed at all the new sights he enjoyed each step of the way.

Zacchaeus (19:1-10)

A chief tax collector ... wanted to see who Jesus was (2, 3). Jericho was on an important travel route and would have been used for the transport of commercial goods. Zacchaeus was not an ordinary tax collector,[71] but a commissioner of tax collecting at this commercial crossroads. No doubt, he had heard of Jesus and His frequent contact with the tax collectors. All of this increased his desire not only to get a close look at Jesus, but to come to know Him. He was separated from Jesus, however, by his being a "sinner," by his great wealth, by the dense crowd, and by his own short stature. But he was willing to try to get close to Him.

---

[71]*Tax collector* is used six times in Luke, and each time with some element of favor in the reference: 3:12; 5:27; 7:29; 18:10, 11, 13. The word in Luke 19:2 is an intensified form of this same word, *"chief" tax collector.*

Climbed a sycamore-fig tree (4). This is not the sycamore tree known in the North American area. It is known as a sycamore but has fruit like the fig and leaves like the mulberry. Its trunk is short and wide with lateral limbs convenient for climbing. When Jesus came to the spot beneath Zacchaeus, He looked up and called to him, "Zacchaeus, come down." Jesus did not use the derogatory terms applied to the hated publicans, but personally called him by name and informed him that He planned to come to his house that day. Zacchaeus was delighted. The distance of separation had lessened remarkably.

I give half . . . I pay back four times (8). Luke does not say so, but Jesus must have preached a sermon at the home of Zacchaeus, where He was a guest. The action of the tax collector fits the conclusion of such an occasion. He stood up to make his announcement.

"*Look, Lord![That is, Listen to this!] Here and now,* not next year or on a monthly pledge—I am going to do it right now—I give half of what I possess—not my income, but my capital—to the poor. Furthermore, if I have cheated anybody—and you know very well this has happened sometimes—I will pay the amount fourfold." (See Exodus 22:1; 2 Samuel 12:6; cf. Proverbs 6:31.) The barriers of separation were continuing to fall. Note that Jesus did not answer that this was not enough. He had recently told a wealthy young ruler he must sell everything and give it to the poor and come follow Him. That was what separated him from God. But Zacchaeus was not keeping that barrier there; he had already put his wealth down to its proper place on the list. Jesus did not make the same demand of him.

Today salvation has come to this house (9). What welcome words to the ears, not only of Zacchaeus, but of his whole household. This meant eternal life and the kingdom of God (Luke 18:17, 18). He was a son of Abraham, a Jew recognized in his cherished circle with Abraham after being an outcast for so long. He was the lost sheep that had been found (Luke 15:5), the prodigal who had returned (Luke 15:24). The Son of Man had found him. Rejoice!

Parable of the Ten Minas (Pounds) (11-27)

A man of noble birth went to a distant country to have himself appointed king (12). This parable was given soon after the declaration of Zacchaeus, either still in his home or along the way for the last seventeen miles to Jerusalem (or Bethany, nearby). The setting to the parable sounds strange. Why would a nobleman go to a distant country to be established as king in his own country? But this is just what had happened to Herod the Great, and to his sons, also.[72] They were dependent on Rome for appointment, and these trips had been made on several occasions. So the setting was quite realistic to Jesus' hearers.

So he called ten of his servants and gave them ten minas. (13) This parable has considerable similarity to the parable of the talents found in Matthew 25:14-30, but the differences should be carefully noted. (1) The settings are different: In Luke, Jesus delivered the parable publicly as He approached Jerusalem. In Matthew, the parable of the talents was delivered privately to the disciples, some days after the triumphal entry. (2) In Luke, a nobleman leaves home to gain a kingship. In Matthew, an owner is away from home for a period. (3) In Luke, the minas are distributed equally to ten servants. In Matthew, the talents are given out to three unequally. (4) In Luke, rewards are given as rulerships of cities, but the one servant is punished by having his mina taken away and given to the one who has ten. In Matthew, the servant who gained five talents and one who gained two are put over many things; the servant who had one talent (no increase) has it taken from him and given to one with ten. (5) In Luke, a number of new items are introduced about gaining his throne, opposition, and punishment of the enemies.

Ten minas. Sixty minas equaled one talent (Matthew 25:15), and a mina equaled 100 drachmas. Thus the sum given each slave was quite different from the large sums trusted with the three in the parable of the talents. The ten minas would be about three months' wages. The slaves were instructed to put the money to work until the nobleman returned.

When he did come back, two were rewarded for their good use of their opportunities, but a third had simply laid his mina aside and not used it. For this, the mina he had was taken from him and given to the one who already had ten. Some might puzzle at

---

[72]Archelaus, son of Herod the Great, went to Rome in 4 B.C. to gain permission to reign. This was opposed by a delegation of Jews, but Rome supported Archelaus. (Josephus, *Antiquities,* xvii, 9, 3-7; 11, 1-4; *Wars,* ii, 1, 1—2, 7; 6, 1-3.)

airness of such a decision, but the lesson is found in the ical result: the one who uses his opportunities will end up with even those opportunities that another has refused to take. This is still more evident in the spiritual values of life.

More lessons are intertwined with the leading one. A delegation had been sent to oppose the nobleman, and upon his return, they were destroyed. This is particularly linked to the kingdom of God and the coming rejection of Christ, and finally the future return of the king and the fate of the adversaries.

Choose Your Subject

Did Jesus choose what He talked about, or did He allow the vital needs of His audience to dictate His subject matter? Did the remarks and requests of the crowd introduce the topics? Some estimate that more than half the time, Jesus let His audience introduce the subject. Even when the people introduced the question, however, Jesus often took His hearers to unexpected thoughts they had no idea would be involved.

In this final stage of Jesus' journey to Jerusalem, many types of subjects appear. This in itself is unexpected. Some, however, one might expect. He gave a prediction of His coming death (Luke 18:31-34) and spent time explaining something of the nature of the kingdom and the time when He will come again (Luke 17:20-37). Life after death was included in His parable about Lazarus and the rich man, but the main thrust of the lesson was the proper use of present opportunities (Luke 16:19-31). This is true also of the ten minas (Luke 19:11-27). The importance of not allowing money to occupy the top place on one's list of values was emphasized again and again (Luke 18:18-30; 19:1-10). But who would have thought we would receive lessons on prayer from an unjust judge or in seeing opportunities from a dishonest steward (Luke 18:1-8; 16:1-12)? For that matter, one would not expect a lesson on ingratitude from the healing of the ten lepers (Luke 17:11-19). The need for humility cannot escape our notice when we read Jesus' story of how the Pharisee acted in the temple (Luke 18:9-14), and then of how Jesus held up the example of a little child (Luke 18:15-17). Of the blind beggar who was made whole at Jericho, Luke writes words that apply to each of us: "He received his sight and followed Jesus, praising God" (Luke 18:43).

Part Four:
The Final Week and Resurrection

Luke 19:28—24:53

CHAPTER TEN

The Surprise Beginning
Luke 19:28—20:47

There is a road one can take from Motueka, on the South Island of New Zealand, and drive north and westward paralleling the northern shore of the island. The road curves back and forth as it ascends the hills and goes on up the mountain. In the winter, the highway is treacherous with snow and ice; but after the driver reaches the summit and descends on the other side, he enters a new world. The sun is shining in the valley, the streets of Takaka are bathed in warmth, the rhododendron are in bloom, and the ugly weather on the cold side of the mountain is soon forgotten.

This was the kind of change Jesus and the disciples must have experienced when Jesus descended the Mount of Olives on the day of the triumphal entry. It became a new world as they entered Jerusalem. It was not a change in the weather, but in the climate of emotions. Before, the group had been weighed down with the certainty of coming death. The threats of the religious leaders of the Jews had reached deadly intensity. The people watched each step of the mounting drama, ready to explode at whatever direction the action took. When Jesus mounted the donkey and began His ride into the city, the crowds broke loose in ecstasy. This was what they had been waiting for. Here was positive indication that Jesus claimed to be the Messiah, and this was made public at the very threshold of the Holy City itself. No ordinary pilgrim coming to the Passover entered riding on an animal. That was reserved for proud generals following a military conquest or for returning heroes after a deed of national proportions bringing salvation to the citizens. It was even prophesied of the Messiah that He would make this kind of entrance (Zechariah 9:9; Matthew 21:5).

235

The Beginning of the Week

The disciples must have been surprised. For months they had been prepared to go one last time to Jerusalem and, if need be, to die there (John 11:16). Even the night before, the disciples and Jesus had eaten in the home of Simon the Leper, and Mary had anointed Jesus (Matthew 26:6; Mark 14:3; John 12:7). Jesus had defended her action by saying she had anointed Him for His burial ahead of time. He had predicted His death, but the disciples could not see how it would come about and hoped against hope it would not happen. But in their wildest dreams, they had not anticipated Jesus' daring to take the initiative and enter the city in a victorious way.

The crowds were surprised. They had been listening to Jesus for more than three years now. Some had even tried to take Him by force and make Him king (John 6:15). He could work miracles, which established His word as endorsed by God. His message told of a kingdom they had not perceived before. He challenged them to follow Him, but in a way that dared them to change from their selfishness and their lust. They did not know whether they were ready to give up their favorite sins. If only Jesus would plainly say, "I am the Messiah." It was rumored He had said it to individuals, but why not include it in His messages to the crowds? And if He wanted to make the announcement in the most effective way, why not make it in Jerusalem (John 7:3, 4)? Their enthusiasm for Jesus rose and fell. One time, all but His closest disciples deserted Him (John 6:66). The animosity of the Pharisees and scholars in the law was so great that one hesitated to be identified with Jesus—unless He really was the Messiah. In that case, they certainly wanted to be on His side. Perhaps something would be settled at the Passover this year—if He came. Did He come? Did he ever! He entered as the Messiah riding on a colt. This is what they had been waiting for. But what a surprise just now!

The Pharisees, the Sadducees, and the other religious leaders were surprised. They had been at enmity with Jesus from the outset. John the Baptist had not received their endorsement, and he had been a forerunner of Jesus. When Jesus stopped the sale of animals and the money changing in the temple area—so profitable to the Sadducees—He met immediate resistance (John 2:14ff). When Jesus unmasked the hypocrisy of those who claimed to be pious and were not, He fanned the flames. At every step of Jesus' campaigns, the Pharisees were present in the audience ready to raise objection to Jesus' message and procedures. Finally, they had determined He must be stopped and sent out word for the people to let the authorities in Jerusalem know where Jesus was so that His arrest could be made (John 11:57). Now, as Jesus came down the Mount of Olives accompanied by the throngs, the religious leaders could see where He was, but no arrest was made. They were too surprised, and fearful of the throngs of the people following Jesus.

Content Notes

When Jesus Arrived (19:28-44)

As he approached Bethphage and Bethany at the ... Mount of Olives (29). East of Jerusalem lies the deep Kedron Valley. To the east of Kedron, the Mount of Olives forms a ridge about two miles long. About one-half mile from its summit on the southeast slopes of the Mount lay the village of Bethphage, and about a mile further to the east was located the town of Bethany. Both of these sites were on the road between Jerusalem and Jericho. Bethphage means "place of unripe figs" and Bethany was the home of Mary, Martha, and Lazarus (John 11:1, 18).

Go to the village (30). Which village Luke does not specify, but Matthew names Bethphage (Matthew 21:1). In 1877, a stone was found here with frescoes and inscriptions, one picture showing two disciples untying a donkey and its colt. Luke tells only of the colt, but Matthew records about the two (Matthew 21:2). Jesus rode the colt "which no one had ever ridden" (Luke 19:30). This in itself was remarkable—both that the colt would leave its mother and also allow itself to be ridden without causing any noteworthy interruption. As Jesus was to be laid in a tomb in which no other body had been placed, so He entered the city on a colt which had not been ridden before. Whether the use of the animal had been arranged ahead of time or whether this was part of the miracle, the owners were willing to allow the two disciples to take it.

Blessed is the king (38). Although the description sounds as though the people led Jesus to mount the donkey, this does not mean the triumphal entry was something Jesus was forced into. He had given instructions concerning the procurement of the donkey. All was progressing according to His plan. They proclaimed Him king (Psalm 118:26), Messiah (Zechariah 9:9), and Son of David. "Hosanna [save]!" they cried.

The stones will cry out (40). The Pharisees were beside themselves trying to devise some way to stop this demonstration, which was honoring Jesus and proclaiming Him the Messiah. Finally, they insisted to Jesus himself that He must reprimand His disciples and quiet them down. But Jesus replied if they were quieted, then the very stones would be shouting the news. This is how exciting, how important, how vital the message is.

As he approached Jerusalem . . . he wept over it (41). In deep contrast with the rejoicing crowds, Jesus had to pause as He came within view of the city. This was the scene He had kept as His final goal. He wept because He knew what the future held— not only of His own suffering, but of the fate in store for this thriving city stretched out before His eyes.

If you . . . had only known . . . what would bring you peace (42). Some were welcoming the source of peace, Jesus Christ. But not long from then, the hostile forces would have their way and, through rejection of Christ, would seal their own doom "because [they] did not recognize the time of God's coming to [them]" (Luke 19:44). Forty years from the time Jesus uttered these words, the Romans were building an embankment around the city, and before the siege was over, the city with all its inhabitants, including the children, suffered hunger, fire, terrible blood and carnage, and destruction. Jesus wept because of the three years of ministry that had not been able to redirect the path of this nation and cause all to follow Him. Especially here in Jerusalem, where the center of the enmity lay, was the situation desperate.

Cleansing the Temple (19:45-48)

Then he entered the temple area (45). Mark makes clear that Jesus entered the city following His triumphal approach, but all He did at that time was observe what was going on (Mark 11:11). Since the hour was late, He and His twelve disciples went back to Bethany to spend the night. On the next day, which was Monday, Jesus returned and drove out those who were carrying on a highly profitable business selling animals and exchanging money. Jesus referred to them as a den of robbers. The Sadducees themselves were in charge of the temple profits, and this loss of business infuriated them all the more.

Every day he was teaching at the temple (47). From the Gospel of Luke, it is impossible to count the passage of days. Starting with the information in John's Gospel, we know that Jesus was present at the dinner in His honor in Bethany six days before the Passover (John 12:1). Probably this was Saturday evening when the Sabbath, by Jewish calculation, would be over at 6 P.M. The next day (John 12:12), Sunday, was the day the triumphal entry was made. Then on Monday, He cleansed the temple (Mark 11:12, 15) and on Tuesday, He was back again teaching the people (Mark 11:20, 27). The teachers of the law and the chief priests were furious because of Jesus' popularity, and they wanted to kill Him, but they were powerless to threaten Him in front of the people.

Day of Questions (20:1-47)

By What Authority? (1-8)

If the religious leaders could not attack Jesus with their soldiers, at least they could engage Him in verbal battle and show they were the ones in control in the temple. Without their approval, He had no right to stop trade, to teach about the kingdom, or to come riding into Jerusalem in a victor's march. He had no priestly authority, He had no authority of a man of wealth and vast holdings. He certainly had no royal claims either from the Herodian family or the Hasmonian rulers before them. Another thing was sure: He had no authority from Rome, and He should have feared the watchful eyes of the Roman guards who walked their posts along the walls above the temple area, the same as everyone else feared them. Surely He would not stoop to claim an authority from the peasants of the land; they were scorned by the high-class Jews in control. Where did He get any authority at all? If He claimed to be the Messiah or even God's Son, Pharisees and Sadducees alike were determined to attack this as false and make claims of blasphemy.

John's baptism — was it from heaven, or from men? (4). Jesus answered their question by asking them a question. It sounded quite simple. John the Baptist was still admired by the people of the land, for they had accepted him as a prophet of God. He had stood against the powerful Herod and told him of his sins. He had died a martyr's death; and who would deny that his message, as well as the baptism he preached, had come with the authority of God himself? He was a prophet of God; this was the obvious answer the people expected. But the Jewish hierarchy in Jerusalem had not endorsed John any more than they were endorsing Jesus. They had not gone out to be baptized by him. In fact, if they now admitted that his authority was from God, the next question would be, "Then why were you not baptized?" On the other hand, if the religious leaders insisted, as they did in their hearts, his authority was from man, the people would turn against them in anger because they cherished the word and memory of John. So they felt compelled to refuse to answer Jesus.

Neither will I tell you (8). Jesus replied that since they would not answer His question, neither would He answer their question. In this way, Jesus effectively silenced them and forced them to withdraw in embarrassment. At the same time, He had actually answered their question, and they knew it. John's authority was from God, and Jesus' authority was likewise from God. Just as they refused to recognize John, they were now rejecting the Christ.

What Have You Done With the Son? (9-19)

Jesus had unmasked the members of the Sanhedrin,[73] who must have been representing Jewish leadership in the temple area. He had revealed their hypocrisy by asking a question they refused to answer, and the people could see through their fear of detection. Then Jesus proceeded to tell a parable that followed their unmasking by a denunciation for their disobedience.[74]

A man planted a vineyard, rented it to some farmers and went away for a long time (9). Although Jesus aimed this parable at the adversaries who had just been seeking a way to beat Him in debate, nevertheless He delivered this story to the people as a whole. Even though this is given as a parable, it has strong marks of the allegory type, having parts of the story fitting real persons and activity. It is similar to lessons taught in the Old

---

[73]That is, the judicial group composed of chief priests, teachers of the law, and elders (Luke 20:1; cf. Luke 19:47; 5:30; Matthew 15:1).

[74]Matthew reveals that Jesus told two additional similar parables at this point: the parable of the two sons (Matthew 21:28-32) and the parable of the wedding garment (Matthew 22:1-14).

Testament (cf. Isaiah 5:1-7). God is the owner who planted the vineyard. The Jewish nation is represented by the privileged farmers who were entrusted with the care of the vineyard for the owner, who expected returns from his land. The ordinary rental system would establish a fixed amount of the harvest (⅓ or ½) agreed upon by the owners and renters.

At harvest time he sent a servant ... another servant ... still a third (10-12). These servants were sent to collect the share of the fruit owed to the owner. But the tenants beat the servants, who represented the prophets God had sent on numerous occasions, only to be rejected by Israel, God's chosen people. (See Nehemiah 9:26; Jeremiah 7:25f; 25:4-7; Matthew 23:34; Acts 7:52; Hebrews 11:36-38.)

I will send my son (13). Finally, the vineyard owner determined to send his own son. Surely the vicious, unfair tenants would honor the son. But instead, they threw him out and killed him.

What then will the owner ... do to them? (15). In the account in Matthew (21:41), the people replied to the question. This is not clear in Luke or in Mark (12:9), but the answers are all the same. The results are twofold. The wicked tenants must be killed, and the vineyard must be entrusted to others. The lesson was clear. The Jewish leaders were pressing for the death of Jesus, who claimed to be the Son. In the parable, the son died, but the perpetrators of the crime would die, also, and the vineyard would be given to another people for tending.

May this never be! (16). This exclamation of the people might have been directed at the horror of the death of the son or the withdrawal of the vineyard from the care of the nation of Israel and the assignment to another people. Perhaps this was a reaction to both of these.

The stone ... rejected has become the capstone [cornerstone] (17). The cornerstone in antiquity had three functions. It could be of special use because it was a large, solid stone that could be put at a spot that needed strength to endure the stress and weight at a particular point. It was also important because it provided the starting point for all measurements from one immovable object. Sometimes it had a third use, the place of a capstone that helped hold everything else in place. So it might have been in the foundation or it might have been used in finishing the work to bind the parts together. Jesus, who was rejected by the people who killed Him, was indeed to be the center of all (Psalm 118:22, 23; Acts 4:11; Romans 9:33; Ephesians 2:20; 1 Peter 2:7).

Will be crushed (18). Those who reject the Christ will be as a pot, dashed and broken against the cornerstone (cf. Isaiah 8:14, 15) or as an object beneath a falling keystone, crushed and destroyed (cf. Daniel 2:44). The teachers of the law and the chief priests knew they were the objects of this application and tried all the more to find a way to destroy Jesus.

What About Taxes to Caesar? (20-26)

Since the first assault had proved a failure, the teachers of the law used another approach. They sent men who pretended to be honest seekers for the teaching of Jesus, but who were actually looking for some way they could put Jesus at odds with the Roman government. An explosive subject of real concern was the payment of taxes. Not only was the collection frequently made in an unfair, oppressive way, but it was a mark of submission to a foreign, Gentile world.

Is it right for us to pay taxes to Caesar or not? (22). They thought they had Jesus in a dilemma. If He said, "Yes, pay the taxes," the people would be disappointed in Him, but if He said, "No, do not," then Rome would arrest Him as a rebel.

Show me a denarius (24). As the drachma was a Greek coin used at one time or another for a day's wage, so a denarius was a Roman coin used also for a day's wage. It regularly had the likeness of the Roman emperor on one side. At this time, it would have been Tiberius Caesar. When Jesus received the coin and held it in front of His viewers, they agreed it was Caesar's likeness. If, then, Caesar was the source, let it go back to Caesar. But, Jesus added, if it bears the stamp of God, return this to Him. The more one thinks about this, the more he sees the hand of God in his life and the greater his debts become to his Creator. Especially this is true after hearing the parable of the dishonest tenants who had refused to pay their debts to the vineyard owner. But the main point in this answer is that it is right to pay taxes to Rome. After all, they provided law and order, protection, roads for travel, and daily benefits to the land. Certainly, all was not ideal, but some debts were owed. But what an inescapable reminder that Caesar had some place in their lives because they used his money.

Surely Not Seven Husbands to One Wife? (27-40)

Since the spies of the chief priests and experts in the law were unable to trap Jesus, the Sadducees[75] came on their own to see whether they could succeed in at least putting Jesus in a ridiculous position. To do this, they built a hypothetical case to make their point.

Now there were seven brothers (29). The first brother married but died without having any child. According to the levirate law, his brother should marry the widow to have children for the first brother so his name would not perish in the coming generations (Deuteronomy 25:5ff; cf. Genesis 38:8). Then the Sadducees carried on the imaginary situation where each brother died without children even to the seventh brother. Finally, the woman died. But now whose wife will she be—if there is a resurrection?

As recorded in Matthew, Jesus began His reply with a simple but telling truth we need to be reminded of constantly: "You are in error because you do not know the Scriptures or the power of God" (Matthew 22:29). The ridiculous picture of a woman with seven husbands in Heaven suddenly vanished when Jesus said they will neither marry nor be given in marriage in Heaven.

Account of the bush (37). Jesus did not leave the subject by dismissing the argument of the Sadducees, but rather introduced an argument of His own. Since the Scripture in Jesus' time did not have any chapter or verse divisions, the citation would be made by an outstanding incident in the context of the passage. So "the account of the bush" would refer to Moses' experience with the burning bush (Exodus 3:1—4:17). In this passage, reference is made to "the God of Abraham, and the God of Isaac, and the God of Jacob" (Luke 20:37). But there is only one God, and He *is* (not was) the God of Abraham, Isaac, and Jacob—they are all still living, and He is their God. There must be life after death.

Well said, teacher (39). Despite the bitter animosity of the Pharisees toward Jesus, they could not refrain from applauding

---

[75]The Sadducees did not believe in a resurrection after death, or any angelic beings, or the oral tradition added to the written law of Moses (Josephus, *Antiquities* 13, 297).

Jesus when He made His point against the Sadducean denial of the resurrection and life after death. From this time, no one was brave enough to come with a question to ensnare Him (Luke 20:40).

From Matthew and Mark, however, we learn of a further question that a Pharisee asked about the most important commandment. When Jesus gave His answer, "Love God and love your neighbor," the Pharisee commended Him. Jesus, in turn, commended the Pharisee, "You are not far from the kingdom of God" (Mark 12:34).

Whose Son Is the Christ? (41-44)

Now that the questions of Jesus' opposition had ceased, Jesus had a question for them. He quoted Psalm 110:1, where David says, "The Lord [God] said to my Lord [Messiah]...." The question was how could the Messiah, who was the Son of David, be addressed by the king David as "Lord" if He is his son. A father does not call a son "Lord." Jesus was in this way making another claim to deity. A word, such as *Lord*, used twice in the same line has a connotation of the *same kind*. Jesus deliberately pointed this out. The Messiah must be something more than David's son if David referred to Him as *Lord* the same way he referred to God as *Lord*. The Pharisees could see this, but they were not ready to admit deity even to David's Son, especially when the claims of Jesus were associated with such a person. So the silence hung heavy over the heads of those who had started the day of questions. This ended the questions.

Beware of the Teachers of the Law (45-47)

Jesus concluded His continued debate of the day with explicit condemnation of certain qualities found in the teachers of the law (the scribes).

Show. They liked to be seen in their flowing robes that set them apart as a special group of superior religious distinction (Luke 20:46). For a show, they made lengthy prayers (Luke 20:47).

Importance. They loved to be greeted in the marketplace. This gave them satisfaction that they were well known, were popular, and had high reputation.

Honor. They occupied the chief seats in the synagogues and banquets. This was a common failure that Jesus had pointed out before (Luke 14:7ff).

Fraud. "They devour widows' houses" (Luke 20:47). They were not only selfish, but they took advantage of defenseless individuals for their own gain. In addition to their misdirected attention, they stooped to deceit and dishonest means to gain their ends.

Such men will be punished most severely (47). In the judgment, all the accounts will be settled. Those who enjoyed a high position in the estimate of people will be responsible for living up to their glowing reputations. The more opportunities one received and then failed to make use of, the more severe judgment will be meted out. The more hypocrisy (Matthew 23:1-36), the greater the condemnation will be.

No One But Jesus

After Philip of Macedon had conquered the whole of Greece, his son, the prince Alexander, was visiting in southern Greece attending the Isthmian games at Corinth. The Greeks were a proud and exclusive people. They would allow only Greeks to participate in their athletic contests. Even the Macedonians were considered non-Greeks and could not enlist in the games. While Alexander was in attendance watching the events, one bold young Greek said to him, "Too bad you are not a Greek. If you were, you could participate with us in the contests." Alexander replied quickly, "Too bad you are not all princes; then you could participate with me."

Jesus had immeasurably higher claims than Alexander. Jesus was not simply the son of *a* king; He was the Son of the King of kings, almighty God, everlasting Father. Jesus was the Prince of Peace. Still, He was rejected of men, and they denied His authority for what He was doing. They did not want Him to participate in their circle, but no one had authority to compare with Jesus, God's Son.

No one but Jesus could answer the attacks of the Pharisees and religious authorities the way He did.

The Triumphal Entry (19:28-44)

He came as a pilgrim to observe Passover week, as the Jews were commanded to do each year, but He entered riding a colt that had never been ridden before. He accepted the praise and acclaim of the multitudes as they hailed Him as the Messiah, the Son of David. He received this honor in the face of opposition He had withstood for years. He defied the resistance of the hierarchy that threatened to kill Him. He startled the people by giving this unmistakable indication that He was indeed the Messiah. He fulfilled prophecy in the action of this day.

The Cleansing of the Temple (19:45-48)

The city was crowded at Passover time. Josephus' estimate of two to three million people in Jerusalem on some occasions is an extreme exaggeration. More likely would be a number close to 200,000.[76] But with thousands in the temple area, Jesus dared to drive out the animals being sold for sacrifice and those who were doing the selling. He condemned them for robbing the people in their dealings and desecrating the holy temple of God. To emphasize further His rightful place of authority, He returned each day and taught in the temple precincts. No one but Jesus could stand practically alone against all the power of the priestly authority.

The Great Day of Questions (20:1-47)

Each time the teachers of the law came to attack His teaching, Jesus not only proved them wrong but laid more stones in the foundation for His claim to be the Son of God. One group after another came to ask Him questions: members of the Sanhedrin, the Pharisees, the Herodians (Matthew 22:16), the Sadducees, and the Pharisees again. No one could answer their questions the way Jesus did. The proof of the effective testimony Jesus gave was the inability of the Jewish leaders to divert the people from supporting Jesus in His claims. They could object to the statements of Jesus, but they could not withstand His logic and His power. No one could teach with the authority Jesus showed.

All this has application to our own lives. Do we choose circles that would exclude Jesus and question His credentials for our

---

[76] Joachim Jeremias, *Jerusalem in the Time of Christ* (Philadelphia: Fortress Press, 1967), pp. 77ff.

course of life? When Jesus established His claims in Jerusalem, He established them in our lives as well. Do we refuse to acknowledge our debts to God and send His Son away empty-handed? Do we treat His messengers with disdain and fail to bring fruits as a nation dedicated to God's principles and service? No one but Jesus has lived among us but proven His place beside God. He was the rising sun who shone upon us from Heaven "to shine on those living in darkness and in the shadow of death, to guide our feet into the path of peace" (Luke 1:79).

CHAPTER ELEVEN

The Last Days
Luke 21:1—22:38

Mt. Vesuvius erupted in A.D. 79, leaving its mark on Roman history.

> Day was turned into night, and light into darkness—an inexpressible quantity of dust and ashes poured out, deluging land, sea, and air, and burying two entire cities, Herculaneum and Pompeii, while the people were sitting in the theater.[77]

Hysteria struck the city as half its population jammed the roadway from the city to the port. They groped in the darkness and fought to gain escape via the boats along the shore.

In Bulwer Lytton's *The Last Days of Pompeii,* a blind girl leads her friends to safety. The Thessalonian blind girl, Nydia, had already found her way to the seashore with the trusty staff she always carried. Darkness was nothing new to her; it was her natural world. But then she went back to the city to find Glaucus and his lover, Ione. They had despaired and lay waiting death beneath an arch in the forum. But Nydia encouraged them and led both to the sea by another route. Only the blind could lead in a darkness such as that. She was willing to risk everything to lead Glaucus to safety.

The True Guide

Fifty years before the eruption of Vesuvius, at the eastern end of the Mediterranean, the time of crisis had come for all mankind. Jesus was not a blind leader; He could see paths others did

---

[77]Dion Cassius, *lib.* 66.

not know were there. He saw battles fought beyond the sight of man, and provided the way of escape from darkness and destruction. During this final week of His earthly life, He was striving to prepare His disciples for the ordeal He knew was just ahead both for himself and also for His followers—in the immediate future as well as through the ages. Not only was He concerned about His disciples within the sound of His voice in the temple area each day, but also the throngs of people, and not just this people at the Passover in A.D. 30. He was anxious because He wanted to lead all people everywhere from darkness to light, from bondage to freedom.

Content Notes

Discern the Truth (21:1-7)

Gifts into the temple treasury (1). This scene comes as an unexpected interlude in the middle of Jesus' major bouts with the Jewish leaders and His last-minute instructions to His disciples. You cannot miss the significance. Jesus always had time for the ones who were pushed aside by the hurry and importance of the prominent. This time, Jesus paused to sit down (Mark 12:41) and quietly observed what was going on during this calm in the midst of the storm. This was probably one of the outer courts, such as the Court of Women, where donation boxes were located. They were shaped like inverted megaphones. In this way, people could place rather large gifts, such as precious jewelry or works of art as well as money. Jesus had nothing to say about the gifts of the wealthy, even though some of them represented large amounts of money.

This poor widow has put in more than all the others (3). She only gave two lepta. This would represent less than half a cent and was the minimum for what would be acceptable as a donation. How could Jesus say she had given more than all the rest? Two principles must be remembered. First, the worth of a gift is not measured by the sum given, but by the sum one keeps for himself. The widow gave everything she had to live on, but the others had given gifts that represented only a small percent of their total wealth. It had been no sacrifice to them, but the widow gave the only sustenance she had. This leads to the second point: the spirit in which a gift is given makes a difference. Certainly the widow was generous, but other qualities are also evident. She must have realized a real dependence on God, which makes a person stronger than when he looks to himself. Finally, she had both faith and love for God.

Some of his disciples (5). The siege with the questioners was over. Jesus was relaxing in the temple area with His disciples, and they could not help but admire the magnificent buildings surrounding them. They looked particularly imposing after Jesus' warning. "Your house is left to you desolate" (Luke 13:35), and, "They will not leave one stone on another" (Luke 19:44). At this moment, however, they remarked about the beautiful stones, some of them over sixty feet in length, and "whatever was not overlain with gold was purest white" (Josephus, *Wars,* 5, 210), and the special gifts presented to make the scene still more breathtaking. For example, Herod had provided a golden cluster of grapes which extended "as tall as a man' (Josephus, *ibid,*).

Not one stone will be left on another (6). Jesus, however, only repeated His description of complete destruction for this majestic temple in Jerusalem.

When will these things happen? (7). From the accounts given in Matthew and Mark concerning this episode, one can add more details to Luke's description. The question about when this destruction would come was asked by Peter, James, John, and Andrew (Mark 13:3). This request for more information came after they had left the temple area and ascended the Mount of Olives. The Gospel of Matthew (24:3) makes clear that they also included in their question a request for the sign of His coming again and the end of the age. No doubt, the disciples were so impressed with the permanence of the buildings in the temple area that to think of their being destroyed before the end of time was impossible. Therefore, they associated all three events together: the destruction of the temple, the coming of the Lord, and the end of the age.

The Fall of Jerusalem (21:8-24)

Watch out that you are not deceived (8). In Jesus' answer, He paid attention to all three queries, plus the request for any warning sign (miracle) to indicate the time was at hand. At the outset, Jesus attempted to quiet their fears and at the same time to alert them to false claims that would deceive some. "Do not follow false Christs. Do not be discouraged by wars and revolutions.

TEMPLE AREA

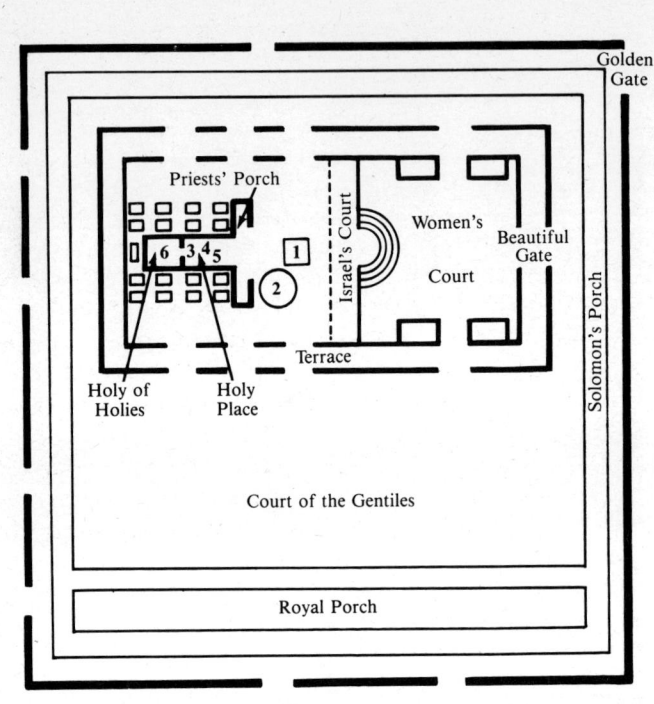

1. Altar of Burnt Offering
2. Laver
3. Incense Altar
4. Table of Showbread
5. Candlestick
6. Ark of the Covenant

They must take place. There will be earthquakes, famines, and pestilences in various places." Indeed, the times before the destruction of Jerusalem did include frightful events, but the disciples were not to panic because of them. Tacitus *(History,* 1, 2) wrote about those days:

> I am entering on the history of a period rich in disasters, frightful in its wars, torn by civil strife and even in peace full of horrors. Four emperors perished by the sword. There were three civil wars; there were more with foreign enemies. There was success in the East, and disaster in the West....

But before all this, they will ... persecute you (12). Not only were the disciples to resist false claims and expect difficult conditions, but they must be prepared to endure trials in synagogues (used by the Jews as places of ecclesiastical tribunal) and before kings and governors. One sees the beginning of fulfillment of these predictions in the accounts of Peter and John's being before the Sanhedrin (Acts 4:3) and of Stephen's being killed (Acts 7:54-60). Paul stood trial before King Agrippa and Governor Festus (Acts 25:13ff). Peter and Paul probably stood trial in Rome and died in martyrdom. (See 1 Clement 5.) Jesus warned, "They will put some of you to death" (Luke 21:16). But how could Jesus continue to promise: "By standing firm you will gain life"? He could say this with full assurance because of the ultimate salvation that lies beyond physical death, beyond the Judgment, and into the eternal salvation of Heaven.[78]

When you see Jerusalem ... surrounded by armies ... flee to the mountains (20, 21). For those who were in Judea, Jesus had a special message in answer to their first question, "When will destruction come to Jerusalem?" The natural inclination to seek safety from an advancing Roman army would be to flee to the protection of a walled city. Instead, they were to flee from the city into the country. At the siege of Jerusalem, which led to its fall in A.D. 70, the Christians did just that and went to Pella, on the east side of the Jordan. Since the Christians were given this instruction for the occasion, this makes obvious the teaching

---

[78] See the favorite saying: Matthew 10:39; 16:25; Mark 8:35; Luke 9:24; 17:33.

does not refer to the second coming of Christ. To flee to the mountains will be a useless gesture at the end of time.

Until the times of the Gentiles are fulfilled (24). The Gentiles were to receive the opportunity for spiritual blessing and inclusion in the invitation of the gospel (Mark 13:10; cf. Luke 20:16; Romans 11:25). But also they were predicted to control Jerusalem for a period of time. But these times seem to have been limited.

The Second Coming (21:25-28)

There will be signs in the sun, moon and stars (25). At this point, Jesus carried His prediction of judgment upon the Jewish nation and Jerusalem on to the final Judgment and the coming of the end. This was an answer to the remaining intended questions of the disciples (Matthew 24:3) concerning Christ's second coming and the end of time. (See Revelation 6:12.)

The Son of Man coming in a cloud (27). (See Acts 1:9-11; Matthew 26:64; Daniel 7:13; Revelation 1:7.) Just as the paragraph before has spoken of the destruction of Jerusalem (v. 24), so this paragraph speaks of the return of the Son of Man. They are two different occasions and are interwoven in the answer Jesus gives His disciples. If the question about the fall of Jerusalem is designated "a" and the Lord's return labeled "b," Jesus' answer (Luke 21:8-36) can be divided in this way: (a, b) 8-19; (a) 20-24; (b) 25-28; (a) 29-33; (b) 34, 35; (a, b) 36.

Stand up and lift up your heads, because your redemption is drawing near (28). The followers of Christ will be neither downcast nor uncertain at the coming of the Lord. Joy and confidence will be uppermost. Christ completed His work of redemption in His death, burial, and resurrection, but the individual's reception of redemption will be fully realized at the final Judgment.

Look at the fig tree (29)

One knows that summer is coming when he sees the green foliage appearing on the tree. Even so, the disciples would be able to tell when the destruction of Jerusalem was approaching by the fulfillment of the signs Jesus gave (Luke 21:20-24). To apply this figure to the coming of Christ does not fit. Christ's coming will be instantaneous, like the snap of a trap (Luke 21:34). There will be no time for the greening of the tree.

Kingdom of God is near (31). The establishment of the church on the day of Pentecost was only a little over fifty days away. As already noted, the *kingdom* can be used in different ways, but this usage fits the context best here. That is the immediate phase John the Baptist and Jesus had proclaimed (Matthew 3:2; 4:17; Mark 1:15; Luke 10:9).

This generation (32). If this refers to the destruction of Jerusalem, which occurred about forty years from the time Jesus declared this, the ordinary meaning of *generation* can be understood here. Some, however, maintain that the second coming of Christ is referred to. They would render the word *race* rather than *generation.* In that case, it would refer to the Israelite race, which will retain its identity to the end of time. The fact that two questions were being answered and Jesus' treatment of them alternated back and forth strongly supports the normal meaning of *generation,* within the next forty years. The passage does not mean that Jesus was saying He would return for His second coming in the present generation. He did indicate that all the things predicted for the generation of time leading to the destruction of Jerusalem would happen as surely as His words are eternally true.

Be careful, or your hearts will be weighed down (34)

Jesus was preparing His disciples for the trying days ahead. He wanted to lead them away from the depression, not only of sin, but the very anxieties of life. Now Jesus spoke not only of the fall of Jerusalem, but of the long journey to the final apocalyptic closing of the coming of the Lord. "Do not be discouraged. Live in hope and trust" (cf. Luke 21:14).

Be always on the watch (36). Two events had been presented: the fall of Jerusalem and the coming of the Son of Man. The one was close at hand, the day and hour of the other was not known (Matthew 24:36; Mark 13:32), but the Lord's return will be sudden and complete. For the one event (the fall of Jerusalem), Jesus prayed they would be able to escape all that was about to happen, and for the second coming—whenever that will be—that they may be able to stand before the Son of Man.[79] Thus,

---

[79]M. J. Lagrange, *The Gospel of Jesus Christ,* Vol. 2. (London), 1938, pp. 183f.

the closing statement summarized by applying one affirmation to one part of the answer and a second to the other part. They must not be deceived and fall to false teaching. They must not be faithless and fail in the trials of persecution. They must be alert and ready.

Each day Jesus was teaching (37). From the Sunday of the triumphal entry to the Thursday of the Passover meal, Jesus had been at the temple instructing the people and guiding His own disciples through the mounting tension of the week. Each evening, Jesus and His disciples had returned to the quiet of the olive grove on the mount to the east of Jerusalem across the Kedron Valley.

Plans to Betray (22:1-6)

The Passover was approaching (1). To the Jews, the Passover week was the highlight of the annual observances in Jerusalem. Although they were commanded to attend three feasts each year (Passover, Pentecost, and Tabernacles), the long distances separating many Hellenistic Jews from Jerusalem made this impossible. But at least they tried to attend one Passover in a lifetime and more if possible. Pilgrims came from Galilee, Perea and other parts of Judea. The city was jammed at these occasions. If trouble was brewing, it usually came to a head when these large crowds gathered for special feasts in Jerusalem. The Romans were apprehensive about this, and the Roman governor frequently came from his usual quarters in Caesarea to Jerusalem for the extent of the special season. He wanted to be on hand if any mob action should be undertaken or if some popular leader should decide to make an unauthorized move. This particular Passover in A.D. 30 had all the marks of danger. The chief priests and teachers of the law had made threats against Jesus in their attempt to stop Him. Jesus had arrived almost a week early for the Passover. The Jewish leaders would like to have arrested Him then, but they were afraid of violent objections from the people. This was doubly dangerous to the leaders. They did not want to pit themselves against the people, and if they did, trouble would result that would bring the Roman authorities into the matter. The Jewish religious leaders were poised ready for action, but waiting for the right chance to move against Jesus.

Then Satan entered Judas (3). One of Jesus' twelve apostles, Judas, brought the offer that started the action. Judas was the one apostle from Judea; all the rest were from Galilee. Luke was careful to help the reader by putting a note beside Judas' name in his listing of the apostles at the outset: "Judas Iscariot, who became a traitor" (Luke 6:16). A popular move today attempts to heroize Judas. After all, he did what he had to do. He was predestined for the role of traitor. Somebody had to fill the part, and Judas carried it through. Some have gone so far as to conjecture that he had Jesus' interest at heart; he thought he could force Jesus to declare himself as Messiah and take a more daring action against Rome. He thought Jesus would use His power to save himself. The record gives no hint of this motive. In fact, John makes clear that Judas was a thief (John 12:6). He had already made choices that led to God's selecting him for the task of betrayal. Satan entered him on more than one occasion (also John 13:27), and he chose to follow his course. God made His selection of Judas upon the basis of His foreknowledge. The source of Judas' action shows no sign of having high motive for service or commitment to Jesus. He went to the priests and accepted the price (Matthew 26:15). Somehow they wanted to arrest Jesus when no crowd was present.

A Supper to Remember (22:7-38)

The day of Unleavened Bread (7). The Feast of Unleavened Bread was used to designate the seven days following the Passover meal when no leaven was allowed in the house (Exodus 12:15-20; 13:3-7). The words could be used to designate the same week and by New Testament times were used interchangeably with Passover. The *Passover* was used to designate (1) a meal begun at twilight on the fourteenth of Nisan (Leviticus 23:4, 5); (2) the lamb prepared for the meal (Deuteronomy 16:2); and (3) the week following the Passover meal (Ezekiel 45:21).

Go and make preparations (8). Jesus sent Peter and John to make arrangements for keeping the Passover that evening. This would include locating the place, going to the temple for the killing of the lamb, purchasing the supplies for the meal, supervising the roasting, and having all things ready when Jesus and the rest of the disciples arrived. Jesus did not tell them where the house was that they would be using for their Passover observance. Rather, they were to follow a man carrying a jar of water, and he would lead them there. Men rarely carried jars of water, only women, so the identification could not be confused. The owner of the house would be expecting them. In this way, Jesus avoided telling any of the disciples where He planned to keep the Passover ahead of time. If anyone at all knew, Judas might find out and pass the word to the Jewish authorities. The time of the Passover meal would be a clever hour to seize Jesus because the crowds would be dispersed to various homes and occupied for the whole evening. But Jesus did not want to be interrupted in His final hours with the disciples, and He did not allow the location to be known to Judas before He arrived there that evening with the rest of the disciples.

Found things just as Jesus had told them (13). Jesus was the true guide. He was leading the disciples through a maze of difficult plots and pressures. The hostile rulers wanted to kill Him, and the impetuous crowds wanted to make him the kind of Messiah they wanted. In the midst of the turmoil, the uncertainties, and the awful apprehension for what the future would hold, Jesus could arrange for an upper room all furnished and ready for an evening alone with His disciples for the institution of a supper to be observed for all posterity. One does not know whether this was done by miracle or by former contact with a dedicated follower. Mary, the mother of John Mark, must have owned a spacious home because the church later met there (Acts 12:12). This may have been the house with guest quarters on the second floor adequate for dining thirteen men. How ever it came about, all things were just as Jesus had told them.

When the hour came (14). The Jews began their days at sundown in the evening. Thus the preparation for the Passover was on the fourteenth of Nisan, and the observance began on that day but extended through the night, perhaps as late as 2 A.M. on the fifteenth of Nisan. Since the fifteenth of Nisan was the day of "Preparation" (the Jews called Friday "Preparation for the Sabbath"), Jesus' crucifixion was on Friday (Mark 15:42). Thus, it was Thursday evening when the disciples were with Jesus to keep the Passover. Some conjecture this as an early observance for the Passover because the next morning, the Jewish leaders did not go into Pilate's judgment hall so they would not defile themselves and be unable to keep the Passover (John 18:28). But this need not mean the Passover meal had not been eaten. The *Passover* is used of the whole seven days, and reference is made here to some observances later in the week.[80] No real obstacle forbids this feast Jesus was observing from being the regular Jewish Passover begun on the fourteenth of Nisan and, on this year, a Thursday evening observance.

I have eagerly desired to eat this Passover (15). The Greek explanation used to describe this feeling of Jesus is striking. He has yearned for this moment to arrive, just before His great suffering was to begin. This was to be His last occasion of fellowship and instruction with His closest friends and companions. He wanted to strengthen them for the ordeals ahead.

Until it finds fulfillment in the kingdom of God (16). In contrast with His previous statement, here Jesus said He would not eat it again until its *fulfillment.* The Passover commemorated deliverance from death and bondage in Egypt. Ultimate redemption from death and the bondage of sin was in the sacrifice of Jesus on the cross of crucifixion. He was our Passover lamb (1 Corinthians 5:7), to be killed on the day following this statement. In the kingdom established in His church, we commune with Him at each observance of the Lord's Supper as we commemorate His death, and finally, our fellowship will be complete in the Messianic banquet in Heaven as well (Revelation 19:9).

After taking the cup (17). Usually, a Passover observance began with a prayer of thanksgiving by the head of the house and then the drinking of the first of four cups of the fruit of the vine. Probably, Luke refers here to the prayer and the first of these cups. The general order of an ordinary Passover Feast next observed the eating of bitter herbs as a remembrance of the bitter slavery in Egypt. Regularly, a young boy then would ask, "Why is this night distinguished from all other nights?" The father's narrative of Israel's exodus from Egypt would follow. After this, the singing of the first part of the Hallel (Psalm 113, 114) would accompany the washing of hands and the drinking of the second cup. After this, the lamb was eaten and the unleavened bread was shared. The continuation of eating the meal followed

---

[80]For example, the special *Chagigah.* See Hendriksen, *New Testament Commentary,* pp. 401ff. It is also possible that the Sadducees were planning to keep the Passover later because they had been engrossed in planning Jesus' arrest when they should have been keeping the Passover (H. Mulder).

until all were satisfied. This was concluded with the third cup. Finally, the singing of the last part of the Hallel (Psalm 115—118) and the fourth cup marked the end.

And he took bread (19). At this point, Luke does not appear to be following the outline of the Passover meal. Matthew and Mark simply report, "While they were eating" (Matthew 26:26; Mark 14:22). Paul, however, describes Jesus as taking the cup "after supper" (1 Corinthians 11:25). Luke probably intended his reference to the first cup as representative of the whole of the Passover meal and its order of observances. At the close of this, Jesus took bread and the cup to institute the Lord's Supper.

The bread that was used in the Passover meal was no doubt broken and passed at this time. It was unleavened bread because of the circumstances of the night the Passover commemorated. They were to prepare and eat the meal in haste (Exodus 12:11). There was no time to wait for the working of yeast. As the feast was commemorated throughout the years, leaven was even removed from the house from the first through the seventh day (Exodus 12:15-20; 13:3-7). The lamb and the unleavened bread were the major elements in the Passover observance. This was commanded as a memorial to Israel's deliverance from bondage in Egypt. Jesus caused the bread to symbolize His own body. Despite His using the words, *"This is my body,"* there was no doubt that He used this in a figurative way because His body was standing there, and the bread was there also—they were distinguishable. Later this very evening, He would be saying, "I am the vine" (John 15:5), but this did not mean He became a vine. Beside the bread's representing the body of Jesus, it represented a particular role that particular body filled. The phrase *given for you* is all important and adds another dimension to the meaning. Some might attempt to limit this to a martyr's death in order to benefit other individuals in some general way. But other information must be taken into account. Both Matthew and Mark use the word "ransom" in the claims of Jesus (Matthew 20:28; Mark 10:45). The Son of Man had come "to give his life as a ransom for many." He was providing the price for buying back souls locked in the guilt of sin. Luke also records the words of Paul to the Ephesian elders (Acts 20:28), "Keep watch over ... the church of God, which he bought with his own blood." The epistle to the Hebrews explains Jesus' words *given for you* (Luke 22:20): "He did not enter by means of the blood of goats and calves; but he entered the Most Holy Place once for all by his own blood, having obtained eternal redemption.... How much more, then, will the blood of Christ, who through the eternal Spirit offered himself unblemished to God, cleanse our consciences from acts that lead to death, so that we may serve the living God!" (Hebrews 9:12-14). Paul sums up the gospel in one brief statement: "that Christ died for our sins according to the Scriptures, that he was buried, that he was raised on the third day according to the Scriptures" (1 Corinthians 15:3, 4). When Jesus said His body was given for you, He meant more than a martyr's death. He meant an offering made for our sins even as it had been prophesied: "The punishment that brought us eace was upon him, and by his wounds we are healed" (Isaiah 53:5).

The Passover was a memorial to the freedom Israel gained from Egypt. It looked forward to the Lamb of God, who takes away the sin of the world (John 1:29). It was fulfilled when "Christ, our Passover lamb [was] sacrificed" (1 Corinthians 5:7). The Lord's Supper is a memorial to freedom from sin and death, a memorial that is offered to all and looks back on its association with the Passover in the past.

Do this in remembrance of me (19). The Western text-type in the Greek omits these words, as well as the next verse. This should not cause as much debate as it has. Some textual scholars, finding the words in 1 Corinthians 11:24, 25, feel that a scribe, familiar with Paul's words in Corinthians, may have written them into the text of Luke. This is highly unlikely. (1) The vast majority of the manuscripts and text families have it. (2) The omission might be explained by a puzzled scribe who, not knowing that the first cup could be part of the Passover observance, tried to reduce the cup-bread-cup arrangement (17-20) to just one cup. But this leaves an unlikely situation. The order would be the cup first and then the bread. This is contrary to most other references (Matthew 26:26, 27; Mark 14:22, 23; 1 Corinthians 11:23-26; but note an exception: 1 Corinthians 10:16). If, however, the first cup is recognized as one of the cups of the Passover observance (which is most likely), then the impossible situation is left with Luke's reporting the passover cup and then the Lord's Supper loaf and no Lord's Supper cup at all. So the passage is best accepted with the last part of verse 19 and verse 20 understood as part of the original writing, and the first cup a Passover observance and the bread and cup, in that order, the Lord's Supper observance.[81]

The new covenant (20). As Moses had confirmed the covenant at Sinai with the sprinkling of blood, so here Jesus announced a new convenant sealed with the shedding of His own blood. The word *covenant* in the Greek can be used in two ways: an agreement between two parties, or a testament (will), a particular type of covenant put into effect at the death of a testator. (See Hebrews 9:15ff.) Both of these can be applied to God's dealing with man. The old covenant (testament) looked forward to the time when it would be replaced by a new covenant (Jeremiah 31:31).

Him who is going to betray me (21). Luke's account of the final week is briefer than the other three Gospel writings. At times, he adds individual details that are not found elsewhere, but he also summarizes much of the time. This is true of his description of Jesus' announcement that one of the Twelve was going to betray Him. Not only is it briefer than the others, the Lord's Supper was instituted after the discussion about the traitor; but in Luke, the Lord's Supper was instituted earlier. Luke does not specify when Judas left the room as John does (John 13:30). This is one of the places where Luke is not chronological but prefers to recount the events in other ways. Most important in this final gathering is the occasion, the Passover, and the instituting of the Lord's Supper. So Luke tells of these immediately. Then he groups the secondary subjects: Judas, the discussion over who will be greatest, and Peter. What Luke says about Judas fits into the description John gives. The announcement must have come while they were still eating the main meal, and Jesus indicated that the one who dipped his hand in the bowl would be the betrayer. If Judas were seated next to Jesus, probably no one would notice this as it happened. It was the custom to dip a portion of bread in the gravy and pass it to the next person.

The disciples deserve credit for not looking around and picking out someone else as a likely candidate for the traitor. Each looked to himself as the only possible weak link (Mark 14:19). No one thought of Judas. Not long after Jesus told Judas he was the one (Matthew 26:25), Judas left. This was before the instituting of the Lord's Supper.

---

[81]See Metzger, *Textual Commentary,* pp. 274ff.

Which of them was considered to be greatest (24). This is another unexpected incident. How could these disciples who loved Jesus and were ready to die with Him be talking about who was greatest at such a time as this? Yet this is true to life. Luke has grouped three disappointments together—Judas, the discussion over who is the greatest, and the prediction of Peter's denials. Perhaps Judas was responsible for the discussion about the greatest. If Judas rushed in when they were being seated and took the place next to Jesus, this may have offended Peter—and others as well. So the seating for the feast may have started the discussion. Then when no one was willing to be the servant and wash the disciples' feet, another problem was faced. Jesus performed the task himself, and there must have been many guilty hearts after that episode (John 13:4ff).

Kings of the Gentiles lord it over them (25). Jesus found it necessary at this emergency hour to return to a basic subject. True, the world loved to exercise authority as prominent figures, but Jesus' followers were taught the opposite. To serve was better than to subjugate. The first will be last and last first (Matthew 20:16, 27; Mark 10:44; Luke 13:30). Those who rank the highest will be those who suffer the most.

Benefactors. This was one of the honorary titles voted to the Hellenistic rulers who supposedly brought assistance to a city or to individuals. More often than not, it was a way to flatter a ruler into bestowing favors.

I confer on you a kingdom (29). For the trials and sacrifices His followers endure, Jesus will grant high positions of responsibility, not simply empty titles. They will be judges over all those included in the kingdom (twelve tribes in a figurative sense).

Simon, Satan has asked to sift you (31). Men of faith and courage draw the attacks of the devil. Jesus wanted to warn the impetuous but lovable Simon. He was ready to die for Jesus, but sometimes Satan puts the trials in such a way that a person does not realize the significance of a word or a deed until it is too late. Jesus wanted to prepare Simon for what was coming, and even it if did not succeed in keeping him from stumbling, this would be an encouragement to get up and try again. Jesus knew more about Simon than Simon knew about himself, but Jesus still wanted to help him, and through him, to help the others: "And when you have turned back, strengthen your brothers" (Luke 22:32).

Purse . . . bag . . . sword (36). These instructions are greatly revised from their former ones for evangelistic campaigns (Luke 9:3; 10:4). On those campaigns, they expected hospitable reception and good treatment along the way. Conditions were going to be different now. They had to have money for supplies and lodging and could not count on homes along the way. They must be ready to protect themselves.

Two swords . . . that is enough (38). That Jesus was saying two swords are enough for the group is unlikely. Not long after this, He reprimanded Peter for using the one he had. *Enough* in this context indicates that Jesus was not pressing the subject further. They simply did not understand.

The Faithful Son

The question that closed the debates in the temple area was asked by Jesus, "Why did David call his son, Lord?" (Luke 20:44). The answer the Pharisees would not give, and that Jesus wanted to emphasize, is clear—because the Son of David, the Messiah, was to be the Son of God. By what authority did Jesus come? His authority was from Heaven, not from men (Luke 20:2ff). This was the opening question from the priests and lawyers. The answer is basic to the teaching and action of Jesus as He led men through the closing hours before His death.

Jesus did not come to His death because of the plots of man or the power of suggested measures from over-zealous friends. He was in complete control to the end and only accepted those moves that carried Him toward the goal He had before Him and at the timetable the Father had allowed (Acts 1:7).

Jesus wanted to impress this upon His disciples. He did not spend these closing precious moments discoursing with his companions on the subject of rest at the end of labors or the blessed advantages in the world to come. He warned them of coming trials. "Do not be discouraged when Jerusalem is destroyed." "Do not be misled by false prophets and false teaching." The very fact that He foresaw these events removed the fears that they lay beyond the control of God. Rather, it was a part of judgment for the rejection of the Son. God would provide help for His followers in the face of trials and persecution. He would provide escape from the scene of carnage at Jerusalem. But they were not to confuse this with the ultimate coming of the Son of

Man. This will come suddenly without further possibility of preparation. The faithful followers will rejoice, but the unprepared will be sealed in their condemnation.

All along, Jesus had been looking forward to the Last Supper alone with the Twelve. This would mark the beginning of the end. On the morrow would be the moment of truth on the cross. Judas had to be shown that his role was known to Jesus. Peter must be forewarned of his weakness that would help his strength to win out in the end. Encouragement must be given to all, and lessons of service, humility, and trust. A memorial needed to be established even before the giving of His body and the shedding of His blood. It was a living memorial to endure to all posterity, not growing old as any material monument must. The fact that it was given beforehand is one more mark of assurance that God was in control and that the Son would be faithful to carry out His mission. No one could take away Jesus' life except that He voluntarily gave it up (John 10:18). "This command I received from my Father."

The applications of these last days to our own lives are numerous and priceless. Walk with Jesus in the temple area. You are there. Hear Him speak of the widow's gift to God and look at yourself. Do not dismiss the teaching about the destruction of Jerusalem just because it has already occurred long ago. You stand somewhere between that time and the coming of the Son of Man; but the lessons from both apply. You must beware of discouragement and false teachings. You must recognize that in trials and temptations, God still provides ways of escape (1 Corinthians 10:13). "He will not let you be tempted beyond what you can bear." Do not delay preparing your life to meet Jesus, on His terms. Be ready, because when He comes, it will be too late to try to make changes. It will be sudden. The lessons in the upper room flood upon you. In the matter of betrayal, you ask with the rest, "Is it I, Lord?" To the command, "This do in remembrance of me," are you faithful? Have you become mechanical rather than mindful? Can you sit through the scene in the upper room without remembering Zacchaeus earlier and wanting to stand up with him to make some special promises?

For Jesus, one thing remained before the trials and crucifixion. He had experienced these moments alone with the disciples, but now He craved some moments alone with His Father in Gethsemane.

JERUSALEM

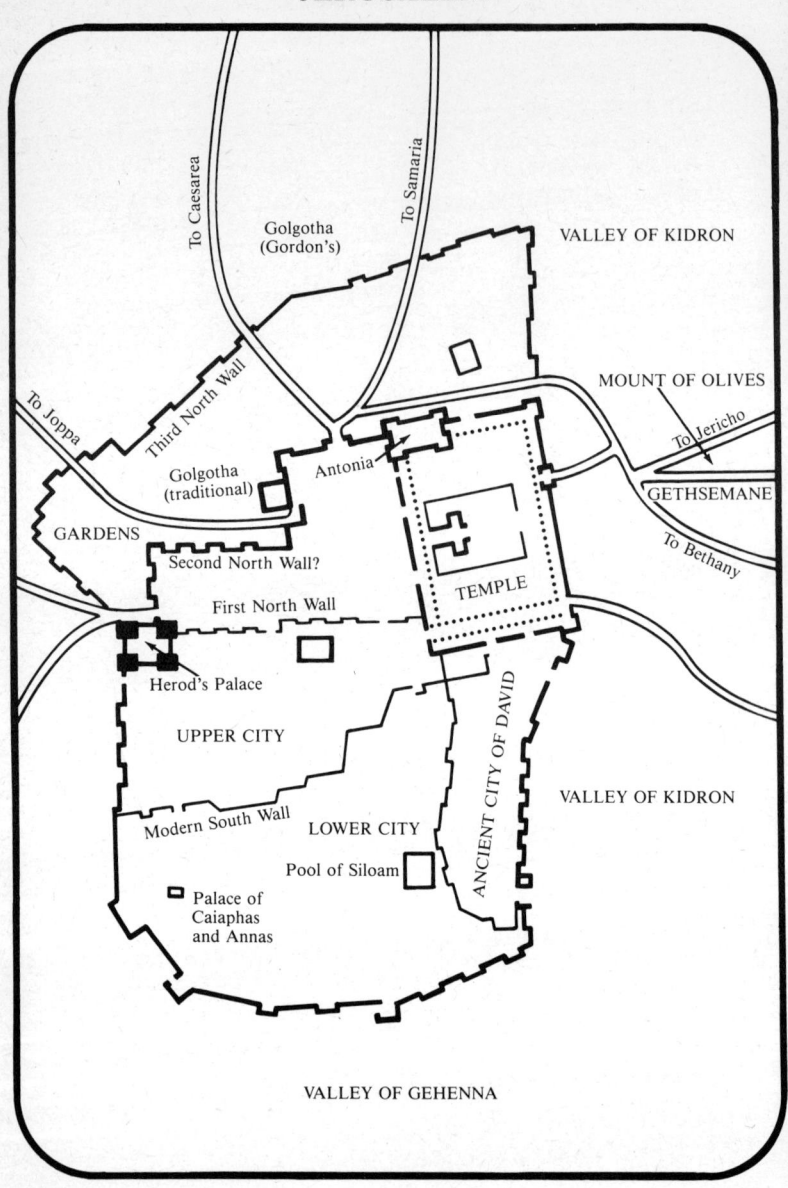

CHAPTER TWELVE

Trials and Crucifixion
Luke 22:39—23:56

"Was it hard for Jesus to do right?"
"Did He really feel temptation to do wrong?"
"Was He so strong that everything came easy for Him?"
These were questions a little boy put to his father. The sage father stopped the writing he was doing in his study, and told the boy to sit down on the floor. He emptied a shelf of books, lined them up on the floor, and sat down on the floor beside his son. He stood two large books upright on the floor. They were facing one another, with a little space between them. Next, he started laying books one on top of the other with the two standing books supporting them underneath. He told his son that the two upright books represented a person who was being tempted and the books piled on top were the temptations. When the pile had reached six books, the bottom books toppled over. Then father and son tried it again, being more careful this time, and reached the number nine before it gave way underneath. The father explained that some people were better than others. Some resisted temptation more, and the load was heavier before they yielded and fell. The father told the boy, "Now imagine a time when an individual was tempted, but He never gave in to temptation, not once. You could go on piling the books up to the sky, but He never gave way." Then the father asked the boy, "Who would have carried the heaviest pressure—those who gave in, whether sooner or later, or the one who never gave in?" Of course, the answer was the one who withstood all temptation. "This was Jesus," the father explained. "He was tempted the way we are, but without sin." Still the weight became tremendous in resisting all temptation.

The father continued by pointing out one way Jesus was not like us—He had never sinned and did not know the feeling of having sinned or the temptation that comes from former sin. But there was one time in His life—at His crucifixion—when He took everybody else's sin for himself. Then the father asked his little boy which person would feel the guilt and weight of sin more, the one who sinned along the way and had grown accustomed to its presence, or the one of sensitive nature who had never known sin in His own life before. "Oh," the little boy answered, "it would be harder on the one who had never sinned before." The father went on to point out that Jesus carried the weight of temptations beyond anything that we know because He never came to a yielding point; and He carried the weight of the sin of all mankind before and after when He died on the cross. "This was not easy."

The little boy gasped, "How could He ever do it?"

The father replied simply, "Being God, He could carry the load; but being man, He felt the full extent of its weight."

Why Did He Have to Die?

The reasons for Jesus' death and the charges of His trials are related, but they are not the same. The very fact that He had so many trials and in such a short time raises suspicion that additional reasons were present beneath the surface of the charges. Luke gives an abbreviated report of the trials, as he does for all of the happenings of the final week. So to consider an overview of all four Gospel narratives regarding the trials and charges would be helpful to an understanding of Luke's report.

Jesus' arrest took place in Gethsemane, on the western slope of the Mount of Olives. From there, He was taken to the palace of Caiaphas where probably at least two trials took place. One was before Annas, high priest from A.D. 6 to 15. (After he was deposed by the Roman Gratus, one after another of Annas' sons gained the official sanction of Rome for the high priesthood, but Annas still retained considerable control. Among the Jews, he was still respected as their choice.) Caiaphas, Annas' son-in-law, and one of those from his family circle who held Roman-approved high priesthood, was in power in A.D. 18-36. So after Jesus was brought before Annas (John 18:12-14, 19-23), He was taken to the court of Caiaphas. This was probably in the same building. Peter in the courtyard may have seen them taking Jesus from one court chamber to another.

After the trial before Caiaphas (Matthew 26:57ff; Mark 14:53ff; Luke 22:54ff; John 18:24), a trial before the Sanhedrin was necessary (Matthew 27:1; Mark 15:1; Luke 22:66ff). No conviction calling for the death penalty could be acted upon without a trial before this highest council of the Jews. Actually, it was only a type of official stamp put on the decisions coming from Annas and Caiaphas. This trial must be held in daylight hours, a measure trying to avoid just what was being done in Jesus' case. They wanted to hurry a death sentence through before others knew about it and could raise objection. This trial was held at the first vestige of daylight—if they even waited that long for its convening. The regular hours would be from the time of the morning sacrifice to the evening sacrifice. Another possible irregularity in the Sanhedrin trial of Jesus was the place of meeting. The usual location was in the temple precincts,[82] but Jesus seems to have been conveniently tried in the palace of the high priest, where the other two trials before the Jews had been held.

Jesus was next taken to Pilate. The Jews were under Roman rule, and no execution could take place without a Roman decision in the matter. To gain this stamp of approval, the Jewish leaders got Pilate out of bed and insisted on an early trial on the pavement in front of the Roman quarters at the Tower of Antonia, the Roman Praetorium in Jerusalem. When Pilate learned that Jesus was from Galilee, he saw a possible escape from rendering a guilty verdict on a man he considered innocent. Herod Antipas was in Jerusalem because of the Jewish Passover, also. So Pilate sent Jesus and His case to Herod for a decision because Herod had jurisdiction as a Roman appointed ruler in the area of Galilee (Luke 23:6, 7).

Herod was unable to draw any response to his questions to Jesus. After more beatings and insults were poured on Jesus, He was sent back to Pilate (Luke 23:8-12).

Finally, Pilate gave in to the demand of the Jewish leaders and Jesus was led away for crucifixion. This was a matter of six different trials Jesus submitted to in the hours between two and six in the morning. The agony and distress mounted in those

---

[82]According to Mishna (Mid. 5:4), in the "chamber of hewn stone."

hours just before the cross. One must take this into account when he attempts to understand the condition Jesus was in as the final suffering on the cross began.

Charges

Each trial emphasized different charges, but they all narrowed down to the specific accusation of blasphemy.

Blasphemy. To the Jew, blasphemy was the gravest of sins and worthy of death. Either an attack upon God (disrespect toward Him, or an insult to Him) or, on the other hand, a claim to have prerogatives that belong to God alone (for instance, the forgiving of sins) might be declared blasphemous. They accused Jesus of blasphemy both against the temple and against God.

Perverting the People. The Jews recognized that the charge of blasphemy was not that serious as far as the Romans were concerned—so long as the god blasphemed was not Roman. What did concern the Roman authorities was anything that might disturb the peaceful flow of business and contentment among the people. Any figure who attracted a large gathering of the populace was considered a potential danger. Especially was this true if He questioned the authority of Rome or incited people to action contrary to Roman policy. On the other hand, the Jewish leaders were just as jealous of any move that did not have their approval, but was gathering great crowds and teaching contrary to the current traditions. To them, this was perverting the people, and at the same time, it was a note of unrest to the Romans.

Claiming to be king. Since the Messiah was to come as the Son of David and establish a kingdom, any claim to Messiahship would be a claim to be king. The term *king* was more meaningful to the Roman authorities; so it was used at this point to emphasize Jesus' association with the ambition to establish himself as king. This meant one thing to the Jew and something else to the Roman. Jesus convinced Pilate that His kingdom was "not of this world," and was not to be set up with fighting legions of military soldiers.

Presenting himself as the Son of God. This point was of great concern to Pilate. He was not so much worried about the welfare of Rome in this charge as to the possibility that Jesus really was the Son of God. The prospect of rendering a charge of guilty upon one who might be divine was not at all appealing to Pilate.

A threat to Rome. When the charge that Jesus claimed to have

God as His Father failed to bring conviction, then the Jewish authorities used the severest pressure they could to gain the decision they were determined to get. Jesus was a threat to Rome because He was setting up a kingdom and the people were following Him. What was new about this charge was that the Jews threatened to send a delegation to Rome and accuse Pilate of supporting a move against Rome by not convicting Jesus. Pilate could not bear to think of a Jewish appeal in Rome against him, and he gave in. He let the Jewish hierarchy have its way, and Jesus was crucified.

Reasons for Jesus' Death

Beside the charges brought against Jesus in court, deep-rooted factors must be realized to understand what was happening when Jesus died.

The religious leaders demanded it. Throughout the Gospel of Luke, one sees the running battle that transpired between Jesus and the Pharisees, the teachers of the law, the elders, and the Sadducees. They were unmasked, they were losing face in the estimate of the people, their control and revenue were threatened in the temple, their traditions were being challenged. They felt they must stop Jesus, and the only way was to kill Him.

The Roman authorities preferred it. The Roman Pilate did not want anything to disturb the *status quo* while he was trying to maintain law and order in the province. Any cause that involved a stir among the people was suspect. If it was a matter of choice, Rome preferred that the leader of any eventual threat to Rome be removed. Execution was preferable to trouble later on.

The people allowed it. Different sentiments were represented among the people. The people who were supported by the wealth of the priestly leaders stood dutifully by and cried, "Crucify Him." Most of the people had slept late that fateful morning because they had kept the Passover the night before, and some observances may have continued until 2 A.M. They had been in their homes when at midmorning the word began to circulate. Jesus was already carrying His cross to Golgotha. Those favorable to Jesus were stunned. They did not know what to do. It was reported that Peter had drawn a sword when Jesus was arrested; but Jesus reprimanded him for doing it. What could one do? Jesus' friends fled. They were like sheep without a shepherd. Those who had shouted God's praises at the coming of the Messiah in the beginning of the week were silent. They had hoped Jesus would redeem Israel, but now He was going to die. They simply let Him.

Satan supported it. The most important battles of all are not a matter of historical record because they were not observed by human eye. But a note or two assures us that Satan was busy participating in the course of events. Judas made his choice to go Satan's road, and Satan used him as the traitor. Satan was delighted to see Jesus' seeming defeat in death. This was Satan's highest achievement, he thought, the crucifixion of God's Son.

God ordained it. The reason Jesus died ends ultimately in the mind of God. He knew there was no other way to redeem mankind. As sin had come through one and death passed to all, now through one, God's own Son, life would return (Romans 5:12-21; 1 Corinthians 15:21, 22). Jesus came for the very purpose of giving His life a ransom for many (Mark 10:45). God was in control all the while. This does not lessen the sin of those who chose an evil role in the fulfillment of God's plan, but this is the reason one can speak of "Good" Friday in the midst of pain and tragedy. Satan did not realize that he was not gaining his way; he was being used to fulfill God's purpose. The religious leaders, the Romans, and Judas simply chose their roles in the working of God's plan. No one is to do evil that good may come (Romans 3:8); but God is able to turn even evil to support a good result. Why did Jesus have to die? Because God loves the sinner, you and me, enough that He sent His own Son to die in our stead. So in a sense, we have had our hand in the evil that was done the day Jesus died; but by the grace of God, we can receive of the good that was accomplished.

Content Notes

Jesus in Prayer (22:39-46)

Mount of Olives (39). Jesus had stayed some of the time in Bethany with Lazarus, Mary, and Martha during His trips to Jerusalem (Luke 10:38, 39). It was ordinary for pilgrims coming to a religious festival to look up some friends who lived in or around Jerusalem and share lodging with them. Luke, however, points out that Jesus had been staying overnight on the Mt. of Olives after each day of teaching in the temple area (Luke 21:37). Here He could find quiet, away from the people, and the distance was not far. John tells the place was a grove across the brook Kedron (John 18:1). Matthew (26:36) and Mark (14:32) specify the place as Gethsemane ("oil press").

Pray that you will not fall into temptation (40). From the Matthean account, Jesus left eight of the disciples—probably at the gate—and gave them instructions to pray. He was concerned about their trials after He was gone. Then Jesus took three disciples with him (Peter, James, and John; Matthew 26:37). They, too, were told to pray—"keep watch" (Matthew 26:38)—while Jesus withdrew alone. Luke alone adds that Jesus went a "stone's throw" still farther (Luke 22:41). He wanted to be alone with His Father to give vent to His feelings. The three were closest to Him on other occasions that Luke notes (the Mount of Transfiguration, 9:28, and the raising of Jairus' daughter, 8:51).

Knelt down and prayed (41). The more usual posture for prayer was standing (Luke 18:11; Matthew 6:5; Mark 11:25; 1 Samuel 1:26). In times of special humiliation, kneeling is noted (1 Kings 8:54; Ezra 9:5; Daniel 6:10; Acts 7:60; 9:40; 20:36; 21:5; Ephesians 3:14). On this occasion, Matthew and Mark describe Jesus as He "fell with his face to the ground"; "fell to the ground" (Matthew 26:39; Mark 14:35).

Take this cup from me (42). All the Synoptic Gospels preserve this prayer of Jesus (Matthew 26:39; Mark 14:36; Luke 22:42). He must have said many things to God in these moments, but Luke, who abbreviates the most, still includes this request for the cup to be removed. The "cup" can be used as a figure of joy (Psalm 23:5) or a note of sorrow and suffering (Matthew 20:22; John 18:11). Here it must indicate the depths of agony.

If you are willing. From these words emerge three truths. (1) God's will held first place in every consideration Jesus made. (2) Jesus' sufferings and temptations were real or He would not have been looking for an alternative to the way events were going. (3) There must have been no other way or God would not have allowed His Son to die as He did.

An angel . . . strengthened him (43). An angel had appeared at the close of Jesus' fasting and temptations (Matthew 4:11; Mark 1:13), but Luke does not include the note. Here, the presence of the angel is told by Luke but not by the other Gospel writers.

Drops of blood (44). Either Jesus' sweat was in large drops of perspiration, like blood, or He actually sweat the drops of blood (hematidrosis) because of the anguish.

Exhausted from sorrow (45). The disciples were asleep when Jesus came to alert them to the approaching enemy. The disciples were going to face trials of their own. But note that Jesus had suffered immeasurably more than His followers, and He, too, must have been exhausted even before the court trials began.

When Darkness Had Its Way (22:47-62)

Jesus Under Arrest (47-53)

A crowd came up (47). This word *crowd* denotes a rather disorganized mob, and from its different elements, it would have numbered at least two hundred people. The temple soldiers would include the captain and officers of the temple guard (Luke 22:52). The chief priests and elders would include leaders of the priestly class and the Sanhedrin. Pharisees were there, too (John 18:3). At least a detachment of a Roman cohort was present (John 18:3); but from the weapons named, "swords and clubs" (Luke 22:52), civilians had also come prepared for trouble. Since four hundred soldiers (beside seventy horsemen) were used to start Paul from Jerusalem to Caesarea by night (Acts 23:23), this may be some indication of the need for numbers in crucial situations. The Jewish leaders knew this was an unpredictable, hazardous undertaking. They had tried to arrest Jesus before and had failed (John 7:32-46).

Judas. . . . approached Jesus to kiss him (47). In all probability, Jesus had already identified himself (John 18:4, 5), and the prearranged signal to be given by Judas was no longer needed. But Judas, determined to carry through his part of the bargain, proceeded to kiss Jesus anyway (Matthew 26:49). This is another indication that Judas was not bent on doing Jesus a helpful favor by forcing Him to assert himself, but rather by deceitful display of affection, he made a mockery of his former role of comrade.

One of them struck the servant of the high priest (50). Of the canonical Gospels, not until John is the name of Peter given to identify the one who cut off Malchus' ear (John 18:10). Luke the physician, alone of the Gospel writers, tells of Jesus' restoring the ear to its former condition (Luke 22:51). Jesus' rebuke reflects His refusal to resort to force to spare His life. He was voluntarily giving it up (John 10:18). This cannot be used, however, as an argument against law and order and the necessity of defending it with the sword (cf. Romans 13:4).

This is your hour (53). Jesus recognized this as the climactic period when the force of evil would reach its height. Darkness reigned. Wrong-doing prefers the darkness (John 3:20), ignorance lives in darkness and cannot comprehend the light (John 1:5), and the lost will be thrown into darkness (Matthew 8:12).

Peter in Despair (54-62)
Peter followed Jesus and even had the courage to enter the very courtyard of the high priest and to stand alongside the enemies of Jesus—just to see what was happening. He did not anticipate, however, how difficult it would be to confess Jesus when all odds were against him. Peter denied he knew Jesus, first to the maid servant, then to a man, and finally to another man just as the cock crowed. His courage had drained away, and now remorse took over. He went out and wept.

One Trial After Another (22:63—23:25)
Jewish Trials (63-71)
Mocking and beating (63). Luke gives the account of Jesus' death in careful blocks of material. Peter had denied Jesus during the trial time, but Luke tells about the incident in a section by itself (Luke 22:54-62). Then Luke gives only a summation of Jesus' trials before the Jews. He does not record how Jesus was first taken to Annas (John 18:12ff), then Caiaphas (Matthew 26:57ff). Finally, at the earliest break of day, the automatic stamp of approval for Jesus' conviction was given by the Sanhedrin (Matthew 27:1). But Luke in summary tells only of the ill-treatment from the guards (Luke 23:63-65) and the accusations at the Sanhedrin Council (Luke 23:66-71).

If you are the Christ . . . tell us (67). The Jewish leaders wanted to condemn Jesus upon His own direct affirmation that He was the Messiah (the Christ). But Jesus refused to conform to their preconceived pattern of establishing guilt. They did not want a basis for beliefs, they wanted grounds for the death sentence. Instead of giving the answer they wanted, Jesus reproved them for their unbelief and added a still higher claim than they gave to the Messiah whom they were looking for. Jesus claimed He would soon have God's approval and the highest of authority as He would be seated on the right hand of God.

Are you then the Son of God? (70). Jesus was claiming to be not only the Messiah on the throne of David, but the Son on the throne of God. So Jesus' antagonists asked for a still more daring admission: was He claiming to be divine?

You are right in saying I am. This reply to their question was an idiomatic expression of an emphatic affirmative. It was used on several occasions during the trials (Matthew 26:64; John 18:37). We can be sure the phrase was used as an affirmative because a parallel passage in Mark uses the phrase "I am" (Mark 14:62), and the reaction of the Jews shows that Jesus was making an affirmation they regarded as a claim to divinity (Matthew 26:65; Luke 22:71). If He had not been the Son of God, if He had not been divine, the claim would have been blasphemy. If His claim is true, receive Him; do not crucify Him.

Roman Trials (23:1-25)

The whole assembly rose and led him off to Pilate (1). Here Luke begins his description of the Roman phase of Jesus' trials. The Jewish leaders had initiated the procedures to bring about Jesus' death, and they kept pressing to the very end to make sure their determined plans were carried out. The Romans were a necessary part of the plan because permission had to be gained from the ruling power in Palestine.

The Romans must bear a part of the responsibility for Jesus' death for agreeing to the sentence of death for an innocent man and for accepting the role of executioner. But all of mankind shares the responsibility for His death because it was our need for redemption that called for the incarnation, and it was the individual sin of all of us that causes each to have a shameful hand in the suffering and death of God's Son on the cross. The details from the trials do not treat the whole of the proceedings as much as the difficulties that were experienced in order to convict an innocent man.

We have found this man subverting our nation (2). The charges brought against Jesus before Pilate were put in different words than those presented in the Jewish trials. Rome was always cautious about allowing revolutionary forces to gather within her borders. So the Jewish leaders tried to accuse Jesus of being a revolutionary. He was not.

He opposes payment of taxes to Caesar. This, too, was not true. (See Matthew 22:15-22.)

And claims to be Christ, a king. The Messiah would be king, the son of David. The term *king* was particularly repulsive to Roman ears because of painful experiences with Etruscan monarchs centuries before. In addition to this, they were always apprehensive that the rise of some local king would become a threat to the power of Rome. Although the term *Christ,* or *Messiah,* would not be understood in Roman society, when the Messianic title *king* was used, extreme attention would be given by the Romans. On this score, truly Jesus was the Messiah, King, but He was not the kind of king that was a threat to the government of Rome. Pilate realized this and maintained that Jesus was innocent. Luke notes Pilate's affirmation of Jesus' innocence throughout the trials (Luke 23:4, 14-16, 20, 22).

He started in Galilee (5). The report to Pilate that Jesus had started His activity in Galilee introduced the thought about a trial before Herod. After all, Herod Antipas (see Luke 3:1, 19, 20; 9:7-9) was also in Jerusalem for the Passover. Pilate saw a way of escape from convicting Jesus by sending Him to the Roman representative of rule in Galilee, a member of the Herodian family. Since Jesus was a Galilean, Pilate would let the Galilean ruler decide His fate.

He plied him with many questions, but Jesus gave him no answer (9). Herod had long wanted to see Jesus (Luke 23:8), and here was his chance. Jesus must have been taken through the streets at this early morning hour, perhaps 4-5 A.M., to Herod's Jerusalem palace near the eastern gate of the city. However, Jesus would not reply to their charges. They put an old royal robe on Him and made fun of Him in a cruel and taunting way. When He would give no answer to their ridicule, they sent Him back to Pilate on the western side of the city.

That day Herod and Pilate became friends (12). Until this occasion, these two had been adjoining rulers, one in Galilee, the other in Judea and Samaria, but in their jealous apprehension of one another, they had kept their distance. Now they were brought together by their common fear of the growing threat from the power of Jesus.

Pilate called together the chief priests, the rulers and the people (13). Again Pilate maintained that Jesus did not deserve death. He would nevertheless have Him beaten and then released.

Release Barabbas to us! (18). The crowd, pressing in on the outdoor trial of Jesus, insisted that Jesus should not be released.

Rather they accepted the alternative of Barabbas. The Gospel of John makes clear that Pilate had made the suggestion of Jesus' release upon the basis of a Passover custom to release one prisoner on the occasion (John 18:39). The Gospel of Matthew also indicates that he made this offer, giving the crowd the choice between Jesus and Barabbas (Matthew 27:17). No doubt Pilate assumed they would not want to see this rabble-rouser, a murderer and a highway robber (Luke 23:19), free to roam the streets, a menace to all. Modern attempts to picture Barabbas as a freedom-loving demonstrator against the oppression of Rome is not justified by the details given in the Gospel accounts. Pilate seemed to have chosen this alternative in the hopes they would be forced to pick Jesus, who was such a contrast to the despicable character, Barabbas. But the crowd, no doubt following the signals of the chief priests and leaders, chose Barabbas and insisted on the death of Jesus.

Crucify him! (21). For the third time, Pilate tried to satisfy the rhythmic chant demanding crucifixion by promising to beat Jesus and then release Him. In fact, other Gospel writers indicate he did have Jesus scourged before the sentence was given and brought Him out in His brutally beaten condition (John 19:1-4) in hopes that the people would soften their demands. But still they wanted crucifixion. Finally, since all else was of no avail, Pilate yielded to the demands and started the procedures for crucifixion.

Jesus on the Cross (23:26-49)

As they led him away, they seized Simon from Cyrene (26). Jesus was crucified outside the city (Hebrew 13:12), and as He started for Golgotha, He was carrying His own cross (John 19:17). Since Matthew records that Jesus was going out (Matthew 27:32) and Luke describes Simon as coming in from the country, it may have been at the gate where they laid Jesus' cross on the shoulders of Simon. This may not have been the whole cross, but the crossbar of the cross. Cyrene is the country in North Africa, west of Egypt and east of Libya. This was the place Simon had originally come from, not necessarily meaning an arrival from such an extended trip. Just now he was simply coming from "the country" (Luke 23:26). Mark adds that he was the father of Alexander and Rufus (Mark 15:21). Since it was customary to designate an individual by his father and not by his sons, these sons must have been known to the generation of the original writing of Mark's Gospel.

Women who mourned and wailed for him (27). Luke alone notes the presence of women along the road to Golgotha and the words of Jesus to them. He warned that future suffering was in the offing. It was going to be so terrible that the women would be fortunate not to have more children to experience the trials. This has reference to the days of the destruction of Jerusalem forty years from Jesus' time.

When the tree is green (31). This part of the proverb refers to the green trees, difficult to burn, and the dry, which allow the fire to spread instantaneously. Jesus referred to His own time, when the fire had been kindled with difficulty, but later, the flames would destroy in a devastating sweep.[83]

Two other men, both criminals (32). As though death by crucifixion were not shameful enough in itself, the execution included two robbers. This enabled those pressing for Jesus' death to insist that birds of a feather flock together. By association, Jesus' death involved common criminals.

The place called the Skull (33). Golgotha is the Aramaic, Hebrew-related word for skull, and *Calvary* is the Latin-related word. The designation may have reference to the shape of the hill or to an association with death and skeletal remains in the vicinity.

And they divided up his clothes by casting lots (34). The clothes of the executed were commonly divided among the executioners, but casting of lots was not normal. The fact that Jesus' essential garment was without seam introduced the lots to avoid tearing the seamless garment (cf. John 19:23ff). Unwittingly, the soldiers were fulfilling Old Testament prophecy (Psalm 22:18).

About the sixth hour ... darkness ... until the ninth hour (44). By the Jewish designation of time, this would be from 12 noon until 3 P.M. The Roman designation of time is included when John writes for the people of Ephesus toward the end of the first century. Thus, in John, the sixth hour describes the time

---

[83] See Joseph A. Fitzmeyer, *The Gospel According to Luke, X-XXIV* (New York: Doubleday, 1985), pp. 1498ff for a list of interpretations.

when Pilate's trial drew to a close, 6 A.M. (John 19:14).[84] Then Mark 15:25 tells the time of Jesus' crucifixion—the third hour—which must be Jewish time and indicates 9 A.M. To sum up the passage of time: the trials were completed about 6 A.M.; the crosses were in place by 9 A.M. At 12 noon, darkness began and extended to 3 P.M.

The curtain of the temple was torn in two (45). The sanctity of the temple was strictly observed. One of the basic principles establishing the divine presence in the Holy of Holies was its separation from the Holy Place by a veil or "curtain." Only the High Priest could enter and only once a year. No one was to set eyes on the Holy of Holies except the High Priest and on one solemn occasion a year, the Day of Atonement. By the rending of the veil—from top to bottom (Matthew 27:51), as one might expect if the power to rend came from above—the Holy of Holies was laid open to other human eyes. This may be symbolic of Christ's opening the way directly to God for all believers (Hebrews 9:3, 8; 10:19ff). This may be a dramatic way to demonstrate how the law was nailed to the cross and rules of the Old Covenant were no longer binding (Colossians 2:14). Likewise, it may visually portray the removal of the wall of partition separating the Jews and the Gentiles, as explained by Paul to the Ephesians (2:14-18). Although Luke does not record further marvels occurring at this time, Matthew includes earthquakes, tombs broken open, and bodies leaving the tombs. These resurrected bodies were not seen until after the resurrection of Jesus, however (Matthew 27:51ff).

He breathed his last (46). After He committed His spirit to God, Jesus died. This must have been about 3 P.M.

Surely this was a righteous man (47). The centurions who have individual roles in the New Testament invariably have something good reported about them. The centurion directing the crucifixion of Jesus is no exception. After he saw the way Jesus died, he reached his own conclusion. He praised God and gave a confession that Jesus was the "the Son of God" (Matthew 27:54; Mark 15:39), "a righteous man" (Luke 23:47). Some are disturbed by the difference in the wording. The difference, however, may not

---

[84]B. F. Westcott, *The Gospel According to St. John* (London: J. Murray, 1882), pp. 281-283.

be as great as one might see at first glance. Luke had special interests. The number of times he records that Jesus was innocent shows an interest in establishing that fact. When he said that Jesus was "right," he was saying that Jesus was innocent. It may also be true that the pagan Roman soldier would have difficulty in speaking of *the* son of God when he believed in many gods. But one must remember that the centurion had been there in front of the cross all day. He had heard the charges and the ridicule. He had drawn the conclusion that Jesus was precisely what He claimed to be. Furthermore, he may have known much of what Jesus had been teaching and what the Jewish people had been hearing. Luke reports what the meaning of the centurion's remark would be.

Including the women who had followed him from Galilee (49). Although the darkness must have frightened away a number of those witnessing the crucifixion of Jesus, some friends were still watching from afar. Luke mentions particularly a band of women who had come from Galilee. Mary the mother of Jesus, Mary Magdalene, Mary the mother of James and Joses, and the mother of the sons of Zebedee were all there (Matthew 27:56; Mark 15:40; John 19:25). Salome was probably the sister of Jesus' mother. This would make James and John the cousins of Jesus, and explain some of the words and actions in His ministry. (See also Luke 8:2, 3.)

The Burial of Jesus (50-56)

Joseph, a member of the council. . . . from the Judean town of Arimathea (50, 51). This site has been identified with Ramathaim-zophim, ten miles northeast of Lydda and ten miles southeast of Antipatris. Joseph was a member of the Sanhedrin but did not agree with their attack on Jesus. He must have been a man of considerable means because he had a rock-hewn tomb and it was but recently constructed, since it had not been used. When they made a tomb like this in antiquity, they would construct it for the whole family; thus we understand the note—"in which no one had yet been laid."

Joseph was a daring man. He went to Pilate and asked for Jesus' body. Ordinarily, a criminal who had been crucified was taken from the cross and left alongside the road or deposited in a pauper's field. Sometimes, however, a loved one would come to request the body that a decent burial might be given. More often than not, in the case of hardened criminals, only a mother would be the one to ask for the body. This note might suggest the total collapse of Mary and the necessity of John's care. Jesus had made the explicit commitment to John because He knew of the particular need that was rising. Mary the mother of Jesus was not named among those who saw where He was buried nor among those who came to complete the burial on the first day of the week.

Pilate was not expected to grant permission for burial in every case of crucifixion. In fact, if treason or a peril to the state was involved, the ruler did not have the right to assign the body to anyone. With this limitation, Pilate's allowing Joseph to take the body was extraordinary because the charge of Jesus' being a king could be interpreted as a peril to the state. The Jews, no doubt, were caught in an unexpected development when they heard that Pilate had already allowed Joseph to have the body. Since Joseph was a member of the Sanhedrin, Pilate might claim his credentials were good. Probably Pilate gave the body to Joseph as an act to even up for all the times the Jewish authorities had forced him to make decisions he did not want to make.

Wrapped it in linen cloth (53). Joseph removed the body from the cross, wrapped it in burial cloth[85] and placed it in a tomb excavated out of the native rock in the side of a hill. The burial procedure was begun but not completed. Nicodemus had been able to obtain about seventy-five pounds of myrrh and aloes (John 19:39), and Joseph had purchased some linen cloth to wrap around the body. The tomb must have been rather close to the place of execution (John 19:42) because no more than three hours (3 P.M. to 6 P.M., or sundown, when the sabbath day would begin) were allowed for the trip to the tomb, positioning the body, washing the wounds and the whole of the body, the application and distribution of the myrrh and aloes on the body and in the wrapping of the linen. Before the men, Joseph and Nicodemus, left, they rolled a big stone across the entrance to keep out animals or intruders. Some of the women (Mary Magdalene and Mary, the mother of Joses) sat watching across from the tomb (Matthew 27:61; Mark 15:47; Luke 23:55), so they

---

[85]Some believe the shroud of Turin is this cloth. See the Excursus after this chapter.

would know where to return when the Sabbath was over, and they could continue the work for final burial.

The Sayings of Jesus on the Cross

No one Gospel has all of the recorded sayings of Jesus given from the cross. In fact, only one saying is given in more than one Gospel: "My God, my God, why have you forsaken me?" but this does not appear in Luke. One must resort to listing what is most likely in an attempt to put the sayings in their chronological order.

	Matthew	Mark	Luke	John
1. Father, forgive them....			23:34	
2. Today you will be with me....			23:43	
3. Dear woman, here is your son....				19:26
4. I am thirsty.				19:28
5. My God, my God....	27:46	15:34		
6. It is finished.				19:30
7. Father, into your hands....			23:46	

Jesus' first thought, in the early moments on the cross before pain and the weight of sin had taken their toll upon His senses, was a plea on behalf of those who were responsible for His death. This is the ultimate in love and concern. How could He think of forgiveness to them in a time like this? "For they do not know what they are doing." A continued and deliberate ignorance does not make a sin excusable, nor does forgiveness come without repentance; so Jesus' prayer does not assure the results following His request. Nevertheless, Jesus shows His loving, forgiving spirit, and He becomes an example to all who hear His voice. (See Stephen's words, Acts 7:60.)

Jesus' promise to the thief (Luke 23:43) must have come early also while they were still able to talk back and forth. Some have been disturbed that, in the Gospel of Matthew, one learns that the robbers as well as the chief priests, the elders, the people, and the soldiers mocked Jesus and heaped insults on Him (Matthew 27:44). Does this contradict the picture given in

Luke, when the one thief rebukes the other for hurling insults at Jesus? Not necessarily. The thieves, both of them, followed the example of Jesus' enemies when they taunted Jesus: "Let him save himself." The thieves, however, had a deeper motive—if Jesus came down from the cross and saved himself, He would make the miracle still greater if He would save the thieves along with himself (Luke 23:39). But one of the thieves could not bear the unfairness of the taunts and came to Jesus' defense. Then he gave his own request to be remembered when Jesus came into His kingdom. Jesus' reply was not a promise for the distant future: "Today you will be with me in paradise." *Paradise* is a Persian word that passed into the Greek, but its meaning of garden or park is best portrayed in its Septuagint use of Genesis 2:8 or Nehemiah 2:8. This is a place of beauty, joy, and bliss. In the New Testament, its only uses are here (Luke 23:43) and 2 Corinthians 12:4 and Revelation 2:7. *Paradise* designates the temporary place occupied by the righteous before the final order of things in eternity. That Jesus went to Paradise from the cross does not allow for the terminology, He "descended into hell." The latter is found nowhere in Scripture, but has been frequently maintained because of the erroneous wording in the Apostles' Creed.

In the next saying from the cross, Jesus committed the care of His mother to John. This is further indication that Mary's husband, Joseph, had died some years earlier and that the brothers of Jesus were not believers in Him at this time (cf. John 7:5) and could not be counted on to help their mother in this situation. Therefore, John, the beloved disciple, was given the responsibility of giving comfort, strength, and guidance to Mary during these trying days.

The words "I am thirsty" came later in Jesus' suffering when His speech was less coherent. The people misunderstood one of His statements, for some thought He was calling for Elijah (Matthew 27:49). Jesus had been offered drink earlier, but He had refused it. This had been the ordinary sedative type of drink given to help deaden the pain. Jesus did not want to have His senses artificially reduced in the least. When He requested a drink in the midst of His final sufferings, however, He accepted the sour drink of a soldier, probably on hand to quench the soldier's thirst during the day. Other offers of drink, offered in derision, seemed to have been declined (Luke 23:36).

The most moving statement of all, and one whose depths we are not able to plumb, is found in both Matthew (27:46) and Mark (15:34): "My God, my God, why have you forsaken me?" This does not mean that God had deserted Jesus in an absolute way, but it certainly indicates that Jesus had to accomplish His task by himself, and He felt a loneliness He had never known before. That Jesus was identified with sin in a unique way at this time and that God is separate from sin in a unique way may well have an association with Jesus' cry at this moment.

John alone records the momentous words: "It is finished" (19:30). This was not simply the end of breath, the end of life, or the end of an episode. This was the completion of Christ's task in the redemption of man. He had completed the purpose for which He had come to earth.

Now we return to Luke for possibly the last of Jesus' words on the cross: "Father, into your hands I commit my spirit" (Luke 23:46). This shows that the separation from God was not absolute. He still heard Jesus' words. He still was ready to receive Him at death. They would be together in a way that had not been enjoyed during the earthly life of Jesus.

Luke records three sayings of Jesus on the cross (the first two and the last). John also records three statements. Matthew and Mark record but one saying each, and it is the same saying in both of them.

EXCURSUS

The Shroud of Turin

Seldom has one ancient artifact provided such a challenge to science and an interest to faith as the shroud of Turin. This is a linen cloth more than fourteen feet long and three feet, seven inches wide that bears the discernible figure of a man, evidently lying in repose after a violent death. One-half of the cloth shows the front view of the person, and then, as though the fabric passed over the head of the individual, the cloth carries the rear view of the same figure on the other half of the long strip. The linen is sepia in color and has stains of blood seeming to have come from wounds in the body. Wrists and feet seem to show nail marks, and specks of blood encircle the head. The back and legs show signs of lashing. The knees are bruised and torn.

The Case for the Shroud

Some maintain this is the very cloth purchased by Joseph and used to cover the body of Jesus. In some inexplicable way, the impression of Jesus was left on the surface of the linen as He lay in the tomb. So the claim is made, and an impressive defense follows.

Known from antiquity. This is not a medieval invention, some claim, because evidence of its existence goes back to as early as the second century (to Braulio of Seville). Tradition tells of Thaddeus' taking a mysterious cloth with the imprint of Jesus' face to Edessa (in what is Turkey today). In 1357, the shroud surfaced in Lirery, France. After a century in a castle belonging to the House of Savoy, it was brought to Turin, Italy, where it has remained since about 1580.

Matching the Scriptural data. The condition of the body outlined on the cloth is much what one would expect as a result of the treatment described in the Gospel accounts: the scourging, the crown of thorns, the nails in wrists (hands?) and feet, and the wound in the side.

A unique testimony. This shroud is different. It is not like other grave coverings, which shared signs of the decomposed bodies they had held. Other shrouds do not carry the impressions of the bodies they held. But Christ's resurrection was unique. This may be another miracle that accompanied the resurrection, some claim.

The Case Against the Shroud

All, however, do not accept the shroud of Turin as the unique grave clothes of Jesus. They point out flaws in the position of those who argue for the truth of the identification.

Too many claims. Besides the various claims about the grave shroud of Jesus, there were similar attempts to identify the Holy Grail and to collect the wood of the cross and nails that were driven into Jesus' hands. There are so many claims, however, it is obvious that all could not be genuine, and this casts suspicion on any remains of this nature. Thus, it is impossible to establish that the shroud of Turin is indeed the linen that was talked about in the earlier traditions from different parts of the world, let alone establish it as the cloth purchased by Joseph for Jesus' body.

Too similar, but not a match. One is struck by the possibility of an individual's reading the Gospel narrative and drawing a figure that reflected the treatment seen in the New Testament. Rather than an evidence of authority, this becomes a hollow example of inventive illustration of the very details recorded in the canonical Gospels. Furthermore, there are Scriptural details that do not fit. For example, the *grave clothes* of Jesus are mentioned in the plural, which seems to demand a number of strips that were wrapped around Jesus. Especially in contradiction to the claim for the Turin cloth, the reference to the head napkin (John 20:7, *soudarion*) denotes that Jesus' head was covered in the burial with a separate cloth and would not have left the facial impression on the Turin linen.

Not unique enough. The Turin shroud is different, but similarities to the middle ages speak against its authenticity. For example, the face and the hands have a prominence that approach an artist's work. The type of beard and characteristics of the lifeless figure reflect an artist's concept of the middle ages. The report that the blood stains check out as genuine human blood is impressive, but when one notes that the blood is flowing in the wrong direction, as though the man were standing up when he is actually pictured as lying down, this raises suspicion. The age of the cloth and the dating of the blood have not been determined. One is tempted to conclude this is the work of an artist and not a miracle.

The fact still remains, however, that no one knows the process that was used to gain these results. Surprising details remain to be explained: the possibility of coins in the two eyes, and the attempt to identify them as denarii from Pilate's time, the pollin detectable in the woven cloth identified as coming from the territory of Israel and Turkey. But it still remains the shroud of Turin and not of Jesus. It may be associated with different parts of the world, but it falls far short of the body of Jesus and A.D. 30.[86]

---

[86] For one who accepts the shroud as authentic, see Gary R. Habermas, "The Shroud of Turin and its Significance for Biblical Studies," *Journal of the Evangelical Theological Society,* 24 (March, 1981), pp. 47-54. For one who considers the shroud as the product of later devotional art, see Robert A. Wild, "The Shroud of Turin—Probably the Work of a 14th Century Artist or Forger," *Biblical Archaeology Review,* 10 (March/April, 1984), 30-46. For one who doubts, but admits uncertainty and includes a bibliography on the subject, see Fitzmeyer, *Gospel According to Luke, X-XXIV,* pp. 1527-29.

CHAPTER THIRTEEN

Victory

Luke 24

To celebrate a major victory, the Romans held a triumphal procession through the streets of Rome. On this occasion, they honored the conquering general and displayed evidences of the conquest. Prisoners of war walked in chains behind chariots or floats depicting scenes from former battles. Samples of booty were shown and examples of bravery portrayed. A Roman triumph was frequently the most memorable event of the year.

One of the outstanding processions of all Roman history followed the conquest of Judea in A.D. 70. Its fame has been preserved in scenes that can be viewed today on the arch of Titus located at one end of the remains of the ancient forum in Rome. The chariot servants are shown carrying the spoils of the great temple of Jerusalem (the trumpets, the table for the showbread, and the seven-branched lampstand). These reliefs are considered among the highest achievements of Roman imperial art. A rare feature of this procession was that father and son shared the triumph together. The son, Titus, completed the conquest; but Vespasian, his father and Roman emperor from A.D. 69, had begun the campaign.

The greatest triumph of all, however, was won at the crossroads of mankind in Jerusalem in A.D. 30. The victory procession was not witnessed by human eyes, but evidence of its occurrence was clear when Jesus rose from the dead three days after His crucifixion and burial. God the Father and the Son, Jesus Christ, shared the victory. In the New Testament, the Greek word *thriambeuo,* meaning "lead in a triumphal procession," was used twice (Colossians 2:15; 2 Corinthians 2:14), and in each instance, it refers to God's victory through Christ. At this time, when Satan felt he had scored his greatest victory in the death of Christ, he found that the very deed he had supported was the means of releasing the captives in sin and disarming the supernatural powers of evil.[87] "[Jesus] made a public spectacle of them, triumphing over them by the cross" (Colossians 2:15). The victory was sealed in the bodily resurrection from the grave.

Another Look

What was happening in the death, burial, and resurrection of Jesus was kept secret until it took place. Prophets who spoke of these matters searched intently "trying to find out the time and circumstances ... [of] the sufferings of Christ and the glories that would follow" (1 Peter 1:11). "Even angels long to look into these things" (1 Peter 1:12). This "look" the angels were taking was a particular kind of look. The Greek word is *parakupto,* and it means to bend over to gain a clear glance, to look carefully into.[88] This is the same word used in the Gospel of Luke to describe the look Peter gave to the empty tomb of Jesus. Peter stooped over to peer into the place where the strips of linen were lying by themselves (Luke 24:12). John also used the word twice in his Gospel to describe the same look into the empty tomb. The first time, John was looking intently into the darkened interior of the tomb (John 20:5); and the second time, Mary Magdalene was crying as "she bent over to look into the tomb" (John 20:11). Only one other time is this word used in the New Testament—James 1:25. The previous verses—James 1:23, 24—picture the man who looks in a mirror and turns away, forgetting the changes he should make. There, another word for *look* is used ("to look at, with reflection"), but verse 25 states: "But the man who looks intently *[parakupto]* into the perfect law that gives freedom, and continues to do this, not forgetting what he has heard, but doing it—he will blessed in what he does."

---

[87]See William Hendriksen, *Philippians, Colossians, and Philemon* (Grand Rapids: Baker, 1979), p. 123.

[88]See Walter Bauer, William F. Arndt, and F. Wilbur Gingrich, *Greek-English Lexicon of the New Testament* (Chicago: University of Chicago, 1957, 1979), p. 619; cf. G. C. Wilke, C. L. W. Grimm, and J. H. Thayer, *Greek-English Lexicon of the New Testament* (New York: T. and T. Clark, 1886), p. 292.

The uses of the word *parakupto*, "to look intently into," are a challenge to each reader to take another look at the resurrection of Jesus, to view the empty tomb and feel the impact of its meaning, to review the resurrection appearances and know the reality of the victory, to apply the promises to our own lives, and to follow the look with action.

The Resurrection Appearances

To Mary Magdalene. Although Luke records only four of a possible twelve appearances of Jesus, an overview of all the recorded appearances helps to understand Luke's testimony better. Jesus' first appearance was to a woman at the tomb. How she happened to be here, and alone, is a matter of conjecture, but it is not difficult to suggest how the details given in the four Gospel narratives could result in just such a circumstance. All four accounts open with the activity on the first day of the week, Sunday, the day after Saturday, the Sabbath. Early that morning, while it was still dark, a group of women (this included Mary Magdalene, Mary the mother of James, Salome, and Joanna) started out from Bethany with supplies to complete the burial preparations for the body of Jesus. Because the Sabbath day had begun (sundown on Friday) soon after Jesus had been taken down from the cross, His body had been left in the central area of the rock-hewn tomb. Later, it would have been placed in one of the loculi, a niche where the body would be put and sealed permanently, but for the time being, it was left waiting the completion of adding spices and perfumes to those already used in haste on Friday. By the time the women arrived at the tomb, a distance of several miles, it was becoming light. Mary Magdalene had rushed on ahead and arrived at the tomb before the others. She found the stone rolled away, and the tomb empty. Immediately, she ran into the city of Jerusalem to tell the apostles. She found only two, Peter and John. They came running as fast as they could to see the empty tomb for themselves. Meanwhile the women from Bethany had arrived at the tomb, received the message from the two angels and started back the way they had come, expecting to spread the news as quickly as possible. After Peter and John had viewed the grave cloths collapsed in place and the head napkin neatly folded and lying along side, they were convinced. He was alive.

After Mary's first run to inform Peter and John, she returned

RESURRECTION APPEARANCES

Possible Order	Place	Citation
1. Mary Magdalene	Jerusalem	John 20:14; Mark 16:9
2. The women	Jerusalem	Matthew 28:9
3. Peter (Simon; Cephas)	Jerusalem	Luke 24:34; 1 Corinthians 15:5
4. Cleopas & friend	Emmaus Road	Luke 24:13-35
5. Ten apostles	Jerusalem	Mark 16:14; Luke 24:36; John 20:19
6. Eleven apostles	Jerusalem	John 20:26
7. Seven disciples by the lake	Galilee	John 21:1-24
8. Five hundred brothers	Galilee(?)	1 Corinthians 15:6
9. Apostles/Great Commission	Galilee	Matthew 28:16-20
10. Apostles/Commission repeated	Jerusalem	Mark 16:15-18
11. James	Jerusalem(?)	1 Corinthians 15:7
12. Ascension/Further Commission	Mt. of Olives	Mark 16:19, 20; Luke 24:44-50; Acts 1:3-12

to the tomb, perhaps by a different route. By the time she arrived, the women had long since departed; Peter and John had also gone. This time, Mary spoke to two angels and then turned to ask the gardener if he knew where the body had been taken.

He spoke her name, and she recognized Him. She was speaking to Jesus. This was His first recorded appearance following His resurrection.

To the women. As the women who had come from Bethany left the tomb to run and deliver the angels' message to the disciples, Jesus appeared to them along the way. They clasped His feet and worshiped Him. He gave them a message to deliver informing the brethren that He would meet them in Galilee (Matthew 28:10). Probably this appearance took place at some point on the road back to Bethany. Mary Magdalene had not found any more of the disciples than Peter and John. Perhaps these women knew where more of them were staying (Luke 24:9).

To Peter. Sometime between the appearance to the women and the meeting of the disciples that evening, Jesus appeared to Peter. Perhaps this was similar to His appearance to the women along the Bethany road. Peter had been on his way to tell of the empty tomb, and Jesus gave Him greeting. This was not only reported that evening (Luke 24:34), but Paul left note of it in his Corinthian letter over twenty years later (1 Corinthians 15:5).

To Cleopas and another disciple. Throughout the trial, crucifixion, and resurrection appearances, Luke gives an abbreviated account of Jesus' activity. At this point, however, he shows how he can describe a scene in warm and sensitive detail (Luke 24:13-35). This appearance starts along the road, but ends with recognition in a house in Emmaus. These two, Cleopas and his friend, hurry the seven miles back to Jerusalem to tell the good news to the disciples.

To ten apostles. Sometimes the number *twelve* was used as a title for all the apostles even after Judas was no longer counted among them. It was used as a designation for the group whether there were twelve or not. The same thing was true of *eleven*. This may have been used to designate the group not counting Judas, even if some were missing from the meeting of the group. Thus, the designation "the Eleven" could still be used for the band of apostles even though only ten were present. This is the case in Luke 24:33f, when Jesus first appeared to a meeting of the group, but Thomas was not present (John 20:24). This was on the evening of that first day of the week when Jesus rose from the dead. Although the doors were locked, Jesus came and stood among them. To correct any false assumption they might have had that His body was no longer physical, He asked for physical food to feed His physical body (Luke 24:41).

To eleven apostles. After a week had gone by, Jesus appeared to the apostles again, and this time Thomas was present (John 20:26).

To seven disciples by the Sea of Galilee. The disciples had gone to Galilee to wait for Jesus as He had instructed (Matthew 28:10). While waiting, seven had decided to go fishing (John 21:3). This was no reflection on their faithfulness. They could work and be waiting at the same time. They recognized Jesus on the shore, and the note of joy resounds.

To five hundred brethren. In Paul's first epistle to the Corinthians, an appearance is noted that we do not identify with those recorded in the Gospel narratives (1 Corinthians 15:6). Some have maintained that this is on the same occasion as the appearance to the Twelve on a mountain in Galilee (Matthew 28:16ff). One is unable to verify or deny this. Neither can it be established whether this occurred in Galilee or the environs of Jerusalem, or some other place. Lest one question the value of such a reference with no more details than this, Paul added his word of assurance to his original readers that many of those were still alive at the time of his writing. They were available for questioning. It would add considerably to a person's life to be marked as one who had seen the resurrected Lord in the flesh. In fact, this adds assurance that Jesus' appearances were not all to a few individuals behind locked doors, but to a considerable number at one time.

To the eleven on a mountain in Galilee. Since this appearance was on a mountain, reminiscent of Jesus' preaching in the out-of-doors because of the great crowds that had come to hear Him, it may suggest there were more present than just the apostles. Especially when the note is interjected that some doubted (Matthew 28:17), one might expect that more than the eleven disciples were there. Jesus had convinced Thomas, seemingly the only remaining doubter among the apostles, on the second Sunday after Jesus' resurrection. This mountain in Galilee is the scene of Jesus' issuing the Great Commission to make disciples of all nations.

Commission repeated. The Gospel of Mark ends abruptly at 16:8 in two of the early manuscripts. But because of the grammar of the Greek and the sense of what is said, it seems impossible that the Gospel could have ended there. Furthermore, Mark would be a Gospel without a resurrection if it ended at 16:8. By far, the best attested ending is the longer one indicating verses 9-20. The report of the resurrected Jesus in this section seems to be a composite picture of several appearances of Jesus. The appearance in Mark 16:14 sounds much like the first time Jesus appeared to the gathering of apostles (ten without Thomas) and He rebuked them for their lack of faith (Luke 24:38). The next verse (Mark 16:15) reflects a different scene and lacks the unbelief of the first. This time, it resembles the Great Commission passage given in Galilee (Matthew 28:16-20). But the closing of Mark leaves no room for material about Galilee. After all, it is likely that the Great commission was repeated more than once. In all likelihood, the Commission was given on an occasion in Judea, near Jerusalem, as well. Then Mark goes immediately to the ascension scene. Two of the appearances, the first meeting of the apostles on the first day of the week and the last one at the ascension, were in Judea. But this presentation of the Commission seems to reflect a different meeting in Judea not reported in the others.

To James. What James, which place, and when, are not spelled out in this passage (1 Corinthians 15:7). We do know that the brothers of the Lord did not believe on Him during His earthly ministry (John 7:5), but soon after the ascension they were among the believers (Acts 1:14). James became a leader of the church in Jerusalem (Galatians 2:9), and Paul had opportunity to visit with James the brother of the Lord when he was in Jerusalem (Galatians 1:19). That this refers to a resurrection appearance to James, the brother of the Lord is most likely. Since his ministry was centered in Jerusalem, this is the probable area where he must have talked with the Lord.

Ascension. Further commission. Luke ties together his Gospel and the book of Acts by closing one work with the ascension of Christ and opening the next volume with the same scene. From Acts, we learn Jesus had been on the Mount of Olives and that all of these appearances occurred in a forty-day period. "After his suffering, he showed himself to these men and gave many convincing proofs that he was alive" (Acts 1:3). The variety of reports we have is astounding, but rather than cause doubt, this should inspire faith. They were not giving a mechanical rehearsed account. These were individual eyewitness reports of what happened in those days immediately following the death, burial, and resurrection of Jesus.

Content Notes

Evidence of Victory (1-8)

They found the stone rolled away from the tomb (2). When the women, Mary Magdalene, Joanna, and Mary the mother of James (see Luke 24:10; cf. Matthew 28:1; Mark 16:1), came to the tomb early on the first day of the week, they discovered the first of a series of indications that events were no longer proceeding in the natural order of death, preparation for burial, and final interment. The women had brought more spices, no doubt purchased after the Sabbath had ended on Saturday evening, and they were ready to complete the preparation of Jesus' body for the final placement in one of the *loculi* opening on the central room of the tomb. But the stone, round enough to roll and shaped enough to fit into a groove extending in front of the tomb, had been moved away from the entrance to the tomb. Who could have done this, and for what purpose?

Did not find the body (3). Luke had stated at the opening of his Gospel narrative that he was writing to assure the certainty of the things he recorded. Now we see Luke lining up the evidence of Jesus' resurrection step by step. The women found the stone rolled back; then they entered the tomb and found that the body of Jesus was not there. But what did this mean? Many possibilities may have been suggested. Enemies could have taken the body. Friends could have come for the body. Thieves could have stolen the remains. Or could it be that Jesus meant what He said—that He would rise again?

Two men in clothes . . . like lightning (4). The women were not left to guess without any positive explanation. Two "men" had an announcement. By Luke's description, they were not ordinary men. They appeared suddenly; they were clad in dazzling apparel. The women were not only startled but filled with fear, and turned their faces to the ground. Then they heard the message.

He is not here; he has risen! (6). This was not an announcement based on wishful thinking or even introduced from deductions gained from circumstantial evidence. This was an announcement by one who knew that Jesus was no longer dead but alive, and the women should not expect to find Him in the tomb. Of course, it was hard to believe. Of course, it was not the normal outcome to be expected three days after death. So the men gave further indication to help the women accept the fact.

Remember how he told you.... Now Jesus' predictions become doubly meaningful. Jesus' followers had been told while they were still in Galilee that He must die, but He would be raised to life (Luke 9:22, 44; cf. 18:31-33). He had proven himself right on so many occasions, there was no excuse for not accepting His predictions without reservations. But then, what did He mean by resurrection? Could it be a kind of spiritual resurrection in a Heavenly world? They may well have accepted His words but doubted a visible, bodily fulfillment of the prediction. With this announcement, joined to the absence of the body, they could see that Jesus meant this in a literal, physical way. But the prediction understood in this way also gave strong support to the actuality of His being alive. The power who could foretell the event was also the power who could bring it to pass, though unnatural by the standards of human limitation. The predictions helped Jesus' followers to see what had happened and helped them believe it when it had happened. "Then they remembered his words" (Luke 24:8).

Compare the accounts. Some consider it naive to accept the Gospel reports at face value without submitting them to critical analysis. Truth has no fear of any analysis as long as the analysis is truthful in itself. It must not be based upon false assumptions or employ an erroneous methodology. Its conclusions must be founded properly upon the findings, not claiming too much and not introducing unrelated deductions. Unfortunately, the value of the Gospel accounts has been lessened for some because of the type of demands put upon the Gospel writers. If their reports are similar to one another, some suggest one copied from the other. If the accounts are different, these same individuals claim the writers were dependent upon some variant tradition, which removes the report one step further from what actually happened. The form of the supposed tradition is reconstructed, the authors are denied, and mythological redactors or editors are put in their places. Too often the accounts lose their luster, not because they are shown up to be fabrications, but because the attention has been diverted to unfounded denials rather than focused on the message the Gospel writers seek to convey.

Earlier in this chapter, we made an attempt to show how the variant reports can possibly fit together. Now let's consider an example of one scene, noting the similarities and differences in the other accounts. But instead of looking for literary patterns or redactional material, we will notice how the combination of elements true to life with the unexpected may be used to capture the genuine thrust of the passage.

In Matthew's account (Matthew 28:2, 3), the reader is introduced to action that preceded what is recorded in the other Gospel narratives. An angel came to roll back the stone. His appearance was as lightning and his clothes white as snow. In Mark (16:5), the women saw a young man dressed in a white robe after they had entered the tomb and found Jesus' body missing. In Luke (24:4), two men appeared like lightning and their clothes were dazzling as the women stood in the tomb. In John (20:11, 12), Mary returned to the tomb, having told Peter and John that the tomb was empty, and two angels in white were seated at the head and the foot of the place where Jesus' body had previously been placed. All of these accounts are different, but they all give a similar testimony. In two accounts, the figures are called "angels" (Matthew and John). However, when Luke relates the report the women gave, he, too, uses the term *angel* (Luke 24:23). In fact, all four accounts describe the appearance of the men/angels as striking in the whiteness of their apparel. This is the same description given of the appearance of Jesus and the glorious splendor of Moses and Elijah on the Mount of Transfiguration (Luke 9:29). Luke described the scene at the time of Jesus' ascension in similar language when "two men" dressed in white appeared to deliver a message (Acts 1:10). In the book of Revelation, the heavenly figures are described in scene after scene dressed in white (e.g. Revelation 3:5; 4:4; 7:9; 15:6; 19:8). Because their physical form resembled men, angels were so designated in Luke and Mark, but because they were angelic figures, their dazzling apparel was noted to make this clear. There is no contradiction but a variety of descriptions given of this scene in the Gospels.

But what of the difference in number? In Matthew and Mark, one figure is reported, and in Luke and John, two are described. The hermeneutical rule bears repeating, which specifies that a contradiction occurs only when one passage affirms what another denies, but unless it is that explicit, it may remain a difference without being a contradiction. The latter is the case here. No passage of the form says that two not one appeared, nor one not two. In a number of instances two figures have been involved in an incident, but one is the spokesman or plays a prominent role so that at times his presence alone is noted in the report.[89] At this point, Luke is eager to register the testimony made more sure by two angels even as two witnesses were the minimum required for verification under the old law (Deuteronomy 17:6; 19:15). The differences in the accounts are not contradictions. Rather, they strengthen the assurance that these were not stereotyped recitals of one traditional report, but rather independent accounts.

The detailed differences but overall agreement continue in the words of the angels, also. Luke does not have the initial reassuring admonition from the angels (not to be afraid) as found in Matthew and Mark; but Luke does note the fright of the women. He chooses to preserve another portion of the angels' words not found in the other Gospels: "Why do you look for the living among the dead?" (Luke 24:5). Some commentators conclude that Luke was ignorant of any words or observations found in the other Gospel accounts but not included in Luke's Gospel. This is an unwarranted assumption. Luke would certainly have seen the Gospel of Matthew if it was written fifteen years before, but oftentimes he did not choose to include the same wording. Instead, he chose his particular material to suit his particular purpose, putting the words and happenings in his carefully laid out plan. This does not mean he was unhistorical, but simply selective. Another example of this follows—Luke does not include the angel's instructions to go to Galilee and meet Jesus there because he does not choose to include a note about Jesus' Galilean appearances. This does not mean he is unaware of them, but Luke follows a regular practice of focusing attention. His attention is focused on Jerusalem. He has taken nine chapters to bring Jesus there. He has related the

---

[89]Mark 10:46 and Luke 18:35 report one blind man (Bartimaeus) at Jericho, while Matthew 20:30 reports two. Mark 5:2 and Luke 8:27 tell of one demoniac by the Sea of Galilee; Matthew 8:28 indicates there were two.

death and burial of Jesus, and now he chooses to concentrate on Jerusalem for the closing episodes of his Gospel.

Luke does refer to Galilee but only as the angel gives reference to the place where Jesus' prediction of death and resurrection were given (Luke 24:6). The words of the angel are a summary of all three predictions of Jesus' death recorded in Luke.[90] The last of these, however, was given on His way to Jerusalem, outside the Galilean territory.

Luke alone uses the terminology, "On the third day," He will rise again (Luke 9:22; 18:33; 24:7). The other Gospels state, "after three days." The Gentile Luke, writing to Gentiles, may have chosen to be more explicit time-wise rather than use the idiomatic expression of the Jews, who definitely counted any part of a day as a complete day—thus the expression "after three days and three nights" could be fulfilled as indicating simply three days, and not require a twenty-four-hour day for each fulfillment. It is interesting to note that Matthew (12:39-41) includes this expression in the sign of Jonah, but Luke omits it in his report (11:29-32). Not that Luke is disagreeing with the meaning of the expression, but he may be fearful that some of his readers would misunderstand "after three days"—just as some have done today in attempting to put the crucifixion of Jesus on Wednesday or Thursday because of demanding a seventy-two-hour period. Luke is explicit, "On the third day."

Wonder and Doubts (9-12)

Luke's account continues to build certainty for the happenings he records. The combination of the true to life and the unexpected weave the strong fiber of trustworthy witness. The burial before the Sabbath began, the rest in obedience to the keeping of the Sabbath, the resumption of the burial preparation early on the first day of the week, and the problem of the stone in front of the tomb are all true to the life and time of the happening. The stone removed, the empty tomb, the message of the angels, the reminder of Jesus' prediction—these are the unexpected elements that startled the women[91] and sent them on their way to

---

[90]Luke 9:22, 43-45; 18:31-33. See also Luke 12:50; 17:25.

[91]Besides the women listed here (Luke 24:10), Mary Magdalene,

tell the news. But the result was not immediate presumption of a resurrection. This was too contrary to natural expectations. This was too hard to believe, even of Jesus. Resurrection was too good to be true.

They told all these things to the Eleven (9). Now that Judas had deserted their number and was dead (Matthew 27:3-10), the number for the apostles was eleven. Whether they were together all in one place or not is not clear. From John, it becomes evident that Peter and John were in one location in Jerusalem and perhaps the women went back to tell the rest who were staying close to Bethany. "All the others" would include the seventy (Luke 10:1) or one hundred twenty (Acts 1:15) who were particularly identified with Jesus.

But they did not believe (11). The tragedy and disappointments of the last few days had left the disciples numb and disillusioned. They were not a gullible, easily-swayed crowd living on emotion. Things had to make sense.

Peter ... ran to the tomb (12). From the Gospel of John (20:3), we learn that John ran with him, also. They wanted to see for themselves. No one had actually seen Jesus yet.

He saw the strips of linen lying by themselves. The grave wrappings were so striking they deserved special note. They would not be the extent of yardage nor the same type as found in Egypt on the mummies. The burial customs were different among the Jews in Palestine. But the plural form for cloth is used.[92] This was not a single shroud. It was multiple wrappings. What seemed to be most striking was the way they were lying there. If grave robbers had entered the tomb and made off with the body, one would expect everything to be left in disorder, showing evidence of haste and no concern. This was not the condition of the cloths. Furthermore, if they were wrapped around and around the body, it would be impossible to extricate the body without unwrapping the cloth. It would indeed be

---

Joanna, and Mary the mother of James, Mark (16:1) adds Salome. The "other Mary" of Matthew 28:1 is the mother of James. The absence of Mary the mother of Jesus is noteworthy.

[92]The plural form is also used in John 19:40; 20:5-7. However, it is singular in Luke 23:53.

remarkable if the linen strips were lying collapsed in neat condition with the body gone.

He went away, wondering. Peter made no high claims immediately. He was trying to line up all the possibilities.

Two Disciples See Jesus (13-32)

Now that same day (13). Luke uses great artistry as he unfolds the evidence of Jesus' resurrection. Thus far, he has not told of anyone who has actually seen Jesus alive again. He continues his record of events that took place on that same first day of the week. This time, he tells the incident in detail, although in other instances he only gives a brief summary. The "village called Emmaus" has been variously identified with Abu-Ghosh (nine miles from Jerusalem), El-Qubeibeh (seven miles), and Motza-Illit (three and a half miles—seven miles round trip).

Jesus himself came up (15). John records Mary of Magdala as the first appearance. Since Luke shows an interest in giving place to women's participation in the events in Jesus' life, one might expect him to record that appearance first. But Luke has already introduced the role of the women in establishing the empty tomb and the message of the angels. This is as far as he wants this opening stage of the resurrection to go. So he chooses to introduce the figure of Jesus in a travel scene (one of Luke's favorite themes) and before two witnesses, not one.

They were kept from recognizing him (16). This is no evidence of Jesus' occupying a glorified body. The condition has to do with the eyes and understanding of the two from Emmaus. The ending of this temporary limitation to their recognition is also noted (Luke 24:31).

We had hoped that he was the one who was going to redeem Israel (21). Three steps are major in this appearance of Jesus. This was the first stage, when the discouragement and despair of Jesus' followers over His crucifixion was put into words by Cleopas. He represents the common feeling on all sides. Then he also reported amazement over the very circumstances that Luke has just described concerning the women, the angels, and the tomb.

And beginning with Moses and all the Prophets, he explained (27). This was the second major stage of the episode, when Jesus taught them from the whole of the Old Testament the predictions and the truths concerning the work of Jesus, the Messiah. Note that this teaching was given while they still had not identified Him. If He had announced who He was, the two would have been so excited they would not have heard a word of His instruction. Just as the crowds had been taught throughout His ministry without public, positive affirmation of His Messiahship, so now Jesus had to delay His declaring His identification so they would listen first to His teaching.

Then their eyes were opened (31). This was the third step. This was the highlight. The two clearly recognized the same Jesus they had known before the crucifixion. This occurred as Jesus gave thanks over the bread of their evening meal (Luke 24:35). There is no indication this is an observance of the Lord's Supper. But Jesus disappeared from their presence, and the two returned immediately to Jerusalem.

More Appearances on the First Day (33-49)

There they found the Eleven (33). The two must have made a quick return from Emmaus to Jerusalem and gone directly to the place where the apostles and other close disciples had gathered to exchange news and excitedly wait for the next development. The number *eleven* was used because of the new designation for the Twelve, since Judas was no longer counted; but from John (20:24) we learn that Thomas also was not there.

The Lord has risen and has appeared to Simon (34). Where this happened, we are not told. It must have been some time after Peter and John ran to the tomb and looked inside (John 20:3-10) and before this meeting of the disciples in the evening "with the doors locked for fear of the Jews" (John 20:19).

Jesus himself stood among them (36). This caps the climax of Jesus' appearances on the first day. He appeared as suddenly as He had disappeared shortly before from the presence of the two from Emmaus. This was not much later because they were still talking about the report from Emmaus. Jesus greeted them in a usual way: "Peace be with you." Luke makes no special note of Jesus' refusal to allow the locked door to stop Him; but the disciples' amazement at seeing Jesus alive and at the manner of His entrance was registered in their reaction. They were terrified, and they thought He was some kind of a spirit with no physical body. Jesus was eager to establish His bodily condition, not only that He was the same Jesus who had been crucified, but that He had the same physical body as well. He showed the scars from the nails both in His hands and in His feet (thus indicating He had been nailed in both places), and then He ate food before their very eyes.

Everything must be fulfilled (44). Jesus pointed out fulfillment in two ways. First, His death and resurrection had been predicted in the Old Testament, the Scriptures designated by the three divisions of the "Law of Moses, the Prophets and the Psalms" (the *hagiographa*).[93] Second, He himself had predicted the events (Luke 9:22, 44; 18:31).

Then he opened their minds (45). The difficulty the disciples had in understanding Jesus' prior statements about His suffering, death, and resurrection may not be entirely because of dullness or stubbornness on the part of the disciples. From this statement in Luke, it would seem that God had formerly kept these matters from being discerned clearly, just as the eyes of the two from Emmaus had been kept from recognizing Jesus until the proper time arrived.

And repentance and forgiveness of sins will be preached in his name to all nations (47). Luke is giving a brief summary of important words that will both conclude his Gospel narrative and be a connecting link to introduce his second volume (Acts), which will follow shortly. Luke does not give the Great Commission as found in Matthew 28:18-20, but Jesus' words are fulfilled as Peter preaches on Pentecost and in the household of Cornelius (Acts 2:38; 10:34-43).

I am going to send what my Father has promised (49). In the Gospel of John, one learns of the explicit promises of the coming of the Holy Spirit (John 14:16, 26; 16:7ff). This was associated with fulfillment on the day of Pentecost (Acts 1:5; 2:4). Thus Luke continues to link the close of his Gospel with the opening of his next volume, Acts.

The Ascension (50-53)

When he had led them out to the vicinity of Bethany (50). From Luke's compressed ending of his Gospel, one would be uncertain as to the passage of time between the scene in the house behind the locked doors and the final ascension near

---

[93] For example, from the law: Deuteronomy 18:15; from the prophets: Isaiah 53:1-12; and from the *hagiographa:* Psalm 22:1-31.

Bethany. The meeting with the Eleven and those with them when reports were heard and Jesus himself appeared lasted on into the night. It is out of the question to suggest that the ascension was that very night in the dark. The opening of the book of Acts (1:3) makes clear that forty days intervened between the first appearances and the final scene Luke uses to close His Gospel. This interval allows time for the appearance in Galilee. As to the place of the ascension, Luke records they returned to Jerusalem from the Mount of Olives, and here in the close of his Gospel, Bethany is named; but the Greek preposition used with Bethany denotes a site over toward Bethany rather than in the town itself.

Returned . . . with great joy . . . stayed continually at the temple, praising God (52, 53). Luke's closing note is indicative of his whole Gospel, and gives the setting for the opening of the book of Acts. "Joy" is a favorite theme of Luke. Plummer wrote: "A writer of fiction would have made them lament the departure of their Master."[94] Instead, it was with joy and praises to God that they waited upon the will of God in the temple in Jerusalem.

The Resurrection—in Fact and in Faith

The resurrection of Jesus introduces the highest of hopes and poses the deepest of problems. The difficulty arises from the reluctance of man to accept anything beyond his own experience. He will not even consider Jesus' bodily resurrection a possibility if he limits his faith to the normal works of nature and leaves no room for the supernatural power of God. On the other hand, one cannot naively accept as true everything that has ever been claimed at any time or in any place. His belief must have adequate basis—especially in the case of events that are as extraordinary as a resurrection from the dead. Nor is it proper to exercise wishful thinking and feel a person can make a thing true simply by wanting it hard enough. You need reasons that are sufficiently strong to convince an honest mind, and it would be possible to communicate those proofs to another.

To deny the bodily resurrection of Jesus is not an interpretation of Scripture. It is a denial of Scripture. The skepticism of the humanist who disallows any such resurrection power to God,

---

[94]Plummer, *Commentary on Luke,* p. 565.

the wishful thinking of the existentialist who wants to make it true for himself without being true in fact, the blindness of the disinterested world—all are insisting, "It could not have happened really." But look at the evidence again.

Evidences of the Resurrection in Fact
The Removed Stone

No description is given of Jesus in the act of leaving the tomb. If there were, the persistent skeptic would simply deny the testimony and say that it was an erroneous apparition that could not be tested. On the other hand, the stone that had been placed in front of the grave was something tangible. For days and weeks after the event, people could return to the site and view the large stone that had covered the entrance to the tomb. They could contemplate the possibilities as to how and why it had been moved from its normal place.

Besides its being a lasting material piece of evidence, the stone was part of the verisimilitude of the report—that is, it is true to the time and place being described. Graves of this type were ordinarily closed by a stone especially shaped to serve the purpose. It was round so it could be rolled to close and open the tomb on the rare occasion when another body was being buried within its enclosure; big enough to cover the entrance, usually an opening just large enough to enable the body to be carried in; and heavy enough (at least a thousand pounds or more) that no scheming grave robber could quickly gain entrance, or an animal shove it aside. Furthermore, in Jesus' case, request was made by the Jewish leaders who had brought about His crucifixion that the grave should be secured by a soldier-watch. It was guarded and sealed by the authority of Rome (Matthew 27:62-66).

A rescript found at Nazareth and dated by Monigliano from the time of Claudius (A.D. 41-54) may have a connection with the tomb of Jesus. The inscription served as instruction from the Roman emperor to the local governors (the legate of Syria or the prefect of Judea) to punish any disturbance of graves with capital punishment. Some details do not exactly fit. (1) The date would be at least a decade after the burial of Jesus. (2) The site is Nazareth, not Jerusalem, the place of Jesus' burial. (3) Jesus' case is not one of vandalism or desecration of the dead, but claims a true resurrection with no outside human help.

Although these items are at variance with the Gospel

accounts, one can see how disputes over the stone and the happenings may have caused repercussions all the way to Rome and have been associated with actions there. (1) The discussion over the displaced stone no doubt extended over many decades and finally could have caused Rome to issue a formal decree to aid in any future incidents that might arise. (2) The placement of a marble slab concerning the matter may have been made at Nazareth because of Jesus' having grown up there and the identification preserved in His name, "Jesus of Nazareth." (3) The story the chief priests concocted for the Roman guards to explain why Jesus' body was not in the tomb (Matthew 28:11-15) may have led the Romans to give a special pronouncement concerning such alleged violations.

In any event, whether the rescript is directly related or not,[95] this is an interesting archaeological contribution to help establish the true to life character of the sealing of the tomb and the gravity of disturbing the contents. "For it shall be much more obligatory to honor the buried. Let it be absolutely forbidden for anyone to disturb them. In the case of contravention I desire that the offender be sentenced to capital punishment on charge of violation of sepulture."[96] Who rolled the stone to the side? The Roman guard had not done it, nor could the story they told be true (that someone came and stole the body while they slept), for how could they report what had happened while they claimed to be asleep? If they had been awake, on the other hand, they would have stopped whoever attempted to violate the Roman seal, or die in the struggle. That is, unless it was a power they could not cope with. The word of the angel provides the answer (Matthew 28:2).

The Empty Tomb

Two tombs from antiquity convey two contrasting messages.[97]

---

[95] See E. M. Blaiklock, *The Archaeology of the New Testament* (Grand Rapids: Zondervan, 1970), pp. 75-82.

[96] E. M. Blaiklock and R. K. Harrison, *The New International Dictionary of Biblical Archaeology* (Grand Rapids: Zondervan, 1983), p. 330.

[97] See R.C. Foster, *The Everlasting Gospel* (Cincinnati: Standard Publishing, 1929), pp. 181-190.

One is a tomb in Egypt dating from the New Kingdom period (c. 1570-1150 B.C.). The Pharaoh Tutankhamen was buried there, and with him priceless articles of richly made clothing, elaborate furnishings, various precious metals, and food for the supposed needs of the king in the afterlife. The Pharoah's mummified remains were enclosed in a sarcophagus containing three coffins one inside the other. In 1923, this tomb was entered and its contents found in all their splendor, undisturbed by grave robbers who have rifled every other royal tomb thus far examined from those ancient times in Egypt.

The other tomb is the burial place of Jesus. It is bare. Even the seamless robe, the only valuable clothing possessed by Jesus, was taken by the soldiers. The message of this tomb has reverberated around the world and through ages. He is not here. He is risen. Tutankhamen's is a message of death. After more than three thousand years, his remains still occupied the tomb. After three days, Jesus' tomb was empty; only the grave clothes and the head napkin remained. His is a message of life to this day and forever.

This is the kind of evidence a person can come back to see. This was not simply in the thoughts of a person. A certain type of feeling was not the source. How many people must have come out of Jerusalem in the weeks following the resurrection just to see for themselves. The grave was empty. The very state of the grave clothes gave credence to a risen Jesus. They were not in disarray as they would have been left in a fertive act of theft. In fact, if someone were taking the body, why leave the grave clothes at all? The cloth that remained was simply collapsed in the place where the body had been. This in itself was a marvel. How could the body be extricated from the cloth wound tightly about the body without the cloth's being unwound? And there was the head napkin neatly in place where one would expect the head to have been.[98] No wonder John "saw and believed" (John 20:8). The body was gone. Friend nor foe could have led a person to the corpse if there had been one. But there was not.

The Message of the Angels

But still the morning remained a mystery. The tomb was

---

[98]Merrill Tenney, *The Reality of the Resurrection* (New York, Harper & Row, 1963), p. 119.

empty, but this was a negative note. The angels supplied the positive information. "He is not here; he has risen, just as he said.... He has risen from the dead and is going ahead of you into Galilee" (Matthew 28:6, 7). Mark describes the one who delivered such a message as a young man dressed in a white robe sitting on the right side inside the tomb (Mark 16:5). Luke called them two men "in clothes that gleamed like lightning" (Luke 24:4-8). John records that Mary Magdalene saw "two angels in white, seated where Jesus' body had been, one at the head and the other at the foot." Their only words as given by John were in the form of a question, "Why are you crying?" (John 20:12, 13).

That these reports carry such a variety of information should not arouse suspicion. Since the details of the incident are not contradictory, the variety simply emphasizes the independence of the accounts. A single figure is reported at times referring to the important spokesman, but this does not contradict the two specified at other times when a fuller description is given. At times, they are called angels, and at other reports, they are referred to by their appearance in the form of young men. Always the striking white apparel is noted. From the angels came the positive announcement, "Jesus is risen from the dead."

The Appearances of Jesus

If Jesus was indeed raised from the dead, His followers would hope to see Him. The disciples would immediately associate a resurrection of Jesus with resurrections they had already known: Jairus' daughter (Matthew 9:18ff), the widow of Nain's son (Luke 7:11ff), and especially Lazarus (John 11). They had seen these people after their resurrections, but Jesus had died such a terrible death. Up to this point, the followers of Jesus had every right to be encouraged. They could see someone had removed the stone from the entrance to the tomb, and the tomb was empty. The body was gone. The angels had informed them that Jesus was alive, but no one had seen Him. Then the appearances began, and this was the crowning proof. He was seen at the tomb and along the road, beside the lake and in the mountain, in the city and out in the country. He was seen in closed rooms, and He ate food. He appeared in Judea and in Galilee. Large groups saw Him, and individuals spoke with Him. Under a great variety of circumstances and on at least a dozen occasions over a period of forty days, Jesus appeared to believers. Did He appear only to believers? Who can say that the five hundred who saw Him at one time could not have included any unbelievers at the first of His appearing? Thomas had not believed until he saw Him. Who can say that James was not still an unbeliever as Jesus appeared to Him? But at the sight of Jesus, his old doubts were driven out. The appearances of Jesus brought faith, courage, and determination to the hearts of Jesus' followers, both then and now. It established Jesus' resurrection in fact.

Objections of the Skeptics

You may wonder at including the objections of those who have denied the resurrection in a list of evidence for the fact of the resurrection. But it is true. The objections are so feeble and so strained that their efforts contribute more toward the reality of the risen Christ then proof against it. This is true of both the early objectors and those present today. The early objectors could not produce the body of Christ to prove that He was still dead. This must be combined with the fact they themselves had requested a guard, and they were determined to keep the corpse under their control, but they failed somehow. Add to this their desperate move to cover up the real happening when they talked with the guards after the body was gone. The guards themselves would never have circulated the story they had been asleep and someone stole the body unless someone was willing to guarantee their safety. To be asleep on duty was a certain death penalty for offenders. But the Jewish leaders could not allow a report about an angel and how the guards were afraid. The Jewish leaders invented a story and guaranteed safety to the guards. On the other hand, for the soldiers to be reporting what happened while they were supposed to be asleep is an obvious mark against the trustworthiness of their testimony. It ends in actual support of happenings beyond their control, happenings they wanted to cover up. On the day of Pentecost, after the fifty-day interim, still no enemy could arise to call out against Peter and disprove the resurrection of Jesus. Even Gamaliel had to say all they could do was to wait to see how it all would turn out (Acts 5:38, 39). It sounds as though the facts were standing up well from the beginning.

Early as well as later skeptics have maintained there are inconsistencies in the accounts of the resurrection. To find contradictions in the reports is one thing, and to have differences is another. The alleged inconsistencies turn out to be differences, not contradictions. "Statements directly and positively contradictory as to the main point at issue would undoubtedly justify our rejecting it; but where the main point is admitted by every witness, slighter differences are not only perfectly consistent with its truth, but are of the utmost importance for establishing it."[99]

The further one studies the incredible theories constructed in order to deny the resurrection of Jesus, the more one becomes convinced that the only answer is the fact that Jesus' body was raised again. Claiming that Jesus was not really dead, but just in a coma, is one of these attempts to deny the fact. As though the Roman soldiers would not make sure He was dead when their lives depended upon His actual death. As though after the scourging and exhaustion of the grueling struggle along the way to Golgotha, the hours of suffering on the cross, Jesus became naturally revived in the tomb, worked His way out of the grave clothes, pushed the at-least-a-thousand-pound stone out of the way, overpowered the Roman guard, and proceeded to join His disciples. This would involve a great deal of the miraculous that the theorists who concocted this were trying to avoid. In addition to that, it runs counter to the information we do have. From the time of second-century Celsus to Hugh Schoenfield's *Passover Plot,* people have been trying unsuccessfully to make a deliberate hoax out of the whole matter. This does not match what Jesus preached and what the disciples continued to preach and live, even to a willingness to die for their testimony. Likewise, the claim of possible confusion of tombs, the suggestion of a spiritual resurrection while Jesus' remains decayed in the grave, as well as the various vision and hallucination theories without any physical grounds—all fail woefully to meet the picture unfolded in the Scripture.[100]

---

[99]William Milligan, *The Resurrection of our Lord,* 4th ed. (New York: Macmillan, 1927), p. 57.

[100]See Josh McDowell, *The Resurrection Factor* (San Bernadino: Campus Crusade, 1981), pp. 76-101.

As Beyschlag truly says: "The faith of the disciples in the Resurrection of Jesus, which no one denies, cannot have originated, and cannot be explained otherwise than through the fact of the Resurrection, through the fact in its full, objective, supernatural sense, as hitherto understood." *(Leben Jesu,* 1. p. 440) So long as this is contested, the Resurrection remains a problem which rival attempts at explanation only leave in deeper darkness.[101]

The Voice of Prophecy

When a normal event is predicted several days ahead of time, people are impressed that it might be something more than coincidence. When an event contrary to natural experience occurs, and yet it was foretold centuries before it happened, one can be sure it is beyond the working of human power. Such is the case of the resurrection of Jesus. David, a thousand years before the resurrection event, said: "Therefore my heart is glad and my tongue rejoices; my body also will rest secure because you will not abandon me to the grave, nor will you let your Holy One see decay." (See Psalm 16:9, 10.) But is the language specific enough to take this as foretelling the experience of the Messiah? On the day of Pentecost, just fifty days after the Passover when Jesus died, Peter announced this identification (Acts 2:25-28).

Jesus himself predicted His death and resurrection.[102] When the voice of prophecy declares the resurrection with such clarity, it adds weight to the reality of the fulfillment when it occurs.

The Testimony of the Church

No one denies the faith of the early Christians. The belief in the resurrection is a fully established historical fact. Even liberal theologians, who deny the bodily resurrection of Jesus, will readily admit the early belief in His resurrection as historical fact. Granted, this is different from saying the actual event of the resurrection occurred, but it is a recognition that there were those who accepted the resurrection as a real happening from the very beginning. This in itself is an indication of the truth of the

---

[101]See James Orr, *The Resurrection of Jesus* (New York: G. H. Doran, 1908, p. 231.

[102]Luke 9:22; 18:31-33; see also Luke 5:35; 9:43-45; 12:50; 13:32-35; 17:25.

testimony. They lived in a time when the evidence could be put to tests we cannot apply today. Yet the Christians persisted in their belief. The adage is true: "Time is the friend of truth." As time goes on, truth will win out. In this case, the church was not daunted by the attacks made against Christ and His miraculous power, which culminated in His own resurrection. But rather, the church grew and the Christians were strengthened. With the passage of time, any deceit or illusion would tend to surface in the face of constant testing. But the church continued in its conviction. This becomes a testimony to each succeeding generation. One cannot explain the beginning and the continuance of the church apart from the truth of the resurrection of Jesus Christ.

The Resurrection in Faith—and Its Value

"The resurrection is therefore the basis of Christian life, not simply the illustration of it. Faith involves not only the acknowledgement of the event but the appropriation of its meaning."[103]

Assurance. The belief in the resurrection brings assurance to the heart of the Christian. The fulfillment of Scripture is enacted in Jesus' return to life (Luke 24:45, 46). This brings hope to mankind because of His victory. It provides proof of His Sonship (1 Corinthians 15:18, 19; Romans 1:4).

Justification. The purpose of Jesus' resurrection was more than a demonstration of victory over death. It was effective in the forgiveness of sins: "And if Christ has not been raised, your faith is futile; you are still in your sins" (1 Corinthians 15:17). "He was delivered over to death for our sins and was raised to life for our justification" (Romans 4:25).

New Life. The resurrection is used in a figure to describe the Christian's change at baptism. "We were therefore buried with him through baptism into death in order that, just as Christ was raised from the dead through the glory of the Father, we too may live a new life (Romans 6:4; see 8:11).

Guarantee. When Jesus was raised from the dead, it was not only evidence of resurrection, but this was a promise and guarantee that believers would be raised as well. "But if it is preached

---

[103]Tenney, *The Reality of the Resurrection,* p. 71.

that Christ has been raised from the dead, how can some of you say that there is no resurrection of the dead? If there is no resurrection of the dead, then not even Christ has been raised. And if Christ has notbeen raised, our preaching is useless and so is your faith.... For as in Adam all die, so in Christ all will be made alive" (1 Corinthians 15:12, 13, 22).

The resurrection of Jesus Christ was not something that just happened and was later made to fit into God's way of salvation. Rather, the resurrection was a vital part of God's eternal plan, a central moment of truth in the redemption of mankind. Paul wrote: "For what I received I passed on to you as of first importance: that Christ died for our sins according to the Scriptures, that he was buried, that he was raised on the third day according to the Scriptures" (1 Corinthians 15:3, 4).

This is the heart of the Gospel—the resurrection of Jesus Christ is true in fact and in faith.

CONCLUDING NOTES

Luke: the Author and the Gospel

After we have read and reread Luke's narrative about Jesus, what have we learned about Luke himself? It would be convenient if we had a cover to this book that would introduce us to the writer—as we are accustomed to find on many of our current works. But since we do not have this help, we must draw our own conclusions concerning his personality, his interests, and his purpose in writing, and recognize—from our own appreciation—his success.

The Author and His Interests

Luke the Person

Was Luke really a medical doctor? Paul said he was (Colossians 4:14), and Luke's language at least allows for this profession. W. K. Hobart[104] maintained that Luke's vocabulary proved he was a doctor, but H. J. Cadbury[105] showed that the physician's use of words in antiquity was not as technical as today. Thus, one cannot establish Luke's medical training by his language alone, but some of Luke's interests and expressions (4:38; 5:12; 8:43) gain particular significance from the information that Paul gives: Luke was a physician.

Was Luke a sailor? His description of Paul's shipwreck (Acts 27:27ff) is so accurate and vivid that James Smith[106] felt he must

---

[104]W. K. Hobart, *The Medical Language of St. Luke* (Dublin: Hodges, Figgis, & Co., 1882).

[105]H. J. Cadbury, *The Style and Literary Method of Luke* (Cambridge: Harvard University Press, 1920).

[106]James Smith, *The Voyage and Shipwreck of St. Paul,* 4th ed. (London: Longmans, Green, 1880).

have had nautical experience. Furthermore, one notes that the "we" passages in the book of Acts (where Luke includes himself in the action described—Acts 16:10-17; 20:5—21:18; 27:1—28:16) indicate that Luke was accompanying Paul more often on the voyages than any other time. But this does not prove Luke was a sailor. He is so accurate in his details at all times, whether he is describing a Roman official in Corinth or the high priest in Jerusalem, that his careful description of a ship at sea is to be expected.

Was Luke an historian? There is considerable difference between a storyteller who enjoys retelling accounts he has heard and an individual who has made a study of writing history and has investigated sources, examined witnesses, visited sites involved in the happenings, and even been present at some of the scenes included in the action of the narrative. High tribute has been given to "Luke the historian" by an outstanding German scholar, an historian himself, E. Meyer, who compares Luke to the great Greek historiographers, such as Thucydides.[107] Luke was an historian in the fullest sense of the word.

Was Luke a litterateur? Once again Luke excels. Jerome considered him the best writer in the Greek of the four Evangelists. He has a larger vocabulary than any other New Testament writer. He has great variety in style. Whereas the prologue to the Gospel of Luke is considered among the passages nearest classical Greek in the New Testament, the rest of chapter one and all of chapter two provide examples of a Semitic tone that is stronger than in any other part of the New Testament. Throughout his writings, Luke's shifts in style are not arbitrary changes for the sake of variety nor are they dependent upon a slavish use of different sources. He shifts his style because of his keen historical and literary sensitivity to the land and people he is describing. When Luke pictures Peter in a Jewish background, he uses more Semitic language than when he tells of Paul in a Hellenistic setting.[108] Luke was an accomplished writer whose beautiful language cannot be adequately translated into the English.

---

[107]See Ellis, *Gospel of Luke,* p. 5.

[108]See H.J. Cadbury, *The Making of Luke-Acts* (London: S.P.C.K., 1927), pp. 221ff.

Can one speak of Luke as a theologian? Certainly, insofar as each person's beliefs about God are considered his theology, Luke was a theologian with everyone else. He did not, however, make a systematic treatment of the subjects listed today in the field of theology, nor did he leave a doctrinal treatise nor form a creed. He did have his special interests and carefully marshalled his material to present it in a way to serve best the purposes he had in mind. Wherever the Gospel writers have shown their individualism, the tendency today is to label this as material coming from their theological views. Unfortunately, once it is assigned to the theological arena, it is dismissed from the historical and considered a creation to satisfy the favorite motifs of the author.[109] Each Gospel writer has his theology; but this does not necessitate the violation of truth to support it, whether in the area of history or theology. Luke is trustworthy in both.

The presence of the Holy Spirit is another dimension to the work of Luke. Were the writings of Luke produced with the inspiration of God? The early church thought so, or Luke-Acts would never have been included among the canonical books of Scripture. The first question asked in receiving a book as the Word of God and authoritative in the life of the Christian was whether it was fully inspired or not. Another question related to this was whether it was apostolic or not. In Luke's case, he himself was not an apostle, but in the eyes of the early church, Luke's close association with Paul was much in his favor. Some affirm his occupying the prophetic office in the church. Two other questions were whether the work had always been accepted and in every place. A final area of concern inquired whether it was harmonious with the rest of Scripture. The two volumes written by Luke were recognized as truly inspired Scripture. The fact that Luke was not an apostle simply meant that the testing was all the more severe in the other areas; but the decision of the earliest times stood in each succeeding generation and has persisted after the discussions over the canon closed in the fourth century.

That Luke's writings were inspired of God did not relieve

---

[109]Hans Conzelmann, *The Theology of St. Luke* (Philadelphia: Fortress, 1961); but compare Plummer, *Critical and Exegetical Commentary . . . Luke,* p. xxxvi.

Luke of all his research work to determine what actually happened and what was actually said. Neither was Luke's literary ability put on hold while a dictated message was written down. God required the full effort and use of individual abilities on the part of His messengers, but He gave them full assurance of the truth of their message. Although it is difficult to measure the guidance of the Spirit or to draw a line between the role of the individual and the direction of God in the inspired writings, one must recognize Luke as even more than a good historian, and also more than a perceptive theologian, all because of the Spirit of God who led him.

Was Luke the companion of Paul? Three references in the New Testament directly link Paul and Luke. While Paul was under house arrest in Rome waiting trial, he wrote three epistles and sent them out together: Colossians, Ephesians, and Philemon. In two of these, he included greetings from Luke (Colossians 4:14; Philemon 24). Then from his final days in prison at Rome, Paul sent his last epistle to Timothy. In this letter, he included the sad note, "Only Luke is with me" (2 Timothy 4:11). The "we" passages in Acts also link Luke and Paul. Beginning at Troas on the second missionary journey, Luke joined Paul, but when Paul went on to Thessalonica, Luke was left at Philippi. He was picked up there six years later and continued with Paul to Jerusalem and waited with him during Paul's two-year imprisonment in Caesarea. After this, he shared Paul's shipwreck and arrived with him in Rome.

Did Luke write both the third Gospel and Acts? The style and language of the third Gospel and of the book of Acts are so much alike that all are agreed the same author must have written both. Furthermore Acts, the second volume, makes reference to the first volume (Acts 1:1, 2) and both works were sent to Theophilus, who would have been aware of the author. Then within the lines of Acts, the author is found using the pronoun *we* in certain passages. Up until now, we have assumed this meant the author was present, and that the author was Luke. But is that a fair assumption? Could the author not have been using an editorial *we* or have merely been quoting a first-person account of the events? And what assurance have we that the author, even if he was present at the events cited, was Luke? The extreme precision shown in the use of words in Luke-Acts assures us that the author's choice of "we" is not simply a quirk of accident or variant sources, but is the intention of the writer to include himself in these scenes. One of these times is when Paul was waiting trial in Rome (Acts 27:1—28:16). It was a time period during which one knows that Luke was there, also. (See Colossians 4:14.) From this point, one must appeal to external testimony. From the earliest notices in the church concerning the authorship of the third Gospel, the testimony has been uniform that Luke is the author. From the closing decades of the second century, one source after another makes reference to the Gospel according to Luke.[110] The New Testament references point to Luke, the external notes identify the author as Luke, and the literary characteristics found in the writings themselves corroborate the name that is written over the third Gospel—Luke.

In all probability, Luke was a Gentile. When Paul listed his fellow workers in Rome, he designated those who were Jews (Colossians 4:10, 11), but Luke was listed with those who were not Jews. All the other writers of the New Testament were of Jewish background. When one reads the Gospel according to Luke, he will watch for any signs of particular Gentile interests in Luke's report.

The name *Lucius* appears twice in the New Testament (Acts 13:1; Romans 16:21), but must refer to another person or persons than Luke. The form of the name is different. In Romans, he was a Jew ("my kinsman," Romans 16:21). In Acts, his home country was Cyrene, in North Africa, and he is named in the book, which would exclude him from the identification with the author because Luke used the first person (plural) when he included himself in his record.

Notices concerning Luke outside the Bible are late and have little to commend their trustworthiness. That he was one of the seventy-two of Luke 10 is unlikely, since he makes no claim as an eyewitness of Jesus' ministry. The same objection can be raised to the tradition that he was one of the two disciples at Emmaus (Luke 24). His place of origin is given as Antioch of Syria in the Anti-Marcionite Prologue, Eusebius, and Jerome. Philippi has also been suggested, since the "we" passages in Acts leave Luke at Philippi for a considerable length of time and Luke's descrip-

---

[110]*Canon of Muratori* (A.D. 180), *Anti-Marcionite Prologue* (A.D. 160-180), Irenaeus (A.D. 180).

tions of the area seem to show special acquaintance with and appreciation for the district. Suggestion has been given that he received his medical training at Philippi. The Anti-Marcionite Prologue affirms that following Paul's martyrdom, Luke lived on, "serving the Lord in a blameless manner.... He died in Boeotia, filled with the Holy Spirit, at the age of eighty years."[111]

Special Interests

Since many of the same episodes from the life of Jesus are told in more than one of the Gospel narratives, one would expect similarities in their accounts. Where differences are found, however, one notes these as marks indicative of the independence of that account from the others. When these differences are repeated and can be grouped under particular headings, they are listed as characteristics of that author. The following subjects are ones that seem to have had a special interest to Luke. Any reader can add his own observations to these. We can only conjecture why these emphases appear. The background of the writer, the need of the immediate readers and of the continuing church, and the call of the very purpose for which Luke writes all have their influence.

Universality. One might expect that Luke, a Gentile, would be interested in emphasizing the inclusion of all people, both Jew and Greek, in the unfolding and goal of the Gospel. That expectation is justified at several points. The genealogy of Jesus (Luke 3:23ff) is traced to Adam and does not simply start with Abraham (cf. Matthew 1:1ff). "And all mankind will see God's salvation" is stressed from the prophecy of Isaiah (Luke 3:6). Non-Israelites are given as good examples: the Good Samaritan (Luke 10:25-37), the Samaritan leper who was healed (Luke 17:11-19), and the centurion with great faith (Luke 7:9; see also Matthew 8:10).

The Divine Imperative. When Jesus predicted His death, He used terms showing the necessity of this event. He had come for this purpose in answer to the divine imperative. This element of

---

[111] For a collection of the material on Luke from early tradition, see H. J. Cadbury in Foakes-Jackson and Lake, *The Beginnings of Christianity,* Vol. 2 (Grand Rapids: Baker, 1979; [original version published in 1932]), pp. 209-264.

necessity is found in all the Gospel narratives (for example, Mark 8:31), but in the Gospel of Luke this same word for *must* is used far more often in association with Jesus' ministry (Luke 2:49; 4:43; 9:22; 13:16, 33; 17:25; 22:37; 24:7, 26, 44). This was part of the plan of redemption, and Jesus' was servant to the divine purpose. Jesus came as the Son of Man, Savior, Lord, Messiah, and Son of God. Luke makes clear who the Servant of the Lord is. In no less than seven passages of the Gospel, references are made to the prophecies of Isaiah 40—66 (2:25, 30-32; 3:4-6; 4:18, 19; 6:20-22; 7:22; 22:37).

The Role of the Holy Spirit. The working out of God's purpose included also the role of the Spirit. He had His role in the birth of Jesus (Luke 1:35), descended upon Jesus at the time of His baptism (Luke 3:22), led Him to the test of temptations from the devil (4:1), and went with Him to Galilee in the unfolding of His ministry (4:14, 18).

Prayer. All the Gospel narratives show Jesus at prayer during especially important scenes in His life, for example, the Last Supper and the Mount of Olives. But Luke tells of Jesus in prayer at frequent occasions, when the other Gospel writers have not paused to give note. Jesus was in prayer at His baptism (Luke 3:21), during His ministry (Luke 5:16; also Mark 1:35), before the selection of the Twelve (Luke 6:12), before the confession of Peter (Luke 9:18), at the transfiguration (Luke 9:28), upon the return of His disciples (Luke 10:21), before the Model Prayer was given (Luke 11:1), for strengthening Peter (Luke 22:32), at His crucifixion (Luke 23:34, 46), and with the two at Emmaus (Luke 24:30).

Joy. The announcement of good news, the gospel, is accompanied throughout Luke with an atmosphere of joy. In Heaven, there is joy when one sinner repents (Luke 15:7, 10). The disciples would rejoice despite whatever came because of their reward in Heaven (Luke 6:23). Mary's visit to Elizabeth (Luke 1:41, 44), the birth of John (1:58), and the announcement to the shepherds (2:10)—all these are examples of joyful news. Also the disciples returned from their evangelistic tour with joy (10:17), Jesus rejoiced (10:21), and defined the motive for joy (10:20). The crowd had joy in Jesus (13:17), Zacchaeus was joyful (19:6), followers were joyful at Christ's entry into Jerusalem (19:37), at Emmaus (24:31f), later in Jerusalem (24:41), and after the ascension (24:52).

Women. Another indication that Luke was a physician may be his interest not only in men but in the whole family of women and children as well. They occupied a more prominent place than was ordinary in the Jewish circles at that time. Mary, Elizabeth, Anna, and the widow of Nain are but a few. The sinful woman who was left unnamed (Luke 7:36ff), the women who followed Jesus even to the cross (23:55; 24:10-12), Mary and Martha (10:38-42), the woman who could not straighten up (13:11-16), the women of Jerusalem (23:27ff), and the women in parables (15:8-10; 18:1-8) all add to the evidence that Luke has given special notice to the role of women.

Rich and Poor. Although Luke notes that some of the rich were among the followers of Jesus (Joseph of Arimathaea, Luke 23:50; and Joanna, wife of Herod's steward, 8:3), nevertheless the poor were the closest to Him. The shepherds came at His birth (Luke 2:8); the sacrifice in the temple was that allowed for the poor (2:24); and Jesus described himself as having nowhere to lay His head (9:58). The Pharisees were not only filled with conceit (18:14), but they were fond of money (16:14). Lazarus the poor man (16:20) and the poor widow who gave all she had to live on to the Lord (21:1-4) were moving examples.

Sinners. Luke depicts Jesus as the friend of those deeply entangled in sin and farthest from God's fold. This is the picture found in all four Gospel narratives, but Luke alone gives the illustrations of Christ's promise to the thief on the cross and His visit with Zacchaeus. The parables of the prodigal son and the good Samaritan are only found in the pages of the third Gospel.

Family Circles. One might consider Luke's warm interest in describing incidents from the homes of Galilee and Judea as an insight into the real humanity of Jesus. Luke alone tells of the scene in Martha's home where Mary chose to listen at the feet of the Master rather than aid her sister in serving (Luke 10:38-42). One reads of the meal in the house of Simon (Luke 7:36ff), a Pharisee (11:37ff), his visit with Zacchaeus (19:1-9), and the blessing offered at the table of the two in Emmaus (24:30). Jesus partook of the food as a man in the flesh even after His resurrection, and Luke stops to describe a specific instance (24:41-43).

Purpose and Plan

Luke's Statement

One of the most difficult tasks for a writer is to sum up a

major work and give the purpose of it all in a simple opening sentence. This, however, is the scholarly thing to do, and Luke does it. He states his purpose to Theophilus quite clearly: "so that you may know the certainty of the things you have been taught" (Luke 1:4). John saves his purpose sentence for the close of his Gospel: "But these are written that you may believe that Jesus is the Christ, the Son of God, and that by believing you may have life in his name" (John 20:31).

If theology is what is believed—and it may be just as true as it can be—and history is what happened, then Luke is more anxious to give history than to deal with theology. Luke wants to tell us what happened, what Jesus actually "began to do and to teach." These are the words Luke uses to sum up his Gospel as he opens the book of Acts (1:1). In his work, he plans to emphasize the historical as a basis of faith. In other words, he would want the reader to keep the history of his Gospel uppermost in mind rather than an analysis of its theology. This is one of the reasons for not translating Luke's phrase in the prologue as some do translate it, "a narrative of those things which are most surely believed among us" (1:1). It rather has the significance, "most surely took place among us." Still better is the translation, "the things that have been fulfilled among us," because this relates the happenings to fulfillment of prophecies from the past.

Unfortunately, when a person writes down his history, he can never include everything that happened, all of the causes that brought it about and all of the results that followed, as well as all the details that accompanied it, to say nothing of the unnoticed and unknown factors. So the historian, in his selection of material, and in the way he arranges his information, in fact, becomes an interpreter of what happened rather than a cold pipeline from the happening to the reader. After all, the history of an event becomes involved with the theology of the historian. But this is what makes it so rewarding to read the history of Luke. With his training, his ability, and the guidance of the Spirit, he is an historian plus much more, and an extraordinary theologian. The more one studies Luke, the more he finds designs and patterns in the unfolding of his account. This does not make this account untrustworthy; rather, it highlights this history told with a purpose.

One can use the scene of Jesus' rejection at Nazareth (Luke

4:16-30) as an example of Luke's use of an historical episode to fill several purposes. He places it as the opening illustration of Jesus' ministry in Galilee. It is obvious, however, that His ministry had already been underway for some time because Jesus himself made reference to their knowledge in Nazareth of all the miraculous works He had been doing in Capernaum (Luke 4:23). In fact, both Matthew (13:54-58) and Mark (6:1-6) tell of a visit to Nazareth at a much later time, but this may well be the same visit. If so, why does Luke insert it at the beginning of Jesus' ministry? Several advantages become evident: (1) It gives an example of the synagogue preaching that characterized Jesus' ministry in its early stages in Galilee. Especially the Gentile reader would be helped by having this description. (2) It gives the reader an understanding that despite the excitement and popularity associated with Jesus' ministry in Galilee, there was an ever-present resistance as well. It was realistic to inform the reader at this early point concerning opposition in order to avoid a false impression of wholehearted, complete support of Jesus throughout His Galilean campaigns. (3) It introduces the type of ministry Jesus was undertaking and associates it with the prophecy of Isaiah (61:1, 2), again helping the reader to understand the whole of Jesus' ministry to follow. (4) It gives an understanding of the self-claims of Jesus. By declaring the fulfillment of this Messianic prophecy, Jesus was informing them they were in the presence of the Messiah. This was no conclusion reached decades later upon reflection of the disciples of new heroizing tendencies of the early church. Luke records it as a happening in Nazareth. (5) It gives evidence of the power of Jesus and how He used it. Indeed, Jesus did not use His healing power at this time in Nazareth, but when the people of Nazareth tried to kill Him, He passed from them unharmed. His power was not diminished.

Luke helps the understanding of the reader in a great many ways by placing the rejection of Jesus in Nazareth to open His ministry in Galilee. Because it may not be in chronological order does not mean that it did not take place. It is no less historical, but it serves many purposes in the position where Luke puts it. It is a careful arrangement to serve the understanding of the truth of the history of redemption in Jesus.

Apology

Some maintain that Luke's primary purpose was to present a

defense for the Christian beliefs in the first-century world. If this is saying that Luke wished to establish a firm basis of fact for the Christian faith, this is true enough. The word *apology,* however, may be a poor choice to describe this since this type of defense became commonplace in the second-and third-century writings of the Christians who sought to meet the attacks of both Jewish antagonists and pagan accusers. Luke's work is not in this category. On the other hand, Luke was against the thought that Jesus did not come in the flesh and gave particular information to deny such a proposal (Luke 24:39). He was against the thought that Jesus must be coming back immediately, and he gave words of Jesus concerning this (Luke 21:8). Luke, however, saw the thrust of Jesus' message that was good news for all—Jew and Gentile. In some ways, it was apologetic.

If one knew more about the situation of Theophilus, it would be helpful. He probably was a Christian who already had a commendable commitment but needed more facts to build on. The presentation in Luke answers what would be expected if it were written by a Gentile for Gentiles. Explanations are given that are unnecessary for a Jew (for example, Luke 22:1). This Gospel aims at fullness. It begins before the birth of Christ and continues through His ascension. Jesus is the Savior of the Gentiles as much as He is the promised Messiah of the Jews. As Luke established the historical incidents and the significance of the events, he naturally built a defense against the attacks that had arisen or were likely to arise concerning these things fulfilled among them.

Missionary Motive

Included in the purposes reflected in Luke's writing must be the repeated notations of the universal goals that Jesus taught. He wanted the Gospel taken to the Gentiles eventually; He included the whole world in His concern. As the Christian evangelists went out to win people to Christ, the Gospel of Luke was a valuable source to introduce the Lord Jesus as well as to deepen the conviction and understanding of the convert (Luke 24:47, 48).

Testimony

Some have suggested that the Gospel of Luke was first written to be a type of court brief to be presented to the Roman court on behalf of Christians (specifically Paul) arraigned there. Dependent upon the date and occasion of writing,[112] this association with the courts has certain attractions to the possibility. In the final analysis, however, even if it were so used, this was neither the sole purpose nor the primary purpose for its writing.

When Luke wrote the Gospel, he probably had full intention of continuing with a second volume. So the purposes for writing the Gospel should also include the purposes for Acts. In fact, the final form may have included a third volume, the earliest collection of Paul's epistles. Such a prepared body of material would have been an admirable testimony to the court to establish that Christianity was not a subversive sect. Just criticism has been given, however, that much of the material would be outside the interest of the court; and, on the other hand, what material there is would have been more specifically focused for such a need. This is like the apologetic purpose of the writing. It could be used in such a way to meet an attack or a false teaching, but it was not designed for that specific purpose.

Peter wrote his first epistle to the Christians in the provinces of Asia Minor. He was preparing them for coming persecution and trials. In this context, he told them: "Always be prepared to give an answer ... for the hope that you have" (1 Peter 3:15). Luke supplies the answer for the testimony of the Christian.

In Orderly Manner

The plan followed by Luke in writing his Gospel is described by one Greek word in his prologue (Luke 1:3). The word means "in orderly manner." But then the question is, "What order?" He probably meant logically, in a systematic narrative continuous in itself; it was "successive," but not necessarily chronological.[113]

Geographical. One becomes aware at the first reading of Luke that much of the action takes place in Galilee, but that the closing chapters have Judea (Jerusalem) as its setting. Without more information, one might think the whole of Jesus' time was spent in Galilee before going up to Jerusalem for the last Pass-

---

[112] See the discussion on the date and occasion of Luke below.

[113] Cadbury, *Making of Luke-Acts,* p. 345.

over. When one reads the Gospel of John, however, it becomes evident that Jesus had an early Judean ministry not recorded in Luke. As one studies Luke, he will watch for the significance of grouping events geographically. He should avoid, however, assigning the geographical extreme symbolic proportions.[114]

Chronological. Far more often than not, Luke gives events in the order of their occurrence, but he is not bound by the chronological order. The example of Jesus' rejection at Nazareth has already been cited. Luke's order of the temptations is different from Matthew's, and it is more likely that Matthew's is chronological. The seeming presence of Judas at the instituting of the Lord's Supper may also be related to a grouping of subject matter without regard to chronology.

The study of Luke becomes more absorbing when one plumbs the reasons for the order that is used in individual sections. Our own culture has come to accept the sequence of time as the expected order of recounting events, but there are many other possibilities, and they cannot be arbitrarily declared wrong nor considered unhistorical upon the basis of another arrangement.

Synoptical. The first three Gospels—Matthew, Mark, and Luke—are called the Synoptic Gospels because they can be "viewed together." These three Gospels have striking similarities in the selection of the material recorded, in the wording of many of the blocks of narrative, and also in the very order in which the episodes are given. This is only half of the matter, however, because there are also considerable differences that make each of the Gospel writers distinctive in his own work. The immediate question is whether or not Luke received his order of material either from one of the other writers or from a type of Synoptic tradition shared by all three. The answer is obviously negative on both counts because no two of the writers agree in their order of events. Some maintain that Mark was used by the other two because, although they vary in order, seldom if ever do both Luke and Matthew disagree with Mark at the same time. So the claim is made that Mark is the standard. This, too, cannot be established. Mark is chronological, or very nearly so, and it may well be that the chronological is the standard the other two are

---

[114]Conzelmann, *Theology of Luke,* pp. 18f is an example of such extremes.

approximating and not Mark at all. There may also be a decided influence from apostolic preaching and years of oral proclamation of the Gospel that left its mark in the selection of subject matter and the order used. All three of the Synoptic writers have the major part of Jesus' ministry confined to Galilee except for the final week. But there are distinct differences, too. Luke has a large section of his Gospel (Luke 9:51—19:27) devoted to Jesus' final trip to Jerusalem, not found as such in the other two Synoptics. On the other hand, Luke does not have material found in Mark 6:45—8:26 (Matthew 14:22—16:12). It is impossible to say that Luke is dependent upon either of the others for the "orderly manner" he speaks of in his prologue.

Topical. Luke made a practice of putting together material of the same nature or on the same subject. The famous string of parables in chapter 15 is an example. At times, he gave groups of sayings tied together by a catchword (Luke 11:33-36). Herod is an example of a figure who is woven into Luke's account where he fits best. Luke even tells of Herod's arresting John the Baptist before the baptism of Jesus. He does not say it occurs then, but he knows it will interrupt his plan to tell it at a later time (Luke 3:19, 20). In a similar way, Luke does not announce the news of John's death as one learns of it (Matthew 14:1-12), but he gives the information by telling of Herod's concern at a later time that Jesus was John the Baptist returned (Luke 9:7-9). These are a few examples of the way Luke weaves together events and sayings in order to present the facts in a memorable, understandable manner best fulfilling his purpose—to assure the Christian of the facts pertaining to Christ and redemptive history.

Date and Occasion

Time of Writing

No single reference gives the precise date of writing for the Gospel of Luke, but a string of data helps to locate the general time. Since the book of Acts is the second volume to the Gospel, one would expect the first volume to have preceded it. The dating of Acts has been disputed, but detailed studies such as by A. Harnack[115] have maintained that the book was written near the

---

[115]A. Harnack, *The Date of Acts and the Synoptic Gospels* (New York: G. P. Putnam's Sons, 1911).

completion of the last events related in Acts. No allusion is made throughout the book that would indicate a date later than A.D. 62, 63. If the Gospel was completed before this, some date such as A.D. 60 would be indicated. This would provide Luke with an admirable opportunity to pursue his investigation into the reliable basis for the details of his work, for he was in Palestine with Paul during Paul's two years of imprisonment there. He could visit the places where the events occurred. He could sit down and talk with individuals who heard and saw what he was writing about. Then Luke accompanied Paul to Rome when he appealed for a trial before Caesar. Thus the Gospel could have been completed in Rome sometime before A.D. 62.

Early Testimony

Early arrangements of the four Gospels generally put Luke in the third place (Canon of Muratori, Origen, and Jerome). Clement of Alexandria and Irenaeus, however, put Luke in the second position. In the order in the manuscripts, Luke is found in the second place in the so-called Ambrosiaster (c. A.D. 380), in a Catalogue of the Sixty Canonical Books, in an Old Latin codex, and in the cursives 90 and 399.

Regarding the date and place of Luke's writing, the testimony from the early church is not uniform. But it gives some grounds[116] corroborating Luke's composition of the Gospel in Rome while Paul was there. This would agree with the possible date between 60-63. This would date Luke earlier than the Gospel of Mark, if that Gospel is to be associated with Peter and in Rome, because the ancient notices about Peter in Rome indicate he was there not earlier than A.D. 64 nor later than 68. While such a sequence has some support from antiquity, it is definitely out of favor with much literary criticism of today.

Source Thoughts

Although the early notices are not uniform in their testimony, nevertheless they support a date somewhere in the 60s. But this

---

[116]Eusebius, *History of the Church,* 2, 33 and Jerome, *Lives of Illustrious Men,* vii. Earlier, however, Jerome had agreed with Irenaeus and the Anti-Marcion Prologue in dating Luke after the death of Paul and in the vicinity of Achaia.

scarcely satisfies many of the modern theories concerning Luke's use of sources. (1) Some maintain that Luke used Josephus, which would necessitate a date in the late 90s. (2) Others believe Luke's relationship to Marcion's Gospel or Justin's use of a common source with Luke indicates a date between 115 and 130 for Luke-Acts. (3) Still others hold that the Gospel of Luke must have been written after Mark because of theories that Luke and Matthew copied from Mark. But none of these particular source theories can be confidently established, so dating Luke at a later time because of them is not proper.[117]

Internal Indications

Luke records the words of Jesus: "When you see Jerusalem being surrounded by armies, you will know that its desolation is near" (Luke 21:20). This is a key passage because its interpretation brings to light the viewpoint of the interpreter. If one denies the possibility of predictive prophecy, then he will insist this is an indication that the Gospel was written after A.D. 70, when Jerusalem fell to the Romans; and these words were not actually given by Jesus but later put down in the writing after the event had occurred. However, if one accepts God as capable of foretelling the future through His Son or other spokesmen, and he finds the words of Luke a trustworthy account of what actually happened, then these words of Jesus become an indication of an earlier date of writing, at least before A.D. 70; for in all likelihood, Luke would have made mention of the fulfillment if it had already taken place. An example of this practice is seen in Acts 11:28, where Luke notes Agabus' prophecy of a famine and its fulfillment in the days of Claudius.

The date 60-63 fits best the factors involved in the writing of Luke's Gospel. Those who insist on later dates invariably appeal to indications that are based upon false suppositions regarding alleged sources and denial of prophecy. Notices from the earliest sources corroborate the early date.

---

[117]See Donald Guthrie, *New Testament Introduction: Gospels and Acts* (Chicago: Intervarsity Press, 1965), p. 106; Geldenhuys, *Commentary on Luke,* pp. 27f; R. C. Foster, *Life of Christ,* pp. 59ff; Lewis Foster, *Standard Bible Commentary: Acts,* Orrin Root, ed. (Cincinnati: Standard Publishing, 1966), p. xii.

The Synoptics, John, and Sources

Matthew, Mark, and Luke

The special acceptance and association of the four canonical Gospels is undeniable. They present a plurality of witnesses to the life of Jesus, not simply one. There is enough similarity to see the emphases and gain a remembrance by repetition, and enough difference to assure an independence in testimony. If one simply copied the other extensively, no plurality of witness could legitimately be claimed. Two are apostles (Matthew and John) and two are not, but come from the generation that overlaps the life of Jesus (Luke and Mark). One apostle writes first, and one apostle writes last. One is noticeably different, and three are so much alike that they are known as the Synoptic Gospels.

Similarities. The first three Gospels are similar in more than one way. Of all the deeds and sayings of Jesus, much the same ones are recorded. Furthermore, much the same order has been followed in describing these episodes. Oftentimes, the same wording is used for recounting situations and conversations as well as the speeches. Many have concluded, "Somebody has copied from somebody."[118] It is estimated that fifty-one percent of Mark's words appear in Matthew and fifty-three percent of Mark's words appear in Luke. Also, there are 200 verses common to Matthew and Luke not found in Mark.

Differences. To gain a picture of the whole, the similarities must be studied alongside the differences. Fifty-nine percent of the material in Luke is different from that in the other two Synoptics. Forty-two percent of Matthew is different and seven percent of Mark. Whole blocks of material are given by Luke that do not appear elsewhere. Even in those sections the Synoptics have in common, Luke's individual characteristics are apparent. Furthermore, there are surprising omissions if one is simply copying the other. Material from Mark 6:45—8:26 does not appear in Luke at all. In the final analysis, fully two-thirds of Luke's Gospel does not reflect Marcan material.[119]

---

[118]Caird, *Gospel of Luke,* p. 18.

[119]See Plummer *Critical and Exegetical Commentary . . . Luke,* p. xxvii; Hendriksen, *Luke,* p. 22; William Hendriksen, *Matthew* (Grand Rapids: Baker, 1973), pp. 6-54.

GOSPEL COMPARISONS

The Problem

Since the early centuries of the church, Christians have puzzled over the relationship of the Gospel narratives to one another. Some maintain that the similarities are so great that one must have been copied from another. On the other hand, the differences are so great that others conclude that one Gospel writer could not have seen the others or the omissions and variant treatments of the same episodes would not be made as they are. The following charts are presented to help you see at a glance the amount of parallels and the amount of material peculiar to each single Gospel.

The Similarities

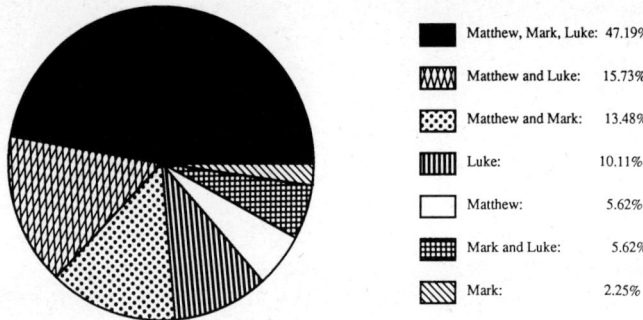

Matthew, Mark, Luke:	47.19%
Matthew and Luke:	15.73%
Matthew and Mark:	13.48%
Luke:	10.11%
Matthew:	5.62%
Mark and Luke:	5.62%
Mark:	2.25%

Eighty-nine total sections

The pie chart, based on the statistics given by Archbishop Thompson,* divides a total harmonization of the Gospels into 89 sections. Matthew reports a total of 73 of these sections; Mark, 61; and Luke, 70. The chart shows how much of this material is shared by the Synoptics.

Almost half (47.19%, or 42 sections) of the material appears in all three Synoptic Gospel narratives. The reports common to Matthew and Luke, but not to Mark, amount to 15.73% of the total (14 sections). This material is what some have labeled as "Q," an imagined document of the proponents of two major sources (Mark and Q) for the writing of Matthew and Luke. Whatever is common to Matthew and Luke, they believe, must have been copied from a common source, and if that source is not Mark, it must have been something else; thus, Q. The sections common to Matthew and Mark but not in Luke, however, amount to almost the same proportion (13.48%, or 12 sections). But the material in Mark and Luke but not in Matthew is considerably less (5.62%; only 5 sections).

Relationship. From these few details concerning the similarities and differences among the Synoptic writings, how would one sum up the relationship of these books to one another?

The Differences
The pie chart also notes that Luke has 9 sections (10.11% of 89) peculiar to itself, Matthew has 5, and Mark has 2.

To this data we add the calculations of B. F. Westcott** on the graph below. This is necessary to balance the picture of similarities and differences. Thompson used 89 sections, but he did not note the different lengths of the sections. Thus, the 9 sections peculiar to Luke yield 10.11% of the total 89 sections; but Westcott shows that these 9 sections are actually 59% of Luke's total Gospel. His interest was in how much of each writer's report was peculiar to that writer. He compared the amount of material, not the number of sections. Thus we see that 59% of Luke's material is found only in Luke. In like manner, 42% of Matthew's report is only in Matthew, and 7% of Mark's is only in Mark. In striking contrast with the Synoptics, 92% of John is new material.

Conclusion
In light of such a combination of similarities and differences (though without actual contradictions), it is safer to conclude that the Gospel narratives, regardless of which is earliest and whether one writer saw another's work, were not copied but represent independent reports of the same good news.

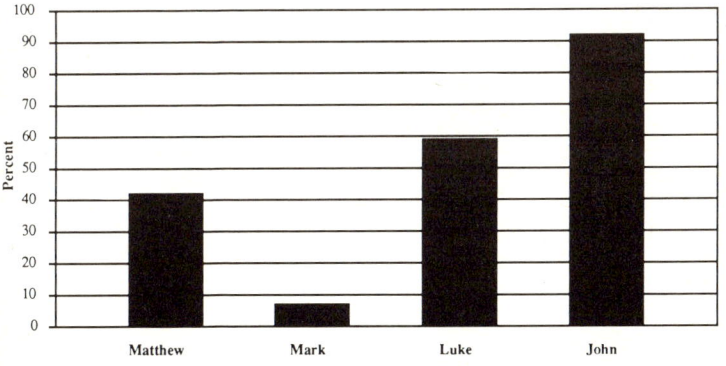

INDIVIDUAL SUBJECT MATTER

*Henry Thiessen, Introduction to the New Testament (Grand Rapids: Eerdmans, 1950), p. 101.

**B. F. Wescott, Introduction to the Study of the Gospels (London: Macmillan, 1895), p. 195.

Three avenues of approach can be used in answering this question, and it would seem necessary to use a combination of all three without dismissing any one of them: historical notices, literary data from the Gospel narratives, and feasible reconstruction.

In the historical early notices about these writings, Matthew is the earliest Gospel, written perhaps in the Aramaic first and then in the Greek by A.D. 50. Then Luke was written second about 60, and Mark was third at about 65. In the reconstruction following this indication, one would recognize the probability that Luke, who had investigated the accounts about Jesus while he was in Palestine during Paul's Caesarean imprisonment, would have known about the Gospel of Matthew, written in Palestine especially for those of Jewish background. When Luke went to Rome with Paul, he could have taken his Gospel with him or even sent it off to Theophilus after his arrival there. While in Rome, Luke would have been in the company of Mark, also (Colossians 4:10, 14). Mark certainly would have been aware that Luke had written a Gospel about Jesus and was working on a second volume about the establishment and spread of the church. Then, after the burning of Rome (A.D. 64), upon the appeal that the preaching of Peter be written down, Mark undertook the writing of his Gospel. Luke had worked in the company of Paul, but Mark had written in the company of Peter. The available literary data is not incompatible with this reconstruction. Thus, Luke may well have been acquainted with Matthew, but he did not derive his plan and structure from him nor yield his own identifiable characteristics in favor of Matthew's. Mark may well have known both Matthew and Luke, but he did not follow their style or structure. Mark used a historical-note-style, which means he wrote in near chronological order. Matthew and Luke do not always follow chronological order, but when they do, they are much the same as Mark. So Mark need not to have been written first; the similarity can be explained by chronological order and not by borrowing. The so-called primitive style of recording and the use of Greek need not be an indication that Mark was written before the others, but may well reflect the influence of Peter, whether written early or late.

The Fourth Gospel

Supplement. How does the fourth Gospel, the one written by the apostle John, fit into the picture? It seems to have been written later, about A.D. 90. This is an addition, important for many reasons. One of them is the example it gives of a Gospel that is written so much later that one can be assured the author was acquainted with the three other Gospel narratives. One is eager to see what use he makes of them. He certainly does not copy them. Ninety-two percent of his material is new, but the points of contact with the Gospel of Luke are noticeable. Jesus' visit at the house of Martha and Mary (Luke 10:38; John 11:1ff) and His appearance to His disciples (Luke 24:36; John 20:19-25) are examples.[120]

John's important role is to be a supplement to the Synoptics. He supplies information the Christians through the ages would have missed sorely if he had not given this added dimension to the person and words of Christ. One would not know details of the early Judean ministry of Jesus (John 2:13—3:36), or His ministry in Samaria (John 4:1-42). Even the length of Jesus' ministry would be far less certain if one could not count the feast days (especially Passovers) noted in John, for they are not recorded in the Synoptic accounts (John 2:13; 5:1; 6:4; 10:22; 12:1).

Alleged contradictions. The new material in John raises again the question of trustworthiness. Is the information accurate? The criticism is made that because the portrait of Jesus is so different in John from the Synoptic Jesus, they both could not be true; therefore the fourth Gospel could not have been written by one of the disciples. It is true the pictures have different emphases and one sees other sides of the figure of Jesus, but they are not contradictory; and, put together, the fuller picture is not distorted, but made clearer. Both Plato in his *Dialogues* and Xenophon in his *Memorabilia* give independent pictures of their teacher, Socrates. The pictures are quite different, but this in itself does not discredit the authorship or establish one right and the other wrong. They supplement each other. Another contradiction is claimed in the time of the cleansing of the temple (early in John 2:13-22; but in the last week in the Synoptics: Luke 19:45-48). Once again, this need be no contradiction but a definite help in understanding why opposition rose so early in the ministry of Jesus. The Synoptics did not tell about it because they related nothing of Jesus' activity in this period. On the

---

[120]See Arndt, *Gospel According to Luke,* pp. 20, 21.

other hand, John did not choose to relate the second cleansing in the final week because the Synoptics had already covered it sufficiently.

Sources

Eyewitnesses and Servants of the Word. In all fairness to Luke, it is well to begin one's search for his sources in his own statement. He affirms he traced the course of all these matters from the beginning and that he received his information from eyewitnesses and those who were dedicated to giving their witness to the gospel (Luke 1:1-4). Many use this prologue of Luke to indicate that his reference to the many who had undertaken to write an account of these things shows that he used all of these attempts as sources. Luke does not say this. Rather, it is his dissatisfaction with these that calls forth his work. Certainly he does not say he is going to sit down and copy them.

Apostolic Preaching. The facts of the Gospel were not kept under wraps for thirty years and suddenly brought to view for the first time when a written Gospel was produced. These matters had been proclaimed in the marketplace, they had been preached in the temple area, they had been debated in the synagogue, and they had been argued on the philosopher's porch. In fact, in antiquity, there was a decided preference for the oral over the written. Papias wanted his information from the living and abiding voice of the eyewitnesses. When these matters had been told and retold, it would be difficult to determine what had come to a definite form orally even before it was finally preserved later in writing. Luke sought out those who preached these accounts as they worked in the service of the Lord (Luke 1:2), and, no doubt, sat down with the eyewitnesses and listened to them tell what they had seen and heard.

Short Written Accounts. The good news was so important and so vital to the lives dedicated to Jesus, that one can be sure that many letters were written to loved ones, many notes left from concerned individuals to their bosom friends, and many favorite stories written for future use. These would have been snatches of the total picture. This type of record would have been frustrating to Luke. He wanted the whole picture from beginning to end. He wanted a dependable record without disconcerting discrepancy in details. He did not want simply to put these fragments together and call it his Gospel. He might, however, get a lead to a teaching of Jesus or to a warm, loving example in His life from one of these short accounts.

Major works. But did Luke use longer, written works as sources for his Gospel? What has been maintained in this section is that Luke did not sit down and copy someone else's testimony without producing a work that shows his characteristics at every turn and his own purposes in the structure of his Gospel. His Gospel is not a patchwork, but a beautiful robe of one whole cloth.

To pursue a detailed study concerning the literary evidence for one Gospel's use of another is beyond the scope of this work, but the lack of demonstrable proof in this area forbids the insistence of some that the dating of the Gospel accounts be governed by the literary relationship. Without this unwarranted insistence, there is no reason for denying the majority of the ancient notices that put Matthew first and then Luke and Mark. If Matthew was written about fifteen years before Luke, it is not conceivable that Luke would have been unaware of his work. The stark differences between Matthew and Luke on some accounts do not justify the conclusion of some that neither one has known the other. Instead, the differences and the similarities are of that nature and in such proportion to warrant the conclusion that the authors were independent writers, each with his own special interests, but with enough sameness to assure corroboration of the facts.

Luke is not a redactor, but an author. He writes an account of the good news about the greatest life ever lived. His word does not return empty. Through the ages, he fulfills his purpose—to bring certainty to all those who love God and seek diligently after Him.

From The Library of Greg Cheatham

INDEX

A

Aaron 40
Abigail 51
Abijah 40
Abila 72
Abraham 63, 67, 68, 73, 100, 200, 217, 230, 243, 322
Achaia 331
Adam 63, 68, 103, 316, 322
Agabus 332
Alexander the Great 30, 111, 245
Angel(s) 34, 44, 45, 47, 48, 49, 207, 216, 217,
                      292, 293, 294, 295, 300, 301, 302, 304, 310, 311
Anna 13, 40, 51, 57, 324
Annas 64, 268, 269, 275
Antioch 31, 42, 321
Apostles 15, 31, 75, 108, 112, 145, 145, 154, 187,
                      218, 256, 257, 284, 293, 294, 295, 296, 297, 303, 305, 333
Arrest 19, 66, 146, 163, 237, 242, 257, 260, 268, 274, 274, 320
Asher 57
Augustus 41, 42, 43, 46, 53, 70, 72
Authority 42, 70, 72, 81, 85, 86, 88, 90, 92, 93,
              95, 100, 107, 110, 115, 117, 120, 123, 132, 137, 139, 150, 157, 173,
                      183, 208, 239, 240, 245, 246, 263, 264, 270, 275, 288, 308

B

Babylonia 73
Baptism 23, 59, 63, 64, 66, 67, 69, 73,
                      74, 75, 73, 74, 75, 76, 81, 86, 109, 225, 239, 315, 323, 330
Beatitudes 112, 113, 117, 174
Beelzebub 18, 61, 156, 181, 182

341

Bethlehem .... 23, 41, 42, 43, 45, 48, 52, 53, 71 (Map), 80, 162
Bethsaida Julius .... 71 (Map), 99 (Map), 147, 172
Bethsaida .... 71, 99 (Map), 146, 147, 170, 172
Blasphemy ...., 103, 104, 239, 270, 270, 276
Blind 17, 18, 89, 92, 116, 121,
124, 181, 202, 228, 229, 232, 249, 301
Boeotia 322
Burial 17, 19, 60, 121, 164, 167, 170, 189, 191, 236, 254, 281,
281, 282, 283, 288, 291, 292, 293, 298, 302, 303, 308, 310

C

Caesar 41, 42, 70, 80, 276, 331
Caesarea 71, 72, 256, 274, 320
Caesarea Philippi .... 71 (Map), 72, 149, 152, 153, 320, 321, 322
Caiaphas 64, 268, 269, 275
Calming the wind 14
Capernaum ...... 13, 72, 90, 92, 93, 94, 95, 97, 98, 99 (Map), 101, 102, 103,
105, 109, 117, 118, 120, 122, 126, 140, 142, 162, 170, 171, 202, 326
Centurion's servant 14, 97, 111, 117
Chronology 17, 53, 64, 72, 76, 80, 81, 120, 218, 329
Chuza 133
Claudius 72, 308, 332
Cleansing the temple 19, 238, 246, 337, 338
Corinth 245, 318
Crippled woman 17, 198, 196, 202
Crucifixion 19, 69, 81, 103, 106, 147, 258, 259, 265, 267, 269,
272, 278, 279, 280, 281, 282, 291, 295, 302, 304, 305, 308, 323

D

Damascus 72, 105
Dating of Acts 330
David 42, 43, 45, 63, 67, 68,
77, 78, 94, 107, 238, 244, 246, 264, 270, 276, 277, 314
Day of questions 239, 246
Dead Sea .... 25 (Map), 39, 64, 66, 125, 162, 228
Death 14, 15, 17, 18, 39, 40, 51, 60, 64, 66, 70, 73, 76, 79, 80,
121, 142, 144, 146, 150, 155, 161, 164, 165, 167, 168, 170, 185, 187,
189, 191, 193, 197, 205, 207, 211, 212, 216, 217, 219, 221, 227, 231,
232, 235, 236, 239, 241, 243, 244, 247, 249, 253, 254, 259, 260, 261,
268, 269, 270, 271, 272, 275, 276, 277, 278, 279, 283, 285, 287, 291,
292, 298, 299, 302, 306, 310, 311, 312, 313, 314, 315, 322, 330, 331
Deborah 51

Deity of Jesus 37, 46, 138, 140, 151, 225, 244

Demon(s) 18, 93, 94, 122, 139, 140, 141,
156, 158, 172, 173, 181, 182, 183, 198, 201

Disciples 10, 14, 15, 16, 18, 19, 40, 45, 75, 85, 93, 94,
97, 102, 104, 105, 106, 107, 108, 109, 112, 121, 123, 131, 132, 135,
138, 139, 143, 145, 146, 147, 149, 150, 151, 154, 155, 156, 164, 165,
168, 171, 173, 174, 178, 188, 189, 191, 192, 194, 199, 202, 212, 216,
217, 218, 221, 222, 223, 224, 228, 235, 236, 237, 238, 250, 251, 253,
254, 255, 256, 257, 258, 265, 273, 274, 294, 295, 296, 303, 304, 305,
306, 311, 313, 314, 321, 323, 326, 337

Discipleship 167

E

Egypt ..... 24, 43, 54, 71 (Map), 79, 162 (Map), 259, 260, 261, 278, 303, 310

Eli 77

Elijah 27, 34, 90, 122, 146, 149, 153, 154, 166, 284, 300

Elisha 90, 122

Elizabeth 27, 28, 35, 37, 38, 39, 48, 323, 24

Emmaus .... 19, 40, 71 (Map), 162, 294, 295, 304, 305, 306, 21, 323, 24

Essenes 39, 74

Esther 51

Evil spirit 14, 15, 85, 87, 93, 138, 140, 145, 54, 183, 184, 198

Ezekiel 79, 206, 257

F

Faith 27, 33, 55, 58, 59, 90,
100, 101, 102, 114, 117, 120, 121, 125, 129, 138, 143, 144, 146, 148,
154, 155, 164, 203, 214, 218, 219, 220, 223, 225, 251, 263, 287, 297,
307, 307, 312, 314, 315, 315, 316, 322, 325, 327

Fasting 51, 69, 78, 105, 106, 112, 226, 273

Feast of Dedication 172, 181

Feast of Tabernacles 57, 172, 181

Feeding the five thousand 14, 15, 146, 147, 149

Fish 14, 98, 100, 148, 180, 228

Fishermen 15, 66, 105

Forgiveness 39, 47, 67, 73, 107, 110,
129, 179, 189, 218, 224, 283, 306, 315

G

Gabriel 23, 27, 28, 29, 33, 34, 35, 36, 37, 38, 48

Gadara .... 71 (Map), 99 (Map), 140

Galilean ministry .... 13, 86, 96, 97, 158, 169 (Chart), 181, 326, 330

Galilee .... 13, 14, 15, 25 (Map), 32, 35, 38, 40, 71 (Map), 72,
   75, 83, 86, 92, 95, 96, 97, 99, (Map), 102, 108, 109, 122, 123, 126, 131,
   145, 161, 162, 163, 164, 168, 169, 201, 228, 256, 257, 269, 277, 282,
   294, 295, 296, 297, 299, 301, 302, 307, 311, 323, 324, 326, 328, 330

Genealogy 23, 63, 67, 68, 76, 77, 78, 322

Gentile(s) 32, 35, 45, 46, 50, 51, 54, 60, 65, 68, 90, 91, 92, 104,
   117, 118, 120, 139, 141, 145, 149, 165, 166, 169, 326, 327, 328 (Chart),
   171, 185, 187, 200, 227, 42, 252, 254, 263, 280, 302, 321, 322

Gerasa 140

Gerasene .... 14, 301 (note)

Gerasenes 139, 140

Gergasenes 140

Gerasene demoniac 14

Gergsa 140

Gerizim .... 71 (Map), 165

Gethsemane .... 19, 153, 265, 266 (Map), 269, 273

God-fearer 32

Good Samaritan 18, 164, 176, 177, 194, 322, 324

Great Commission 214, 296, 297, 306

H

Hannah 28, 51

Healings 14, 17

Heaven 17, 34, 37, 41, 45, 76,
   120, 131, 133, 153, 156, 165, 166, 172, 173, 179, 182, 185, 181, 189,
   192, 206, 207, 208, 214, 239, 243, 247, 253, 259, 264, 323

Hebron 35

Herod

  Agrippa I 64, 73

  Antipas .. 16, 32, 64, 66, 72, 75, 76, 105, 117, 122, 123, 131, 133, 146, 149,
   200, 201, 239, 269, 277, 330

  Philip 64, 66, 72, 76, 147

  the Great 32, 39, 52, 53, 64, 66, 72, 75, 80, 228, 231, 251

Herodias 66, 75

Holy Spirit 33, 34, 37, 38, 50, 56, 59, 66, 67, 75, 76, 78, 79, 87,
   102, 181, 184, 189, 190, 214, 261, 306, 319, 320, 322, 323, 325

Huldah 51

I

Inspiration 189, 319

Isaiah 59, 65, 73, 76, 88, 92, 100,
   122, 124, 135, 157, 211, 241, 242, 261, 306, 322, 323, 326

Iturea .... 71 (Map), 72

J

Jacob 37, 77, 120, 200, 243
Jairus 14, 40, 142, 143, 153, 311, 273,
James
  the Lord's brother 79, 136, 137, 294, 297, 312
  the apostle 15, 40, 97, 100, 104, 144, 153, 166, 251, 273
  the father of Judas, Thaddaeus 108
Jericho .... 18, 25 (Map), 71 (Map), 161,
        162 (Map), 163, 166, 176, 219, 228, 229, 232, 237, 301
Jerome 136, 318, 321, 331
Jerusalem ..... 13, 14, 23, 25 (Map), 28, 35, 40, 43, 51, 52, 56, 58, 71 (Map),
    72, 86, 92, 95, 99 (Map), 102, 112, 123, 135, 150, 152, 153, 162, 163,
    164, 165, 168, 169, 174, 175, 176, 177, 181, 188, 197, 201, 220, 221,
    226, 227, 235, 236, 237, 238, 239, 240, 246, 247, 251, 253, 254, 255,
    256, 265, 266 (Map), 269, 272, 274, 277, 279, 291, 293, 294, 295, 296,
    297, 301, 302, 303, 304, 305, 307, 308, 310, 320, 323, 324, 328, 332
Jesse 42
Jesus' brothers 136
John
  the apostle 13, 15, 40, 41, 79, 97,
      100, 104, 144, 153, 56, 166, 173, 175, 251, 257, 273, 274, 281, 282,
        284, 292, 293, 294, 295, 300, 303, 305, 310, 333, 336
  the Baptist 16, 29, 31, 32, 34, 35, 38, 39, 52, 56, 63, 64,
      65, 66, 72, 73, 74, 75, 76, 80, 105, 106, 109, 111, 122, 123, 124, 125,
        126, 132, 145, 146, 149, 178, 200, 215, 236, 240, 255, 323, 330
Jonah 164, 302
Jordan .... 25 (Map), 64, 71 (Map), 73,
        99 (Map), 147, 161, 162, 168, 219, 228, 253
Joseph
  Jesus' stepfather 13, 32, 36, 38, 42, 43, 4, 49,
        52, 56, 57, 60, 61, 68, 76, 77, 78, 131, 136, 284
  Jesus' brother 136
  of Arimathea 40, 281, 282, 287, 288, 324
Josephus 35, 53, 72, 73, 75, 79,
        102, 140, 147, 231, 243, 246, 251, 332
Judah 35, 37, 40, 43, 77
Judas
  the son of James 108
  Iscariot 108, 256, 257, 258, 262,
        263, 265, 272, 274, 295, 303, 305, 329
Jude (Judas, Jesus' brother) 136, 137
Judea .... 32, 39, 41, 42, 64, 71 (Map),

72, 95, 96, 98, 108, 109, 122, 162, 291 (Map), 163, 168, 172, 201, 219, 253, 256, 257, 277, 297, 308, 311, 324, 328

Judging 115

Judgment Day 185, 217

Judgment 34, 63, 64, 66, 73, 75, 115, 124, 136, 170, 170, 171, 185, 189, 192, 193, 217, 222, 245, 253, 254, 258, 264,

K

Kedron (Kidron) Valley .... 71 (Map), 79, 197, 237, 256, 266 (Map), 273

Kingdom of God 170, 255, 259

Korazin (Chorazin) .... 71 (Map), 99 (Map), 170

L

Last Supper 323

Lazarus 237, 272, 311

Leper 14, 236, 322

Leprosy 14, 17, 90, 97, 101, 122, 124, 219, 220

Levites 49, 87

Lord's Supper 259, 260, 261, 262, 305, 329

Lucius 321

M

Man with dropsy 17, 196, 202

Martha 18, 163, 177, 178, 237, 272, 324, 337

Mary
  Magdalene 133, 281, 282, 292, 293, 294, 295, 298, 300, 302, 311

  mother of Jesus 13, 28, 29, 34, 35, 36, 37, 38, 40, 42, 43, 44, 45, 46, 47, 51, 52, 54, 56, 57, 58, 59, 61, 68, 76, 77, 78, 136, 137, 184, 281, 282, 283, 284, 303, 324,

  mother of James 293, 298, 303

  sister of Martha 18, 185, 163, 177, 178, 236, 237, 272, 324, 337

  mother of James and Joses 281, 282

  mother of John Mark 258

Messiah 15, 34, 36, 46, 49, 50, 54, 56, 63, 64, 65, 66, 67, 74, 76, 87, 88, 89, 90, 92, 93, 94, 101, 122, 124, 126, 132, 157, 235, 236, 238, 239, 244, 246, 257, 258, 270, 272, 275, 276, 278, 304, 314, 323, 326, 327

Michael 34

Miracle(s) 14, 15, 16, 27, 34, 58, 59, 79, 86, 87, 90, 91, 93, 94, 97, 102, 104, 107, 111, 117, 118, 119, 120, 121, 122, 131, 132, 137, 139, 141, 144, 147, 148, 156, 158, 164, 181, 183, 185, 198, 201, 202, 202, 236, 237, 251, 258, 284, 288, 289

Miriam 51

Mount Hermon 120, 153
Mount of Olives .... 71 (Map), 99 (Map), 197, 235, 237,
251, 266 (Map), 268, 272, 294, 297, 307, 323

N

Nazareth 13, 28, 35, 40, 43, 51, 52, 59,
71 (Map), 86, 88, 90, 92, 94, 95, 99 (Map), 102, 120, 124, 131, 157,
162 (Map), 166, 229, 308, 309, 325, 326, 329

Nazirite vow 33
Nicodemus 175, 282

P

Palestine .... 25 (Map), 32, 35, 71 (Map), 73, 87, 95, 102,
104, 122, 134, 151, 162 (Map), 169, 172, 276, 303, 331, 336

Papyrus 17
Parable(s) 13, 18, 106, 106, 112,
132, 133, 134, 135, 136, 138, 164, 177, 179, 180, 181, 182, 183, 184,
190, 191, 192, 194, 202, 206, 207, 212, 213, 214, 216, 217, 222, 223,
224, 230, 230, 231, 232, 240, 241, 242, 324, 330

Paralytic 14, 101, 102, 104, 202
Passover 19, 52, 57, 81, 147, 163, 166, 169, 172, 235, 236, 239, 245,
246, 250, 256, 257, 258, 259, 261, 269, 271, 277, 278, 313, 314, 329

Pastoral Epistles 46
Paul 14, 41, 45, 58, 59, 60, 88, 94, 116, 170, 253, 260, 261,
274, 280, 295, 296, 297, 316, 317, 318, 319, 320, 321, 328, 331, 336

Pentecost 19, 57, 66, 75, 152, 255, 256, 306, 312, 314
Perea .... 17, 32, 71, 75, 95, 161, 162 (Map), 201, 219, 228, 256
Perean ministry .... 168, 169 (Chart)
Peter 15, 37, 40, 46, 75, 94, 97, 98, 100, 104, 105, 108, 132,
141, 144, 149, 152, 153, 154, 171, 190, 199, 203, 207, 221, 227, 228,
242, 251, 253, 257, 262, 264, 265, 268, 271, 273, 274, 275, 292, 293,
294, 295, 300, 303, 304, 305, 306, 312, 314, 318, 323, 328, 331, 336

Pharisee and the publican 18, 223, 224
Pharisee(s) 15, 16, 18, 39, 45, 66, 85, 92, 102, 103, 104, 105,
106, 107, 116, 118, 126, 128, 131, 158, 164, 182, 183, 186, 187, 188,
193, 194, 196, 198, 201, 202, 203, 206, 207, 209, 212, 215, 216, 220,
221, 232, 236, 237, 238, 239, 243, 244, 245, 246, 264, 271, 274, 324

Philip 171
Physician 14, 89, 94, 101, 274, 317, 324
Pilate 64, 72, 197, 269, 270, 271, 276, 277, 278, 281, 282
Prayer 34, 50, 51, 67, 87, 108, 112, 143, 148, 153, 164, 177,
178, 179, 180, 181, 212, 223, 232, 259, 272, 273, 283, 323, 323

Prediction of Jesus' coming death 15, 89, 150, 155, 212, 227, 228, 232

347

Priests 27, 32, 34, 40, 64, 87, 88, 131, 150, 221, 227,
 239, 240, 242, 243, 252, 257, 258, 264, 274, 277, 278, 283, 309

Prodigal son 18, 207, 208, 209, 230, 324

Prophets 18, 29, 64, 87, 88, 90, 122,
 132, 149, 153, 164, 187, 215, 241, 264, 292, 304, 306

Psalms 28, 29, 306

Q

Quirinius 54

R

Repentance 34, 63, 64, 65, 67, 73, 75, 85,
 105, 105, 110, 129, 131, 179, 185, 208, 209, 223, 283, 306

Resurrection 13, 17, 19, 37, 59, 60, 69, 120, 133, 137,
 147, 152, 164, 170, 185, 189, 191, 203, 217, 233, 243, 244, 254, 280,
 288, 292, 293, 294, 295, 296, 297, 298, 299, 301, 302, 303, 304, 308,
 306, 307, 308, 310, 311, 312, 313, 314, 315, 316, 324

Rich man and Lazarus 18, 217, 232, 261

Rich ruler 171, 175, 225, 226

Rome 39, 40, 42, 53, 64, 66, 72,
 104, 109, 116, 123, 201, 222, 224, 231, 239, 242, 253, 257, 268, 270,
 271, 276, 277, 278, 291, 308, 309, 320, 321, 331, 336

S

Sabbath 16, 17, 35, 87, 88, 92, 94, 97, 107, 127,
 186, 196, 198, 202, 239, 258, 283, 282, 293, 298, 302

Sacrifice 28, 48, 49, 50, 56, 151, 205, 246, 250, 259, 269, 324

Sadducees 39, 66, 102, 131, 236, 238, 239, 243, 246, 259, 271

Salvation 29, 31, 38, 39, 49, 51, 56, 65, 80, 89, 97, 103, 108,
 110, 175, 177, 206, 209, 211, 219, 222, 230, 235, 253, 316, 322

Samaria .... 25 (Map), 32, 71 (Map), 95,
 161, 162, 163, 165, 166, 169, 219, 277, 337

Samaritan 61, 181, 219, 220, 227, 322

Samaritan territory 17, 161, 165, 166

Samson 33

Samuel 28, 29, 33, 36, 52, 106, 107, 229, 230, 273

Sarah 51

Satan 34, 68, 69, 70, 78, 79, 93, 138, 139, 156, 172,
 179, 181, 182, 183, 184, 192, 193, 256, 257, 263, 272, 291

Savior 38, 39, 45, 46, 113, 114, 126, 130, 158, 209, 323, 327

Sea of Galilee .... 25 (Map), 35, 98, 99 (Map), 100, 117, 133, 138,
 139, 146, 147, 153 (Map), 161, 162 (Map), 171, 219, 296, 301

Septuagint 140, 284

Sermon on the Mount 18, 97, 112, 113, 114, 116, 174, 178, 191
Sermon on the Plain 13, 112, 114, 129
Servant of the Lord 89, 323
Sidon 13, 71, 90, 168, 171
Signs 52, 98, 164, 183, 185, 254, 287, 288, 321
Simeon 13, 32, 40, 50, 56
Simon
    Jesus' brother 136
    of Cyrene 278
    Peter 157, 263, 294, 305
    the leper 236
    the Pharisee 16, 112, 126, 127, 128, 324
    the Zealot 109
Simon's mother-in-law 14, 94, 97, 100, 202
Socrates 109, 337
Son of David 45, 67, 95, 229, 238, 244, 246, 270
Son of God 28, 37, 38, 44, 46, 49, 58, 59,
    60, 70, 76, 95, 104, 132, 139, 140, 154 158, 189, 194, 227, 239, 245,
        246, 270, 272, 273, 275, 276, 280, 291, 323, 325, 332
Son of Man 107, 113, 117, 125, 130, 131, 150, 155, 157,
    189, 192, 220, 221, 222, 223, 254, 255, 260, 264, 265, 323
Synagogues 13, 86, 87, 95, 102, 244, 253
Synoptic Gospels 18, 45, 65, 67, 78, 94, 96, 97, 102,
    134, 139, 273, 329, 330, 333, 334, 335, 337, 338,
Syria 54, 70, 90, 153, 308, 321

T

Taxes 65, 104, 105, 104, 109, 242, 276
Temptations 63, 65, 68, 69, 78, 78, 79,
    86, 179, 218, 265, 267, 268, 273, 323, 329
Theophilus 10, 31, 32, 139, 320, 325, 327, 336
Tiberias .... 40, 71, 92, 99 (Map), 133, 171
Tiberius Caesar 70, 72, 80, 81, 242
Trachonitus .... 71 (Map), 72
Transfiguration 15, 152, 153, 273, 300, 323
Trials 19, 23, 32, 72, 103, 179, 218, 228, 253, 256, 263, 264,
    265, 267, 268, 269, 273, 274, 275, 276, 275, 276, 277, 279, 280, 328
Trip to Jerusalem 13, 16, 23, 159,
    161, 162, 163, 164, 165, 166, 168, 169, 171, 172, 177, 182, 194, 201,
        209, 211, 219, 224, 227, 228, 231, 232, 330
Triumphal entry 19, 201, 231, 235, 237, 238, 239, 245, 256

The Twelve ..... 15, 16, 51, 97, 107, 108, 112, 117, 120, 131, 135, 145 (Note), 146, 147, 150, 156, 172, 191, 218, 227, 238, 262, 265, 296, 305, 323

Tyre 13, 71, 168, 171

V

Virgin birth 35, 36, 58, 59, 60, 61, 66, 76, 89

W

Washings 74, 186

Widow's son 14

Widow's gift 250, 265

Wise-men 80

Women .... 19, 35, 43, 51, , 60, 108, 133, 148, 250, 258, 279, 279, 281, 282, 293, 294, 295, 300, 301, 302, 303, 304, 324, 324

X

Xenophon 109, 337

Y

Year of Jubilee 89

Z

Zacchaeus 18, 229, 230, 265, 323, 324

Zebedee 100

Zechariah 23, 27, 28, 29, 31, 33, 34, 35, 37, 38, 39, 40, 45, 46

SUGGESTED READING

Arndt, W. F. *The Gospèl According to St. Luke.* St. Louis: Concordia, 1981 (reprint).

Cadbury, Henry J. *The Style and Literary Method of Luke.* Cambridge: Harvard University Press, 1920 (Kraus reprint).

Foster, R. C. *Studies in the Life of Christ.* Grand Rapids: Baker, 1971 (reprint, 1986).

Geldenhuys, J. N. *Commentary on the Gospel of Luke.* Grand Rapids: Eerdmans, 1979 (reprint).

Godet, F. *Commentary on the Gospel of Luke.* Grand Rapids: Kregel, 1981 (reprint).

Hendriksen, William. *Exposition of the Gospel According to Luke.* Grand Rapids: Baker, 1978.

Hobart, W. K. *The Medical Language of St. Luke.* Grand Rapids: Baker, 1954 (reprint).

Marshall, I. Howard. *The Gospel According to Luke.* Grand Rapids: Eerdmans, 1978.

_____ . *Luke, Historian and Theologian.* Grand Rapids: Zondervan, 1979.

Morris, Leon. *The Gospel According to St. Luke.* Grand Rapids: Eerdmans, 1974.

Plummer, A. *A Critical and Exegetical Commentary on St. Luke*. Edindurgh: T. & T. Clark, 1896, 1922 (reprint, 1978).

Ragg, Lonsdale. *St. Luke*. London: Methuen, 1922.

Ramsay, William. *Luke the Physician*. Grand Rapids: Baker, 1979 (reprint).

Robertson, A. T. *Luke the Historian*. Grand Rapids: Baker, 1979.

Stonehouse, N. B. *The Witness of Luke to Christ*. Grand Rapids: Eerdmans, 1951.